To Change the World

TO CHANGE THE WORLD

The Irony, Tragedy, and Possibility
of Christianity
in the Late Modern World

James Davison Hunter

UNIVERSITY PRESS

2010

OXFORD
UNIVERSITY PRESS

Oxford University Press, Inc., publishes works that further
Oxford University's objective of excellence
in research, scholarship, and education.

Oxford   New York
Auckland   Cape Town   Dar es Salaam   Hong Kong   Karachi
Kuala Lumpur   Madrid   Melbourne   Mexico City   Nairobi
New Delhi   Shanghai   Taipei   Toronto

With offices in
Argentina   Austria   Brazil   Chile   Czech Republic   France   Greece
Guatemala   Hungary   Italy   Japan   Poland   Portugal   Singapore
South Korea   Switzerland   Thailand   Turkey   Ukraine   Vietnam

Published by Oxford University Press, Inc.
198 Madison Avenue, New York, NY 10016

www.oup.com

Oxford is a registered trademark of Oxford University Press

Library of Congress Cataloging-in-Publication Data
Hunter, James Davison, 1955–
To change the world : the irony, tragedy, and possibility
of Christianity in the late modern world
/ by James Davison Hunter.
p. cm.
ISBN 978-0-19-973080-3
1. Church and the world. 2. Christianity—United States. I. Title.
BR517.H86 2010
261′.1—dc22
2009028991

10 11 12 13 14 15 16 17 18 19

Printed in the United States of America
on acid-free paper

For Dogwood

CONTENTS

PREFACE

THE QUESTIONS THAT ANIMATE this book are both broadly academic and deeply personal. The basic academic question is simply, how is religious faith possible in the late modern world? From this, of course, many others follow—Is it possible? How does the encounter of religious faith with modernity change the nature and experience of faith? Or, for that matter, modernity itself? These questions have puzzled scholars for several centuries and they will continue to do so long into the future.

The more personal question is a variant of the academic one; simply, how do believers live out their faith under the conditions of the late modern world? In searching for an answer to that question, one discovers endless complexity. As a Christian believer, I find many perplexing disparities between the Christian faith that I have come to know and what I see acted out in the world. Within those disparities, there are elements of irony and tragedy, but also assurance and possibility. (The reader will eventually discern that the title itself is ironic and yet also suggestive of latent possibility.) The three interconnected essays that make up this book are an attempt to make sense of these bewildering realities in a way that, I hope, will contribute to scholarship on these enduring questions as well as be useful for believers.

It is impossible to acknowledge the full debt I owe to so many for their help over the years. I have benefited enormously from the research assistance of Kristen Deede Johnson, Matthew Mutter, Patrick LaRochelle, Emily Raudenbush Gum, Robert Loftin, Heather Dill, Alan Faulkner and Julie Ryan. They have been able researchers and good friends and to each I am very grateful. I am profoundly grateful to Peter Berger, Chuck Mathewes, John Seel, Josh Yates, Nick Woltersorff, Christian Smith, Jeff Dill, Greg Thompson,

Ashley Berner, and Mark Berner, who engaged the argument in detail and from whose knowledge and erudition I received valuable advice for improving the manuscript. I have also benefited from innumerable conversations with a wide range of other friends and colleagues over the years—Joe Davis first and foremost, Richard Horner, Ken Myers, Glenn Lucke, Josh Benoit, David Franz, Felicia Song, Ed Song, Justin Holcomb, John Weiser, Dave Kiersznowski, Demi Lloyd, Peter Brooks, Jan Karon, David Lumpkins, Kate Lumpkins, Tom Gilliam, David Turner, Mike Metzger, Tom Nelson, Tom Streeter, John Yates, John Yates Jr., Corey Widmer, Sandy Willson, and David Henderson. Their fingerprints are found throughout. I am indebted as well to Cynthia Read at Oxford, who graciously worked with me on this project and saw it through to the end. Needless to say, the issues at the core of this book have dogged me for years. There is one group of friends who have engaged them with me longer and more patiently than any others. Jim Seneff, Don Flow, Tim Keller, and Skip Ryan have challenged, goaded, encouraged, and supported me as good friends will do, and from them I have received great wisdom and insight. More than anything else, these essays come out of my ongoing conversation with them. Finally, there are my children, Whitney, Colin, Kirsten, and Matt, and my wife, Honey, from whom I have learned most about faithful presence.

Essay I

CHRISTIANITY AND WORLD-CHANGING

Chapter One

CHRISTIAN FAITH AND THE TASK OF WORLD-CHANGING

OUT OF NOTHING, "GOD created the heavens and the earth" (Gen. 1:1). This was the beginning, the primordial act, the culmination of which was the creation of human life. The spirit that God breathed into his creation was life itself, not only in its manifest beauty and delight but also in its potentialities. The goodness of his creation, then, was anything but inert. It was dynamic, vibrant, and full of latent promise. But what of that vitality and promise?

"Then the Lord God took the man and put him into the Garden of Eden to cultivate it and keep it" (Gen. 2:15). In the Hebrew derivations, the key verbs are *abad* and *shamar*. The former can be translated as work, nurture, sustain, and husband; the latter means to safeguard, preserve, care for, and protect. These are active verbs that convey God's intention that human beings both develop and cherish the world in ways that meet human needs and bring glory and honor to him. In this creative labor, we mirror God's own generative act and thus reflect our very nature as ones made in his likeness.

In the Christian view, then, human beings are, by divine intent and their very nature, world-makers. For Christian believers, an obligation accompanies God's gift of life, an obligation by no means negated by human sin—man's rebellion against God. Indeed, it was reaffirmed in God's covenant with Noah (Gen. 9), and then with Abraham (Gen. 12–17), and then with Moses (Exod. 19), and then finally with Jesus Christ, the last Adam (1 Cor. 15:45), the first born of the New Creation (Rom. 8:24; Eph. 1:20). People fulfill their individual and collective destiny in the art, music, literature, commerce, law, and scholarship they cultivate, the relationships they build, and in the institutions they develop—the families, churches, associations, and communities they live in and sustain—as they reflect the good of God and his designs for flourishing. To be sure, active renunciation of the world can be found from time to time in various places and traditions. Even today, there are some who hold to a "lifeboat theology," seeing the world as a sinking ship on its way to judgment and hell; in this view, the goal of the Christian is to rescue as many as possible on the lifeboat of salvation.[1] There are also some who see their faith merely as a coping strategy for dealing with the complexities and difficulties of life.[2] As a rule, though, indifference toward the world is quite rare in the history of God's people. The passion to engage the world, to shape it and finally change it for the better, would seem to be an enduring mark of Christians on the world in which they live. To be Christian is to be obliged to engage the world, pursuing God's restorative purposes over all of life, individual and corporate, public and private. This is the mandate of creation.

Needless to say, the *actual* legacy of Christians in relation to this mandate is ambivalent, to say the least. Willful negligence of moral and spiritual obligations, the abuse of power, and corruption through self-aggrandizement result in the exploitation of other human beings and the destruction of the resources of the social and natural environment. At the same time, there is a record of extraordinary good; of service to all and in honor of God. The ambivalence is what it is. There is much for Christians to be inspired by and much of which repent.

This legacy of ambivalence, however, has done nothing to lessen the eagerness of Christians to fulfill this mandate in our own time, nor should it. To be sure, Christian believers of all traditions can be found calling each other to engage the world and to change it for the better. Consider the number and range: The Presbyterian Church USA aims at "renewing the church to transform the world,"[3] The Episcopal Church declares that a "revolution" (of justice and peace) "is precisely what God's work, God's mission, is all about."[4] The mission of the Evangelical Lutheran Church in America calls for "transforming the structures of society, working for justice, and preserving the earth."[5] And the U.S. Catholic Conference of Bishops declares that influencing the political world is important because "Our faith demands it. Our teaching calls us to it. Our nation needs it and others depend on it. We can make a difference."[6]

Besides the denominational bodies, there are the para-church ministries—both Catholic and Protestant. The Wilberforce Forum declares, "it is vital for us to prepare ourselves to become God's agents in shaping this culture and bringing biblical truth to bear on all of life." The Wilberforce Forum leadership ministry, the Centurions Program, is "designed to develop and equip an ongoing fellowship of Christian men and women who will be trained . . . to restore our culture."[7] Campus Crusade's explicit message to recruit and motivate its staff has been, from the beginning, to "help change the world." The

Focus on the Family Institute's purpose is "to equip today's student leaders to impact culture for Christ," to give "each student the inspiration and ability to change lives while shaping culture." The Legionaries of Christ and Regnum Christi both involve priests "determined to change the world for Christ." The Pinnacle Forum exists to "transform lives and the culture." The Trinity Forum's charge is to "contribute to the transformation and renewal of society." Christ for the Nations has a program for "training world-changers." Summit Ministries aspires to equip people "to have a positive influence on the society in which they live." The Aftershock Web Community exists as a "community of Christians who want to love God and love people [in order to] . . . grow and change the world for the good found in Christ." The Promise Keepers invite participants to "be a part of a revolution that changes a life of imitation and mediocrity into one of passion and character . . . a radical revolt that will forever change the world." There is a "Change the World School of Prayer." And then there are colleges, such as Christendom College, Indiana Wesleyan University, Bethel University, and Abilene Christian University, that publicly declare their intention to train students who will "change the world," or "reclaim our culture for Christ and His Church."[8] One could go on.

It is fair to say that in each organization and all the people they represent, differences notwithstanding, the idealism about fulfilling the mandate of creation is sincere, the efforts are earnest, and the intentions are undoubtedly honorable. But is that enough?

In this essay, I consider the ways in which Christians in much of their diversity actually think about the creation mandate today, examining the implicit theory and explicit practices that operate within this complex and often conflicted religious and cultural movement. Let me emphasize that I am not just talking about Evangelicals and Fundamentalists, in spite of the fact that they have been the loudest, most energetic, and most demanding of all Christians in recent decades. This essay and the ones that follow are concerned with Christianity in its variety—at least much of it: conservative as well as moderate and progressive, Protestant as well as Catholic. The subject of these essays is the social imaginary that serves as a backdrop for the ways in which the majority of those in America who call themselves Christian engage the world. I contend that the dominant ways of thinking about culture and cultural change are flawed, for they are based on both specious social science and problematic theology. In brief, the model on which various strategies are based not only does not work, but it cannot work. On the basis of this working theory, Christians cannot "change the world" in a way that they, even in their diversity, desire. But this is just the beginning; the entry point for a longer reflection on the Christian faith and its engagement with the world.

Chapter Two

CULTURE: THE COMMON VIEW

To understand how to change the world, one must begin with an understanding of what is to be changed. In short, everything hinges on how we understand the nature of culture. What is meant by culture, and what it is composed of, are of critical importance, as we shall see.

One can find a range of opinion about culture these days, but one perspective on the matter has gained predominance in the public imagination. This view is echoed by politicians in their campaign rhetoric and reinforced through the popular media. Wittingly or unwittingly, people of faith (and not just Christians) and the institutions that represent and serve them have also embraced it.

The substance of this view can be summarized something like this: The essence of culture is found in the *hearts and minds of individuals*—in what are typically called "values." Values are, simply, moral preferences; inclinations toward or conscious attachment to what is good and right and true. Culture is manifested in the ways these values guide actual decisions we individuals make about how to live—that is, how we spend our time; how we work; how we play; whom we marry, and how and why; how we raise our children; whom or what we worship; and so on. By this view, a culture is made up of the accumulation of values held by the majority of people and the choices made on the basis of those values.[1]

A slightly more sophisticated version of this is found in the view of those who speak of "worldviews." A worldview, as Charles Colson has defined it, is "the sum total of our beliefs about the world, the 'big picture' that directs our daily decisions and actions. . . . [it] is a way of seeing and comprehending *all* reality."[2] In this way, Christianity is not just a set of doctrines and beliefs and the values based on them but a wide-ranging and inclusive understanding of the world; a worldview in competition with other worldviews. Where do worldviews come from? In his words, "It is the great ideas that inform the mind, fire the imagination, move the heart, and shape the culture."[3] Mind. Imagination. Heart. Though driven by ideas, worldviews exist primarily in the hearts and minds and imaginations of individuals and take form in choices made by individuals. As Colson puts it, "Our choices are shaped by what we believe is real and true, right and wrong, good and beautiful. Our choices are shaped by our worldview."[4] In this light, he can conclude, "history is little more than the recording of the rise and fall of *the great ideas*—the *worldviews*— *that form our values and move us to act*."[5] "If we're going to succeed in restoring a moral influence in American culture," he says, we need to "cultivat[e] a Christian mind" and "live out a biblical worldview."[6]

What all of this means is that if a culture is good, it is because the good values embraced by individuals lead to good choices. By contrast, if a culture is decadent and in decline, it is because the values or worldviews held by individuals are mistaken at the least, or even immoral, and those corrupt values lead to bad choices. Cumulatively, those mistaken ideas, corrupt values, and bad choices create an unhealthy, immoral culture.

Colson's book *How Now Shall We Live?* has been particularly influential in Christian circles in promoting this perspective and is therefore worth further consideration. One illustration he offers to explain how worldviews work is the case of secular evolutionary theory—in a word, Darwinism. Colson argues that our view of our origins profoundly shapes our understanding of ethics, law, education, and even sexuality. If humans are the products of evolutionary forces, then "morality is nothing more than an idea that appears in our minds when we have evolved to a certain level." "If Darwinism is true, there is no divine law or transcendent moral order," and "law is reduced to a managerial skill used in the service of social engineering." "If human beings are part of nature and nothing more . . . then the mind is simply an organ that has evolved from lower forms in the struggle for existence . . . and its value depends on whether it works, whether it enables the organism to survive."[7] In short, Darwinism is at the heart of the modern worldview and explains so much of the relativism that prevails in our culture and the dangerous ideologies that have sprung from it. Yet Darwinism, Colson explains, has a variety of empirical and scientific problems with it. Most importantly, secular evolutionary theory cannot explain the irreducibly complex structure in nature. Given the flaws in its logic and science, why then, he asks, "is Darwinism still the official creed in our public schools?" Colson answers his own question: "Because the real issue is not what we see through the microscope or the telescope; it's what we adhere to in our hearts and minds. Darwinism functions as the cornerstone propping up a naturalistic worldview."[8] The heart of the controversy over human origins "is not science; it is a titanic struggle between opposing worldviews—between naturalism and theism. . . . Only when Christians understand this," he argues, "will we stop losing debates."[9]

Here you have it in a nutshell. Bad ideas have been adhered to in our hearts and minds—and not just those of most scientists, lawyers, ethicists, and educators—and bad consequences have followed in due course. Throughout the book, Colson offers other interesting illustrations from the ideas of Jean-Jacques Rousseau, René Descartes, Alfred Kinsey, and others. The point is always the same. Bad ideas form the basis of destructive values and these, in turn, lead to bad choices. In the end, these all cumulatively lead to an unhealthy and declining culture.

But the same ideas work in the reverse. If we want to change our culture for the better, we need more and more individuals possessing the right values and the right worldview and, therefore, making better choices. As Colson argues, "A virtuous society can be created only by virtuous people, whose individual consciences guard their behavior and hold them accountable." And so he poses the question directly: "How do we redeem a culture? . . . from the inside out. From the individual to the family to the community, and then outward in ever widening ripples."[10] The decisions that ordinary individuals make are of critical importance. "We easily forget that every private decision contributes to the moral and cultural climate in which we live, rippling out in ever widening circles—first in our personal and family lives, and then in broader society."[11] The matter lies in the choices we make. "In every choice and decision we make, we either help to overcome the forces of barbarism . . . or acquiesce to the forces."[12]

With this framework in mind, Colson then lays out four objectives: "First, Christians must be good citizens. Second, Christians must carry out their civic duty in every walk of life. Third, Christians must be engaged directly in politics. Fourth, the church must act as the conscience of society, as a restraint against the misuse of governing authority."[13] He summarizes the strategy in this way: "if our culture is to be transformed, it will happen from the bottom up—from ordinary believers practicing apologetics over the backyard fence or around the barbeque grill. . . . *the real leverage for cultural change comes from transforming the habits and dispositions of ordinary people.*"[14]

While influential in certain Christian circles, Colson is by no means alone in taking this perspective on culture and cultural change. Commenting on the Second Vatican Council, the political scientist Robert George has written that it instructs in the ways that the "work of transformation of minds and hearts necessarily includes work of cultural transformation."[15] Carl Anderson, the Supreme Knight of the Knights of Columbus, echoes this sentiment in his book *A Civilization of Love: What Every Catholic Can Do to Transform Culture*, when he declares that "the responsibility of Christians in our own time remains as it was in Paul's—to radically transform culture, not by imposing values from above, but through a subtler yet more powerful process—living a vocation of love in the day-to-day reality of our lives."[16] Indeed, we hear this general perspective everywhere within the Christian tradition (Protestant and Catholic) and outside as well—"we can change the world one life at a time";[17] "shap[e] the culture from the ground up—one person at a time";[18] indeed, "ordinary people can achieve extraordinary results."[19] Not surprisingly a cottage industry has arisen in response to the desire for "worldview training:" There are worldview summer camps, worldview institutes, homeschool curricula, and an endless number of books on the subject.[20] This is, for example, the explicit objective of "The Truth Project" spearheaded by James Dobson's Focus on the Family: "We believe this one project represents the possibility for exponential change within the body of Christ, as we expect that thousands will be transformed by this curriculum. As it has been throughout history, God continues to call ordinary people to make an eternal difference in our world."[21]

Indeed, this view has a long history and remains widespread in American public opinion as well. As a man of the Enlightenment, Thomas Jefferson himself gave voice to his generation's shared ideal: "Enlighten the people generally," he wrote in 1816, "and tyranny and oppressions of body and mind will vanish like evil spirits at the dawn of day."[22] This was the foundation for Jefferson's commitment to public education and it is a sensibility and commitment that continue to motivate many people of good will today. Change the values of the common person for the better and a good society will follow in turn.

Values and the Tactic of Evangelism

It is this implicit view of culture that motivates certain communities of Christians, especially Evangelicals, to focus on evangelism as their primary means of changing the world. Evangelism is not only a means of saving souls but of transforming individuals and, in a roundabout way, the culture. The logic behind this position is the belief that the problems society faces can be traced back to a loss of spiritual vitality and moral propriety. Whether the problem is corporate greed and malfeasance, crime, sexual promiscuity, abortion, homosexuality, violence in the schools, decadence portrayed in the popular media, or whatever, each indicates the unhappy truth that people have lost their moral bearings. Only by changing the hearts of individuals who engage in such acts or who sanction them, then, can real headway be made in stepping back from the precipice of social degeneration. As the logic goes: if people's hearts and minds are converted, they will have the right values, they will make the right choices, and the culture will change in turn. As James Boice argues, "We need to be reminded that genuine conversion does make profound differences in a person's life. And it is just those persons the country needs. Laws change nothing. People do."[23]

Let's consider an example. Among conservative Christians, the late Bill Bright of Campus Crusade for Christ initiated annual "Fasting and Prayer" gatherings for Christian leaders with this purpose in mind. Bright explains,

> America as a nation is losing its soul. Our abundance has led to greed. Our freedom has become license to turn away from God. Our national religious heritage is being forgotten or ridiculed as irrelevant or old-fashioned.
>
> America has become one of the most sinful nations in the world. Crime, abortion, divorce, violence, suicide, drug addiction, alcoholism, teen pregnancy, lust, pornography, fornication, adultery and sodomy run rampant. Through pornographic films and literature we have done more to destroy the morality of other countries than any nation in history.
>
> Powerful forces within our country want to make it illegal to mention the name of Jesus, carry Bibles, display religious pictures, or wear Christian emblems in schools. The judgment of God is upon America, but I believe God wants to spare our nation and I am confident that He is going to send a great spiritual awakening to North America and the world.

To this end, Bright invites Christian leaders "to fast and pray for spiritual revival throughout America and the world."[24] Spiritual revival is the key to changing America. The logic, as he puts it elsewhere, is this: "In my opinion, the only way to change the world is to change individuals. Changed people, in sufficient numbers, will produce changed campuses, changed communities, changed cities, changed states and nations—yes, in a very real sense, a changed world. Jesus Christ is the only One who can change people from within. We can help change the world by introducing people to Jesus Christ."[25]

One could find many examples from the Evangelical world that illustrate this tactic.[26] Yet Evangelicals are not the only ones who embrace spiritual renewal as the centerpiece of cultural change. Different traditions within historical Christianity offer different articulations of the same idea. A Presbyterian ministry consultant, for example, articulates this strategy this way: "God's paradigm for cultural change" is modeled in the life of Jesus. "Jesus' strategy for change [is]: A. Come follow me (Matthew 4:19), B. Come be with me (Matthew 26:38), [and] C. Go! (Matthew 28:19)."[27] Abiding in Christ, imitating him, and then modeling his example to others in one's life is the biblical plan for generating a culture of peace.

One finds this theme articulated by Catholics as well. Addressing a congress of young people, the late Pope John Paul II argued, "Part of Christian realism is to understand that great social changes are the fruit of small courageous daily choices."[28] They "can be like leaven in the dough, capable of changing the grand metropolis, the large cities, the intellectual environment. And [they] can build a better future, because it is man who builds that human reality. Indeed, if man allows himself to be prompted by God, if he walks together with Him, he is capable of changing the world."[29]

This is not a complex theological point but one shared by the average priest. As a parochial vicar argued in his own words, "Live the faith and Change the World." "You and I," he argues, "are called to live the faith to such a degree that we bring change, radical change to our world by paving the way for God's Kingdom to Come."[30] The spiritual dimension is critical to this dynamic force. Mother Teresa herself put it this way, "People ask me: 'What will convert America and save the world?' My answer is prayer. What we need is for every Parish to come before Jesus in the Blessed Sacrament in Holy Hours of prayer."[31]

Everyone recognizes that much is at stake. As Billy Graham put it, "The greatest need in America at the moment is for a moral and spiritual renewal. This comes, I believe, *only* as we turn in repentance and faith to the living God, Who stands ready to forgive and renew us from within."[32] Evangelical social critic Os Guinness echoes the individualist "hearts and minds" argument: "The integrity and effectiveness of America's future in the world depends ultimately on the integrity and effectiveness of the faith in the hearts and lives of Americans."[33] To this end Guinness argues that "our time is one we need to remember" ..., "repent of ...," "resolve to ...," "take responsibility for ...," and "be realistic. ..." Only when Americans in enough numbers respond in this way can there be the "reformation and revival" America needs if it is to avoid social disaster and, he warns, the judgment of God.

Values and the Tactic of Political Action

Interestingly, this emphasis on values, choice, and spiritual renewal has also predisposed nearly everyone to focus on politics as the central means of changing the world. The reasoning goes like this: bad law is the outcome of bad choices made by individual politicians, judges, and policy makers.[34] Thus, changing the world requires that individual Christians vote into office those who hold the right values or possess the right worldview and therefore will make the right choices. Colson's four-step strategy points in just this direction, and many share his view. Thus, even a small organization like The Center for American Cultural Renewal, based in Rutland, Vermont, aspires to "educate, inspire, recruit, and train grassroots activists with the goal of renewing the culture through the ballot box and personal involvement in public affairs. We want to empower those citizens who are frustrated with the increasingly bankrupt moral and ethical climate in America with the knowledge and strategies enabling them to step up, be heard and make a difference."[35] What are those strategies? Prominently, they include lobbying "elected and appointed government officials and legislators, encouraging the passage of good laws."[36]

At one level, there is nothing exceptional about the effort to change the world through politics. Christians of various traditions and of both conservative and liberal political persuasion embrace the logic of a political strategy for change. They would readily affirm that politics is a legitimate sphere of activity for Christians. "The proper role for the Christian citizen," as one Evangelical puts it, "is to participate in government as fully as his calling and skills can take him, whether it be limited to voting or as an active government official."[37] "Christian people," he continues, "have an equal opportunity to set good public policy, not merely to protest after bad policy has been set."[38] Again, believers from the range of traditions in historical Christianity would find little, if anything, to object to in this.

At the same time, many Christians, while endorsing a political tactic for changing the world, also recognize and warn against the limitations of this tactic. Samuel Johnson is often quoted favorably and correctly in this regard, by Catholics, Evangelicals, the Reformed, the Mainline, and the Orthodox alike: "How small of all that human hearts endure, that part which laws or Kings either cause or cure."[39] Indeed, most Christians would agree that politics cannot solve all the problems in the world and, even further, would affirm, as a matter of theological principle, a distrust of all worldly power. Christ's kingdom, indeed, is not of this world.

These qualifications notwithstanding, the reality is that politics is the tactic of choice for many Christians as they think about changing the world. This has been most conspicuously true for Evangelicals, though it has also been as true for Christians in the Mainline Protestant traditions. It is not an exaggeration to say that *the dominant public witness of the Christian churches in America since the early 1980s has been a political witness*. This remains true today, again, particularly among the Evangelicals who, through innumerable para-church ministries, assert themselves into one political issue after another and into electoral politics as well. One Evangelical politician spoke for many in this tradition when he said, "America is the land of the Bible. I am convinced that only the Bible can provide the ultimate standard, the benchmark, by which we may hold our public policy and our political leaders accountable. It is the only standard that has the authority, relevance, precision, and power by which we may reform the thought-life of this country."[40]

For those of the so-called Religious Right, it was the dominance of secular humanists in the judiciary especially, but also in the legislature, that led to the outlawing of prayer and Bible reading in public schools, emptying them of religiously based values; to the legalization of abortion-on-demand; to the easing of sodomy laws; to the liberalization of restrictions on pornography and violence in popular culture; and so on. This being the case, the task must be to increase the number of Christians working in the realm of law and public policy at all levels of government and, short of that, to mobilize popular indignation to pressure politicians to support the policies and laws compatible with Christian principles. For some the logic is simple: if Christians can only get their people into office and maintain their laws, all will be well. As James Dobson of Focus on the Family explained, "The side that wins gains the right to teach what it believes to its children. And if you can do that, you write the curricula, you tell them what to believe and you model what you want them to understand and *in one generation*, you change the whole culture."[41]

Consider, in this regard, the view of one prominent Christian politician, Tom Delay. In public pronouncements during the 2000 presidential election cycle, this congressman argued that Americans must step up their resistance to the degradation of moral values. "We must transform our resistance into an aggressive counterattack," he said. "It's time to put our politics to work to renew our culture, to defeat the mounting effort to expel all religious belief from public life."[42] "What Congress can accomplish with a Republican President will be incredible. It will be nothing less than a rediscovery of the values that made America a great nation and that have made Americans a good people."[43] These are high expectations for what politics can accomplish but they are not his expectations alone.

This rationale has long animated all of the major legal and political conservative Christian organizations in distributing voter guides, initiating litigation, lobbying politicians and so on—groups such as Focus on the Family, the Christian Coalition, the Family Research Council, the Rutherford Institute, the American Center for Law and Justice (or ACLJ), the Center for Christian Statesmanship, and the now-defunct organizations, the Moral

Majority, Christian Voice, and the Religious Roundtable. This purpose has inspired the public affairs wing of the more moderate National Association of Evangelicals as well.[44] Acknowledging that the nation has been "caught in a profound culture war," the organization has insisted, "Evangelical Christians possess the weapons to win that war." "The NAE believes that the combination of more intense prayer and increased voter participation can have a significant impact on the cultural crisis in our national life." To this end, the NAE's Board of Administration approved initiatives "to stir evangelicals more fully to meet their civil and biblical responsibilities as citizens, and thus to strengthen their influence in public life." In particular, their objective has been to "recruit millions of evangelicals to pray more specifically and knowledgeably for their political leaders, and register one million new voters."

This rationale has inspired the major organizations of progressive Christian commitment as well. As Jim Wallis, the head of the Sojourners Community, puts it in *The Soul of Politics*, "The fundamental character of the social, economic, and cultural renewal we urgently need will require a change of both our hearts and our minds. But that change will demand a new kind of politics—a politics with spiritual values."[45] In the same vein, the antidote to the crisis offered in "The Cry for Renewal," for example, is "renewed *political* vision." This vision, it is made clear, "depends upon spiritual values," for only these values can provide "the moral direction and energy" required to renew "our impoverished political process." "By seeking the biblical virtues of justice and righteousness," the manifesto reasons, "the Christian community could help a cynical public find new political ground." In all, the objective of Christians is to offer "a *political* vision with spiritual values that transcends the old and failed categories that still imprison public discourse and stifle our creativity." The particular aspiration of this manifesto is to make it possible for other Christians to compete with the Religious Right: "the issues of political morality we now confront are too important to be left to only one voice. We testify that there are other visions of faith and politics in the land. New voices are critically needed. We especially appeal to the media to let new voices now be heard. We appeal to the politicians to listen to the voices of religion rather than seeking to manipulate them."[46]

Values and the Tactic of Social Reform

A third tactic that emanates from this working theory is a tactic of changing the culture through a renewal of civil society—the institutions that mediate between citizens and the state and market. The premise of this tactic is the recognition that politics and public policy, while they have their place in the larger scheme of things, are limited in what they can actually accomplish. Don Eberly, perhaps the most eloquent advocate of this tactic, puts it this way: "The most pressing issues of our time are social and cultural in nature, for which easy government solutions are not available."[47] Given the weaknesses of politics, "the solution is to recover the individual person in civil society," "to revive the spiritual and moral dimensions of democracy," "to effect a broad-based moral, civic, and democratic renewal." "Democracy's survival depends on the presence of just such a democratic disposition, habit, and outlook among the members of society." How is this accomplished? Eberly argues, "there is a strong hint in the pages of history that voluntary associations became the means of social correction when other forms of public action, such as legislative change, fell short. Private associations and moral reform movements have often produced progress after the realization set in that government either could not or would not do these things."[48]

This tactic, then, focuses on "broad-based voluntary reform movements led by citizens and community leaders permeating the character-shaping sectors of society."[49] In this tactic, the culture is improved through social movements of moral reform addressing particular problems within the family, schools, neighborhoods, and civic associations. What these movements all have in common is "a common desire to instill character by treating the individual as capable of and responsible for exercising self-control."[50] Illustrations of these voluntary social movements include, among others, the fatherhood movement, the marriage movement, the character movement, and the teen-abstinence movement. In more recent arguments, Eberly hopes to export this "bottom-up" strategy globally.[51]

In one bipartisan initiative entitled "Renew Our Culture," seven cultural indicators are listed as "measurable actions" that would be fundamental to the development of a healthy culture. These include: increasing parental involvement, increasing volunteerism, sustaining strong marriages, protecting children from drugs, creating greater safety for children and communities, reducing the consumption of violent and perverse entertainment, and reducing the number of abortions and out-of-wedlock births. At the heart of the plan is the goal of "empower[ing] individuals to assume responsibility for changing lives and communities."[52]

In Sum

It goes without saying that the spiritual, political, and social tactics for addressing the present challenges and perplexities of our time are not mutually exclusive. Most Christians would argue that these initiatives can work in concert. One of the reasons that they are compatible is that, different as they may seem, they share the same fundamental assumptions. *Cultures change when people change* or, as Charles Colson puts it, "transformed people transform cultures."[53] This happens substantively and lastingly only when there is change to the heart and the mind of the person, through the values and ideas that people live by.

There are several important elements implied in this view. First, real change must proceed individually—one by one. Even in the tactic of social reform, its advocates aim to "remak[e] the culture and the country one soul at a time."[54] "Our greatest strides in the world of cultural renewal will be made not in the arena of politics, but in the families, communities, churches, and charities of America—one person at a time."[55] Though they want to impact the institutions of civil society, "cultural transformation is brought about by *personal* transformation."[56] Second, cultural change can be willed into being. Cultural change, then, is purposeful and planned, insofar as the decisions that transformed individuals make are rational and consistent, and their choices conscious and deliberate. As the spokesman for "Renew our Culture" puts it, "where there is a will for healthier culture there is a way."[57] "Dare we believe that Christianity can yet prevail?" asks Charles Colson. "We must believe it. . . . this is an historic opportunity."[58] Third, change is democratic—it occurs from the bottom up among ordinary citizens, ordinary people. In this light we can see how one person can make a significant difference in the world. One person can stand at the crossroads and change things for good—such as Martin Luther, John Calvin, Charles Wesley, Jonathan Edwards, or William Booth, Bishop Tutu, John Paul II, Dorothy Day; or for ill—such as Frederick Nietzsche, Adolf Hitler, Joseph Stalin, Pol Pot, and so on.

If there is an exemplar whose life mission touches all of these themes and strategies—and who is celebrated as such—it is William Wilberforce (1757–1833). Wilberforce was a member of the British House of Commons and spent over forty years seeking to end slavery and "reform the manners" of his society. He was a devout Christian who believed that true personal change came through salvation by faith in Jesus Christ, and his ideals were fed by his deep faith. As an activist, he led a social movement committed to the moral reform of British society and against much opposition eventually prevailed in abolishing the legalized slave trade. Wilberforce was indeed, a great man and a model of what one courageous person willing to step into the fray can do.

At the end of the day, the message is clear: even if not in the lofty realms of political life that he was called to, you too can be a Wilberforce. In your own sphere of influence, you too can be an Edwards, a Dwight, a Booth, a

Lincoln, a Churchill, a Dorothy Day, a Martin Luther King, a Mandela, a Mother Teresa, a Vaclav Havel, a John Paul II, and so on. If you have the courage and hold to the right values and if you think Christianly with an adequate Christian worldview, you too can change the world.

This account is almost wholly mistaken.

Chapter Three

THE FAILURE OF THE COMMON VIEW

B EFORE GOING ANY FURTHER, it is important to be explicit about what I am saying and what I am not saying. First, for the Christian, evangelism is central to their identity and purpose in the world. To share the Gospel is to share the gift of life; the making of disciples is foundational to the Christian faith. And peoples' lives do change profoundly when they receive the gift of grace—their attitudes and behaviors are transformed and, in turn, they can and often do have a positive effect on those around them. In a similar vein, no one would deny that law, public policy, and politics are worthy vocations for Christians to pursue. The pursuit of justice and righteousness in these vocations can give glory to God and provide great service to many. Finally, social movements oriented toward moral reform have done enormous good in the past and still do in the present. All of these things are good and great good can come from them.

But do they change the world?

The answer is both yes and no; but it is mostly no. Cultures simply do not change in these ways, or at least not in the way people think they do.

A Fatal Flaw

To explain more fully, the focus of my attention is not on evangelism or politics or social reform per se but rather *the working theory* that both undergirds these strategies and approves them as the primary if not only means for changing the world. For all the good that actually comes from these particular strategies, the working theory of culture and cultural change on which they are based is fundamentally flawed.

To begin to make a case, I simply offer a few key illustrations—I make no effort to be comprehensive here.

I begin with faith in America. Consider, first, the fact that communities of faith have been a dominating presence in American society for the length and breadth of its history. There is some evidence that suggests that there are even more Americans who are worshipping as part of a congregation today than in the past.[1] As late as 1960, only 2 percent of the population claimed not to believe in God; even today, only 12 to 14 percent of the population would call themselves secularists. This means that in America today, 86 to 88 percent of the people adhere to some faith commitments. And yet our culture—business culture, law and government, the academic world, popular entertainment—is intensely materialistic and secular. Only occasionally do we hear references to religious transcendence in these realms, and even these are vague, generic, and void of particularity. If culture is the accumulation of values and the choices made by individuals on the basis of these values, then how is it that American public culture today is so profoundly secular in its character?

A second illustration follows from the first. In American history, the greatest number of religious people and the greatest vitality of religious observance tend to be among the traditional adherents. Evangelical and orthodox Catholics are especially prominent. Even today, they outnumber their liberal counterparts in Protestantism and Catholicism, and the vitality of their piety is extraordinary. Take charitable giving, for example. The conservative members of these faiths are not wealthier than their more liberal counterparts (quite the opposite, in fact), but they are far and away more generous—the majority giving over 8 percent of their income away every year and almost half giving 10 percent or more every year. Or take church attendance. In recent years, white Evangelical Protestants were about twice as likely to have attended church in the past week as their mainline counterparts, according to a survey by the Baylor Institute for Studies of Religion.[2] They were two and a half times as likely as mainline Protestants to read the Bible once a week or more, and half again as likely to pray that often.[3] And when it came to church activities, black and white Evangelicals were again twice as likely to participate, far outweighing mainliners in everything from prayer and Bible study groups to church choir and sports leagues.[4] Yet despite such enthusiastic participation, the history of the conservative faith traditions over the last 175 years has been one of declining influence, especially in the realm of ideas and imagination. It is true that their political influence has undulated over the years; presently, it is quite high in certain sectors. But culturally, these faith traditions have moved from a position of offense to one of defense. Once prominent in almost all spheres of American public life, setting the agenda and framing public goals, conservative believers have fallen to relative impotence. Indeed, in some arenas, they now have no presence and exert no influence at all. So, if culture is really just what exists in our hearts and minds and manifests itself through the choices that we make, then the values of the largest and most vital groups should be the values that assert the greatest sway. Needless to say, they are not.

Consider, by contrast the experience of the Jewish community in America. Except for a brief period in the middle of the twentieth century, Jews have never comprised more than 3.5 percent of the American population. Yet, as David Hollinger has shown, the contribution of the Jewish community to science, literature, art, music, letters, film, and architecture is both brilliant and unrivaled.[5] And these contributions were made in a context often defined by open, aggressive, and malicious anti-Semitism; an anti-Semitism manifested in restrictions and quotas against Jews in private schools, camps, colleges, resorts, and places of employment, in public denigration by some of the most respected leaders of the time (including Henry Ford), and in physical assault on Jews, especially young Jews. Yet despite these obstacles, (obstacles often generated and perpetuated by Christians themselves), their influence in the shaping of high culture has been quite disproportionate to their size. The debt America owes to this small community is immeasurable.

A similar story of influence can be told of the gay community. At most 3 percent of the American population, their influence has become enormous; again far disproportionate to their size. It is worth pointing out too that most of the gains in visibility, legitimacy, and legal rights by the gay rights movement were made during the twelve conservative years of the Reagan and Bush presidencies. Those advances continue largely unabated through the present—a time when a majority in the general population has remained privately troubled by homosexuality. In only the past few years, we have witnessed the rapid transformation of gay marriage from an almost unthinkable hypothetical for most Americans to the subject of a raging debate at the center of American public and political life. In 2000, Vermont moved to recognize civil unions between gay and lesbian couples. In 2003, Texas sodomy laws were struck down by the U.S. Supreme Court. And in 2004 same-sex marriage was legalized in Massachusetts, sending tremors throughout the rest of the country. And this was only the beginning. One finds similar transformations taking place in Canada, Spain, and other countries, as well as in the American Episcopal Church. The same is true for American popular culture. Over the past decade, an ever-increasing number of prime-time sitcoms have begun to highlight the gay and lesbian lifestyle. *Ellen*, *Will and Grace*, *The L-Word*, *Queer Eye for the Straight Guy*, the list goes on. Gays and lesbians are now a staple of comedy and drama in everything from talk shows to film. By contrast, at least in mainstream American media, there is now little or no space for the voicing of questions of moral and social concerns about this movement. Homosexuality has become a fact of our collective life and social reality such that the only legitimate question is how we are to learn to live with it.[6]

In both of these latter instances, the question is the same: if culture were simply a matter of hearts and minds, then the influence of various minorities—whoever they are and whatever that may be—would be relatively insignificant. But again, in these instances and in many others we can draw from history, we know this is not the case.

In the previous chapter, Charles Colson is cited posing the question "why is Darwinism still the official creed in our public schools?" He argues that "the real issue is not what we see through the microscope or the telescope; it's what we adhere to in our hearts and minds." Yet according to survey data, Colson has it all wrong. In a recent Gallup poll, there was an even split between those who said that Darwin's theory of evolution is supported by evidence and those who said it is not supported by evidence, with each side garnering 35 percent of the respondent pool. The rest either didn't know enough to say, or had no opinion at all on the issue. In the same poll, 45 percent of respondents agreed with the statement that "God created human beings pretty much in their present form at one time within the last 10,000 years or so"; and 38 percent opted for a form of evolutionary creationism in which the development of human beings from less advanced forms of life was divinely directed. Only 13 percent said that God had no part in the process.[7] This raises an observation and a question. The observation is that the "hearts and minds" of most Americans are with Colson on this issue—83 percent of all Americans take some form of providentialist view of origins. The question is, if educational policy is a matter of hearts and minds, as Colson contends, then education would reflect the complex views of the population. Why doesn't the curriculum reflect that view; why has secular evolutionary theory really become the official creed in the public schools?

A similar scenario exists on the question of abortion. If we are to listen to the special interest groups, the issue of abortion leads to a clear choice. From one perspective, we must choose between *life* and *death*; from the other, it is *choice* versus *oppression*. When the stakes are so high, compromise is an evasion. These binary oppositions are institutionalized into our legal system. Abortion is legal—or, given a few new Supreme Court judges, it will become illegal. For many, *Roe v. Wade* represents the stranglehold of "the culture of death." For many others, it is a beacon of freedom and hope for all women. The reality is, however, that when one examines the hearts and minds of ordinary Americans, one finds more of a spectrum of opinion on abortion than a stark contrast. Indeed, the majority of Americans hold a more complex and in some ways, incoherent view of the place of abortion in our society. In a recent survey by the Pew Forum on Religion and Public Life, only 15 percent of respondents said that "Abortion should be . . . *always illegal.*" Thirty-five percent said that abortion should be *"legal and up to women to decide."* Fifty percent of those surveyed, however, responded that abortion should be legal in only *some* circumstances—with 33 percent of the total saying that it should be "legal in few circumstances" and 17 percent saying that it should be "legal in many circumstances."[8] Clearly, then, laws and policies do not simply follow or mirror majority opinion. If they did, moderates would win the day, and abortion would only be legal in some circumstances. But as the debate over partial-birth abortion has clearly shown, even attempts to limit the most extreme forms of abortion are too highly controversial, and moderates have little place amid the heated rhetoric of our national conversation over the fate of the unborn.

And so it goes. In example after example, we find evidence that culture is in fact a much more complicated phenomenon than we normally imagine. Indeed, it often seems eerily independent of majority opinion.

The Apparent Problem

But why? The advocates of the dominant strategies of cultural change all tend to agree, in effect, that the reason Christians do not have more influence in shaping the culture is that Christians are just not trying hard enough, acting decisively enough, or believing thoroughly or Christianly enough. Consider the following statements: "Significant changes in any society come . . . *only* as Christian people hear the word of God and determine to obey it."[9] The lesson: believers simply need to be more determined and to work harder. "If Christians do not seize the moment and act on the cultural commission, there soon will be no culture left to save. But *when we do our duty*, we can change the world."[10] And so, the lesson is that believers must work harder at their God-given duty. *"Once we understand who we are and whom we serve,* we will have the means to find our moral compass and bring the ship of state back onto its true course."[11] Here the lesson is that for these things Christians must achieve clarity. "Our generation *must cultivate morality anew.*"[12] To this end, believers must strive more vigorously. "The [culture] war is winnable *through the witness of our faith and through the commitment of each individual to take up spiritual arms* against 'the darkness of this world.'"[13] The lesson here is that people of faith need to shore up their spiritual commitment. "When we *truly understand our faith*, we can begin to share it with others with authority and passion."[14] Christians need, therefore, to understand more carefully and more fully the claims of their faith on their lives. Consider another illustration from Focus on the Family.

> Why does a biblical worldview matter? If we don't really believe the truth of God and live it, then our witness will be confusing and misleading. Most of us go through life not recognizing that our personal worldviews have been deeply affected by the world. Through the media and other influences, the secularized American view of history, law, politics, science, God and man affects our thinking more than we realize . . . However, *by diligently learning, applying and trusting* God's truths in every area of our lives—whether it's watching a movie, communicating with our spouses, raising our children or working at the office—we can begin to develop a deep comprehensive faith that will stand against the unrelenting tide of our culture's non-biblical ideas. *If we capture and embrace more* of God's worldview and trust it with unwavering faith, then we begin to make the right decisions and form the appropriate responses to questions on abortion, same-sex marriage, cloning, stem-cell research and even media choices.[15]

Here too the lesson is that because most Christians are befuddled, Christians must be more diligent in learning and embrace more of God's worldview. Only then will things turn around. It is this logic that has provided the basis for Focus on the Family's "Truth Project." Dobson explains,

> This is the "cosmic battle." Unfortunately, in our culture, the lies of the world, the flesh and the devil bombard us from every quarter. And, when we fail to recognize them as lies and instead accept them as true, the consequences are significant . . . and devastating. Sadly, the vast majority of believers in our culture are ill-prepared to fight in this battle. We suffer from the same pathologies the world does and, statistically, at roughly the same levels: divorce, sexual addictions, eating disorders, depression, worry, apathy, discontent, anger, abortion, poor media viewing habits, pornography . . . and so on. How can this be? Quite simply, we are falling for the counterfeits.[16]

The answer, according to Del Tackett, the director of The Truth Project:

> By embracing the reality of who God is and His Truth claims for all of life, we can stand up against every giant that threatens us. Our all-powerful God has promised us, through the prophet Isaiah, that "no weapon forged against you will prevail, and you will refute every tongue that accuses you" (Isaiah 54:17). Our prayer is that *The Truth Project* will provide you with the knowledge and insight you need in order to be a vessel for change in our fallen world.[17]

In all of these instances, the burden of responsibility and action resides with the individual Christian and it is up to them to be better and do more to change the world.

The apparent problem, in brief, is twofold: First, Christians just aren't Christian enough. Christians don't think with an adequate enough Christian worldview, Christians are fuzzy-minded, Christians don't pray hard enough, and Christians are generally lazy toward their duties as believers. By the same token, there are not enough people who *do* fully embrace God's call on their lives, praying, understanding, and working to change the world.

But is this it? Does this explain why it is that the world seems to be changing inexorably in the "wrong" directions for these believers? Does this account for why Christians seem to have such little effect on the direction of history? Or, is there more to the nature of culture and cultural change that is presently missing from the popular understandings of these matters?

The Real Problem

The real problem of this working theory of culture and cultural change and the strategies that derive from it, originate from a tradition deep in Western thought. This tradition reaches back to Plato, though it finds its most modern and powerful articulation in the German Enlightenment—the philosophical thinking of Immanuel Kant, Gotthold Lessing, Johann Gottfried Herder, Johann von Goethe, Friedrich Schiller, and, most importantly, Georg W. F. Hegel. In a word, "idealism."

Without going into an elaborate discussion, idealism is a principle and tradition in metaphysics that maintains that something "ideal" or nonphysical is the primary reality. It isn't as though nature or the material world doesn't exist or isn't important, but what has greater ontological significance and is certainly prior to nature and the physical, are ideas—in short, the "mind." We know this, say advocates, in part because material reality cannot be known independent of the conscious and knowing self. In the basic (and, if you will, Platonic) formulation, physical objects are just pale imitations of the ideas and ideals that represent them.

This being so, it is ideas that move history. Though Herder is credited with the insight, it was Hegel who developed the idea systematically and who gave the larger argument credibility. As with many things in the history of ideas, the specific formulations of Herder, Hegel, or anyone else is far less important than the general and overarching point about the significance of ideas in human history.[18] What is finally relevant is the translation of academic idealism in Christian thinking into a pedestrian Hegelianism.

We see this illustrated in many places. Consider, for example, the argument from Colson's *How Now Shall We Live?* about the range of conflicts in our political culture.

> The culture war is not just about abortion, homosexual rights, or the decline of public education. These are only skirmishes. *The real war is a cosmic struggle between worldviews*—between the Christian worldview and the various secular and spiritual worldviews arrayed against it. This is what we must understand if we are going to be effective both in evangelizing our world today and in transforming it to reflect the wisdom of the Creator.[19]

Nancy Pearcey, who cowrote *How Now Shall We Live?*, argues much the same point in her own book, *Total Truth*: "It has become commonplace to say that Americans are embroiled in a culture war over conflicting moral standards. But we must remember that morality is always derivative—it stems from an underlying worldview."[20] To engage the *culture* war, she contends, "we have to be willing to engage the underlying *cognitive* war." Here again, it is the mind that matters, the ideas that are operative in culture.

It makes sense, then, to trace the history of, say, sexuality in terms of the changing ideas about sexuality. As Colson explains in Chapter 25 of *How Now Shall We Live?*, the problem begins with Jean-Jacques Rousseau, is amplified by Sigmund Freud, becomes championed by Margaret Sanger, is justified "scientifically" by Alfred Kinsey, is popularized among the educated classes by the psychologist Wilhelm Reich and the fiction of Robert Rimmer, and finally is translated for ordinary school children through the work of Mary Calderone, the architect of contemporary sex education.[21] This is but an illustration of his earlier contention that "history is little more than the recording of the rise and fall of the great ideas—the worldviews—that form our values and move us to act."[22] Colson is not alone in his unqualified idealism. This is the convention among most American Christians.[23]

Having said this, I would be remiss if I didn't mention two other elements that give idealism a distinctly American and Protestant flavor. For one, woven into idealism is the element of "individualism," the view that the autonomous and rational individual is the key actor in social change.[24] The tradition of individualism is actually much broader as it reaches down from the Protestant Reformation into its more contemporary secular manifestations; as a principle and tradition in epistemology and ethics in which the unique, unrepeatable person (as opposed to any sort of collective entity) is seen as the primary cause and beneficiary of action. Linked integrally with these two is yet a third element, "Christian pietism," the view that the most important goal in life is having one's being right before God. Theologically, there is nothing exceptional to this, but as an element of a working theory of culture, that is something else altogether. In this light, pietism is sympathetic to idealism in the way that it extends idealism into the realm of the religious, spiritual, and supernatural conceptions of reality. Mind and spirit are fused. For the Christian, pietism is a natural link to both idealism and individualism. But in the end, the larger source of the problem with the prevailing view of culture and cultural change is idealism.

The Perils of Idealism

On the face of it, there is significant merit to the emphasis given to ideas, to the individual and to personal piety. Yet filtered through the legacy of German idealism, they have prejudiced our larger view of culture and cultural change in ways that are fundamentally problematic. The image this perspective offers is of culture, somehow, free-floating in the ether of consciousness. Change consciousness and one changes culture. But are ideas, values, and worldviews singularly important to cultural change? Are ordinary individuals with conviction the main carriers and agents of that change? Is rational consistency the best way to resist worldviews different from one's own and the most effective way to persuade others?

In fact idealism misconstrues agency, implying the capacity to bring about influence where that capacity may not exist or where it may only be weak. Idealism underplays the importance of history and historical forces and its interaction with culture as it is lived and experienced. Further, idealism ignores the way culture is generated, coordinated, and organized. Thus, it underrates how difficult it is to penetrate culture and influence its direction. Not least, idealism mistakenly imputes a logic and rationality to culture where such linearity and reasonableness does not exist but rather contingency and accident. In all, it communicates the message that if people just pay attention, learn better, be more consistent, they will understand better the challenges in our world today; if they have the right values, believe the right things, embrace the right worldview, they will be better equipped to engage those challenges; and if they have the courage to actually jump in the fray and there choose more wisely and act more decisively, they will rise to and overcome those challenges and change the world.

There is an irony in this perspective. One of the great virtues of the "worldview" approach to culture is its rejection of "dualism"—the division between secular and sacred, public and private, objective and subjective; the idea that the truth of Christianity is really only religious truth, relevant to one's personal life but mostly irrelevant to other spheres of life. As Nancy Pearcey says, Christianity is "total truth." It encompasses all reality. Dualism is, in fact, pervasive and it is toxic and it must be rejected. So the advocates of the worldview approach are to be commended. The irony is this: *the idealism expressed in the worldview approach is, in fact, one manifestation of the very dualism its proponents are trying to challenge. Idealism reinforces that dualism by ignoring the institutional nature of culture and disregarding the way culture is embedded in structures of power.*

In sum, idealism leads to a naïveté about the nature of culture and its dynamics that is, in the end, fatal. Every strategy and tactic for changing the world that is based on this working theory of culture and cultural change will fail—not most of these strategies, but all. As I said at the start of this chapter, this is not to say that the renewal of hearts and minds of individuals is not important; nor is it to say that worldview education is not a good thing and will not have beneficial effects; nor is it to say that social reform and political engagement are not worthy goals. It is simply to say that these things are just not decisively important if the goal is to change the world. Thus, if one is serious about changing the world, the first step is to discard the prevailing view of culture and cultural change and start from scratch.

Coda: Culture as Artifact

Deep from within the Evangelical world, a new perspective on culture and cultural change has been introduced in part as a response to the idealism that pervades the dominant perspective on culture. This view recognizes that culture is more than just a worldview. The heart of culture, rather, is constituted by things; the things we create. As its chief protagonist, Andy Crouch, has put it, culture is constituted by "actual, concrete stuff—material, corporeal, physical. It's the very tangible product of human activity."[25] He echoes this point repeatedly: "If we want to understand culture, then, it's always best to begin and end with specific cultural goods."[26] "Culture is the accumulation of very tangible things—the stuff people make of the world."[27]

Crouch's view operates from within some of the assumptions, though not the ideology or practices, of a certain tradition in anthropological theory called cultural materialism. What his perspective mainly shares in common with this theoretical approach is the priority given to the materiality of culture and to the demographic forces involved in producing material culture.[28] "We talk about culture, he writes, "as if it were primarily a set of ideas when it is *primarily* a set of tangible goods."[29]

Crouch is not merely a materialist, though. He clearly recognizes that culture also entails beliefs, values, and ideas—indeed, it requires them for it is only through them that material goods are understood and interpreted. But the priority is obvious, "We make sense of the world by making something of the world. The human quest for meaning is played out in human making: the finger-painting, omelet-stirring, chair-crafting, snow-swishing activities of culture."[30] In short, ideas, symbols, ideals, worldviews, and the like are not free-floating and autonomous from lived reality. They are, rather, mediated through things. It is the vast array of cultural artifacts—from omelets, chairs, and snow angels to highway systems, from the Pill to iPods—that finally shape the way we encounter and make sense of the world.

The priority he gives to the materiality of culture means that his focus is on the artifact as an artifact, and its power to shape the way that people imagine and experience the world. As Crouch puts it, "culture requires a public: a group of people who have been sufficiently affected by a cultural good that their horizon of possibility and impossibility have in fact been altered, and their own cultural activity has been spurred, by that good's experience."[31]

Given this view of culture, how do cultures change? It stands to reason that "[c]ulture changes when new cultural goods, concrete, tangible artifacts, whether books or tools or buildings—are introduced to the world."[32] Put more succinctly, "The only way to change culture is to create more of it."[33] As Crouch puts it,

> culture changes when people actually make more and better culture. If we want to transform culture, what we actually have to do is to get into the midst of the human cultural project and create some new cultural goods that reshape the way people imagine and experience their world. . . . We seek the transformation of every culture but how we do it is by actually making culture.[34]

Importantly, the proper sphere of culture making is local and shared—it is never a solitary affair. "Every cultural good, whether a new world, law, recipe, song, or gadget, begins with a small group of people."[35] The same can be said of cultural change. As he concludes, "for any given human being in a particular cultural environment, all it takes to change their world—to change the horizons of possibility and impossibility for them—is to change the culture right around them."[36]

Cultural power, he argues, is defined "as the ability to *successfully* propose a new cultural good."[37] The paradox, for Crouch, is that while we all share the imperative to be culture makers, we finally cannot change the world because we cannot anticipate or dictate how any cultural artifact will be accepted by others. Crouch grounds this view on the assumption that societies are, in effect, constituted by the aggregate of individuals consuming a range of cultural goods, thereby influencing each other's horizons of possibilities. It is for this reason that he argues that the best strategy for Christians is to invest in creative cultural production. "Investing is basically a way of placing bets on which cultural goods will grow in world-changing importance."[38]

This perspective has generated a good deal of positive interest, especially among younger Evangelicals. But does it adequately account for the movements and configurations of contemporary culture? Take, for example, his own faith tradition—Evangelicalism. Over the twentieth century, Evangelicals have been distinguished by their massive cultural output in books and book publishing, magazines, radio, music, bible studies, theology, Christian education at all levels, and so on. Given the success of these ventures, it is clear that consumption has matched production. Without doubt, this creativity has far outmatched the cultural output of probably any other faith tradition in America. It is true that Evangelicals have not been active in high art or in film, but these facts alone do not account for their dramatic marginalization in American society, not least since other much smaller minorities have had a much greater influence. Is it merely that Evangelicalism has failed to market their cultural products well? Or, that as a movement, it has not operated in the "right" markets? Too many questions are left unanswered.

There are certainly aspects of this perspective and Crouch's specific take on it that are laudable. It does seek to provide a corrective to the excesses of idealism attending the dominant view. Crouch's theology of gospel and culture is also a welcome relief to the focus on politics as a means of engaging the world. Yet, in the end, this view still suffers from fundamental flaws that render it inadequate for understanding the complexity of the world and Christianity's relationship to it.

For one, the attention placed on the material qualities of culture and the embodied qualities of cultural production is all to the good. Yet the near exclusive focus on the explicit, visible, tangible, and conscious aspects of culture minimizes the more implicit, intangible, preconscious, inherited, and thus more encompassing nature of culture. He sees the tip of the iceberg, but not the mass of ice below the surface.

For another, this perspective fails to recognize and address the relationship of culture to the dynamics and structures of power that operate in the world (and in the culture itself). It fails to consider the importance of the social location of cultural production and the symbolic meaning attached to different cultural objects. All cultural production and all cultural objects are not, in the end, equal; some are of much greater influence than others. There are reasons for this that Crouch's model cannot explain. The market model which his approach to culture assumes is not, in fact, a free market at all, for human desire is rooted in a normative framework; that is, the structures of human desire are framed and shaped by historical and sociological forces that are, as sociologists will often say, "relatively autonomous" from the market. What this means, in other words, is that the "things" created are not culturally neutral, and neither is desire, but both are infused with a moral significance that operates somewhat independently from though always through the market itself. There are many ways this plays out, but the most obvious contemporary example is the phenomenon of "branding." These powerful realities and the dynamics that give them traction are unaccounted for in this approach to culture.

What is more, while this view does acknowledge the social and communal nature of cultural production, it falls short of adequately understanding the powerful institutional (and not just organizational) nature and dynamics of culture. In this view, the social dimensions of culture are comprised of the efforts of individuals working together—creating, acting, initiating, and so forth. *The model of cultural change on offer, then, implicitly operates within the framework of a market populism.* Change comes through the random aggregation of individual actions and choices in a free market of options. What matters for the Christian in this approach to culture, is entering into the marketplace with the creation of new cultural goods. The direction and purpose and coherence of cultural creation matter less because, in the end, it will be the market that determines what succeeds or fails. On the face of it, this is naïve.

Finally, the market populism that underwrites this perspective is reinforced by the absence of the church itself from the discussion. For individual Christians there is much to do, but for the church—as an institution, a set of inherited practices, a source of discernment, and a guide for wisdom, or as a locus of vision, innovation, formation, and mobilization—there is little if any place or role.

In the end, this view of culture and cultural change shares many of the basic problematic assumptions of the dominant view. This perspective is individualistic—cultures are constituted by and changed through the actions of aggregated individuals. Though an impersonal market finally determines the outcome, cultural change can be willed into being—through the investment and creation of cultural goods. And cultural change is democratic—it occurs through the actions of ordinary people, from the bottom up.

When all is said and done, though offered as a new approach to culture and cultural change, the "culture as artifact" perspective also falls far short of providing an adequate account of the complexity of culture and Christianity's relationship to it. Once again, we are left with the need for an alternative.

Chapter Four

AN ALTERNATIVE VIEW OF CULTURE AND CULTURAL CHANGE IN ELEVEN PROPOSITIONS

THE PREVAILING VIEW of culture is a weak view and the strategies for change that emerge from it are ineffective, largely because they fail to take into account the nature of culture in its complexity and the factors that give it strength and resilience over time.

To address this failing, however, is to go right to the heart of social theory. Needless to say, this arena of scholarship can be highly esoteric—any truly detailed elucidation would require tomes. To lay it all out, then, would be possible but, in the end, it would be a distraction from the argument at hand.[1] And so I will simply lay out the heart of an alternative approach in eleven propositions—seven about culture itself and four about cultural change. Here again, more could be said about each one, but these propositions and their short descriptions cover the major highlights that suggest a different and, I believe, better direction.

Seven Propositions on Culture

PROPOSITION ONE: CULTURE IS A SYSTEM OF TRUTH CLAIMS AND MORAL OBLIGATIONS

Culture is, first and foremost, a normative order by which we comprehend others, the larger world, and ourselves and through which we individually and collectively order our experience. At the heart of culture is a *complex* of norms, as social scientists are prone to call them. But these norms are better understood as *commanding* truths, which define the "shoulds" and "should nots" of our experience and, accordingly, the good and the evil, the right and the wrong, the appropriate and the inappropriate, the honorable and the shameful.

Accordingly, culture involves the obligations to adhere to these truths, obligations that come about by virtue of one's membership in a group. Put differently, culture is a system of truth claims and moral obligations.

All of this said, these truth claims and moral demands do not exist as a set of propositions. It is true that they mostly can be expressed as aphorisms or old adages but people rarely if ever grasp them within consciousness as a series of recipe formulations. Rather, they are embedded within narratives that often have overlapping themes and within various myths that often reinforce common ideals.

Only in a highly abridged sense, then, is culture a worldview. Perhaps the most important thing to realize is that this "worldview" is so deeply embedded in our consciousness, in the habits of our lives, and in our social practices that to question one's worldview is to question "reality" itself. Sometimes, we are self-conscious of and articulate about our worldview, but for most of us, the frameworks of meaning by which we navigate life exist "prereflectively," prior to conscious awareness. That is, our understanding of the world is so taken-for-granted that it seems utterly obvious. It bears repeating that it is not just our view of what is right or wrong or true or false but our understanding of time, space, and identity—the very essence of reality as we experience it.

This is so because the frameworks of knowledge and understanding (and thus culture, in this sense) are largely coterminous with language. Language, the most basic system of symbols, provides the primary medium through which people apprehend their conscious experience in the world. Through both its structure and its meaning—its syntax and semantics—it provides the categories through which people understand themselves, others, and the larger world. To acquire language is to see the world and oneself in it, meaningfully.

This is why one cannot merely change worldviews or question one's own very easily. Most of what really counts, in terms of what shapes us and directs us, we are not aware of; it operates far below what most of us are capable of consciously grasping.

PROPOSITION TWO: CULTURE IS A PRODUCT OF HISTORY

If language provides one reason why culture is settled so deeply into consciousness and social practice, history is another reason. Culture takes form as the slow accretions of meaning in society over long periods of time. In this sense, culture is much less an invention of the will than it is a slow product of history.

A bit of jargon can help here. In his development of the old Aristotelian and Thomist concept of *habitus*, the French social theorist Pierre Bourdieu offers an insight into just how important the interaction of history with culture is. Bourdieu defines habitus as a system of dispositions shared within a society or within a community. Experienced as internal law and external necessity, habitus represents "the past which survives in the present" or, as he puts it elsewhere, it is "history turned into nature,"[2] *second* nature, if you will. It organizes a way of being, and not just a course of action, and it does so in a way that makes our understanding of the world and our way of life seem natural. For these historical reasons, culture is highly resilient, durable over time.

This does not mean that cultures are closed systems and impervious to influence and change. Obviously enough, they are open and variable and always given to some modification, adaptation, and alteration. It is just that they are not easily changed in these ways or changed in the direction we want them to change. The inertia built into culture by virtue of its relationship to its long history tends to make it lumbering and erratic at the same time.

PROPOSITION THREE: CULTURE IS INTRINSICALLY DIALECTICAL

There are two ways in which this proposition plays out. The first has to do with the relationship between ideas and institutions. Given the pervasive tendencies toward idealism, we are prone to view culture in terms of its leading ideas. We often speak of these as though culture was like a gaseous vapor—you can't see it but you know it is there because people are inspired by it or infected by it (as the case may be). Yet ideas are not free-floating in consciousness but are grounded in the social world in the most concrete ways. To put it bluntly, culture is as much an infrastructure as it is ideas. It takes shape in concrete institutional form. One must view culture, then, not only as a normative order reflected in well-established symbols, but also as the organization of human activity surrounding the production, distribution, manipulation, and administration of those symbols. Another way to say this is that culture is intrinsically dialectical. It is generated and exists at the interface between ideas and institutions; between the symbolic and the social and physical environment.

Ideas are important, of course, but without understanding the nature, workings, and power of the institutions in which those ideas are generated and managed, one only understands half of what is going on in culture. It is better to think of culture as a thing, if you will, manufactured not by lone individuals but rather by institutions and the elites who lead them. Institutions such as the market, the state, education, the media of mass communications, scientific and technological research, and the family in its socializing capacities are not organizationally neutral but have their own logic, place, and history that interact with the ideas and ideals for which they are carriers. It is the failure to understand and integrate this basic fact that makes most Americans and American Christians effectively "Hegelians" when it comes to culture.

There is another way in which culture is intrinsically dialectical—one that would seem so obvious that it does not need any explanation. This is the relationship between individuals and institutions. Individuals, of course, do possess beliefs and values, and as such they are constitutive of a social order and its institutions. But at the same time, those institutions and the larger social order of which they are a part not only provide the framework of meanings and social relations in which individuals operate but also "act back" on individuals to form the structures of their consciousness.[3] In short, individuals and institutions are inseparable. Institutions cannot exist without the individuals who make them work, but individuals cannot be understood outside of the institutions that form them and frame all of their activity. That said, in the formation of culture, one should not be under the illusion that the dialectic is evenly balanced. While individuals are not powerless by any stretch of the imagination, institutions have much greater power.

PROPOSITION FOUR: CULTURE IS A RESOURCE AND, AS SUCH, A FORM OF POWER

To think of culture institutionally and organizationally allows one to think of *symbols as a resource*. Symbols take the form of ideas, information, news, wisdom, indeed, knowledge of all kinds, and these in turn are expressed in pronouncements, speeches, edicts, tracts, essays, books, film, art, law, and the like. The amount of cultural output, of course, varies considerably by society and by the institutions producing it.[4]

At the same time, symbols in the form of knowledge, technical knowhow, credentials, and cultural accomplishments can also be thought of as a form of capital. Particularly in *the cultural meaning imputed* to such things, culture can be understood as *symbolic capital*. Though, unlike money, symbolic capital cannot readily be transferred from one generation to another, or from one individual to another, like money, symbolic capital can be accumulated. Some individuals, some organizations, and some objects have more and accumulate more symbolic capital than others. For example, a Ph.D. has more symbolic capital than a car mechanic; a member of the National Academy of Sciences has more symbolic capital than a high school science teacher; the winner of a Nobel Prize in literature has more symbolic capital than a romance novelist. Likewise, whatever else one may think about the *New York Times*, it has more symbolic capital than the *Dallas Morning News*, Yale has greater symbolic capital than Bob Jones University, and some say (though it is highly disputed) that the Yankees have greater symbolic capital than the Red Sox. At the risk of droning on, an Oscar has more symbolic capital than a Christian Film and Television Excellence Award, a Rhodes scholarship carries more symbolic capital than a Rotary Club scholarship, and a BMW has more symbolic capital than a Honda. All of these are extreme contrasts but they make the point.

Importantly, culture is not neutral in relation to power but a form of power. In other words, like money, accumulated symbolic capital translates into a kind of power and influence. But influence of what kind? It starts as credibility, an authority one possesses which puts one in a position to be listened to and taken seriously. It ends as the power to define reality itself. As Bourdieu puts it, it is the power of "legitimate naming." Take Alexander Solzhenitzyn as an example. While many people endured the Gulag, some of whom wrote of their experiences, it was Solzhenitsyn's reputation and credibility that was catapulted far beyond his peers. This was in large measure due to his Nobel Prize in literature. This symbolic capital, in turn, gave him the ability to speak on a wide range of other issues far outside the realm of literature with great authority. To give another example, an op-ed in the *New York Times* confers greater credibility and authority than anything opined in the *Chattanooga Times Free Press*. And finally, one might point to the universal practice of "book-blurbing." When one turns to the back cover of a new book by an Evangelical and finds an enthusiastic endorsement by James Dobson or J. I. Packer, the book immediately gains an enormous boost in legitimacy. This occurs whether or not the endorser has any expertise in the subject of the book. Symbolic capital is conferred almost magically on the book simply by virtue of the endorser's celebrity status within the Evangelical Christian community. Indeed, often enough it takes little more than a celebrity blurb and a catchy cover to give an otherwise mediocre book manuscript the power to influence the perceptions and convictions of its readers.

PROPOSITION FIVE: CULTURAL PRODUCTION AND SYMBOLIC CAPITAL ARE STRATIFIED IN A FAIRLY RIGID STRUCTURE OF "CENTER" AND "PERIPHERY"

This proposition is merely an extension of Proposition Four. Let me put it this way: with economic capital, quantity is paramount. In the ways of the world, more is almost always better, and more influential, than less. With cultural capital, it isn't quantity but quality that matters most. It is the *status* of cultural credentials and accomplishment and status is organized in a structure that ranges between the "center" and the "periphery." The individuals, networks and institutions *most critically involved* in the production of a culture operate in the "center" where prestige is the highest, not on the periphery, where status is low.

And so, *USA Today* may sell more copies of newspapers than the *New York Times*, but it is the *New York Times* that is the newspaper of record in America because it is at the center of cultural production, not the periphery, and its symbolic capital is much higher. Likewise, one can sell a hundred thousand copies of a book published by Loyola, Orbis, Zondervan, IVP, or Baker, and only 5,000 copies of a book published by Knopf, but it is the book by Knopf that is more likely to be reviewed in the *New York Review of Books* or the *New Republic*, or the *Washington Post Book World* because Knopf is at the center and Loyola, Orbis, Zondervan, IVP, and Baker are at the periphery. Influence follows accordingly. By the same logic, one may be able to get as good an education at Bluefield State College in Bluefield, West Virginia, as one would at Harvard, but Harvard, as an institution, is at the center and Bluefield State is at the periphery of cultural production. Therefore, someone with a credential from Harvard will find many more opportunities than someone from Bluefield State and will more likely end up in a position of greater influence than the other.

One could give myriad examples but the point is clear: the status structure of culture and cultural production is of paramount importance to understanding culture and cultural change.

PROPOSITION SIX: CULTURE IS GENERATED WITHIN NETWORKS

Most of us are inclined to what has been called the "great man" (or great person) view of history. It is a Hegelian idea of leadership and history, popularized by the nineteenth-century Scottish historian, Thomas Carlyle. In his own words, the history of the world is but the biography of great men:

> For, as I take it, Universal History, the history of what man has accomplished in this world, is at bottom the History of the Great Men who have worked here. They were the leaders of men, these great ones; the modellers, patterns, and in a wide sense creators, of whatsoever the general mass of men contrived to do or to attain; all things that we see standing accomplished in the world are properly the outer material result, the practical realization and embodiment, of Thoughts that dwelt in the Great Men sent into the world: the soul of the whole world's history, it may justly be considered, were the history of these.[5]

For Carlyle, heroes shaped history through the vision of their leadership, the power of their intellect, the beauty and delight of their aesthetic, and, animating it all, a certain inspiration from above. When the world's need is most acute, great leaders rise to the occasion and provide the courage and vision to address that need. "In all epochs of the world's history, we shall find the Great Man to have been the indispensable savior of his epoch."[6] In the realm of the spirit, it was Moses, the Buddha, Jesus, and Mohammed among others. In the case of war, it was Julius Caesar, Alexander, Charlemagne, Napoleon, Washington, Bismarck, and others. In the case of the intellect, it was Plato and Aristotle, St. Paul, St. Augustine, Thomas Aquinas, Martin Luther and John Calvin, Jonathan Edwards, Charles Darwin, Sigmund Freud, Albert Einstein, and the like. In the case of the arts, it was Michelangelo, Raphael, Caravaggio, da Vinci, Titian, Monet, Degas, and the like. All form an aristocracy of knowledge, talent, ability, ambition, and virtue, and so endowed have stood like switchmen on the train tracks of history; it is their genius and the genius of other heroic individuals that have guided the evolution of civilization this way or that; for better or for worse.[7]

The only problem with this perspective is that it is mostly wrong. Against this great-man view of history and culture, I would argue (along with many others) that *the key actor in history is not individual genius but rather the network* and the new institutions that are created out of those networks. And the more "dense" the network—that is, the more active and interactive the network—the more influential it could be. This is where the stuff of culture and cultural change is produced.

In making this case, I don't want to underplay the role of individual charisma and genius. Within any network, there is usually one who provides a certain unprecedented leadership, who offers a greater degree of articulation or who puts more at risk financially, socially, and reputationally, or who provides the connective tissue for the network itself. This is where we do find the greatness of a Martin Luther or John Calvin, a William Wilberforce, a Dorothy Day, a Martin Luther King, and so on. My point is simply that charisma and genius and their cultural consequences do not exist outside of networks of similarly oriented people and similarly aligned institutions.

PROPOSITION SEVEN: CULTURE IS NEITHER AUTONOMOUS NOR FULLY COHERENT

There is a tendency to view the culture as an autonomous and coherent realm of life, a sphere of activity that is independent, cohesive, and self-directing. There are useful reasons to think this way. The fact is, however, one can only separate out culture from other spheres of life and activity in an analytical vacuum. In reality, culture—as ideas and institutions—is mixed together in the most complex ways imaginable with all other institutions, not least of which in our own day are the market economy and the state.

The relationship of culture to the economy is especially complex in contemporary America because so much of what drives and sustains the economy and so much of what it sells is knowledge, information, images, symbols, entertainment, and the like. Long gone is the time when economy was mainly driven by the production and distribution of "things." Since the mid-twentieth century, larger and larger regions of the marketplace are based on the commodification of culture in all its forms—not least of which is Christian culture.

At the same time, the government is inextricable from the work of culture. In some ways, the expansion of the state in the last several decades is due to its growing role in the production of knowledge and information. Science and education are, in the main, appendages of the state, as are the myriad regulatory agencies dealing with health, occupational safety, welfare, and communications among others. So too, of course, is the judiciary. This means not only that the state provides much of the financial, personnel, and administrative infrastructure for the knowledge industry but also that the state can limit dissent through its coercive powers. It is in the realm of education where these powers are most critically at work. Since school attendance is mandatory for all children up to the eighth grade, and since the government has a monopoly on public education, children are required to be educated under the auspices of the state. The only alternatives available, as we know, are for families that have the time to give to homeschooling or the money to afford private education. And then take electoral politics. This has become an industry oriented far more toward the management of images and the marketing of a candidate than to the propagation of political ideals and policies.

These are just two arenas in which the institutions and work of culture are inseparable from other institutional spheres. These institutions have their own logic, dynamics, and direction, as well as their own center and periphery. For these reasons, culture is never fully autonomous.

Culture also is composed of innumerable *fields*—relatively distinct and often-overlapping regions of meaning, activity, networks, and relationships, as well as rules and interests. Religious traditions and ideological movements can be thought of as fields of culture as can publishing, entertainment, education, ministry, and the like. Each of these has its own range of subfields. By their very nature, these too have their own logic, dynamics, and direction, as well as their own center and periphery. The complexity of culture is great indeed but it does not end there.

Beyond all of this there are the relatively distinct, and often competing perspectives that are drawn from different geographical regions of a society, various ethnic groups and social classes, and an infinite range of religious traditions and moral communities.[8] These are not only relatively distinct but they are regularly in tension if not antagonistic toward each other. For these reasons, culture, especially in the modern world, can never be fully coherent.

Ideas Sometimes Have Consequences: Four Propositions on Cultural Change

Culture, it is fair to say at this point, is a knotty, difficult, complex, perhaps impossible puzzle. And what I have offered above is just a sketch; so much more could be said. Still, if I am right in my general description thus far, then the idea that changing a culture mainly by changing the hearts and minds of ordinary people is looking less and less plausible. Yet cultures do change. Yes, they are enduring but they are never permanent. What, then, can be said for how cultures change?

Let us begin with a well-known maxim: "Ideas have consequences." The adage comes from a book by this title published in 1948 by the University of Chicago professor of English, Richard Weaver. It has become a mantra to many people who think about the culture today and it has done so because it is so obviously correct. Even a pragmatic economist like John Maynard Keynes recognized the truth of this insight when he wrote, in his book, *The General Theory of Employment, Interest and Money,*

> The ideas of economic and political philosophers, both when they are right and when they are wrong, are more powerful than is commonly understood. Indeed the world is ruled by little else. Practical men, who believe themselves to be quite exempt from any intellectual influences, are usually the slaves of some defunct economist. Madmen in authority, who hear voices in the air, are distilling their frenzy from some academic scribblings of a few years back. I am sure that the power of vested interests is vastly exaggerated compared with the gradual encroachment of ideas.[9]

It is indisputably true that ideas do have consequences. Yet it is also true that *not all ideas have consequences*, and among those that do, some have greater consequences than others. How is this? What explains the difference? Weaver's statement would be truer if it were reworded as: "*Under specific conditions and circumstances* ideas can have consequences." When these conditions are in place, ideas can inspire greatness, creativity, sacrifice, and human flourishing. But keep in mind, under the very same conditions, other ideas can lead to extraordinary folly or unspeakable destruction.

The question is: What are those conditions and circumstances? A fully adequate answer to this question is not within our reach. There are some provisional observations that we can make, however.

PROPOSITION EIGHT: CULTURES CHANGE FROM THE TOP DOWN, RARELY IF EVER FROM THE BOTTOM UP

It is sometimes true that economic revolts (as in labor protests) and social movements (such as environmentalism) occur from the "bottom up"; that is, through the mobilization of ordinary people. And while they can have tremendous influence, *on their own terms*, the specific ends are often limited and/or short-lived. It is also true that political revolutions (such as the French Revolution, the Communist Revolution in China, and the assortment of revolutions in Mexico, Yugoslavia, Vietnam, Algeria, Cuba, Bolivia, Angola, Mozambique, Guinea-Bissau, and Ethiopia) can take form and spread through the recruitment and organization of popular protest. Such revolutions, however, nearly always involve leadership from the ranks of marginal and disaffected elites who build new organizations that coalesce revolutionary changes around new state and national identity.[10] Here too their influence can be enormous. Yet the deepest and most enduring forms of *cultural* change nearly always occurs from the "top down." In other words, the work of world-making and world-changing are, by and large, the work of elites: gatekeepers who provide creative direction and management within spheres of social life. Even where the impetus for change draws from popular agitation, it does not gain traction until it is embraced and propagated by elites.

The reason for this, as I have said, is that culture is about how societies define reality—what is good, bad, right, wrong, real, unreal, important, unimportant, and so on. This capacity is not evenly distributed in a society, but is concentrated in certain institutions and among certain leadership groups who have a lopsided access to the means of cultural production. These elites operate in well-developed networks and powerful institutions.

Over time, cultural innovation is translated and diffused. Deep-rooted cultural change tends to begin with those whose work is most conceptual and invisible and it moves through to those whose work is most concrete and visible. In a very crude formulation, the process begins with theorists who generate ideas and knowledge; moves to researchers who explore, revise, expand, and validate ideas; moves on to teachers and educators who pass those ideas on to others, then passes on to popularizers who simplify ideas and practitioners who apply those ideas. All of this, of course, transpires through networks and structures of cultural production.

Cultural change is most enduring when it penetrates the structure of our imagination, frameworks of knowledge and discussion, the perception of everyday reality. This rarely if ever happens through grassroots political mobilization though grassroots mobilization can be a manifestation of deeper cultural transformation. Change of this nature can only come from the top down.

PROPOSITION NINE: CHANGE IS TYPICALLY INITIATED BY ELITES WHO ARE OUTSIDE OF THE CENTERMOST POSITIONS OF PRESTIGE

As I argue in Proposition Five, spheres of cultural life are broadly stratified according to relative degrees of prestige. In the broadest terms, one can see this as a division between "center" and "periphery." But it is important to emphasize that "center" and "periphery" are relative rather than fixed concepts. That is to say, prestige is not dichotomous, in the sense that either one has it or one doesn't, but is rather a range with infinite gradations. Thus, within the "center," one can observe degrees of prestige with the very highest levels at the core or nucleus. Thus, for example, among universities, New York University is certainly in the "center" but is not at the very core. Yale would have even higher prestige. Among newspapers, the *Boston Globe* has a great deal of symbolic capital, especially compared to smaller papers in other regions of the country, but it is not at the nucleus of the center, where you would find the *New York Times*. Among public policy think tanks, the New America Foundation is close to the center if not in it, but it does not have the symbolic capital you would find at the Hoover Institution.

These kinds of distinctions are important because change is often initiated outside of the centermost positions. When change is initiated in the center, then it typically comes from outside of the center's nucleus. Wherever innovation begins, it comes as a challenge to the dominant ideas and moral systems defined by the elites who possess the highest levels of symbolic capital. Innovation, in other words, generally moves from elites and the institutions they lead to the general population but among elites who do not necessarily occupy the highest echelons of prestige. The novelty they represent and offer calls into question the rightness and legitimacy of the established ideas and practices of the culture's leading gatekeepers. The goal of any such innovation is to infiltrate the center and, in time, redefine the leading ideas and practices of the center.

This proposition is sympathetic to the insights of the Italian social theorist, Vilfredo Pareto, who argued that change occurs through a "circulation of elites." His theory was fairly complex, though in its simple and sanitized form, he argued that elites were either foxes or lions. Foxes, as he put it, were those who innovated, experimented, and took risks. Lions, by contrast, were those who defended the status quo in the name of social stability. Foxes and lions were in tension over power. When lions were ascendant, foxes challenged their authority and would seek to infiltrate their ranks in order to replace them. Yet because it is difficult for foxes to maintain a stable social order, the lions would eventually replace them or—more interestingly—the foxes would become lions.

PROPOSITION TEN: WORLD-CHANGING IS MOST CONCENTRATED WHEN THE NETWORKS OF ELITES AND THE INSTITUTIONS THEY LEAD OVERLAP

The impetus, energy, and direction for world-making and world-changing are greatest where various forms of cultural, social, economic, and often political resources overlap. In short, when networks of elites in overlapping fields of culture and overlapping spheres of social life come together with their varied resources and act in common purpose, cultures do change and change profoundly. Persistence over time is essential; little of significance happens in three to five years. But when cultural and symbolic capital overlap with social capital and economic capital and, in time, political capital, and these various resources are directed toward shared ends, the world, indeed, changes.

PROPOSITION ELEVEN: CULTURES CHANGE, BUT RARELY IF EVER WITHOUT A FIGHT

Every field of culture and, thus, culture itself represents terrain in which boundaries are contested and in which ideals, interests, and power struggle. By its very nature, culture is a realm in which institutions and their agents seek to defend one understanding of the world against alternatives, which are always either present or latent. That work is the work of legitimation and delegitimation; of naming one normal and right and its competition, deviant, inferior, stupid, inadequate, ridiculous, un-American, politically incorrect, or just plain evil. This is not to suggest that the terrain of culture is even or that struggle is ever fair. It never is. But it is also never uncontested. Even the weak and symbolically disadvantaged, as theorists such as Michel Foucault and Homi Bhabha have noted, have at least some power to delegitimate established cultural authorities. Of course conflict is not the *only* dynamic of culture. Often enough, change will occur through movements of convergence, assimilation, and even concord. Yet conflict is one of the permanent fixtures of cultural change. It is typically through different manifestations of conflict and contest that change in culture is forged.

When there are challenges to the status quo, those challenges must still "articulate" with the social setting.[11] That is, an alternative vision of society—its discourse, moral demands, institutions, symbols, and rituals—must still resonate closely enough with the social environment that it is plausible to people. If it does not, the challenge will be seen as esoteric, eccentric, parochial, and thus either unrealistic or irrelevant. On the other hand, if the challenge articulates too closely with the social environment that produces it, the alternative will likely be co-opted by that which it seeks to challenge and change.

In Sum

Ideas do have consequences in history, yet not because those ideas are inherently truthful or obviously correct but rather because of the way they are embedded in very powerful institutions, networks, interests, and symbols.[12] These factors—overlapping networks of leaders and overlapping resources, all operating near or in the center institutions and in common purpose—are some of the practical dynamics within which world-changing occurs. These are the conditions under which ideas finally have consequences. While it may be pedantic to make this point, let us call attention to the fact that we have ended up with a very different understanding of culture than the one commonly accepted today.

To draw the distinction even more sharply, let me briefly return to the philosophical influences I spoke of earlier, influences that prejudice our views of culture and cultural change. Against idealism, the view that ideas move history, we now see ideas inexorably grounded in social conditions and circumstances (and not just material objects). Against individualism, which influences us to view the autonomous and rational individual—even if a genius—as the key actor in social change, we now see the power of networks and the new institutions that they create, and the communities that surround them that make the difference. Finally, against Christian pietism, which biases us to see the individual's "heart and mind" as the primary source and repository of culture, we now see that hearts and minds are only tangentially related to the movements of culture, that culture is much more complicated and has a life independent of individual mind, feeling, and will; indeed, that it is not so much individual hearts and minds that move cultures but cultures that ultimately shape the hearts and minds and, thus, direct the lives of individuals. The movement between the individual and culture, in other words, goes in both directions and perhaps moves even more strongly in the latter direction.

One Critical Lesson, One Important Qualification

What this overview teaches is that cultures are profoundly resistant to intentional change—period. They are certainly resistant to the mere exertion of will by ordinary individuals or by a well-organized movement of individuals. The idea, suggested by James Dobson, that "in one generation, you change the whole culture"[13] is nothing short of ludicrous. Change in political systems and economic conditions *can* occur relatively quickly but the most profound changes in culture typically take place over the course of multiple generations. The most profound changes in culture can be seen first as they penetrate into the linguistic and mythic fabric of a social order. In doing so, it then penetrates the hierarchy of rewards and privileges and deprivations and punishments that organize social life. It also reorganizes the structures of consciousness and character, reordering the organization of impulse and inhibition. One cannot see change taking place in these ways. It is not perceptible as an event or set of events currently unfolding. Rather, cultural change of this depth can only be seen and described in retrospect, after the transformation has been incorporated into a new configuration of moral controls.[14]

In this light, we can see that evangelism, politics, social reform, and the creation of artifacts—if effective—all bring about good ends: changed hearts and minds, changed laws, changed social behaviors. But they don't directly influence the moral fabric that makes these changes sustainable over the long term, sustainable precisely because they are implicit and as implicit, they form the presuppositional base of social life. Only indirectly do evangelism, politics, and social reform effect language, symbol, narrative, myth, and the institutions of formation that change the DNA of a civilization.

Imagine, in this regard, a genuine "third great awakening" occurring in America, where half of the population is converted to a deep Christian faith. Unless this awakening extended to envelop the cultural gatekeepers, it would have little effect on the character of the symbols that are produced and prevail in public and private culture. And, without a fundamental restructuring of the institutions of culture formation and transmission in our society—the market, government-sponsored cultural institutions, education at all levels, advertising, entertainment, publishing, and the news media, not to mention church—revival would have a negligible long-term effect on the reconstitution of the culture. Imagine further several social reform movements surrounding, say, educational reform and family policy, becoming very well organized and funded, and on top of this, serious Christians being voted into every major office and appointed to a majority of judgeships. Legislation may be passed and judicial rulings may be properly handed down, but legal and political victories will be short-lived or pyrrhic without the broad-based legitimacy that makes the alternatives seem unthinkable.

Such is the story of one of the most powerful transatlantic social reform movements of the nineteenth and early twentieth centuries—the temperance movement. This movement failed, of course, not least because it did not and could not address the culture of restraint on which the particular interest of temperance depended. In the end, the ideal of "temperance" finally expired in derision with the repeal of the Volstead Act in 1933, the word now having disappeared from our public vocabulary. This same logic accounts for the contemporary failure of the Christian Right to stop the growth and legitimation of homosexuality, abortion, and pornography, among other concerns. The passion and earnest resolve generated by all such movements may change people and may effect communities and they may, for a time, change laws, but they generally will not influence the course and direction of the culture as a whole unless they are tied to larger structural changes in the culture.

Culture, at root, provides the very terms by which life is ordered. In our own culture, the inherited categories derived largely from biblical and classical sources by which we understand the most basic aspects of human life have been and are being transformed by very powerful forces over which individuals and social groups have little control, forces such as consumerism, communications technology, and so on. The most humane understandings of personhood, relationships, community, time, space, freedom, obligation, material wealth, cannot be established or recovered through a five-year plan or even in a generation—certainly not through politics, not through social reform, and not even in and through revival. In this light, the call to this generation of Americans to repent and pray for revival to renew the values of the national culture may be welcome, but no one should be under any illusion about its capacity to fundamentally transform the present cultural order at its most rudimentary level. Invitations by Christian leaders to fast and pray are most worthy, but their main effect will be to renew the church rather than keep America from "losing its soul." All such engagement may be worthy, but if the end is to "save civilization," it most certainly is naïve. By themselves or even together, evangelism, politics, and social reform, then, will fail to bring about the ends hoped for and intended.

The important qualification one must make in all of this is that even when successful, change does not always occur in the direction that people propose or with the effects for which people hope. There are almost always unintended consequences to human action, particularly at the macro-historical level and these are, often enough, tragic. The architects of the Enlightenment who understood the power of science and predicted the progressive amelioration of human suffering through it, would never have desired or predicted the development of nuclear weapons. The Protestant Reformers of the sixteenth century never would have imagined that the turn toward individual conscience and moral asceticism would have contributed to an economic system that would "act back" on the culture as a cause of secularization. Likewise, the Puritans who founded Harvard and Yale would have never expected that their schools would become strongholds of secularity. And the missionaries who brought aid to impoverished parts of the Third World would have never wished for the growing cycle of dependency they unwittingly helped foster. And so it goes. One can never quite predict where things will go.

Culture is endlessly complex and difficult, and it is highly resistant to our passion to change it, however well intentioned and heroic our efforts may be. But with that said, one thing is clear: Christians will not engage the culture effectively, much less hope to change it, without attention to the factors mentioned here.

Chapter Five

_____

EVIDENCE IN HISTORY

I T IS ONE THING to assert conceptual and theoretical propositions about culture and cultural change; it is quite another to measure these propositions against the historical record. How does this alternative stand up to the hard realities of history?

What follows is not a comprehensive account of the processes involved in Western Christianity or modern cultural history. Instead, what follows is a brisk overview of certain moments in history that will highlight what is well known to scholars in these fields of study but perhaps less well known to the average reader. For many, history is a blur. Somehow, pagan Rome became Christianized, Europe was proselytized, faith was renewed from time to time as in the Reformation and in various revivals, and fate or God's will must have directed it at every step. In any event, things all turned out the way they were supposed to have turned out.

Indeed, many Christian believers do affirm that God is sovereign in history. And yet that does not mean that the human factor is irrelevant to how history unfolds. Indeed, history unfolds in ways that are contingent on individual action and social processes that are not random but patterned. The purpose of this chapter is to explore some of those patterns as they play out in a few important transitional moments.

The Growth of Christianity

The Christian Church had its origins as a small sect within Judaism at the periphery of the Roman Empire. For a century after the death of Christ, Christianity was little more than a superstition promulgated by a "club" that was only threatening insofar as any association provided an opportunity for social/religious and political unrest to develop.[1] The church lacked financial, intellectual, and cultural resources, it had few defenders among elite classes, and its relationship to the Roman Empire had not been fully articulated. Through this time, grassroots growth was disproportionate to the growth of Christian cultural influence but even this was small. Some estimates put the number of Christians at less than fifty thousand (in a population of roughly sixty million) inhabiting forty or fifty small cities within the Roman Empire. Few had actually heard of Christianity, and fewer still had personal contact with Christians.[2] Needless to say, Christianity changed over the course of three centuries, evolving from an obscure sect to a threat significant enough to warrant persecution and philosophical refutation, and finally to the official religion of the Roman Empire. This move from the periphery to the center of religious and cultural influence in the Roman Empire took centuries, and the dynamics at play were various and complex.

Consider the important part played by aspects of the social, economic, and cultural ecology of the Roman Empire in the growth in the size and influence of Christian presence. Not surprisingly, Christianity's early growth occurred through the interconnected cities of the Greco-Roman empire, cities that were often at the crossroads of important trade routes. The institutional setting of this expansion, however, was the network of Jewish Diaspora synagogues. Its early reputation as a Jewish sect also served to protect it from persecution.[3] All cultural developments at that time depended on the overlapping social networks associated with familial ties, ethnic or geographic origins, occupations, and cultic interests, and Christianity was no different; in this case, its dependence was on the social networks of kinship, work, and faith among Diaspora Jews.[4]

Yet another dynamic was the fact that the Roman world was unified and dominated by Greek language and culture.[5] This was the language and culture of the "center" and those who had influence had facility in the manners, customs, rhetoric, grammar, and idiom of this civilization. Thus, by the time of St. Paul, Jews had been Hellenized for over a generation not only outside of Palestine but also in Palestine itself. It was this Hellenized sector of Judaism that Christian mission turned to first in its evangelism. As Werner Jaeger has written,

> It was that part of the Jerusalem community of the apostles called the "Hellenists" in the sixth chapter of Acts which, after the martyrdom of their leader Stephen, was scattered all over Palestine and started the missionary activities of the next generation. Like Stephen himself (Stephanos),

they all had good Greek names such as Philippos, Nikanor, Phochoros, Timon, Parmenas, Nikolaos, and mostly they stemmed from Jewish families that had been Hellenized for at least a generation or more. The name of the new sect, *Christianoi*, originated in the Greek city of Antioch, where these Hellenized Jews found their first great field of activity for their Christian mission. Greek was spoken in the *synagogai* all around the Mediterranean, as is evident from the example of Philo of Alexandria who did not write his literary Greek for an audience of gentiles but for his highly educated fellow Jews. A large following of gentile proselytes would not have developed had they not been able to understand the language spoken at the Jewish worship in the synagogues of the dispersion. Paul's entire missionary activity was based on this fact. His discussions with the Jews to whom he addressed himself on this travels and with whom he tried to bring the gospel of Christ were carried on in Greek and with all the subtleties of Greek logical argumentation.[6]

Scriptural studies and argumentation cited the Septuagint not from the Hebrew original but from the Greek translation. Indeed, as most everyone knows, the Christian writers of the apostolic age used the Greek literary forms of the Epistle, after the model of Greek philosophers. St. Paul's great lecture at the Areopagus cited in Acts 17 was a direct challenge to the dominant culture of the age, a challenge aimed at its source—the learned philosophers of classical Greek wisdom and erudition. Paul was the apostle to the gentiles and it was his facility with the dominant culture that created the inroads into that population.[7]

The urban centers of the Mediterranean became the foci of cultural production in the growing church. Jerusalem continued to be an important center of ecclesiastical activity in these early years, but there were other cities, which were already centers of Greco-Roman culture and learning, in which the church started to flourish even more. Over the course of the first two centuries of the church, Alexandria in Egypt, Ceasarea on the sea north of Jerusalem, Carthage in Tunisia, Antioch in Syria, Constantinople in Turkey, and Milan in Italy all became places of vitality where Christians took on the challenge of engaging the dominant culture both critically and constructively. Yet it was Rome, *the* center of the empire that became the geographical center of the church too. The importance of Rome was not due to any distinctive theology—something it did not produce until much later—but rather due to its reputation, wealth, and location.[8]

In all of these cities, there are clear indications that Christians had made their way into elite circles of wealth, power, and culture. In each there were

Christians prosperous enough to act as benefactors and the churches relied on them as such.[9] St. Paul himself as well as Eusebius, the father of church history, mentions the presence of Christians in the imperial households and in the Roman upper classes. Some have said that Philip the Arabian, who reigned from 244 to 249—a half-century before Constantine, was likely the first Christian emperor. The persecution under Emperor Valerian in the late second century was aimed at Christians who were part of the imperial household as well as believers who were part of the equestrian and senatorial orders.[10] Even under the reign of the Emperor Diocletian, who initiated some of the most vicious persecutions of Christians, Christians were prominent in his household, including his wife and daughter who either were Christians or were favorable toward the church. It is also not incidental that with very few exceptions, the church fathers—including Justin Martyr, Anthony the Great, Tertullian, Ambrose of Milan, Jerome, Basil the Great, Gregory of Tours, Athanasius, Gregory of Nyssa, St. Cyprian of Carthage, St. Gregory (the miracle worker), Cyril of Jerusalem, John Chrysostom, and Augustine— were born into families that were either prosperous, highly educated, or of high social standing.[11] Of those figures for whom there is little evidence, such as Irenaeus, Clement of Alexandria, Jerome, and Origen, we can infer a certain social privilege by virtue of their extraordinary erudition. (Since only roughly 10 percent of the ancient population was literate, even a small amount of education would have set one apart with distinction.) These were figures who received thorough training in such subjects as Greek, Latin, rhetoric, and jurisprudence, and all became men of considerable intellectual accomplishment.

The urban centers of the Mediterranean also became the setting for various voices in different parts of the empire to be heard and to engage each other. As the home of the Jewish philosopher Philo as well as Bishop Demetrius, Clement, and Origen, Alexandria was especially important as a center of theological imagination. Needless to say, Rome's importance grew by the generation. As Robert Wilken has observed, almost all of the outstanding Christian thinkers in the second century spent some time in Rome: Valentinus, the brilliant Gnostic teacher and author of the Gospel of Truth; Marcion, a radical Christian leader and biblical scholar and fanatical follower of Paul; Hegesippus, an early historian of the Christian movement; and Justin Martyr and Athenagoras, among the earliest and most astute apologists of the Christian faith.

In this story, education was exceptionally important, for much of the spiritual and cultural creativity of the church resided in the establishment and transformation of the schools of that time. Schools were established by the end of the second century in all of the major urban areas of the Mediterranean, in most cases by the leading Christian intellectuals who resided there. Justin Martyr (100–165) in Rome; Pantaenus, Clement (150–211), and Origen (185–253) in Alexandria; Tertullian (160–225) in Carthage. The schools not only were functional in forming potential leaders in the church. They were also the primary settings in which intellectual vitality was generated and influence in the culture was exerted.[12]

There were three factors related to their influence. The first factor had to do with the quantity and quality of intellectual output. By the second century, hostility among Christians to Greek philosophy was beginning to wane. The schools themselves brought together both the catechetical and classical learning by "correlating the higher learning from the Greco-Roman world with the special insights into the nature and purpose of God in the biblical tradition."[13] Christian intellectuals, then, not only understood their own theological and biblical tradition, but also had knowledge of the leading ideas of the culture. Over a period of generations, Christians developed a vibrant intellectual tradition. Scholars who were associated with these schools produced a body of scholarship that was as well reasoned and erudite as anything produced by the pagan philosophers of the time.

Much of the creativity was motivated by intellectual challenges from the outside. At the end of the first century, those challenges were few for little was known about Christianity. For example, Pliny in his letters and Tacitus in his history mentioned Christians, yet they did not see them as a significant presence and thus made little effort to understand what they believed and how they lived. In the middle of the second century, the famous physician, Galen, did take a serious interest in the beliefs, practices, and way of life of Christians and conferred intellectual legitimacy to the faith by recognizing it as a school of philosophy on the same footing as Greek philosophy. By the time Celsus wrote toward the end of the second century, Christianity was still numerically small but emerging as a real challenge to the dominant culture. Celsus, himself not a significant philosopher, nevertheless had considerable influence through his polemic against Christianity, *The True Doctrine*; his diatribe against Christian superstition echoed in several important polemics that followed. Origen, perhaps the most important figure in the Christian church between Paul and Augustine, studied Celsus's polemic, reproduced much of it, and then responded to it point by point. In turn, Porphyry wrote his rebuttal to Christian faith with full awareness of the intellectual achievement of Origen. Yet by the time Origen died in 253, Christianity was no longer merely self-protective.[14] Origen had established Christianity as an intellectually serious but also inspiring faith. His efforts went a long way toward laying a foundation for the conversion of the Greek-speaking provincial aristocracy who were fundamentally Platonist in outlook.[15]

Needless to say, the disputes over Christianity didn't end in the third century, but the terms of engagement had changed. Critics could no longer dismiss it; they recognized that Christianity was here to stay, and thus their effort turned to trying to accommodate it within the existing polytheism of the day. From the learned neoplatonist Porphyry (233–305) to the last pagan emperor, Julian the Apostate (331–363), critics challenged the beliefs of Christian faith, not least the divinity of Christ, and its claims to exclusivity. This was especially well articulated in Porphyry's treatises, *Against the Christians* and *Philosophy from the Oracles*. Here he argued, among other things, that Christianity was simply another religious alternative within the range of Roman religious options. His intention was simply to defuse the threat that Christianity actually represented. His argument was tremendously influential; a century later, Christian thinkers such as Augustine and Cyril of Alexandria were still trying to defend Christianity against this attempt to undermine its bid for Roman allegiance. What is significant in all of this, of course, is that Christians were willing to meet their opponents on the same ground.[16] "That Christianity became the object of criticism by the best philosophical minds of the day at the same time when Christians were forging an intellectual tradition of their own was a powerful factor in setting Christian thought on a sound course."[17]

The second reason for the influence of the schools was institutional. The educational system of the Roman Empire was the *paideia*—in theory, a careful process for educating a young man into his true form for the purposes of citizenship. *Paideia* involved a formal curriculum covering logic, grammar, and rhetoric, yet embedded within it was the means by which the most excellent virtues and habits of the classical heritage were passed on to successive generations. In its social functions, though, *paideia* was a structure for socializing elites within the aristocratic and imperial culture of the empire. As Peter Brown has shown, young males were carefully prepared according to a traditional canon of decorum, civility, and scholarly excellence. Through it, the highly stratified hierarchies of social power as well as the imperial networks (connecting, through patronage, the emperor to local elites throughout the empire) were maintained. The skills of *paideia* were intricate and extremely difficult to master. For this reason, social mobility was severely limited; and yet neither the social hierarchy nor social networks was impenetrable. Through patronage, *paideia* provided an avenue of mobility for men of talent from less-privileged backgrounds. In this way, the organization and exercise of power throughout the Roman Empire was legitimated.[18]

There was very little room for maneuver in this structure. The ability of educated elites to speak their mind was highly constrained. In general, only those who felt that they could count on the protections of the more powerful exercised such freedoms.[19] The exceptions were certain philosophers who, of course, were members of the nobility and shared in their *paideia*, but transcended the need for patronage and friendship. They had access to the imperial court and, in principle, could speak to the powerful without fear of reprisal.[20]

This was the dominant social structure of the Roman Empire and the system that maintained it. It was, therefore, the social setting in which early Christianity emerged. Change took centuries, and it did not occur without conflict. Yet by the late 300s, the church's relationship to this system had changed. In most instances, the bishops who emerged were local notables who were well-born, in possession of *paideia*, and increasingly entrusted with the political autonomy of the philosopher.[21] In some cases, the bishops had been philosophers before their conversion. Either way, the Christian bishop became a *vir venerabilis*, a person deemed "worthy of reverence" by the powerful. As a consequence, bishops began pronouncing on public affairs and more and more Christians began to hold office and exercise influence in the cities of the empire. Secular leaders even began to turn to bishops to control crowds and defend law and order.[22] All the while, the church grew more and more interconnected through frequent councils, travel to Rome, and so on.

What happened in these early centuries, then, was less a dramatic conflict between Christianity and paganism with Christianity winning and more a slow and ambiguous transition. Over a period of centuries, in a process that was rife with tension, conflict, and setback, a subtle shift occurred by which the distinction between Christian faith and non-Christian *paideia* faded. In this, *paideia* was both challenged and affirmed. By late antiquity, as Brown has shown, the Christian church absorbed the Roman *paideia* into Christian catechesis. In this way, *paideia* became a preparatory school of Christian character.[23] At the same time, the church co-opted the imperial hierarchy and its power relations. Far from being a church of the lower classes, the church reflected the sharp divisions in Roman society: its upper echelons were occupied by highly cultivated persons, drawn from the class of urban notables."[24] What this meant was that the new power of Christian bishops amounted more to a "reshuffling" than to a true cultural change.[25] "It was the flesh and bone of access to imperial power that came to count by the fifth century. A groundswell of confidence that Christians enjoyed access to the powerful spelled the end of polytheism far more effectively than did any imperial law or the closing of any temple."[26] The transition from secular to Christian power in the Roman Empire, then, was not quick and decisive but rather gradual and ambiguous.

There was yet another factor in the cultural transformation of the Roman imperium that is only indirectly related to *paideia*. The bishops rejected a central tenet of *paideia*, namely its understanding of and relationship to the social order. In the existing social order, sharp distinctions were made between citizen and noncitizen and between city and countryside. "The poor were defined as those who belonged to no urban grouping."[27] When the bishops declared themselves to be "lovers of the poor," the church was unwittingly offering a new model of society.[28] The care of the poor emphasized a very different and more universal bond of social solidarity, namely, a common humanity. The fact is, the Christian church reached more people. Even though it was still a demographic minority, a church that was seen to reach out to the margins of the social order established its "right to stand for the community as a whole."[29] The "care of the poor became a dramatic component of the Christian representation of the bishop's authority in the community."[30] Constantine's recognition of the bishop's court of arbitration was decisive in this regard, for this court gave reality to the subtle shift by which the bishop, as "lover of the poor," became also the protector of the lower classes.[31] It was by stressing their relationship with the socially and economically marginal that the bishops projected a form of authority within the city that *outflanked* the traditional leadership of the notables.

There was corruption in the way this power was used, to be sure.[32] Even so, extraordinary good was accomplished as well. Both before and after he became a bishop of Caesarea, Basil (329–379) was exemplary in this regard. Basil exploited to the full his status as a local notable and man of *paideia* in order to gain tax exemptions and personal immunities for the founders of poorhouses. Basil's role as a patron of the church's wealth to the poor reached the entire region—organizing relief for the victims of famine, establishing a leper hospital, and providing food for the poor.[33]

The bishops modeled what was already embraced by the entire church—an outreach of charity and care for the poor and disenfranchised. The net effect was revolutionary. Because Christian charities were beneficial to all, including pagans, imperial authority in society was weakened. Julian the Apostate understood this and responded to the problem by attempting to establish an alternative Roman philanthropic system in the hope that it would lessen the people's reliance on Christian charity. Julian's observations were perspicacious:

> These impious Galileans not only feed their own poor, but ours also; welcoming them into their *agapae*, they attract them, as children are attracted, with cakes. . . . Whilst the pagan priests neglect the poor, the hated Galileans devote themselves to works of charity, and by a display

of false compassion have established and given effect to their pernicious errors. See their love-feasts, and their tables spread for the indigent. Such practice is common among them, and causes a contempt for our gods.[34]

In effect, as Brown notes, the bishops sacrificed political authority for spiritual authority, only to gain it back again as the leaders of the church in the new dispensation of the Christianized Roman Empire.

The transformation that had occurred was reflected in the decline of ancient pagan art from the currency and iconography of late antiquity. The image of Jupiter was last put on Roman coins in the early decades of the fourth century, and by the end of the fourth century all pagan art was repudiated. Thomas Mathews writes,

> The dimensions of this revolution are staggering. In effect, a highly nuanced visual language that had been developed over the course of a thousand years to express man's sense of cosmic order, to deal with the forces beyond his control, to carry his aspirations and frustrations, to organize the seasons of his life and the patterns of his social intercourse, was suddenly discarded. The gods and goddesses, nymphs and heroes were roughly thrown aside; their mutilated and decapitated statues were interred in the foundations of Christian churches. Their battered remains still give us eloquent testimony of the violence of their downfall . . .
>
> In their place a new language of images was laboriously composed, selected, assembled, rehearsed, and refined. The criteria of this process were many, but the inherent strength of each new image must have been one of the most decisive considerations in its eventual success. The new images should not be thought of as simply filling up the voids left by the overthrow of the old, but as actively competing with the old images. The lanky Good Shepherd of Early Christian art wrestled with the muscular Hercules and won. . . .[35]

In ways that were convoluted and anything but inevitable, the triumph of Christianity expanded its reach.

The Conversion of Barbarian Europe

As a Jewish sect, early Christianity followed the dispersion of Judaism throughout the Mediterranean. As it became established with its own identity, the dispersion of Christianity increasingly followed the network of urban centers that comprised the administrative framework of *Pax Romana*. In the

Roman Empire, the ecclesiastical provinces were often the same as the civil provinces. And, as we've seen, the influence of the church grew as it penetrated the higher echelons of social life and this was accomplished largely through its penetration and cooptation of the educational system. For all the other problems that followed, the church's social vision was revolutionary, not least for the way it reached out to the poor and socially marginal.

Reinforcing this populist tendency in late antiquity was a new type of leader—the monk, and a new social institution—the monastery. Monks began as hermits, seeking seclusion from the world to pursue a life of spiritual purity. They were spiritual virtuosi and yet they were not necessarily well born nor did they necessarily have the benefits of *paideia*; many didn't. Monks were holy men, highly respected by the masses, and their spiritual status was a direct challenge to *paideia* and the power structure it served. Monasteries first emerged at the end of the third century, were not firmly established as an institution until the middle of the fourth century, and did not flourish until the fifth century. Originally, they were communities of ascetics who had gathered around a holy man to learn from and emulate. Though drawn together, they nevertheless permitted a large degree of seclusion. By the time of Basil, monks lived and worked together in community. These missionary monks and their monasteries varied considerably. They were transplantable largely because they were flexible in their organization and function. As we will see, monasticism was significant for several reasons. For now, this is all backdrop.

When the barbarians invaded the empire in the fifth century, the cities and its inhabitants were terrorized, the territories were fragmented, and the central administrative structure of the empire was profoundly weakened. In sum, the barbarians defeated the Roman Empire militarily and in part politically, yet not culturally. Much of classical and Christian culture remained robust. For one, reading and writing Latin remained at the heart of the literary culture, and the church became its chief patron and defender. The social organization of the church and civil structure were also far better ordered and disciplined than what was found among the barbarians. The authority of the church remained strong as well. Thus, when the Hun king, Attila, entered Italy, Pope Leo the Great went out to meet him and persuaded him to return to Hungary and live at peace with Rome. When the Vandals came into Italy by sea, Pope Leo again went out to meet their leader. While the Vandals did take Rome, out of deference for the pope they did not slaughter the inhabitants or pillage the churches. In terms of civil authority of late antiquity, the church stepped in where Roman civil authority was crippled, especially in the outlying regions of Spain, Gaul, and Britain.[36]

What this meant was that after the fall of Rome, there was a reversal of a sort. What remained of Greco-Roman civilization now tended to follow the tracks of Christianity, mainly through the work of the monasteries and the monks who founded them. The monks were a cultural vanguard, and the monasteries they founded were strong institutions and culturally more developed than anything that existed in Celtic, German, Slavic, and Frankish paganism and culture. This was true not only for knowledge and literature but also for urban life and commerce, law and property rights, and even food and dress. Thus, over the fifth and sixth centuries, a large network of monasteries developed all through Europe. These were mission-oriented and they functioned to extend the geographic reach of the church and its culture.

St. Patrick's life and witness is illustrative of this vanguard effect but also exemplary for the model it provided to other monastics in generations to come. It is said that he was the first to take the call to "teach all nations" literally; meaning, teaching even the barbarians who lived beyond the frontiers of the empire.[37] Ireland was such a frontier. Some records indicate that he founded 365 churches and monasteries in Ireland in the fifth century. Being outside the empire, Latin was a foreign language and the technology of writing was not well known. All of these basic skills had to be learned. In the process, the culture of Roman Christianity was naturalized to the setting. Monasteries, then, functioned as schools for teaching the young Latin grammar and as places for transcribing the Scriptures. From these, other missionaries were sent out to establish monasteries in England and on the Continent. Among these, two were especially important. In the sixth century St. Columba founded the monastery of Iona, which became, a century later, perhaps the greatest center of Celtic Christian learning and influence. It was from here that Scotland and England were evangelized. A generation later, St. Columbanus left Ireland for the continent and started four monasteries, the most important were the Luxeuil monastery in Burgundy and later, Bobbio in Italy. Bobbio became a stronghold of higher learning, while Luxeuil in France became an incubator of missionaries. It is estimated that over sixty of these missionaries went into France, Germany, Switzerland, and Italy, founding over one hundred different monasteries in the seventh century.[38]

The monastic movement was in full force by the sixth and seventh centuries, and it continued to flourish for several centuries. In the first half of the sixth century, Benedict founded and was abbot of thirteen monasteries in a valley north of Rome and later, a monastery in Monte Cassino, south of Rome. In the seventh century, St. Aiden founded the monastery Lindesfarne, also one of the great repositories of European learning during the early Middle Ages (second only to Iona). In the same century, Fructosuosus created a complex of monasteries in Spain. In the early eighth century, St. Boniface built a small network of monasteries in central Germany about the same time as St. Pirmin was creating a confederation of at least twelve monasteries in Gaul, ranging from Bavaria to Lake Constance, from Switzerland to western France. These few cases merely illustrate the sort of energy and resources being poured into the Christianization of Europe.

The influence of the monasteries was multiple. As mentioned, they were centers of learning. Latin and Greek were necessary for the church's sacraments and for theological scholarship, but Latin was also the *lingua franca* of Roman law and civilization. In a context that had no educational system, schools were required to teach language, grammar, literacy, and writing, and the power that came with this learning was obvious to all. The monasteries provided for this need. Though outside of the Greco-Roman world, Ireland's monasteries and those they spawned in England and on the Continent became the premier scholarly and educational centers of the Western world. "The reputation of Irish culture was such that many foreign monks wished to spend some time on the island where 'learning flourished.' In the Irish monasteries, for example, young Anglo Saxons were welcomed in the cells of Irish monks, where they received food and the books they needed at no expense."[39] It was only in the *scriptoriums* that the great classical and biblical texts of early Western civilization were reproduced and preserved.

Equally evident, the monasteries were outposts of evangelization. In this, the monks focused on the regional and local aristocracy rather than on the *rusticus*, the common people. As a rule, the higher up in the social hierarchy, the better for the church, for they were the ones who had the local influence necessary to diffuse the faith among their dependents.[40] Once a king had been converted, then the local nobility and others could convert without fear (though some did convert *out of* fear or in the attempt to win favor from their superiors). Missionaries deliberately followed a strategy of converting a people from the top down.[41] Barbarian kings, such as Clovis (king of the Franks), Ethelbert (king of Kent), Edwin (king of Northumbria), Stephen (king of Hungary), Sigebert (king of Essex), Boris (king of Bulgaria), Peada (prince of Mercia), Vladimir (prince of Kiev), Harald (king of the Danes), Olaf (king of Norway), and James (king of Sweden) were among the most visible and historically important.

The relationship between the church and the landed aristocracy was mutually beneficial. On the one hand, the missionaries depended on the material support of the wealthy and powerful. Throughout Europe—in what became England, Germany, Switzerland, France, Italy, and the Balkans—benefactors not only gave the land on which churches and monasteries were built, but provided staggeringly generous patrimonies in the form of gifts, legacies, endowments, and treasures. This, it is generally agreed, was the single most important factor in the gradual Christianization of major parts of Europe.[42] Indeed, the costs of running a bishopric were exorbitant. In addition to the buildings and furnishings that were constructed and maintained was an entourage that not only included monks and priests but laborers, craftsmen, an armed retinue for protection, and servants as well. The production of books, for example, was essential to evangelization, and this involved a complex process in which animals were slaughtered, turning skin into vellum that could be written on, ink-making, brush and quill making, bookbinding, and so on.[43] The dependency of the church on the largesse of benefactors was not without moral tension.[44] Even so, the resources the nobility provided were essential. And then there was the provision for the needs of the poor and the sick.

By the same token, the barbarian aristocracy that converted benefited as well. They saw in Christendom a more advanced civilization (in terms of wealth, technology, order, and authority) and were drawn to accept the faith as much by greed and *realpolitik* as by inspiration.[45] The aristocracy gained new techniques of rule through literacy and legislation, prestige and legitimacy through association with powerful sacred rituals and actors, and the commercial and political benefits of geographically extensive ecclesiastical networks.

It is not unfair to say that the church in these centuries was an *adelskirche*, a German term that means "the church of the nobility." In short, this was a church managed by and largely for the aristocracy. For all of the obvious sordid complications this entailed, aristocratic dynasties yoked their considerable resources over a period of generations to the work of the church.[46] The ecclesiastical and aristocratic networks overlapped—in many respects, they evolved into the same networks, with bishops, abbots, and the like drawn from the wealthy and nobility. Nearly all of the courageous saints of the time—Patrick, Columba, Columbanus, Boniface, Pirmin, Willibrord, Wilfrid, Aiden, Amandus, Vladimir, among others—came from wealth or noble birth.

In sum, the conversion of barbarian Europe took centuries. The movement of change was from the higher echelons of the social order to the lower; indeed it took multiple generations after royal conversion for Christianization in the culture and among the common people to occur. Looking back, it is easy to be ambivalent about all that occurred. One can find Christian faith that is at its most exemplary—enacted love that is humble, courageous, sacrificial, generous, and so on. One can also find Christianity syncretized with paganism and rife with corruption—forced conversions, bribery, greed, calculating, power-hungry, and exploitative. There is much here to learn from and emulate and every bit as much to detest.

The emergence of Christianity in barbarian Europe implied a competition between Christian and pagan power resulting in conflict that was symbolic and, at times, even violent. Clerics disrupted pagan worship and destroyed pagan sacred objects, and pagans returned the compliment, at times killing Christians in revenge. There was a competition and, therefore, conflict with Muslims and Jews as well. More often than not, there was conflict among different branches of Christianity. This is a chaotic and a regularly unhappy history with both positive and negative results inextricably entwined. But even the most creditable parts of the story would not have happened without the church being at the leading edge of intellectual and cultural production and without the complementary resources of overlapping elites.

The Carolingian Renaissance

Popular history refers to these centuries as the "Dark Ages," a pejorative term referring to a so-called backwardness and cultural stagnation between the fifth and eleventh centuries in which written history and other cultural achievements were thin. Though this was true in much of Western Europe, it doesn't tell the entire story, for there were pockets of cultural activity everywhere. As we have seen, monasteries proliferated and were hives of cultural work and achievement that preserved much of the literature of antiquity and extended the reach of Christian and Roman civilization. In the middle of this period, from the late eighth through the ninth century, there was an exceptional flurry of high cultural production referred to as the Carolingian Renaissance, in which education, literature, law, theology, architecture, art, and music all flourished.

The background to this story is found in the Frankish barbarians who had overtaken Roman Gaul at the end of the fifth century. From that point on through the eighth century, the Franks slowly transitioned from a loosely connected network of independent tribal communities to a somewhat united and at first pagan kingdom under the sacral kingship of the Merovingians. As in other parts of Europe, Christianization was gradual, as a sacral dynasty of pagan war-kings was replaced by a sacral dynasty of Christian war-kings.[47] Christianization, then, had been established, but it was fairly superficial. Indeed, the greater part of the population was still pagan, especially in the rural areas. All that said, the Irish monastics who evangelized the area, built monasteries, and educated the nobility had laid a stable foundation for societal reform of a more genuine Christian character. As the Merovingian power collapsed, the Carolingian "mayors" began to grow increasingly prominent as patrons of the church and its missionary work. It was in this context that Boniface, in 741, launched his reform of the Frankish church and its institutions. One of Boniface's most important contributions was the realignment and unity of the Frankish church, its rulers, and Rome itself. Despite the weaknesses and problems that still remained in their Christianity, the Carolingian dynasty and the aristocracy associated with it expanded the depth and reach of Christianity in their territories.[48]

Central to the reform of the time was the successful mobilization of the Frankish aristocracy by the higher-level leadership of the church.[49] Emblematic of these overlapping networks was the relationship between Charlemagne and Alcuin, an English monk of the Benedictine order.[50] Alcuin was a key figure at court, a beloved teacher, a highly regarded scholar, and in effect the architect of the Carolingian renaissance. As his biographer puts it, "The voice is the voice of Charles, but the hand is the hand of Alcuin."[51] Alcuin himself is said to have taught almost every major scholar of the next generation.[52] Many of them came to occupy important positions in the church and the empire.

Together, Charlemagne and Alcuin brought about extraordinary reform to scholarship and education. For one, they established the seven liberal arts, the *trivium* (grammar, logic, and rhetoric) and *quadrivium* (arithmetic, geometry, music, and astronomy), as the organizational model of higher learning, a model that, in time, became the basis of scholarship and education for all medieval Western Europe. As in modern education, subjects were separated into different classes with specialized teachers for each. Scholars from Italy, Germany, and Ireland descended on Charlemagne's court, as did the young nobility, to participate in the profusion and excitement of intellectual activity. Under Alcuin's leadership, the Palace School became the center of knowledge and culture for the empire and, in many respects, for all of Europe. It is said that though the reach of the church was geographically wide, men and books moved freely and cooperatively through the empire, linked together through monasteries and churches and the many councils and synods they held.

Scholarship was less oriented toward innovation than it was toward making ancient wisdom accessible and practical to a larger population. Thus, one of the primary activities was the preservation of ancient texts as well as their reproduction through a costly program of book production. Charlemagne's court library contained Christian texts such as illustrated Bibles, commentaries from the patristic age, liturgical books, guides to ascetic discipline, and prayer books, but also some of the great pagan texts from ancient Greece through late antiquity—Virgil, Horace, Cicero, Juvenal, Ovid, and Tacitus, among others. Libraries in monasteries and cathedrals possessed similar collections. The intellectual vitality was extraordinary, and there were financial resources to sustain it. One measure of this accomplishment is the fact that seven thousand manuscripts and fragments now remain from the ninth century alone, compared with only eighteen hundred in total from the first eight hundred years of the western Christian era.[53]

The reforms pushed down into the lower orders of priests and monks and to the common people as well. Through a series of royal decrees, all clerics were required to learn how to read and write and be in possession of the basic knowledge necessary for the performance of their clerical responsibilities. To this end, reading-schools were established for the benefit of ordinands, who learned the fundamentals of doctrine and canon, liturgy, the psalter, and music. Bishops, in turn, were required to examine their clergy periodically, to ensure their compliance with these educational edicts.[54] In addition, a scheme for universal elementary education was also established. By royal decree, primary schools were to be established in every town and village with basic education provided by the priests.

Beyond a renewal of scholarship and educational reform, the Carolingian renaissance extended to musical innovation and artistic production. Music was one of the seven liberal arts and it was central to the educational program promoted by Charlemagne and Alcuin. The most important innovation of the time was the Gregorian chant and the ways it was made uniform in liturgy throughout the empire. It came to its ascendancy more through oral practice than written codification but even so, it reflected an emerging and commonly held tradition that did not exist before. Much the same can be said of art, as reflected most importantly in metal work and in the illustration of books—all of which reflected the influence of Celtic design and ornamentation, but appropriated in ways that created the first "court style" of medieval Europe.[55]

Though the court of Charlemagne displayed a love of knowledge for its own sake, it is also clear that education was useful to the effort to build the empire. In the Carolingian empire, the skills of reading and writing were not only the keys to faith but to knowledge and power as well.[56] Latin was employed not only in the liturgy but also in secular administration as a means of binding different and rival people together. Through literacy and the written word, law could achieve some measure of consistency and universality; indeed, there was no aspect of Carolingian society that was untouched by the written word.[57] A common written language and literacy made a common culture possible.

The most prominent characteristic of the Carolingian age was the effort to realize an Augustinian vision of a Christian society, which, like the church, was one, made up of many parts working together in equilibrium. From Pippin the Short's and then Charlemagne's court emerged a political theory of the ordered and just relationship of Christianity and society rooted in canon law. His administration, in which Charlemagne sent out regular *missi* to all parts of the empire, reinforced the proper and harmonious functioning of society according to Christian ideals.[58] One obvious way this was manifested was in the organization of the clergy. Whether a monk, a nun, a canon, a priest, or a bishop, each category of persons had a definable purpose and rule of conduct and held an obligation to live by it. But what applied to the clergy also applied, though perhaps less strictly, to the "order of laymen." As one scholar puts it, "earthly order reflected heavenly order; God's Church was functioning properly only if, in its organization, its habits, and its worship . . . it reflected heavenly practice."[59]

Much more can be said of this extraordinary period and how it unfolded. At its heart, the Carolingian renaissance was an attempt to revive the Roman Christian culture of late antiquity. Yet the great achievement of Carolingians was both renewal and reformation of that tradition in new ways that formed the foundation both for the renaissance of neoclassicism three centuries later and for all of Latin Christendom through the sixteenth century and beyond. Clearly the epoch, like most in human history, was not without corruption, exploitation, violence, and the abuse of power. There is, then, much to criticize and condemn in the actions of the powerful. Yet just as clearly, there is also much that we can admire and commend. In the end, the good that was produced did not come about through literary, textual, musical, and artistic genius alone. Nor was it the result of brilliant administrative initiative. By the same token, neither was it a creation of the extraordinary wealth and patronage of the nobility. It was, of course, a result of the coming together of all three at once.

The Reformation

The success of the Reformation, as Protestants like to tell it, was a result of the triumph of truth over falsehood, true Christian morality over corruption in the medieval church, genuine piety over false piety, and so on. To be sure, there was sham godliness, spiritual and moral corruption, and theological fabrication for which the Reformation stood as a corrective. But there were other reform movements of the late medieval period that contended for the same things as Luther, Calvin, Zwingli, and Hus and yet either failed or were rendered impotent. What made the Reformation of the sixteenth century successful, though, were factors that were not exactly theological or spiritual in nature.

There were several aspects of the social, political and economic landscape that were relevant to the success of this movement. For one, it is important to remember that the Holy Roman Empire—roughly coterminous with the rule of the Austrian and Spanish Hapsburgs—was not politically or administratively centralized. Central Europe, for all practical concerns, was comprised of a collage of more than two hundred relatively self-governing principalities, duchies, bishoprics, archbishoprics, and imperial cities.[60] The entire region was marked by political rivalries and dynastic conflicts that pitted the landed nobility against each other in the endless effort to expand their territorial powers. Among common people, both peasants and artisans, there was a growing discontent with the inequities of power and wealth and many of the oppressive duties imposed on them. There was a tangible yearning for new social freedoms, and this restiveness was never far below the surface of social life. Besides these internal squabbles and domestic tensions, were threats from the expanding Ottoman Empire in the east and tenuous relations with France and England. Imperial authority, then, faced many distractions that kept it from attending to the challenge of the new reformers.[61]

There were changes taking place in the late medieval economy as well. During the sixteenth century, international commerce expanded dramatically. In Eastern Europe and in France, growing revenues accrued to the benefit of the aristocracy who, in turn, used their wealth to solidify their political control over their territory. However, in central and northern Europe, the primary beneficiary of this growing wealth was a class of merchants, entrepreneurs, financiers, and exporters and importers dispersed through a network of cities and towns located along its key trading routes. Cities like Zurich, Geneva, Amsterdam, Rotterdam, Antwerp, Ghent, Strasbourg, Nuremberg, Augsburg, and Cologne were growing in population and linked by lively trade. Less and less was wealth and power concentrated in the nobility and landed aristocracy. The increasing prosperity and self-sufficiency of the towns and cities gave birth to a new and alternative commercial elite that were not only independent of the concentrated power of the church and its defenders, but who were eager to protect their growing political and, ipso facto, religious autonomy. The political autonomy of these towns and cities, combined with their increasing wealth, was a crucial enabling factor for the Reformation.

At its heart, of course, the Reformation was an intellectual and moral revolution, originating within the theological faculty of a German university, which challenged and offered a bibliocentric alternative to late medieval theology and religious practice. Foundational to this revolution was the fact that the leading reformers were all scholars of the first order. In addition to the Bible, they had mastery over the ideas, logic, language, and texts of classical thought and medieval scholasticism. Luther, for one, was well versed in works ranging from Aristotle to Seneca, Augustine to Peter Lombard.[62] Calvin too was broadly educated in the humanities and in law, his first published work being a commentary on Seneca's *De Clementia*. Also foundational to the intellectual success of the Reformation was its strategic alliance with the humanist movement, already well established by the time Luther nailed his ninety-five theses on the doors of the church in Wittenberg. The humanists, represented most prominently by the person and work of Desiderius Erasmus, had a vast and international network in German, Swiss, and Austrian universities. They provided texts, knowledge of languages, and new standards of scholarship, all of which informed the academic formation of the reformers. They also had "softened the ground" culturally and intellectually through their satirical attacks on clerics and scholastics.[63] Not least, they had a disproportionate influence over publishing. Their support was both critical and indispensable. As Alister McGrath puts it, "Without humanism, there would have been no Reformation."[64]

Though Luther and Calvin are given the greatest credit, the movement itself had its roots in and was perpetuated by a wider network of theologians, professors, and students operating through associated universities and academies. The influence of the widespread humanist network has already been mentioned. One of their innovations, eventually adopted by the reformers, was the "academy." As Peter Burke describes it, they were more formal and longer lasting than a circle but less formal than a university faculty. The academy was both an ideal social form in which to explore innovation and a conduit for spreading reformational ideas. Some of these were founded within universities and others eventually gave birth to new universities. As Burke observes, "Little by little these groups turned into institutions, with fixed memberships, statutes, and regular times of meeting. By the year 1600 nearly 400 academies had been founded in Italy alone."[65]

Luther himself was surrounded by a network of others similarly committed, not only in his monastic order but all over northern Germany, not least Joseph von Staupitz, (the man to whom Luther himself attributed the success of the Reformation[66]), Philipp Melanchthon, Johannes Sturm, Martin Bucer, Wolfgang Capito, Johannes Bugenhagen, Justus Jonas, and

George Spalatin. Melanchthon, a professor of Greek, became an especially important figure. Melanchthon not only was a brilliant scholar—he was called "the teacher of Germany" and regarded by many as a close second to Erasmus as the most learned man in Europe[67]—but also was organizationally savvy. He organized and participated in many of the colloquies, congresses, and dialogues of the 1520s–1540s, not least the Diet of Augsburg in 1530, as perhaps the leading negotiator of the Reformation. Maybe even more important than this, Melanchthon was the principal architect of curricular reform in the German universities, reform that redefined higher education in central Europe for over a century.

The networks were even more extensive in Calvinism a generation later. Calvin himself worked within a network of first-rate theologians and churchmen that included Guillaume Farel, Antoine Froment, Pierre Viret, Theodorus Beza, Germain Collodon, Laurent de Normandie, Peter Martyr, John Knox, Bernardino Ochino, and Sabastianus Castellio. In the context of Calvinism, it was the aristocratic Beza who became the critically important figure.[68] Beza was the principal mediator to the German princes in their attempts to reconcile Calvinism and Lutheranism; he led the colloquies between the French prelates and the Reformed theologians, and he was the primary emissary of the Huguenot churches in their ongoing negotiations with the French monarchy.

In 1559 Beza also became the first rector of the Geneva Academy, and under his leadership it grew into one of the main centers in Europe for the training of parish clergy.[69] As Beza claimed, the Geneva Academy was "a nursery garden" for the ministry not only in France and Switzerland but in England and Holland as well.[70] Yet, the importance of the Geneva Academy lessened over time as the Reformed movement matured and as other Reformed academies and colleges were established in multiple places in Switzerland, France, Germany, Scotland, England, and Holland. Of these, many were significant, but the university in Leiden deserves particular mention as a kind of a sixteenth-century version of Johns Hopkins; a model research university. The university was deliberately founded as a Calvinist university in 1575, and through its noble benefactor, William of Orange, extraordinary resources were poured into it in order to attract distinguished scholars with high salaries and low teaching loads. It quickly became one of the leading centers in the subjects of history and politics.[71]

These universities and academies became centers of international activity and association, and through these activities and networks reformed ideas spread quickly. Students from all over Europe traveled to Geneva or Heidelberg or Oxford and the like for their education. Faculty as well often circulated to other academies and universities. The urban and university-based networks served as a catalyst of innovation, centers of meeting, and of course the source of pastoral leadership and clear pastoral training for the growing number of churches serving its expanding population.[72]

The rapid spread of reformed ideas was also encouraged by the fact that the Reformation created a vast number of political refugees exiled from their Catholic homelands—first pastors and then nearly everyone. The unintended consequences of this were hugely favorable to the movement. Graeme Murdock summarizes the dynamic this way:

> The common Calvinist experience of life as a refugee, or of being part of a host community that received refugees, led to lasting international connections between individuals and communities. . . . As churches became established in Switzerland, the Palatinate, Scotland, England and Bearn, and the churches in the Netherlands, France, Hungary and Poland battled for legal recognition and survival, princely courts, noble houses, universities and colleges also became locations for interaction between many Calvinists. Theologians, clergy, students, booksellers, merchants, diplomats, courtiers and military officers became involved in networks of personal contacts, correspondence, teaching and negotiation.[73]

These international connections, then, were most common and had the most benefit among the social and intellectual elite.

It is no accident that universities were located in the growing urban areas along the commercial routes established by merchants and traders. Europe's growing economy expanded from city to city along these roads and rivers. Networks of universities, faculty, students, pastors and their churches, then, were formed along this web of cities and towns. A critical element of this infrastructure was the existence of international networks of Protestant merchants, based in places like Geneva, Hamburg, Frankfurt, Nuremburg, Amsterdam, Middelburg, London, and Antwerp. Their support was not only financial but strategic too. It was the pastors and godly merchants who dominated the reformed communities of the time as ministers and elders, and it is they who are rightly credited with the successful propagation of the Reformation, especially in its Calvinist strain.[74] The net effect was a cosmopolitanism that was rare in history to that time; a cosmopolitanism that had an eschatological feel. "Is it not wonderful," the Calvinist pastor John Bale writes, "that Spaniards, Italians, Scots, Englishmen, Frenchmen, Germans, disagreeing in manners, speech and apparel, sheep and wolves, bulls and bears, being coupled only with the yoke of Christ, should live so lovingly and friendly . . . like a spiritual and Christian congregation."[75]

It was among these merchants and within these urban areas that the new technology of printing flourished. An activity that had once been controlled by the alliance of church and nobility, was no longer their monopoly. For example, because of the capacity of mechanical printing to reproduce text, thousands of copies of Luther's ninety-five theses were produced and distributed within only a few weeks after his posting them in Wittenberg; and five thousand copies of his German New Testament were sold only two months after its completion in 1522.[76] Indeed, it can be said that the Reformation comprised a propaganda war against the Catholic Church and in this, the printing press—in the production of sermons, tracts, pamphlets, commentaries, and Bibles—was used to full advantage. As Robert Wuthnow summarized, between 1517 and 1550, approximately 150,000 new books, with combined sales of 60 million copies, were published—at least four times as many as had appeared during the entire fifteenth century. Between 1517 and 1523 alone, one could find 400 printers, 125 places of publication, and approximately 900 authors.[77]

As is well known, the success of the Reformation depended not only on the support of the emerging commercial elite but also on the protections provided by regional nobility. Religious confession was a life-and-death matter at this time. In France alone, thousands of Protestants were killed for their beliefs.[78] The critical contribution of the nobility, then, was in the provision of safe haven. Luther himself would likely have been executed (as Savonarola had been a generation before and Jan Hus a century before) if Frederick the Wise had not removed him to safe refuge at Wartburg Castle after the Edict of Worms. After all, the Edict of Worms declared Luther an outlaw, banned his writings, demanded his books be burned, and required his arrest so that he would be "punished as a notorious heretic."[79] Protestants sought protection through laws, such as the Edict of January, the Edict of Pacification, the Edict of St. Germain, the Edict of Nantes, and the Edict of Toleration, which could only be formed and enforced by royal decree. Throughout Germany, the Netherlands, England, Switzerland, and France, Protestant communities thrived only as they had the legal, political, and even military protection provided by local but powerful nobility.[80]

Here again, there is infinitely more that could be told about the dynamics of this period, the details of which are endlessly fascinating. Not least of these are the effects of the Reformation on architecture. Even in the thick of conflict between Protestants and Catholics, Calvinists were among the elites of art and architecture who worked in the service of Catholic patrons. Their distinctive style reflected their convictions, and in turn their work encoded criticism and resistance to the dominant religious and political authorities.[81] One must also acknowledge the obvious—that for all of its emphasis on reforming Christianity to a more pure form, one can find stupefying contradiction and hypocrisy. For example, Luther was not innocent of the blood spilled by the Peasant Revolt (1524–1525), and his anti-Semitism and proto-nationalism was to have horrific consequences for later German history. As to Calvin and Beza, both were directly culpable in the execution—by burning at the stake—of Michael Servetus, the Spanish physician and radical reformer, for heresy. The power of the Consistory was staggeringly oppressive to any who violated Geneva's theocratic rule. The freedoms they wanted for themselves they were not prepared to offer others. All of that said, the central point is clear: the Reformation may have been rooted in a desire for spiritual purity and theological truthfulness, but its success depended on factors in addition to if not other than these. Among other things (including historical serendipity), they included the creation of an alternative elite that was not bound tightly within the Catholic network, overlapping with other networks of leaders, drawing from the wealth of resources they brought with them—intellectual, institutional, administrative, financial, and political—all in common cause. All of these were nothing short of decisive.

Successor Movements: Awakenings, Antislavery Reform, Revival

The Reformation was a true revolution in ideas and institutions that challenged and transformed the nature and direction of Western civilization. In its wake were a series of successor movements that were not so much alternative directions but rather elaborations or applications of the same cultural logic as the Reformation. In these cases, the intent was to "push down" or extend into the larger public the theological and spiritual ideals at the heart of reformational Christianity. Because these movements were oriented toward popular renewal or reform rather than a foundational challenge to the social order, the success they enjoyed was either targeted or short term. Even so, many of the same dynamics discussed here were at work in these movements too.

Consider the Great Awakening of the 1730s and 1740s. George Whitefield, Jonathan Edwards, and the Wesley brothers—John and Charles—attract most of the attention from historians and for good reason. Yet they were hardly alone in this effort. These men were part and parcel of a vibrant transatlantic network of relationships committed to the renewal of Christian faith.

The leadership of these efforts in Britain and in the American colonies had varied backgrounds though the movement's most prominent leaders were largely from established families of the merchant and professional classes. They were also, as a whole, exceptionally well educated at elite universities— John and Charles Wesley, George Whitefield, John Gambold, John Clayton, James Hervey, Benjamin Ingham, Thomas Brougham were all Oxford trained; John Erskine and Thomas Gillespie were educated at Edinburgh; Jonathan Edwards, David Brainerd, Jonathan Parsons, Samuel Hopkins, and Joseph Bellamy were trained at Yale; and Thomas Prince Sr., Benjamin Colman, Josiah Smith, and Ebenezer Pemberton, were educated at Harvard. Within the dominant Christian tradition, they formed an alternative elite drawn from communities of English non-conformists, Scottish Presbyterians, and New England Puritans. Perhaps most interesting is the evidence that indicates that these evangelical pastors were connected to each other and aware of one another's activities.

The groundwork for these networks was laid in the late seventeenth and early eighteenth century. For example, Anglican missionaries from the Society for the Propagation of the Gospel in Foreign Parts were well established throughout the colonies by the 1730s, supporting missionaries, providing libraries, and setting up charity schools.[82] These along with the societies for reformation of manners and the Anglican religious societies, all active in the first half of the eighteenth century, were important in preparing the public for the revival.[83] Even more, revivalism already existed locally in New Jersey, New York, Massachusetts, Pennsylvania, and in parts of Wales, Scotland, and England. Though up to that point it had not effectively transcended regions or denominations, there was a common Evangelical message of spiritual new birth through grace and, thus, a shared mission across colonial America and in Great Britain.[84]

More than anyone else, it was George Whitefield who was the catalyst for the broad transcolonial and transatlantic revival that has come to be known as the Great Awakening.[85] One reason was that Whitefield was seemingly ubiquitous. He not only traveled extensively through England and Wales, but he made seven trips to the colonies and fourteen to Scotland. He was also a central figure in a far-reaching epistolary network that included hundreds of ministers, evangelists, financial backers, printers, and ordinary laypeople. Most important, he was personally and regularly in correspondence with the main revival figures in Britain and America. As Susan O'Brian puts it, "When Whitefield sent letters from the colonies to London for distribution, he did so by the trunkload."[86]

In some cases, the purpose of the correspondence was practical, for example, circulating devotional literature, recommending good reading, collecting money for missionary work, and making arrangements for future hospitality. In other instances, these ministers and Evangelists used their contacts for discussing theological matters, the nature of piety, and the practice of revivalism. It is important to note that though this correspondence was often personal in nature, it was public in its intent and consequence. These letters were read to congregations and ministerial associations. They were also published in inexpensive newspapers, some of which existed only to publicize the news of revival and to provide advanced publicity for future events. The distribution of these papers along with journals, pamphlets, and sermons comprised the means by which a transatlantic and intercolonial Evangelical consciousness and movement developed. In this way, the Calvinist revivalists of the mid-eighteenth century created a "community of saints" that reached beyond local geographic and even theological boundaries.[87]

It was these networks of leaders, with their innovations in communication, that launched or supported specific initiatives such as Whitefield's Bethesda, the Georgia Orphan House; donated money to missionaries; and helped to establish the Presbyterian College of New Jersey, which became Princeton University. Not least, these networks initiated and sustained the United Concert for Prayer, an international, interdenominational parish-based movement of prayer that became another of the major legacies bequeathed by the mid-eighteenth century revivals to evangelical Protestantism.[88]

Another important successor movement to the Reformation was British abolitionism of the late eighteenth and early nineteenth centuries. As noted earlier in this essay, Evangelical belief is regarded as the source of spiritual, moral, and humanitarian energy for this movement. As we noted in Chapter 2, with regard to leadership, William Wilberforce is nearly always regarded as *the* heroic figure in the successful end of the slave trade in the British Empire. It was his Christian faith and moral determination that finally won the day and, for this reason, it is Wilberforce who is lionized as the model of what one man, with faith, can accomplish for good. No one studying abolition would deny the critical role played by Wilberforce and Evangelical conviction, yet the larger story of the British abolitionist movement is considerably more complicated, unfolding along dynamics that are now familiar.

For one, the cultural backdrop of the late eighteenth century was defined by the progressive intellectual ideas of the French and Scottish Enlightenment—the thought of John Locke, Montesquieu, Alexander Pope, Samuel Johnson, Adam Ferguson, Thomas Reid, and William Blackstone, as well as Edmund Burke and Adam Smith. Though understood differently within different philosophical schools, the concepts of liberty, happiness, and benevolence in general were all implicitly critical of the ideal and institution of slavery. The cultural logic of Scottish realism in particular, portrayed a moral order that was providentially designed but also one that required human betterment, not least in the area of human liberty. In this respect, the intellectual framework for abolition was already well established; the case for freedom—at least among intellectuals—already won.[89] Politics, however, was another matter.[90]

On this more pragmatic front, the abolitionists made an appeal to the national interests of the British Empire. The thought among many in the political classes was that it was in the interest of Great Britain to at least partially ban the slave trade precisely because a considerable part of the slave trade contributed toward the economic growth of the colonies of Britain's enemies—France, most importantly. This was the argument of the influential book, *The War in Disguise*, by James Stephen published in 1805.[91] Stephen's argument was very influential and carried the majority opinion in Parliament.

It is well known too that Wilberforce was not an isolated actor but was surrounded and supported by a network of friends, associates, and sympathizers. Those closest to him were known as the Clapham Circle. One can count over two dozen leaders from the highest echelons of business, church, literary life, and government and politics who were connected and worked together in this common cause. These individuals either came from or operated within the centers of cultural influence. The majority were exceptionally well educated. Wilberforce, Henry and John Venn, Thomas Clarkson, Charles Simeon, James Eliot Edward, Thomas Gisbourne, Beilby Porteus, Thomas Babington Macaulay, and Claudius Buchanan, for example, were all educated at Cambridge. In this network one finds members of the aristocracy (John Shore, Baron Teignmouth), business elite (such as John and Henry Thornton), literary elite (most importantly, Hannah More, but also Buchanan and Clarkson), and clergy, as well as members of Parliament and key figures in government administration (besides Wilberforce, Thornton, William Smith, Thomas Fowell Buxton, Zachary Macaulay, and James Stephen). It was certainly significant too that Wilberforce, Eliot, Smith, and others were longtime friends with the British prime minister, William Pitt. In and through these networks, they created numerous voluntary organizations, established strategic alliances, and made maximum use of the public media of the day—sermons, lectures, pamphlets, and newspapers.

The abolition of the slave trade and slavery itself may have been their primary concern but it was not their only concern. Among other things, they devoted themselves to everything from the care of the poor and charity schools to prison reform and the prevention of cruelty to animals. In this, they were often paternalistic toward slaves and toward the poor. With fresh stories of popular violence coming from France, many were also deeply suspicious of the excesses of popular democratic reform. Still, they promoted an egalitarianism that was unusual within their social class and, among other things, they did much to make Great Britain more democratic.

Beyond Christianity

It bears repeating: the foregoing is not intended as an exhaustive account of any one of these important moments in the cultural history of the West. Each episode is infinitely more complex than what has been described here—volumes have been written that provide much more careful and nuanced accounts of these periods. Nor am I arguing that these are the only important moments of cultural transformation. The social, institutional, economic, and cultural dynamics I am emphasizing in the alternative model of cultural change I propose, play out just as clearly in critical moments of secular cultural transformation. A few brief illustrations should suffice to make this case.

Consider the Enlightenment.[92] By the second half of the seventeenth century, the power of early modern states in Europe had become increasingly centralized and interventionist under the rising pressures of international economic and political competition. All aspects of economic life—from production through trade—were increasingly systematized and regulated. The net effect of this new mercantilism within each national context was both economic growth and political stability. National treasuries swelled with unprecedented surplus wealth. It was in this way that the state became a source of patronage, channeling its capital into science, architecture, the arts, and philosophy. Both in its own right and through charters it officially granted to private ventures, the state became an employer and a benefactor to a growing cadre of scientists, writers, playwrights, intellectuals, artists, publishers, and printers. They also established professional societies, scientific and literary academies, and salons that were directly or indirectly linked to the monarchy and its offices. Not least, they provided recognition and legitimacy, physical facilities, channels of communication, space for social interaction, and legal protection for those on the cutting edge of intellectual and artistic experimentation.

Where cultural production had remained squarely under the patronage of religious authorities through the early seventeenth century, a new and alternative cultural economy was now developing that competed with and eventually superseded that of the church. In particular, colleges and universities remained under ecclesiastical authority and, as such, they were not only defensive of theological orthodoxy and the social order it implied, but they were resistant to the innovations that naturally accompanied an age of discovery. The salons, literary clubs and societies, and royal academies that developed in the late seventeenth and early eighteenth centuries, in effect, circumvented traditional authority based in the universities and, by extension, in the church.[93] In time, the intellectual culture and mission of the universities themselves were transformed by the innovations of the Enlightenment.

In sum, where the state provided both vast economic and administrative resources as well as freedom for intellectual and artistic innovation—e.g., France, England, Prussia, and Scotland—the Enlightenment flourished. Where the state failed to provide adequate resources (as in the Dutch Republic, Sweden, and Austria), or freedom (as in the case of Spain and Russia), the Enlightenment faltered. What occurred in less than a century was mind-boggling. At the time that John Locke died and Rousseau was born in the early years of the eighteenth century, it was unimaginable that the authority of Christendom would ever be diminished. Its institutions and its authority were unassailable. Yet in less than a century, traditional Christian authority and the regime it spawned and maintained had either been overturned (as in France) or had been forever weakened. In this we see a cultural transformation of world historical significance. To see this only, or primarily, as an evolution in the history of ideas fails to grasp the nature and character of the change that took place. Rather the Enlightenment was a revolution generated by an alternative network of leaders, providing an alternative base of resources, oriented toward the development of an alternative cultural vision (a new anthropology, epistemology, ethics, sociality, and politics), established in part through alternative institutions, all operating at the elite centers of cultural formation.

In a way that is counter-intuitive to the standard way of telling the story, these dynamics also play out in one of the successor movements of the Enlightenment, European socialism between 1864 and 1914. Though the story of Marxism and Leninism is typically recounted as a story of the power of the working class on the periphery of society, European socialism could not have succeeded as much as it did without the elements of transformation we note here.

First, it was a successor to the Enlightenment insofar as it was dependent on the "virtues of science, an awareness of history and sensitivity to its importance as a legitimating motif, skepticism toward religious dogma, and faith in progress."[94] Indeed, theoretically, modern socialism was, in some respects, a logical extension of the principles laid down by the great French philosophers of the eighteenth century."[95] Second, though a grassroots theory, it was articulated and championed by those in the higher echelons of the social order, not least, networks of disaffected intellectuals who came from and drew heavily on the resources and institutions of the society they hoped to overthrow. Both Marx and Engels, for example, came from upper bourgeois society: Engels was the son of a multinational cotton manufacturer and an industrialist himself, who was influenced intellectually at University of Berlin and who participated in the city's intellectual subculture; Marx, a doctor of philosophy from Friedrich-Wilhelms-Universität in Berlin, married to the daughter of a German baron, was mostly dependent on the largesse of his friend and colleague.[96] Other prominent socialists included William Liebknecht, who was trained in philosophy, theology, philology, and history at the universities of Giessen, Berlin, and Marburg,[97] and Jean Jaurés, who was educated at the prestigious *École Normale Supérieure* in Paris. The irony here of course is that Marxism views history as inevitably unfolding toward socialism but its ushering in was done from the top, by powerful cultural intellectuals whose theory was both highly abstract and difficult to read by any but the most intellectually trained thinkers. The role of intellectual elites became explicit with Lenin's organization of the Bolshevik Party.[98] Lenin himself came from relative privilege, his father having been an official with the Russian government; and the Bolshevik revolution was financed in part by private benefactors and even the German government. Third, European socialism depended on capitalist institutions, not least the newspaper industry and other commercialized media. "The leaders of the movement, most notably Marx himself, wrote for commercial newspapers, served as salaried editors, and secured royalties from their books and pamphlets."[99] The print media then served both as a means of disseminating ideas as well as a source of personal and collective income.[100] Here, too, Lenin was explicit about wanting to appropriate capitalist institutions. "We must take the entire culture that capitalism left behind and build socialism with it. We must take all its science, technology, knowledge and art. Without these we shall be unable to build communist society."[101]

The alternative view of cultural change that assigns roles not only to ideas but also to elites, networks, technology, and new institutions, provides a much better account of the growth in plausibility and popularity of these important cultural developments. It also provides a more cogent explanation for other important cultural developments in the modern West, not least for the triumph of Darwinism[102] in the nineteenth century and of Nietzsche,[103] literary modernism,[104] modern art[105] neo-Marxism,[106] and a general secular ethos in education and law[107] in the twentieth century.

Conclusion

As I have repeatedly affirmed, the unfolding of history is infinitely complex. Any attempt to provide a neat summary, therefore, will inevitably fail to grasp the intricacy and subtlety of the reality it seeks to describe. But some historical accounts are better than others and thus provide clearer insight than common knowledge would otherwise offer. In this chapter, I have made no pretense of providing original historical research on these critical moments of cultural evolution in the West. Instead, I have only aspired to provide a fairly concise summary of some of the leading scholarship on these periods.

What one can say now with some conviction is that the common view of cultural change (sketched out in Chapter 2), in fact, does not offer a useful account of any of the major periods of transformation we have reviewed here. Change in a culture or civilization simply does not occur when there is change in the beliefs and values in the hearts and minds of ordinary people or in the creation of mere artifacts. Populism had a place at different points in these dramas and, in some cases, with unintended consequences. In the Reformation, for example, populism manifested itself in the Peasant Revolt, and as such it was the source of extraordinary carnage (up to 100,000 dead!). It also had a place in the Awakenings as well. The beliefs and values of ordinary people, then, are not irrelevant to the story of change. Yet in none of the instances recounted here was change dependent on the popular appeal and acceptance of the alternative culture proposed. The beliefs and values of ordinary people have a place in the unfolding drama; but it is neither the central nor the decisive place in the instigation and direction of change itself.

Neither does change in a culture occur with the mere creation of new artifacts. To be sure, artifacts or cultural goods do have a place in the story of change. For example, the production of books or texts as well as the creation of schools are prominent aspects of most of these episodes, and yet those texts and those schools that were most influential were hardly the result of random production operating within a free market. What mattered was (a) who was writing the text or leading the school, (b) where—sociologically and geographically—the text was produced or where the school was located, (c) what was being communicated in those texts and schools (both content and quality), and finally (d) how much and for whom (the audience). Absent critical sociological conditions surrounding the production and consumption of material goods, artifacts are largely meaningless.

What, then, is decisive? Though the context, configuration, and interrelationship in each historical instance are all quite different, at every point of challenge and change, we find a rich source of patronage that provided resources for intellectuals and educators who, in the context of dense networks, imagine, theorize, and propagate an alternative culture. Often enough, alongside these elites are artists, poets, musicians, and the like who symbolize, narrate, and popularize this vision. New institutions are created that give form to that culture, enact it, and, in so doing, give tangible expression to it. Together, these overlapping networks of leaders and resources form a vibrant cultural economy that gives articulation, in multiple forms, and critical mass to the ideals and practices and goods of the alternative culture in ways that both defy yet still resonate with the existing social environment. These networks of leaders and the various resources they bring may or may not originate in the "center" of cultural production, but they do not gain traction in the larger social world until they do challenge, penetrate, and redefine the status structure at the center of cultural life. Invariably, as we have seen, this process results in conflict. As to politics, where present, it contributes most effectively to the process of cultural change not when it imposes a cultural agenda but when it creates space for a new way of thinking and living to develop and flourish.

To live in a culture is, in most times and places, to experience the world as stable and enduring. This is true even in times of great social change and cultural upheaval. We tend not to experience the change as change but only really recognize it for what it is in retrospect. Whether or not we are aware of what is going on in the world around us, we do know that cultures can and do change in the most profound ways over time. As we have seen, ideas can have revolutionary and world-changing consequences and yet they appear to do so only when the kinds of structural conditions discussed here are in place. If true, it raises significant questions for understanding Christianity in America in our own time.

Chapter Six

THE CULTURAL ECONOMY OF AMERICAN CHRISTIANITY

I N SOME WAYS, the question of Christianity's place in contemporary America is an odd question. From the European view, America remains remarkably Christian, to the point of being weirdly puritanical. A typical view of America from the Middle East would see it as Christian in origin and character, though hypocritical and in a gradual descent toward decadence. And to non-Christians living in America, there is no question that America still *feels* very Christian. What, then, is the point of the question? Isn't the answer obvious?

But my question is not so much about the residual effects of a once robust and pervasive Christianity that continues to define the contours and character of American society but about the capacity of present-day Christianity to reproduce itself in ways that influence the larger world for good. If the nature of culture is as much institutional as it is ideational, if it unfolds along the convoluted, contested, and contingent dynamics I suggest, and if the historical record—incomplete as I have summarized it here—nevertheless affirms an alternative view of culture and cultural change rather than the common view, then how do the movements of historical Christianity in contemporary America measure up to the configuration of factors that I believe create conditions conducive to cultural influence? In the larger social and political economy of culture-formation, how do the culture-forming institutions of historical Christianity relate to the broader field of such institutional gatekeepers?

I would caution at the outset that the observations that follow are not intended to be comprehensive or systematic. It is important for someone to offer such a comprehensive view, but here it would be a distraction from the main line of argument. The landscape I paint here, to use a well-worn metaphor, is painted with a broad brush. The strokes will not capture the detail that would make the picture complete but it will still illustrate the broad contours of the situation.

Preliminary Observations on Politics and Economics

Within social life, one can make broad analytic distinctions between the major realms of social life—the economic, the political, and the cultural. Of course, such distinctions are finally unsatisfactory because, as I have noted, each area infuses the others. Money is inextricably linked to partisan politics, wealth creation is inhibited or encouraged by politics and public policy, and economics and politics not only are shaped by the culture but also are themselves expressions of culture. All of that noted, it is still possible to make observations on the basis of broad analytical distinctions between the economy, polity, and culture.

The first and perhaps most obvious thing to say is that the most visible way American Christianity influences the larger society today is in the political realm. This is especially so among Christian conservatives, though, in recent years, Christian progressives have been regaining influence. What is Christianity's influence here? How are its elites positioned? High-profile Catholic and Evangelical politicians, judges, and operatives may have received most of the attention in recent years but they are not the most important players on the landscape. Christian communities are also represented within the realm of the higher-end public policy think tanks (such as the Heritage Foundation and the Ethics and Public Policy Center) but rarely as such; that is, these think tanks are not explicitly providing the Evangelical view of this issue or the Catholic perspective on that issue. Though very much present within this area, policy-oriented intellectual work is also not the place where Christians of any stripe make their most significant mark. Rather the greatest strength and energy over recent decades has come from faith-based pressure groups and their leaders, again overwhelmingly within conservatism but, again, not exclusively so. Some of these groups and their leaders seek to exert influence on a range of issues (e.g., Focus on the Family, the Christian Coalition, the Family Research Council, American Values, the Cry for Renewal coalition, the Interfaith Alliance, Sojourners, Alliance for Justice, Concerned Women for America, etc.), while other groups are oriented toward one specific issue (such as Priests for Life, the Religious Coalition for Abortion Rights, the National Right to Life, and the Evangelical Environmental Network). These groups are well organized, often strident, noisy, and, at times, effective in shaping the character of different party agendas and in influencing the nature of public debate around specific political issues.

In the economic sphere, the situation is quite different. The collapse of the so-called WASP (white Anglo-Saxon Protestant) establishment in the post–World War II period changed a great deal in America. Protestant domination in economic life dissipated at the least, and if Christians retain an influence *qua Christians* in the corporate world, it is in ways that are more self-consciously pietistic. Indeed, one can find a wide representation of Christian believers in all areas of business and commerce.[1] There are highly accomplished Christian believers (who are known as such) at the head of major public and private corporations and a number of ministries to serve them, such as C12, BBL Forum, Wise Council, and the Christian Business Leaders' Association. There also is a Christian presence in the upper-middle-class professions—law, medicine, architecture, and so on—where Christian professional organizations proliferate (e.g., the Christian Legal Society, the Christian Medical and Dental Association, Christian Medical Fellowship, the Christian Management Association, the Association of Christian Librarians, North American Christian Social Workers Association, the Christian Chiropractors Association, and so on). This representation would seem to be growing especially among Catholics, the Reformed, and Evangelicals. For the most part, however, the Christian presence in business and commerce and the professions tends to be weighted in small to mid-sized firms and organizations in smaller cities and in the suburbs and exurbs. Thus, its economic influence is not in the leadership of American capitalism, but primarily within the middle classes.

What about the sphere of culture?

Cultural Resources

Perhaps the best starting point for understanding the cultural influence of American Christianity in all of its diversity is to look at the scale and orientation of faith-based patronage, for it is here that one finds the main resources that fuel its cultural economy.[2] On the face of it, faith-based philanthropy is impressive. For many years now, nearly forty percent of the total philanthropic giving from all sources in the United States has gone to religious organizations.[3] According to *Giving USA*, Americans gave $93 billion to churches and religious organizations in 2005, accounting for 35.8 percent of total giving.[4] Other surveys show that at least two-thirds of all individual contributions go to religious organizations.[5] But what is the nature of this giving? Upward of eighty percent of religious giving comes from individual donations rather than from foundations or corporations. And the majority of this giving consists of proportionally small individual contributions to an array of ministries and causes.[6]

There are, of course, foundations that contribute to faith-based work. The Foundation Center's report *Grants for Religion, Religious Welfare, and Religious Education* lists 260 foundations that give over one million dollars annually to religious charities, awarding just over one billion dollars. Though the giving is not insignificant by any measure, compared to the larger universe of foundation giving, the amounts are relatively small (see Table 1).[7]

Among the nation's ten largest foundations, only the Ford Foundation and the Lilly Endowment actively seek to support religious agencies and projects with religious purposes.[10] Of the faith-based foundations, most give only to local or regional projects. This is why in the larger philanthropic world, this faith-based philanthropy is considered to be "the special domain of the 'country cousins,' the small religious grant-makers (see Table 2)."[11]

Of the self-described Catholic foundations, most orient their grant-giving to churches, dioceses, parishes, and orders. A substantial amount goes to Catholic education, including seminaries, secondary and postsecondary schools, and monasteries. There is also significant giving to social service organizations. In one case, the Koch Foundation, much of its funding is devoted to Catholic evangelism efforts (see Table 3).

As to self-described Evangelical foundations, the focus of giving has long been on missionary work and evangelism, Evangelical college and seminary education, and welfare organizations engaged in relief, development, and other social services. These foundations have also tended to favor para-church agencies over denominations.[14] This general pattern continues to hold true. In 2004 and 2005, for example, the ten largest Evangelical foundations made 317 grants totaling $103,631,308.[15] Of these grants, $7,717,285 went to an educational institution such as a seminary, Christian college, or Christian school; $12,352,471 was given to social service organizations including the YMCAs; $2,642,995 went to international relief organizations; $31,567,741 went to missions (most of which were for international missions); $18,334,502 were designated for evangelism efforts, from Campus

TABLE 1   Ten Largest Independent Foundations by Total Giving

Foundation	Total Giving[8]	Religious Giving[9]
Bill and Melinda Gates Foundation	$1,356,377,000	$36,069,754
The Ford Foundation	$553,000,000	$11,238,900
The Lilly Endowment	$422,300,000	$105,530,263
The Robert Wood Johnson Foundation	$369,500,000	$6,118,203
W. K. Kellogg Foundation	$329,000,000	$4,839,484
The William and Flora Hewlett Foundation	$319,916,093	$1,236,000
The Annenberg Foundation	$217,414,830	$3,515,785
Gordon and Betty Moore Foundation	$215,827,278	$315,597
John D. and Catherine T. MacArthur Foundation	$194,500,000	$1,247,400
David and Lucile Packard Foundation	$170,381,000	$1,072,000

TABLE 2 Top Ten Foundations in Religion, Religious Welfare, and Religious Education[12]

Foundation	Religious Giving
Lilly Endowment, Inc.	$105,530,263
Bill and Melinda Gates Foundation	$36,069,754
John Templeton Foundation	$29,941,908
Arthur S. DeMoss Foundation	$22,674,687
The Duke Endowment	$17,423,098
The Harry and Jeanette Weinberg Foundation	$16,793,600
H. N. and Frances C. Berger Foundation	$14,534,467
The Richard and Helen DeVos Foundation	$13,299,700
The Maclellan Foundation, Inc.	$12,477,091
Wayne and Gladys Valley Foundation	$12,300,000

TABLE 3 Top Ten Self-Described Catholic Foundations[13]

Foundation	Religious Giving
Wayne and Gladys Valley Foundation	$12,300,000
Florik Charitable Trust	$11,179,799
Koch Foundation, Inc.	$7,170,297
Dan Murphy Foundation	$5,895,750
The Ave Maria Foundation	$5,134,093
Thomas and Dorothy Leavey Foundation	$4,272,000
Carrie Estelle Doheny Foundation	$4,108,361
Connelly Foundation	$4,057,671
Raskob Foundation for Catholic Activities, Inc.	$3,954,589
Norcliffe Foundation	$2,995,000

Crusade to Luis Palau; and $3,817,000 were for a variety of other para-church organizations. Only $14,722,523 went to a church or a denominational organization(see Table 4).

Here a point of contrast may be instructive. In 2004, the Ford Foundation, the Hewlett Foundation, the Annenburg Foundation, and the John D. and Catherine T. MacArthur Foundation gave a combined total of over $200 million dollars in grants to "arts and culture."[18] In the largest Catholic and Evangelical foundations, $10,706,335 was given to arts and culture.[19] As to scholarship, invention, and social innovation, The John D. and Catherine T. MacArthur Foundation gave 12 million dollars for their "genius" fellows awards. In the Catholic and Evangelical foundations noted above, no fellowship program exists at all for supporting the most talented intellectuals,

TABLE 4   Top Ten Self-Described Evangelical Foundations[16]

Foundation	Religious Giving[17]
National Christian Charitable Foundation	$196,678,792
Arthur S. DeMoss Foundation	$22,674,687
Maclellan Foundation	$12,477,091
The Richard and Helen DeVos Foundation	$13,299,700
Lazarus Foundation	$11,433,049
Aimee and Frank Batten, Jr. Foundation	$10,588,200
Open Doors International, Inc.	$9,217,757
The J. E. and L. E. Mabee Foundation, Inc.	$8,858,721
Jack Whittaker Foundation, Inc.	$7,764,847
C.I.O.S.	$7,317,556

artists, or social innovators.[20] This review is hardly systematic or comprehensive, but the preliminary indications suggest that very few resources within the Christian community, in all of its diversity, go to supporting leadership in developing cultural capital in the centers of cultural production.

Cultural Capital

However one evaluates the period—critically, positively, or some mixture of the two—the WASP establishment meant that from the colonial period certainly through the mid-nineteenth century, many if not most of the leading institutions of cultural production in America reflected or were informed by certain assumptions and understandings of historical Christianity. Christian faith had been enormously influential in the culture precisely because it has had a principal if not hegemonic role in the culture-producing institutions of society. This was most obviously true for the churches, the dominant arbiters of spiritual and moral understanding and sensibility. This was also the case, of course, at the founding of elite colleges and universities (e.g., Harvard, Yale, and Princeton, etc.), private schools (e.g., St. Paul's, Groton, Deerfield, St. Mark's, etc.), and even the public schools. All had a self-conscious and distinct Protestant identity. This was the case in the major movements of social reform as well—the temperance movement most prominently. And it was true in popular culture (e.g., hymnology) and, in less explicit ways, in that small but growing realm of high culture—music, literature, and art.

Needless to say, WASP hegemony within the culture-producing institutions has waned. There are multiple and complex reasons for this. Perhaps the most obvious explanation is found in the exponential growth and pluralization of the culture industry as a whole, including the news media, film, television, popular music, the internet, and the like.

In terms of culture-producing institutions grounded in specific traditions, the most striking decline in the last half century has been within mainline Protestantism. There was a time when pronouncements from the National Council of Churches or from the major mainline denominations, such as the United Methodist or Episcopal Churches, would attract enormous public attention and, in turn, generate significant public debate. At one point, *The Christian Century* was a periodical of considerable clout both inside and outside of the Christian community. But those times are long passed. The private schools and colleges established by the mainline Protestant denominations, as a rule, still want to be known as places that foster values, but few will go so far as to identify those values as Christian. There are some exceptions to the rule, of course, but overall, the distinctiveness of mainline Protestant identity has largely dissolved since the 1960s. The cultural production of the mainline tradition now tends to exist within denominational and transdenominational bodies and tends to be oriented to its own internal needs and interests. Its public voice, once prominent and vigorous, has become so marginal that it is nearly invisible outside of its own constituencies.

Cultural production within the Catholic Church is mainly but not exclusively oriented toward serving its lay constituencies. Perhaps the biggest change has been in the decline in numbers of priests and men and women religious, all of which has created staffing shortages for its schools and charities. In the higher reaches of intellectual and literary production in the larger world outside of the Catholic enclave, Catholics have been more successful and better integrated than other Christian traditions. Universities such as Notre Dame, Georgetown, Catholic University, and the Loyola campuses are first- and second-tier institutions that provide an institutional base for much of this production. Journals such as *First Things* and *Crisis* provide a platform for public engagement. Intellectuals such as Michael Novak, Richard Neuhaus, Robert George, Mary Ann Glendon, George Weigel, and Russell Hittinger have been prominent in giving a conservative Catholic voice to key issues. Catholics have a very strong presence in analytical philosophy, history, and ethics and academic theology. And the American Catholic literary tradition (that includes Flannery O'Connor, Walker Percy, and the like) is rich and continues to flourish through the talents of novelists; short story writers such as Tobias Wolfe, Alice McDermott, and Andre Dubus; and poets such as Dana Gioia and Seamus Heaney among others. Within the more traditionalist Catholic community, there are institutions that serve the faithful well, but here again they are on the periphery of public culture. Christendom College,

Thomas Aquinas College, Magdalen College, and Ave Maria College were established deliberately to foster a distinct Catholic identity. Here one can find an extensive array of media that includes publishing (e.g., Baronius Press), periodicals (e.g., the *Catholic Digest*, the *New Oxford Review*, *Envoy* magazine, *Saint Maria's Messenger*, etc.), arts news (e.g., GrapeVine Online), Internet news and features (e.g., cathcom.net, Catholic News Service, Zenit.org, Spirituality for Today), and film production (e.g., Grass Roots Films). Traditionalist Catholics are also heavily involved in the homeschooling movement.

Much of the contemporary Evangelical world was initially created in reaction to the secularization of the mainline Protestant institutions in the mid-to-late nineteenth century. This was especially true in the case of the prominent Evangelical colleges and seminaries—Baylor in 1845, Taylor in 1846, Wheaton in 1860, Calvin in 1876, Gordon in 1889, Biola in 1908, Messiah in 1909, and so on. Many of these institutions are economically viable, and the quality of students, faculty, and scholarship has improved considerably over the decades. These schools draw almost exclusively from the Evangelical community, and as teaching institutions they are embraced by the community and serve its needs well. As scholarly institutions, however, the schools and their faculty are in a tough spot. The schools and faculty operate between the standards of scholarship and career mobility set by the secular academic establishment and the commitments of their faith community. Here they find they are doubly marginalized. Scholars are marginalized from the larger intellectual culture, especially to the extent that they pursue Christian distinctions in their work, yet they are also marginalized within Evangelicalism because of this community's long-standing tradition of anti-intellectualism—a tradition well documented by Richard Hofstader and Mark Noll.[21] It does not help that the teaching loads of most Christian colleges are often twice that of elite secular colleges, not to mention research universities. Many Evangelical scholars are committed to academic excellence, but they work in a community that neither values it highly nor supports it generously.

In terms of general cultural production, Evangelicalism is the standout. Since the late nineteenth century, Evangelicals have invested most of their energies into creating a structure of "parallel institutions."[22] Evangelicals are extraordinarily energetic, generating hundreds of millions of dollars through book and magazine publishing, radio, and television. In Evangelical publishing the most prominent publishers are Eerdmans, Baker Publishing Group, Brazos Press, Broadman & Holman Publishers, Good News Publishers/Crossway Books, Gospel Light/Regal Books, Intervarsity Press, NavPress, Paraclete Press, Thomas Nelson Publishers, Tyndale House Publishers, and Zondervan. In the magazine world, there are *Christianity Today*, *World*, and

Discipleship Journal, among others. In terms of radio programs, there is *Break-point*, *Adventures in Odyssey*, *Creation Moment*, *Family Life Today*, *Focus on the Family*, *Janet Parshall's America*, *Jay Sekulow Live!*, *Money Matters*, and *Our Daily Bread*, among many others. In Evangelical television broadcasting, there is the Christian Broadcasting network, Sky Angel, the Trinity Broadcasting Network, and the Daystar Television Network, each of which offers multiple programs for public viewing. There is also a developing Evangelical film industry that has produced dozens of films such as *The Omega Code* (1999), *Left Behind* (2000), *Jonah: A Veggie Tales Movie* (2002), *Hangman's Curse* (2003), *Woman, Thou are Loosed* (2004), *End of the Spear* (2005), and *Amazing Grace* (2006). In all of this, the production of culture tends to be concentrated in commercial ventures that are often hugely successful.

There are exceptions, of course, yet overall this cultural productivity is characterized by at least three features. First, the works that are produced are almost exclusively directed to the internal needs of the faithful. This insularity is quite striking. The Evangelical world is not only difficult for outsiders to understand (consider the caricatures that abound) but also nearly impossible for them to penetrate. Evangelicals, in other words, offer little by way of a common vocabulary of shared life informed by faith but not exclusive to it. Second, this cultural productivity all tends to operate closer to the margins than to the center of the broader field of cultural production.[23] Evangelicalism boasts a billion-dollar book publishing industry, yet the books produced are largely ignored by the *New York Review of Books*, the *New York Times Book Review*, the *Washington Post Book World*, and other key arbiters of public intellectual argument. Magazines such as *Christianity Today*, *World*, or *Books and Culture* also do well in the Evangelical and Reformed world, yet they do not compete with or counterbalance their secular counterparts, and generally only *First Things* attracts an audience outside of this particular faith community. Christian television is almost all ghettoized in the small viewer hours of Sunday morning or to the backwaters of cable broadcasting. Noncommercialized art by Christians is, as I said, small, vital, and growing through organizations such as *Image*, Christians in the Visual Arts (or CIVA), and the International Arts Movement (IAM), but such efforts are small and constantly underfunded and, like the commercialized art (e.g., Thomas Kinkade), it is typically peripheral to the major galleries and reviews. What is more, this vast commercial empire does not operate in the major centers of culture formation (such as New York City, Washington, Chicago, San Francisco, or Los Angeles) but rather in medium-sized cities on the periphery (such as Wheaton, Illinois; Colorado Springs, Colorado; Orlando, Florida; and Virginia Beach, Virginia). Third, cultural production in the Evangelical world is overwhelmingly oriented toward the popular. Very much like its retail politics, its music is popular music, its art tends to be popular (highly sentimentalized and commercialized) art, its theater is mega-church drama, its publishing is mainly mass-market book publishing with a heavy bent toward "how-to" books, its magazines are mass-circulation monthlies, its television is either in the format of a worship service or the talk show, its recent forays into film are primarily into popular film, and much academic work is oriented toward translation—making the difficult accessible to the largest possible number. While there are exceptions to the rule, overall, the populist orientation of Evangelical cultural production reflects the most kitschy expressions of consumerism and often the most crude forms of market instrumentalism.

As it is with Catholics and mainline Protestants, individual Evangelicals can be found everywhere—in elite research universities, university presses, think tanks and the like—and there they make important contributions. But except for a few areas such as philosophy and American religious history, where they have had a significant presence and influence, their number tends to be very small and their broader impact of no great consequence. Likewise, in literature, there are some talented novelists, poets, and critics in these communities, but here again their number is few and they too tend to be fairly isolated in their respective fields. Much the same can be said about the Evangelical presence in architecture, the visual arts (painting, sculpture, etc.) and the performing arts (e.g., theater, film, dance, music, and the like). In all of these arenas and others (such as journalism and advertising), there are individual exceptions—extraordinary, remarkable, talented exceptions—but they are exceptions, rather than a normal occurrence. These individuals are present in these spheres, it would seem, more by accident than by design; certainly more as a statistical aberration than through the deliberate cultivation of the churches.

In the Halls of Power?

The more important point is institutional. Since the 1960s, none of the movements in contemporary Christianity have been prominent in creating, contributing to, or supporting structures in the arts, humane letters, the academy, and the like; structures that either explicitly express their faith tradition or that are implicitly compatible with or reflect the assumptions of their tradition. And the movement that has had the most vibrant cultural economy—the Evangelicals—has also been the least interested in such efforts.

One way to summarize how the cultural economy of American Christianity is oriented is illustrated in the following chart. This matrix roughly follows the classic Aristotelian distinctions between the true, the good and the beautiful. Each area identifies key spheres of cultural activity, and while these distinctions may begin as philosophical abstractions, they play out within concrete spheres of life; institutions and organizations where the social order is produced and reproduced. Clearly, this matrix is, at best, a crude instrument, inadequate precisely because it defies the complexity that exists in real life but it can help us see where the various communities of historic Christianity tend to put their energy and resources and in this way it helps to demonstrate the present situation.

In the early decades of the twenty-first century as in the last decades of the twentieth, Christian presence in America has been a presence primarily in, of, and for the middle class in everything that this designation means. This is especially true for the Evangelical, Reformed, and Catholic traditions. There are exceptions, of course, but those exceptions tend to prove the rule. Thus, the financial capital that fuels Christianity's religious, social, and political causes is generated primarily from the extraordinarily generous tithing of the ordinary faithful. The considerable political capital American Christianity has amassed exists primarily in its pressure groups and the ability of those groups to mobilize the grassroots, middle-class, church-going voters. The vitality of its cultural capital today is a vitality that resides almost exclusively among average people in the pew rather than those in leadership, on the periphery not the center of cultural production, in tastes that run to the popular rather than the exceptional, the middle brow rather than the high brow, and almost always toward the practical as opposed to the theoretical or the imaginative. There is little taste for "high culture" especially in Evangelicalism, where the tendency has long been toward translation—making things accessible to the largest number of people.

Politics is another matter—and one I shall address in Essay II. *In terms of the cultural economy*, however, Christians in America today have institutional strength and vitality exactly in the lower and peripheral areas of cultural production. Against the prevailing view, the main reason why Christian believers today (from various communities) have not had the influence in the culture to which they have aspired is not that they don't believe enough, or try hard enough, or care enough, or think Christianly enough, or have the right worldview, but rather *because they have been absent from the arenas in which the greatest influence in the culture is exerted*. The culture-producing institutions of historical Christianity are largely marginalized in the economy of culture formation in North America. Its cultural capital is greatest where leverage in the larger culture is weakest.

As I've said repeatedly, there are exceptions, but some observers make far too much of those exceptions.[24] The reason is that the Christians who do operate in positions of social, cultural, and economic influence are neither operating within dense social networks nor working together coherently with common

The Culture Matrix

THE TRUE (Knowledge – What is)	THE GOOD (Morality – What should be)	THE BEAUTIFUL (Aesthetics – What can be imagined)
Theoretical	*Abstract*	*High Brow*
o Academic think tanks o Elite research universities (in the social sciences and humanities) o Elite opinion magazines and journals o Elite NYC and 1st tier book university publishers	o Academic philosophy & moral psychology o Law schools and schools of public policy	o Visual arts o Literature and poetry o Classical & orchestral music o Theater & dance o Museums
→	→	→
High-end Educational	*Activist*	*Upper Middle Brow*
o First & second tier colleges o High-end journalism o **Seminaries & divinity schools** o Elite private schools	o Public policy think tanks o **Special interest groups** o **Innovative churches, synagogues & faith based ministries of mercy** o **Moral education activism**	o Public television o Public museums o Film o Jazz & specialty music o High-end advertising agencies
→	→	→
Practical Everyday	*Grass Roots*	*Low Brow*
o **Journalism (print & electronic)** o The Internet o **Mass-market book publishing** o **Churches, synagogues & teaching ministries** o Public education o Christian schools	o **Local activist organizations** o School boards o **"How-to" publishing** o **Youth organizations & ministries faith-based ministries of mercy** o Moral education	o Prime-time television o Mass market movies o **Popular music** o **Mass advertising agencies** o Cable television o **Mass circulation magazines**

The bolded areas signify the institutional space in which the cultural economy of Christianity is strongest.

agendas, not least because they are largely disaffected from the local church. There are those with fairly high levels of social and economic capital but it is not linked with high levels of cultural capital. It is fair to say, then, that in any social and culturally significant way, Christians are absent from the institutions at the center of cultural production. The cultural capital American Christianity has amassed simply cannot be leveraged where it matters most.

Christianity as a Weak Culture

At one level, it is impossible to deny the extraordinary and genuine vitality in American Christianity today. Ministries of mercy, foreign missions, church planting, and ministries oriented to the care of souls, the needs of the poor, the elderly, and the disabled all flourish and as such, remarkable good is accomplished. But these achievements are largely rooted in and belong to the local church or parish. Para-church ministries have an important place but they are driven by the energy and passion of ordinary Christians and clergy of the local church community. This represents integrity with the best of the tradition. Yet for all of the reasons noted above, the collective impact of the Christian community on the nature and direction of the culture itself is negligible. There are other issues to consider as well.

Earlier I argued that the potential for world-changing is greatest when networks of elites in overlapping fields of culture and overlapping spheres of social life come together with their varied resources and act in common purpose. Is there the possibility of finding common purpose in American Christianity today?

Different people will have different opinions on the matter. Politics has been a realm that has generated some defensive unity among some parts of the Christian community. For example, family law and edge-of-life issues have been sources of political solidarity among conservative Catholics, Evangelicals, and the Reformed. Social justice issues have been the source of political solidarity among their progressive counterparts. Yet apart from politics in these areas, fragmentation seems to be a much more prominent tendency. Clearly, there are ways in which the history of Christianity can be told through the history of its divisions and this has not abated in our time. Insofar as Christianity aspires to maintain certain continuities through time, fragmentation is as much of a challenge as it has ever been. The fragmentation of theology and confession has lessened among the Catholic, Reformed and, in some instances, the Evangelical, though it is as deep as it has ever been and probably more widespread among the conservative and liberal within various traditions. There is no question that Christians in the historic traditions want to be united by common core beliefs, even when their ecclesiology varies—agreement on the authority of Scripture, the sovereignty of God, the status of the unbeliever and the purposes of evangelism, and so on—yet when one goes below the surface, one sees very little agreement at all. Certainly the pressures toward denominational, doctrinal, and social fragmentation are significant. Within the traditions, the very meaning of the terms "Catholic," "mainline," "Reformed," and "Evangelical" are contested. There are disagreements among all who call themselves by these terms as to what the terms mean in the first place.

Nowhere is this disarray more in evidence than among the leadership of the Evangelical movement. As a former president of the National Association of Evangelicals said when asked who the most influential people were giving leadership to the Evangelical movement, "My answer, I think, is nobody. And that's part of the problem. It's amazing the lack of leadership. Evangelicalism is a bunch of personalities who either are so hung up on their own kingdoms . . . or are so anti-intellectual that [issues of vision and leadership] are just out of their purview."[25]

A second matter, in this regard, concerns the strong indications that for all the deep belief, the genuine piety, the heroic faith, and the good intention one finds all across American Christianity today, large swaths have been captured by the spirit of the age. One does not have to review or redo the research of many social scientists to recognize the extent of this challenge. Consumerism, individualism, the therapeutic and managerial ideologies have gone far to undermine the authority of the Christian movement and its traditions. This problem is especially acute among the young, where, as Christian Smith observes, a "moralistic, therapeutic deism" has triumphed over historical creedal faith and practice.[26] It is true that movements like the homeschooling movement and Alpha are attempts to create a protected area free from the compromising effects of the larger world. But these are defensive actions by small communities that simply do not have the resources to go up against the behemoth institutions of modern secular culture.

One can debate the degree to which fragmentation and acculturation have come to characterize American Christianity but even the most optimistic assessment would lead one to conclude that Christianity in America is not only marginalized as a culture but it is also a very weak culture. For all of the vitality and all of the good intention among Christian believers, the whole (in terms of its influence in the larger political economy of cultural production) is significantly less than the sum of its parts. And thus the idea that American Christianity could influence the larger culture in ways that are healthy and humane is, for the time being, doubtful.

Chapter Seven

FOR AND AGAINST THE MANDATE OF CREATION

S O WHERE DOES THIS LEAVE US?
The mandate of creation is central to who Christians are before God. This mandate calls for obedience, yes, but this should not be viewed as a heavy burden. Indeed, in fulfilling this mandate Christian believers become more of who God intends them to be. Importantly, this is not a mandate for a few but for all—*all* are participants, *all* are enjoined to participate in ways framed by the revelation of God's word in the creative and renewing work of world-making and remaking. And it is in the divine nature of this work that vocation is imbued with great dignity.

It is, in part, the appeal to every person, regardless of stature, giftedness, achievement, wealth, power, or personality that makes the Gospel so radical. Every person is made in God's image and every person is offered his grace and, in turn, the opportunity to labor together with God in the creation and recreation of the world. It is of a fabric with the ethic of care central to Christian faith, an ethic that enjoins all Christians to serve the needs of the poor, the widowed, the orphaned, the weak, and the dispossessed. Together these form the basis of a populism made explicit in affirmation and in judgment, exhortations to shun the false idolatries of status, wealth, and power, to disdain the very idea of thinking of oneself as better than others, and so on. In both affirmation and judgment, this biblical ideal finds its ultimate sanction in the life and words of Christ himself. In his own words, "whoever wants to become great among you must be your servant, and whoever wants to be first must be slave of all. For even the Son of Man did not come to be served, but to serve, and to give his life as a ransom for many" (Mark 10:43–45).

The Specter of Elitism

This point bears some emphasis. The significance of every person before God irrespective of worldly stature or accomplishment and the care for the least are the ethical hallmarks of Christianity, for they mark every human being and every human life in the most practical ways with God's image and therefore as worthy of respect and love. Without these, Christianity is a brutalizing ideology. This is why elitism—a disposition and relationality of superiority, condescension, and entitlement by social elites—is so abhorrent for the Christian. Its foundation is exclusion on the implicit (and sometimes explicit) view that people are *not* equal in love and dignity before God. Thus, by its very nature, elitism is exploitative. So far as I can tell, elitism for believers is despicable and utterly anathema to the gospel they cherish.

At the same time, the populism that is inherent to authentic Christian witness is often transformed into an oppressive egalitarianism that will suffer no distinctions between higher and lower or better and worse. At its worse, it can take form as a "tyranny of the majority" that will recognize no authority, nor hierarchy of value or quality or significance. When populism becomes a cultural egalitarianism, there is no incentive and no encouragement to excellence. This too is to be bemoaned.

This brings us to a central dilemma. On the one hand, populism is organic to American Christianity, yet on the other, populism is, in some ways, at odds with what we now know about the most historically significant dynamics of world-changing. In other words, there is an unavoidable tension between pursuing excellence and the social consequences of its achievement; between leadership and an elitism that all too often comes with it. Is it possible to pursue excellence and, under God's sovereignty, be in a position of influence and privilege and *not* be ensnared by the trappings of elitism?

The Question of Power

There is another dilemma that arises from these observations, a dilemma perhaps even more difficult to solve. The creation mandate inevitably leads Christian believers to a transformative engagement with the culture in which they find themselves. Yet by its very nature, this engagement will not be neutral in character. Whether we like it or not, merely engaging the culture implies the issue and exercise of power. The matter of power is unavoidable. One cannot transcend it or avoid it or pretend it isn't there. The only questions are, how will Christians think about power? What kind of power will

Christians exercise? How will Christians, individually and institutionally, relate to the range of powers that operate in the world?

If the analysis I have offered thus far is correct, it would be natural for some to conclude that what is implied here is an alternative way for Christians to pursue, attain, and use *political* power to achieve faith-based ends. It might be natural but it would also be completely wrong and, in my view, an utter distortion of the creation mandate. This is an interpretation of the creation mandate that Christians should reject entirely. Speaking as a Christian myself, contemporary Christian understandings of power and politics are a very large part of what has made contemporary Christianity in America appalling, irrelevant, and ineffective—part and parcel of the worst elements of our late-modern culture today, rather than a healthy alternative to it. On this, more will be said in Essay II.

Let me say further that the best understanding of the creation mandate is not about changing the world at all. It is certainly not about "saving Western civilization," "saving America," "winning the culture war," or anything else like it. The reason is that so much of the discussion surrounding this kind of world-changing is oriented toward the idea of controlling history. The presumption is both that one can know God's specific plans in human history and that one possesses the power to realize those plans in human affairs. There is a fine line between presumption and hope, as Aquinas observed, but in our culture, such presumption nearly always has tragic consequences.

For now, I will only say that the antidote to "seizing power" in a new way is a better understanding of *faithful presence*. Consider it this way: the culture matrix from the previous chapter is not just a visual demonstration of Christianity's lack of influence in the larger culture. It is also, and far more significantly, a visual demonstration of its absence (of people, institutions, and other resources) from key areas of culture; an abandonment of the call to faithful presence—*irrespective of influence*. Not least, the culture matrix is a visual demonstration of where the church is not healthy. A healthy body exercises itself in all realms of life, not just a few. The failure to encourage excellence in vocation in our time has fostered a culture of mediocrity in so many areas of vocation.

There is more to say on all of these matters. For now, one way to summarize the direction of my argument is to say that *theology moves in the opposite direction of social theory*, but neither oblivious nor without reference to its insights. A theology of faithful presence means a recognition that the vocation of the church is to bear witness to and to be the embodiment of the coming Kingdom of God. To paraphrase St. Paul at the end of his letter to the Galatians, "what matters is the new creation" (Gal. 6:15). The new creation he speaks of is a reference to the kingdom of God working in us and in the world; a different people and an alternative culture that is, nevertheless, integrated within the present culture. Whatever its larger influence in the world may be, a culture that is genuinely alternative cannot emerge without faithful presence in all areas of life. This will include networks (and more, communities) of counter-leaders operating within the upper echelons of cultural production and social life generally. These are realms of performance and distinction that may be rare and inaccessible to the average person, but they are still critically important to both the renewal of the church and its engagement with the culture.

RETHINKING POWER

Chapter One

THE PROBLEM OF POWER

THE MANDATE OF CREATION is a source both of glory and of shame for the Christian community. It is a source of glory because it is through the creation mandate that believers understand *how* they are made in the image of God. Even in our fallen state, people reflect his divine nature and thus have the potential to manifest love and mercy and innovative and constructive labor in service to all of God's creation. It is a source of shame because of the astonishing abuse of that potential in acts of exploitation and destruction. Christians have been, at times, the face of manipulation, cruelty, and hardship.

What is the determining factor? Many things, undoubtedly. Yet as Christians seek to fulfill the creation mandate, perhaps the central factor determining the effectiveness and the outcome of their engagement with the world is the dynamic of power. When faith and its cultures flourish, they do so, in part, because it operates with an implicit view of power in its proper place. When faith and its cultures deteriorate, they do so, in part, because it operates with a view of power that is corrupt. The end can only be corrupting.

Cut to the present. Let us assume the best of intentions. Christians today—of whatever stripe—sincerely want to engage the world for good. As we have seen, though, Christians have embraced strategies that are, by design, incapable of bringing about the ends to which they aspire. Christians have failed to understand the nature of the world they want to change and failed even more to understand how it actually changes. Even if they did, Christians in America are not anywhere close to being in a position to do anything about it.

The worst possible conclusion, then, is that what Christians need is a new strategy for achieving and holding on to power in the world—at least in any conventional sense. Such a conclusion is not only wrong on its own terms, it is wrong because Christians operate with an understanding of power that is derived from the larger and dominant culture of the late modern world.

To get to a clearer and perhaps better understanding of power, it is important to come to grips with how power is understood in theory and practice in contemporary America and the relationship of the church—in its diversity—to it. This is the task of Essay II.

Chapter Two

POWER AND POLITICS IN AMERICAN CULTURE

O NE OF THE ENDURING QUESTIONS of the social sciences is the question of how societies hold together. The classic answer to this question was that "traditional" (that is, agrarian, economically undeveloped, and non-urban) societies were held together mainly by beliefs held in common by all of its members. Modern societies, by contrast, are held together through social and economic interdependence. While this general formulation pro-vided a fairly reasonable explanation, upon closer examination, the account did not go far enough. The reason is that just as people and associations in so-called traditional societies depended heavily on each other for the sake of survival, so too do modern societies depend on at least some common beliefs, shared ideals, and collective myths to function smoothly.[1]

The question of how societies hold together gains new poignancy in a world like ours, where even a minimal consensus of sensibilities, disposi-tions, and attitudes seems elusive, where there are even fewer beliefs, ideals, commitments, and hopes held deeply in common, where there are few if any real and meaningful traditions observed or binding public rituals practiced. What else is there to hold such a society together? What remains to bind together its innumerable fragments? The answer, in large part, is power—the exercise of coercion or the threat of its use.

In a democratic regime, of course, individuals or communities cannot exercise force themselves willy-nilly. Rather, the final repository of legitimate force is found in the state. Clearly the state is not the exclusive domain of power in the modern world, nor are its instrumentalities the only means for the ordering of social life. But it is the final repository of legitimate force and in this way it plays an exceedingly important role in modern societies. In its ability to make law, the state has the ability to assert its power positively or negatively on people and communities—to confer privileges or impose sanctions, to provide assistance or create difficulty, to bestow rights or to inflict punishment, harm, injury, and loss.

In principle, of course, the legitimacy of a democratic state to exercise force derives from the sanction of the people. This is part of the meaning of the concept "popular sovereignty." It is also true that democratic institutions have their own ideals, traditions, symbols, and practices, and these too have their own legitimacy and power to bind. These forms of legitimacy are nothing to dismiss lightly for they are the difference between a regime that is tolerable and one that is intolerable. That said, it is important not to forget that at the root of every social order is coercion or the threat of its use. Yet the authority of democratic government is not above challenge and its resilience is not unlimited. Indeed, when the state takes positions that are widely unpopular, if its leaders are corrupt, or if the institutions of government are ineffective, its legitimacy is tested and its capacity to legitimately exercise force is strained. Ideas of popular sovereignty and democratic practices and procedures, then, make the use of state power palatable, but only up to a point.

The Turn to Politics

Why this brief excursion into political theory? The reason is that it provides a starting point for explaining some important developments in American political culture over the last century—and especially since the New Deal: a tendency toward the politicization of nearly everything.[2]

If modern politics is the sphere of leadership, influence, and activity surrounding the state, politicization is the turn toward law and politics—the instrumentality of the state—to find solutions to public problems. The biggest problem is how to create or reinforce social consensus where little exists or none could be generated organically. This is demonstrated by the simple fact that the amount of law that exists in any society is always inversely related to the coherence and stability of its common culture: law increases as cultural consensus decreases. By these lights, the fabric of the common culture in modern America has worn even more thin in the last several decades and the extraordinary amount of litigation we have seen in recent decades is just one place we see it.

Much of that litigation and policy formation simply represents the attempt by institutions and groups to clarify their position or jockey for position in the larger social world. What is implied here should not be passed over too quickly. Politics has become so central in our time that institutions, groups, and issues are now defined relative to the state, its laws and procedures. Institutions such as popular and higher education, philanthropy, science, the arts, and even the family understand their identity and function according to what the state does or does not permit. Groups (women, minorities, gays, Christians, etc.) have validity not only but increasingly through the rights conferred by the state. Issues gain legitimacy only when recognized by law and public policy. It is only logical, then, that problems affecting the society are seen increasingly, if not primarily through the prism of the state; that is, in terms of how law, policy, and politics can solve them.

In short, the state has increasingly become the incarnation of the public weal. Its laws, policies, and procedures have become the predominant framework by which we understand collective life, its members, its leading organizations, its problems, and its issues. There are other forces that frame common life as well—most notably the ubiquitous market—but these are not autonomous from the state but linked integrally with its extensive instrumentalities. This is the heart of politicization and it has gone so far as to affect our language, imagination, and expectations. The language of politics (and political economy) comes to frame progressively more of our understanding of our common life, our public purposes, and ourselves individually and collectively.

Ideology

Politicization is most visibly manifested in the role that ideology has come to play in public life; the well-established predisposition to interpret all of public life through the filter of partisan beliefs, values, ideals, and attachments. How does this come about? My contention is that in response to a thinning consensus of substantive beliefs and dispositions in the larger culture, there has been a turn toward politics as a foundation and structure for social solidarity. But politicization provides a framework of expectations and action and very little substantive content. In a diverse society, ideological polarization is a natural expression of the contest to provide that content.

Consider this from another perspective. There is a tradition in political theory that claims that in a liberal democracy, the state is or should be neutral when it comes to questions of the good. This is wrong mainly because it is impossible. Law infers a moral judgment; policy implies a worldview. Indeed, in a society divided and often enough polarized on basic questions, and where persuasion is ineffective at generating agreements, the state—perhaps unwillingly so—becomes a patron to ideology. Each and every faction in society seeks the patronage of state power as a means of imposing its particular understanding of the good on the whole of society. Thus, the turn toward the power of the state is also seen in the rise of ideologically driven special interest organizations, the geometric growth in policy-oriented litigation, the political conflicts over federal and Supreme Court justices, and the ideological conflict over nearly all public issues: education, the environment, the family, gender, sexuality, art, faith, and so on.

This is part of the reason that every area of civic life has been politicized to one degree or another and strained by ideological conflict. Consider family life. Centuries of practice in marriage, divorce, gender roles, sexuality, child rearing, and children's welfare have come to be contested, and the resolution of these issues has been primarily sought through legal and political means. There is hardly an issue relating to the family that has not been politicized in our day and divided by ideology. Similarly, the realm of education has also become thoroughly politicized. Whether the question is standards of excellence, curriculum, funding policy, or extracurricular life, all are divided politically and contested legally. In higher education, scholarship, hiring, promotion, and tenure (especially in the humanities and social sciences) are also understood and evaluated (in part) through an ideological grid. By the same token, science and technological innovation have become politicized. Whether the issue is the environment, the climate, energy, health care, or human biology, the funding of scientific and technological inquiry depends heavily on government resources and these government-funded inquiries are often framed directly or indirectly by partisan considerations. In some cases, the legality of scientific inquiry is determined by political contest. Not least are the interests of professional organizations. As they represent their memberships to the larger world, teachers, counselors, psychiatrists, psychologists, historians, lawyers, and the like, in recent decades have all come to act more and more like special interest organizations that press their agenda through their political influence. The arts are similarly effected. Then, of course, there is the politicization of the news media. It isn't just that media organizations position themselves and are judged by the public by their ideological orientation (e.g., the *New York Times* is liberal and the *Washington Times* is conservative; CNN is liberal and Fox News is conservative). Unless the topic is a human interest story buried at the end of the newscast or in the back pages of the newspaper or news magazine, news reporting on almost any issue is framed in terms of who is winning and who is losing in the contest for political advantage.[3]

I am not making an evaluation of the costs and benefits of any legal or political disputes, but only observing the increasing importance of law and politics to address them and the role of political partisanship in contesting them. These historical tendencies are remarkable indeed. It is worth recalling that through most of history, political revolutions were palace revolutions. When they occurred, average people were mostly peripheral to the event.[4] The active participation of citizens is rare in history. Now, of course, the commonly accepted view is that everyone must be involved because the primary means to get anything done in society or to effect change in any area of social life, is through law and politics.

Given this turn, it is hardly surprising that the language of partisan politics has come to shape how we understand others. The identity of public actors is determined to a large degree by their partisan attachments, either real or presumed. This is not only seen in how we tend to label people and their actions and motivations ideologically as conservative, liberal, traditionalist, progressive, feminist, fundamentalist, and the like. Such labels credit or discredit depending on the group one is in or the relationships one has. Even categories of identity that are not in themselves political become suffused with political meaning. This is precisely what happened to the categories of race, class, gender, and sexual orientation. Age and disability are evolving in this direction too. It is also seen in how many people understand themselves this way too. Next to their occupation or profession, their commitments as Democrats, or Republicans, pro-lifers or pro-choicers, conservative, liberal, gay, and so on, compete to form the largest part of a person's identity in public. These tendencies are more pronounced within the professional classes than among business people or wage earners but it is a pervasive tendency all the same. Taken to an extreme, identity becomes so tightly linked with ideology, that partisan commitment becomes a measure of their moral significance; of whether a person is judged good or bad. This is the face of identity politics.

The Conflation of the Public with the Political

This turn toward politics means that we find it difficult to think of a way to address public (by which I mean collective, common, or shared) problems or issues in any way that is not political. Politics subsumes the public so much so that they become conflated. And so instead of the political realm being seen as one part of public life, all of public life tends to be reduced to the political. Linguistically, the political becomes effectively synonymous with the public for, in fact, they come to occupy the same space. The primary if not only meaning given to a public act is its political meaning and importance. The same can be said for agendas, strategies, and visions—they too tend to be interpreted in light of how they advance or undermine relative standing in the quest for influence and power. It is difficult to even imagine much less accept the idea that there should be public space occupied by activities or organizations that are completely independent of the political realm. The realm of politics has become, in our imagination, the dominant—and for some the only adequate—expression of our collective life.

In this turn, we have come to ascribe impossibly high expectations to politics and political processes. As I noted before, we look to politics as the leading way to address our common problems and implicitly hope that politics, broadly defined, will actually solve those problems.

Again, my purpose here is not to suggest that the outcome of any particular issue is good or bad but rather to observe the historical tendency, in recent decades, toward the politicization of everything. This turn has brought about a narrowing of the complexity and richness of public life and with it, a diminishing of possibility for thinking of alternative ways to address common problems and issues.

The Will to Power

Democratic ideals, principles, and reasoning provide a framework for making sense of and justifying the bent toward politicization in public life. I assume that this is why few are alarmed by these developments. But let us not lose sight of what is going on here. When one boils it all down, politicization means that the final arbiter within most of social life is the coercive power of the state. When politicization is oriented toward furthering the specific interests of the group without an appeal to the common weal, when its means of mobilizing the uncommitted is through fear, and when the pursuit of agendas depends more on the vilification of opponents than on the affirmation of higher ideals, power is stripped to its most elemental forms. Even democratic justifications are not much more than a veneer over a will to power. The actions themselves may be within the bounds of legitimate democratic participation, yet the basic intent and desire is to dominate, control, or rule.

Of course many "postmodernists" would ask what the fuss is all about. For them, the justifications we create are of no real account anyway; no matter how you dress it up, every aspect of social life comes down to power and domination. It has always been thus.[5] One should simply recognize things as they are and act accordingly. The problem with this Nietzschean perspective is not only that it is nonfalsifiable (e.g., you cannot prove it wrong), but that it also fails to make distinctions in the types of power and the layers of meaning that human beings impute to their own lives, relationships, and circumstances. All of these things matter greatly and the postmodernists discount them too quickly. All that said, there are ways in which public life is increasingly imitating the postmodernist and Nietzschean description of things. The politicization of everything is an indirect measure of the loss of a common culture and, in turn, the competition among factions to dominate others on their own terms. Our times amply demonstrate that it is far easier to force one's will on others through legal and political means or to threaten to do so than it is to persuade them or negotiate compromise with them.

"Ressentiment"

What adds pathos to our situation is the presence of what Nietzsche called "ressentiment." His definition of this French word included what we in the English-speaking world mean by resentment, but it also involves a combination of anger, envy, hate, rage, and revenge as the motive of political action. *Ressentiment* is, then, a form of political psychology.

Though *ressentiment* has historical precedence,[6] it has become the distinguishing characteristic of politics in modern cultures. Nowhere does it find a more conducive home than among the disadvantaged or mistreated as directed against the strong, the privileged, or the gifted. But here an important qualification: perception is everything. It is not the weak or aggrieved per se, though it could be, but rather those that perceive themselves as such.

Ressentiment is grounded in a narrative of injury or, at least, perceived injury; a strong belief that one has been or is being wronged. The root of this is the sense of entitlement a group holds. The entitlement may be to greater respect, greater influence, or perhaps a better lot in life and it may draw from the past or the present; it may be privilege once enjoyed or the belief that present virtue now warrants it. In the end, these benefits have been withheld or taken away or there is a perceived threat that they will be taken away by those now in positions of power.

The sense of injury is the key. Over time, the perceived injustice becomes central to the person's and the group's identity. Understanding themselves to be victimized is not a passive acknowledgement but a belief that can be cultivated. Accounts of atrocity become a crucial subplot of the narrative, evidence that reinforces the sense that they have been or will be wronged or victimized. Cultivating the fear of further injury becomes a strategy for generating solidarity within the group and mobilizing the group to action. It is often useful at such times to exaggerate or magnify the threat. The injury or threat thereof is so central to the identity and dynamics of the group that to give it up is to give up a critical part of whom they understand themselves to be. Thus, instead of letting go, the sense of injury continues to get deeper.

In this logic, it is only natural that wrongs need to be righted. And so it is, then, that the injury—real or perceived—leads the aggrieved to accuse, blame, vilify, and then seek revenge on those whom they see as responsible. The adversary has to be shown for who they are, exposed for their corruption, and put in their place. *Ressentiment*, then, is expressed as a discourse of negation; the condemnation and denigration of enemies in the effort to subjugate and dominate those who are culpable.

Political Culture

Here let us pause. What I am describing is neither the stuff of political theory nor political science. Rather it is a realm one could call political culture—the implicit framework of moral claims and narratives within which ideals (the realm of political theory) and attitudes, institutions, and action (the realm of political science) operate. By comparison to theory and science, this province is not often discussed in academic circles but it is critically important. It brings into relief the nature and character of politics, as opposed to simply the form, process, and ends of politics.

What, then, am I saying about American democracy? Democracy in America has been in existence and flourished for over two centuries, but over this time the political culture has not remained static but changed and evolved. Slowly, often imperceptibly, there has been a turn toward law and politics as the primary way of understanding all aspects of collective life. Nothing catalyzed this tendency more than the Depression-era New Deal. The tendency now effects conservatives every bit as much as it does liberals; those who favor small government as it does those who want a larger government. It has affected everyone's language, imagination, and expectations, not least conservatives who, like others, look to law, policy, and political process as the structure and resolution to their concerns and grievances; who look to politics as the framework of self-validation and self-understanding and ideology as the framework for understanding others. It is my contention that

Nietzsche was mostly right; that while the will to power has always been present, American democracy increasingly operates within a political culture—that is, a framework of meaning—that sanctions a will to domination. This, in turn, is fueled by a political psychology of fear, anger, negation, and revenge over perceived wrongs.

I don't want to overstate the case—clearly what I describe here are not fully and comprehensively established realities; all is not power and *ressentiment*. What makes it more complicated (and interesting) is that there are genuinely public-spirited people on all sides of all issues. Indeed most people are not resentment-filled and power hungry. But consistent with my view all along is the fact that the motives of individuals and the structures of culture are not the same thing. In terms of the structures of our political culture, these dynamics are clearly present and represent increasingly significant tendencies.

The Question of Faith, the Importance of Myth, and a Word on Method

Christians are citizens and have all the legal rights that anyone else has to participate in the political process and undoubtedly they exercise those rights with the best of intentions. To be sure, Christians have shaped American political life for both good and ill for the length of its history; much of it amounts to a legacy of which they can be justly proud.

But how do Christians stand in relation to the present configuration in our political culture? There is no simple answer, for Christians, like any other social group, are not monolithic. Christians approach politics differently. Many individual Christians, of course, are utterly indifferent to politics and are not involved at all. But this stance is rare among Christian organizations and ministries concerned with public issues. As a consequence, faith too has become highly politicized. Non-Christians view Christianity politically and Christians themselves stake out their own positions in ideological terms. Among those leaders and organizations that are active, one finds a range of broad positions.

In this essay, I focus on just three of these positions—the conservative, progressive, and neo-Anabaptist positions—because in contemporary America, these are the most prominent. They are, in effect, "political theologies," and they are powerful in part because they are shrouded by compelling myths that give voice to the ideals and public identities of different parts of the

Christian community. And though the political landscape is changing, these myths provide a source of continuity in the language and logic of their competing positions. In their broad contours, then, these myths and the political theologies that emanate from them provide the primary scripts for thinking about and discussing faith and public life for most American Christians. These myths and the scripts that derive from them cut across confessional and denominational traditions. In principle, then, Catholics, Evangelicals, Fundamentalists, mainliners, Orthodox, and Pentecostals could all be found (and often are found) giving voice to each of these three public theologies. Within these positions, of course, one finds even more variation—denominational tradition, race and ethnicity, region, education, and gender all provide their own emphases. It would be impossible to account for all of the variation and so I focus on the principal script within each position as articulated by its leading spokespeople.

What is interesting in these accounts is not so much their particular ideology, as their disposition toward public life more broadly. A group's ideology may be (and often is) related to its temperament but these are not the same thing. The concern of this essay, then, is primarily with how Christians from different perspectives relate to the larger public culture. In this way I am less concerned with the patterns of Christian political engagement than with the nature and character of that engagement. Yet, one cannot understand the latter without the context provided by the former.

Matters of faith and politics are obviously sensitive. Nerve endings have been exposed and worn raw from rhetorical abrasion. Right and Left and everyone in-between have been criticized thoroughly. It is important, then, to try to understand the concerns each group has on their own terms. My task in the next three chapters, then, is mostly descriptive, laying out the story each group tells, the story that makes sense of their particular engagement with the world they want to change. I will offer as little commentary as possible in the interest of letting various positions unpack the narrative in their own way. Much will be familiar in what follows, but in framing these stories in light of the present configurations of political culture, my hope is to see what is familiar in a new light.

Consider, first, the so-called Christian Right.

Chapter Three

_____

THE CHRISTIAN RIGHT

T HE POWER OF THE Christian Right peaked in the year 2004. Though the movement has lost credibility and legitimacy, it is far from dead. Indeed, because the logic on which it is based is so embedded within the history and consciousness of American Christianity, it will not likely die anytime soon; but it will be reconstituted. But what is the nature of that logic?

Christians who are politically conservative want what all people want: namely, to have the world in which they live reflect their own likeness. The representation of social life they imagine and desire is not a reflection of the reality they live, but rather their highest ideals expressed as principles for ordering individual and collective passions and interests. It is a vision of human flourishing, but one obviously framed by the particularities of their distinct worldview.

In the present world order, many if not most of the principles they most esteem have come under fundamental challenge. There has been a challenge to heterosexuality, to monogamy, to marriage as a life-long commitment, to the sacred responsibility of parenting, to the authority and autonomy of the family. There has been a challenge to the sanctity of human life, most clearly in the earliest stages of life but also life at its most vulnerable and at its end. Not only has there been a challenge to the truths of the Christian faith and the traditions and scripture that express them, but there has been a challenge to the very concept of truth as well. And there has been a challenge to the moral authority of the church. These challenges have been expressed intellectually, educationally, and artistically, but also commercially, through advertising, and in the range of entertainment media. Not least, all of these challenges have also been expressed legally and politically.

There was a time in America and in Europe when the world more closely reflected the ideals and principles that conservative Christians hold dear. Homosexuality was never mentioned except as a shameful act even if it was practiced, most marriages remained intact even if the couple was miserable, the nuclear family was culturally and statistically normative, abortion was rare and the threat of euthanasia not even imaginable. There was a time when the Bible and *Foxe's Book of Martyrs* were the two books that could be found in nearly everyone's home; a time when the church was held in high regard even if its practices were not observed, and its truths were respected, even if they were not embraced. There was also a time when Christians who were open about their faith, the clergy not least, held positions of prominence and influence in the shaping of society. Those times are long past, but the fact that those times existed figures prominently in the collective memory of Christians who are politically conservative. The nostalgia is palpable.

Neither the social origins of American Christianity nor the historical changes it has undergone are in dispute. These are what they are. What *is* far more interesting and important is how this story is told, its moral meaning, and its political consequences. Interpretation is key. There are interesting differences among Evangelicals, Fundamentalists, the mainline, Catholics, and Charismatics, and interesting variations between intellectuals and populists. Overall, though, there are common themes and a basic narrative that will be recognizable to most. Here, the litany of concern and complaint is mostly familiar. Still, it is worth reviewing—and reviewing as much as possible in the verbatim, for the tone is as important as the content.

Myth and History

As a general rule, conservatives are animated by a mythic ideal concerned with the "right-ordering" of society. Politically conservative Christians— Protestant and Catholic—are not unique in this light but draw their political ideals from this logic and philosophical tradition. The question of how society is rightly ordered and the key to the relationship between politically conservative Christians and contemporary political culture is rooted in the particular way that they understand the origins of America. The American founding is the point of reference against which the present is measured. There is variation here but there are also common themes. There are those who believe that America was founded as a Christian nation. The founders were Christian in conviction or, at least, their sentiments and principles were influenced strongly by Christian faith. The founding political documents therefore reflect a Christian worldview. The institutions of the early republic, such as schools, charity, hospitals, and the like, were Christian in character if not in content, and its morality was Christian. In a letter to the editor of *The Washington Post*, one believer explains it this way:

> Ours is a rich heritage passed down by men who had a deep and abiding love for God and for Jesus Christ. One has only to look at men like Franklin, Madison, Sherman, Dayton and Washington to see lives that were directed by their belief in God. The Constitution itself is free of specific references to God and religion not because our forefathers didn't believe in God, but because they wished to create a nation in which people would be free to practice their worship of God without interference from the government.[1]

Rejecting a straightforward account of "America as a Christian nation," a large number of Christian conservatives take the slightly different view that faith (both Jewish and Christian) was an active presence in public affairs in America for the better part of its history. Not only was it the personal reality of the majority of people, it also provided the motivations for public service, the language of public discourse, and the terms for the long pursuit of public justice. No one has been more articulate about this position than the late Catholic intellectual and priest, Richard John Neuhaus, who put it this way:

> The notion that religion is the first political institution of American democracy, it is fair to say, would strike many people today as rather odd. That was, however, the argument made by Alexis de Tocqueville in the 1830s. It was a persuasive argument then, and I suggest that it is no less persuasive now. . . . I take "one nation under God" to mean a nation under judgment. It is in that sense that it is pertinent to understanding why religion is our first political institution. The audacious thing, the unprecedented thing, about the American regime is that it deliberately makes itself vulnerable to a higher sovereignty. . . . The people, however, acknowledge a sovereignty higher than the sovereignty of the state. And, in the American constitutional order, the state places upon itself a self-denying ordinance not to interfere with, not to try to direct or guide, not to establish whatever the sovereign people acknowledge as a sovereignty higher than themselves and higher than the state. This new and audacious thing is called the free exercise of religion. No other regime in human history had ever supposed that it could deny itself the right to attempt to control what its people believed about things most binding. . . . The free exercise of religion is the most

radical form of free speech and free association in that it enables people to speak and act under the auspices of an Authority expressly declared to be greater than the authority of the state, and greater than the authority of the people from whom the state derives its authority. . . . And so the doctrine became established, so to speak, that the state is not to establish doctrine regarding the most binding things. Put positively, the doctrine reads this way: the sovereignty of the state is subject to the sovereignty of the people; the people, in turn, are subject to whatever sovereignty they acknowledge as sovereign. For almost all Americans, then and now, that sovereignty is referred to by the name of God. As in "one nation under God." As in religion as the first political institution of the American democracy. . . . Suffice it for our purposes that "one nation under God" resonates for the great majority of Americans within the vocabulary of the God of Abraham, Isaac, Jacob, and Jesus, and entails what Americans with little difficulty affirm as the Judeo-Christian moral tradition. If American intellectuals are incredulous about the proposition that religion is the first political institution of American democracy, it is not because Americans are less religious or more religiously pluralistic than before.[2]

In this view, the Tocquevillian legacy that celebrates the active role of religion in public extended into the modern age through the abolitionist movement, prohibition, and with the civil rights movement of the 1960s and it extends to the present in the movement against abortion, homosexuality, and the like. In their own view, conservative Christian activists are anything but strange. They are, rather, the "rightful heirs" of progressive Christianity. Now as in the past there is a direct line of reasoning from biblical mandate to public policy recommendation.

These two perspectives define the end-points of a range of opinion rather than mutually exclusive alternatives. Indeed, one will often hear those with a more exclusively Christian understanding of American history take the more inclusive view in their public rhetoric. And most laypeople who are politically conservative have no firm ideas about just how religious or Christian America actually was in the past, but they do sense that something has gone quite wrong.

However it is approached, America's religious legacy is understood as providing, in effect, a "deed of trust," and thus a sense of ownership over America and all the entitlements that go along with it. America belongs to the people of faith. It was the ideal of God's righteousness that provided the principles of ordered freedom. It was the history of providential judgment against oppression that provided the precedents and lessons of liberty and justice. It was the ethic of hard work and discipline rooted in faith that created the framework for America's prosperity. In sum, it was their faith that provided the spiritual and moral foundations for America's greatness. In this view, Christians and Jews (though mostly Protestants) bear the legacy of that history and the responsibility that comes with it weighs heavily.

Harm to America

For politically conservative Christians, America is clearly moving in the wrong direction. Some speak in more dire tones than others, but even for the more temperate the news is not good—"immorality has taken center stage while our Christian heritage has fallen by the wayside."[3] In the most general formulation,

> America today is in a virtue deficit where our standards of right and wrong have become increasingly hazy. Out of this haze have arisen great problems within our society including: hostility towards organized religion, sexual exploitation, the homosexual agenda, the demise of the family, and the culture of death. Sadly, we now live in a country where children kill children, families are broken, mothers have been told that allowing an abortionist to take the life of an unborn baby is simply a matter of "choice," and where the public expression of our nation's religious heritage is considered a crime. These are disastrous trends for our country. If they aren't reversed, America—this great experiment in self-government—will be in jeopardy.[4]

Another leader puts it in even more bleak terms. "The soul of America is dying, its leaders live in decadence, and [people] look on with indifference."[5]

The reason for this moral decline is the "growing hostility towards all things religious";[6] "the secularization of our country."[7] And yet what has and is occurring is not due to impersonal historical forces. The legacy has not just been lost but has been taken away. Put differently, there is intention and active agency in this process most generally by "radical secularists." As one activist put it, "Deep in the nation's capital, America's culture was hijacked by a secular movement determined to redefine society from religious freedom to the right to life. These radicals were doing their best to destroy two centuries of traditional values."[8] The net effect is that "the nation has been taken from us and transformed by secular liberals and humanists into a nation we no longer recognize. . . . People who have a very different agenda for America [than ours] have stripped the nation of its pride, dignity, and honor."[9] Perhaps the most elaborate description of the harm to America brought about by secularists is made by James Dobson in his "Letter from 2012 in Obama's America."[10] Here he speculates about the natural outcome of an Obama presidency—the Left's takeover of the Supreme Court, the unilateral legalization of same-sex marriage and the punishment of all organizations that do not recognize this right, sweeping restrictions on free-speech and free assembly, rampant pornography, the restriction of gun ownership, the outlawing of homeschooling, the elimination of all restrictions on abortion, and so on.

Needless to say, it isn't just people with a secular worldview but specific groups and organizations that are responsible for the decline of American culture.[11] These include "the news media, interest groups on the Left (including militant homosexuals, radical feminists, and Big Government liberals),"[12] the National Organization for Women, the National Abortion Rights League and other pro-abortion groups, the American Trial Lawyers Association, the American Civil Liberties Union (ACLU), and "the rest of the 'criminal rights' lobby,"[13] the National Endowment for the Arts,[14] the Democratic National Committee,[15] and "gutless politicians." What makes this particularly jarring, in their view, is the way in which this "liberal culture has targeted our kids."[16] It isn't just that "Hollywood serves up a steady diet of irresponsible sex and violence, and the pro-abortion crowd gives them condoms and birth control pills."[17] Even worse, "textbooks and liberal education bureaucrats are selling our children the liberal political agenda."[18] Among other things, "the National Education Association . . . opposes parental consent for teenagers getting abortions and promotes distribution of condoms to school children,"[19] and, thus, "moral anarchy pervades America's classrooms."[20]

If there is an epicenter of the problem, though, it is seen in the judicial system—"the last great bastion for liberalism."[21] Some have called "the secular-liberal takeover" of the judiciary the greatest assault representative self-government has ever faced; an assault that is "more dangerous and successful because it comes from within and aims to destroy not just our physical defenses, but the moral ideas, habits and practices that sustain our character as a free people." The principal instrument for their assault has been "an abuse of the judicial system," and in particular the Federal judiciary's assertion of supreme and unchecked constitutional power. In particular, the U.S. Supreme Court has arrogated to itself governmental power that the Tenth Amendment unambiguously reserves to the States, arbitrarily withdrawn the protection of the community from generations to come, interfered with the public celebration of religious festivals and observances determined by the people, and now seeks to remove all references to the Creator, God, from public declarations adopted by the people. The campaign of "liberals and progressive forces" has been nothing less than "insidious."[22] The problem, then, is not just the fact that the courts are complicit in "trying to erase our Judeo-Christian heritage."[23] "The courts have also imposed immoral decisions on the American people."[24] The courts' decisions liberalizing the practice of abortion and homosexuality are particularly galling since the majority of Americans oppose them. Cumulatively, these actions amount to "judicial tyranny."[25]

"Look at what they've done to us"—*The Harm to Christians and Their Faith*

Make no mistake—in this telling, "these groups [and organizations] are sinister—they use misinformation and fear"[26] to accomplish their agenda. The net effect is not only harm to America but harm to Christians and all people of faith. The net effect is a marginalization of Christians in most spheres of public life. This has been very obvious in politics. One Christian leader declared that "Christians have been under-represented, ridiculed and outright ignored by our political leaders for much too long."[27] It is also true in the arts and in entertainment. In the realm of high culture, take as an illustration the work of the National Endowment for the Arts. In the 1990s, it made "a point of funding anti-Christian and pornographic 'art' projects . . . projects designed specifically to offend and outrage Christians and religious people."[28] As to popular culture, it too is hostile to the values that Christians cherish most highly. The world of television and film is especially hostile. The actor Stephen Baldwin declared, "what I have come to understand about Hollywood, the media, Internet porno, and video games, is that a majority of what it does is evil."[29] One observer went so far as to claim that "Hollywood hates you as a Christian." And "How could Hollywood not hate Christians? Christians reject everything Hollywood stands for. Hollywood is very much enemy territory and is destined to remain so."[30] The contempt secularists have toward Christians extends to the family. Indeed, "the entire world conspires to mock and belittle Biblical manhood and womanhood. Great courage is needed to do things which as recently as a century ago would be considered normative."[31] Not least, one finds this kind of hostility in education. One Christian leader observes, "right now Christians are under the most ferocious and vicious attack ever on American college campuses."[32]

Yet the injury suffered goes beyond being ignored or belittled to outright discrimination. Some conservative Christians argue that one can find within the news media, among Democratic politicians, and among left-wing interest groups and in the courts, outright "anti-Christian bigotry."[33] Claims are made that "the public expression and acknowledgement of religion and traditional values have been banned,"[34] that there are efforts to "silence Christian voices and suppress the Christian vote,"[35] that the filibuster, once abused to protect racial bias, is now being used against Christians who have been appointed to the judgeships.[36] Some conservatives contend that the effort to ban the word "Christmas" in public settings is an expression of the same hostility.[37]

Stories are always the most poignant way to communicate to people, and toward this end, politically conservative Christians turn to atrocity stories to capture the peril that Christians face. One ministry leader in higher education declares that he "could give you countless examples like these of how Christian professors and Christian students are being persecuted, purged and silenced on university campuses for their faith. . . . Christian students today are afraid to speak up about their Christian faith on the campus because they know they will almost certainly be laughed at, mocked, or marked down in their grades."[38] Atrocity stories can be especially effective at generating sympathy for those who suffer and generating anger toward those who perpetrate the offence; and in this, they are useful for mobilizing the faithful. "Christian Persecution: Reports from the Front Line"[39] was the name of a panel at one political conference. At such times one hears stories of unfairness, struggle, and sometimes triumph—a college student opposed for starting a creation club at his state university, a Navy chaplain who has been censured for praying in Jesus' name, a pastor who received death threats for holding a "Mr. Heterosexual Contest" in Worcester, Massachusetts, a ministry denied student organization status for not allowing gays in its leadership, a 15-year-old girl suing her school district for discrimination against the Christian club she founded, the Boy Scouts of America sued for its oath to God in the Scout's pledge. The stories are myriad.

From Fear and Anger to Action

The sense of injury to country, culture, and faith is perceived to be unrelenting. "Secularists have worked tirelessly"[40] and thus the unfairness is only getting worse. The fears are found on many fronts.[41] For one, "the threat that we face today is not on a foreign battlefield or from a foe's army—it is a threat from within. It is a threat of our national character. It is divorce, abortion on demand, illiteracy, out-of-wedlock births, crime, drugs, family breakup, violence; it is the lives that it consumes, the hopelessness that it breeds, the dreams that it destroys."[42] In the media, "the liberal news media's attacks against the Christian Coalition are growing even more vicious." In government, "the Left could easily regain control of Congress . . . by winning only a few seats . . . which would put us right back where we started—with radicals back in charge of our government."[43] Indeed, "the largest abortion provider in the entire nation is hard at work to elect their radical pro-abortion allies to Congress this year, and they are using our tax dollars as part of their scheme."[44] In the judiciary, "we are daily confronted with the fact that traditional marriage in a given state or region is never more than one federal judge away from being declared unconstitutional."[45] In social life, the "'new tolerance' [has become] the instrument secularism is using to brand Christians. You will experience criticism, ridicule, censorship, condemnation, litigation, and imprisonment if you don't embrace every view. We may be sent to jail for intolerance. . . . This is exactly what happened, step by step by step, to the Jews in Nazi Germany."[46] Indeed, already "Christian-bashing has become a popular political pastime, and some analysts say that real persecution may start this decade." "Fierce Persecution Will Begin Soon."[47]

The conclusion is unavoidable: "nothing short of a great Civil War of values rages today throughout North America. Two sides with vastly differing and incompatible worldviews are locked in bitter conflict that permeates every level of society."[48] By virtue of their faith, Christians find themselves on one side. As to the other side, James Dobson declares that "most of what those who disagree with us represent leads to death—abortion, euthanasia, promiscuity in heterosexuality, promiscuity in homosexuality, legalization of drugs. There are only two choices. It really is that clear. It's either God's way, or it is the way of social disintegration."[49] The meaning of this conflict is apparent. American civilization is at stake:

> If we fail at this moment of destiny, we will become a secularized nation like Canada or the continent of Europe, whose laws are based on secular humanism, or worse, on post-modernism, which holds that there is no truth, no basic right or wrong, nothing good or bad, nothing evil or noble, nothing moral or immoral. Law then will be a whimsical standard that shifts with the sands of time.[50]

The gravity of the situation calls for a decision. As Beverly LaHaye puts it,

> The challenge stands before us. The question each of us must answer is this: Will I accept this challenge? . . . Christians can change our country . . . You and I have a tremendous opportunity to influence public policy in order to open the doors for the truth of the gospel to be communicated in all areas of our society.[51]

But what would Jesus do in this situation? "Would Jesus have ignored these wicked activities?" asks Dobson. "No, I am convinced that he would be the first to condemn sin in high places, and I doubt if he would have minced words in making the point."[52] So the time for action is overdue. "As Christians, many of us have sat by silently far too long, voicing our complaints about immorality but never really taking any action. I believe one of the primary reasons for this is because many of us have simply not known what to do."[53] But in the minds of the leaders of this movement, the decision is unambiguous. It is time to "Stand up. Say 'NO.'"[54] "ENOUGH!"[55] "We're not going to take it anymore."[56] Michael Steele declared, "It's about action. Are you prepared to go back home and do something; and fight for something? Because if you're not, go; you are bringing the rest of us down."[57] As Stephen Baldwin more colorfully put it, "We are the hands of the Lord. I don't know about you, but I am putting some boxing gloves on mine."[58]

The Turn to Politics

The call to engage invariably is two-pronged: prayer and action. As one activist put it,

> Today, the future of America hangs in the balance. It is up to you and me—the Christians throughout this great nation—to get on our knees and pray, educate ourselves, and mobilize the members of our churches to action. Our nation's future is at stake.[59]

The place of prayer for politically conservative Christians is certainly not perfunctory but most sincere. As the Christian Life Commission of the Southern Baptist Convention puts it, it is essential

> to get Southern Baptists praying more for government leaders and more for crucial cultural issues which affect the church's mission. . . . The first and greatest resource of the citizen Christian is his or her access to God in prayer. James says, 'You do not have, because you do not ask God' (James 4:2). We must not fail to alter our nation's course because we fail to ask God fervently for its rulers, its rules and its revival.[60]

All of the groups in this movement affirm this position.

At the same time, there is a call to action and action means "changing the government policies and laws which create an environment in which immorality and parental neglect are allowed to flourish."[61] In educating its members about engaging the culture, the Southern Baptist denomination has written, that "one type of opportunity for stewardship which is often ignored is the opportunity of using our political influence and our political power. We are as responsible for how we vote as we are for how we use our money. . . . Political apathy is a sin."[62] The spiritual onus is heavy indeed and, given the nature of our times, there is urgency to this call as well. As the National Association of Evangelicals tells its members,

> Evangelical Christians in America face a historic opportunity. We make up fully one quarter of all voters in the most powerful nation in history. Never before has God given American Evangelicals such an awesome opportunity to shape public policy in ways that could contribute to the well-being of the entire world. Disengagement is not an option. We must seek God's face for biblical faithfulness and abundant wisdom to rise to this unique challenge.[63]

For individual believers, this invariably means informed voting. To this end, all of the major players declare that it "is absolutely critical that Christians be registered, be informed and vote our values. As believers, we have a duty to be involved in the democratic process. But our charge is not simply to vote our geographic origins, our denominational affiliation, our party or even our pocketbook. Instead, we must vote our values, our beliefs, our convictions. An informed vote takes effort. The choice is not always easy, but it is always significant."[64] We are admonished to "Pray that Christians in America will register to vote (Matt. 22:21)." "Pray that God would make the choice between candidates clear as voters weigh candidates and their positions with biblical values (Proverbs 3:5–6)." "Pray that God's people would feel the need to engage the culture and be involved in government just as Jesus taught (Matt. 5:13–16)."[65] Given the fact that "much of what we've fought for over the years is won or lost in our nation's courtrooms," it is all the more important to have a legislative branch capable of confirming conservative judges. "The stakes are far too high for us not to get involved."[66] But the argument that trumps all others is the argument grounded in the example of Christ himself. "Would Jesus register to vote? Would he go to the polls? Or would he stay home? Assuming he did vote, which candidates would he support? We know that Jesus expects his followers to be salt and light in our culture, and that he expects us to participate in government (see Matt. 5:13–16; 22:21). Based on his teachings, it would be safe to say that Jesus would register and vote and support the candidates that most closely represent his values. Isn't that what we should do on Election Day?"[67] Rick Scarborough goes so far as to say, "For a Christian not to vote is a sin."[68]

For parishes and churches, the call to action means forming congregants through a process of political socialization. It is difficult to say how much this occurs in local churches or to what degree it is systematized when it does occur. For activists in this movement, the ideal church would be like the West County Assembly of God, a 600-member Evangelical congregation in Missouri. The church's pastor, John A. Wilson, gives sermons that extol the importance of opposing abortion, stem cell research, and same-sex marriage, and he publicly says he supported President Bush's decision to go to war in Iraq. To promote involvement in social issues, the church has a dozen-member "moral action team" that holds open meetings for parishioners each month. They inform church members about socially conservative electoral issues. They register them to vote at stands outside the sanctuary on designated "voter registration" Sundays. During elections, the "moral action team" even drives church members to the polls.[69]

And then there are the political organizations themselves. There are dozens of such organizations, some with greater longevity than others. The Moral Majority and the Religious Roundtable of the 1980s may have faded from memory, but many others have risen to take their place. Christian Coalition, the Family Research Council, Focus on the Family Action, Vision America, Priests for Life, Alliance Defense Fund, Liberty Council, the Foundation for Moral Law, Concerned Women for America, America 21, American Center for Law and Justice, Joyce Meyers Ministries, Vision Forum, Faith and Action, Traditional Values Coalition, Renew America, the Center for Reclaiming America for Christ, and Eagle Forum, are just some of the familiar names. This list is incomplete as it is but it is even more so for not including denominational organizations concerned with politics nor nondenominational agencies, such as the National Association of Evangelicals, that have political action divisions. Overall, they vary considerably. Some have missions that are broad and others that are narrow but all are in general sympathy with each other.

Overall, these organizations defend a prominent role for religion in public life, a traditional nuclear family, and traditional morality. As with the Christian Coalition, they work to identify, educate, and mobilize Christians for effective political action.[70] Their ambition is to achieve what the Christian Coalition claims to have achieved, namely, "more access to administration officials, more influence in congressional and administrative affairs, and more impact on international delegations to the United States government than at any previous time."[71] They proudly announce what all aspire to: "a place at the table again, and a prominent one at that."[72]

The Character of Political Engagement

The turn to politics as the means to deal with the problems they see is significant. There will be more to say about this shortly. What is every bit as important is the *character* of their political engagement; that is, the way in which politically conservative Christians come to and participate in the political process. There are two distinctive features.

The first is the particular nature of the enterprise. The tax code in the United States allows nonprofit status for organizations that are nonpartisan and, to be specific, that do not endorse candidates for elective office. For this reason, as well as for reasons of theological principle, conservative Christian political organizations claim to be nonpartisan. However, they are nonpartisan only in a technical sense. Though not without some qualification, the reality is that they are decidedly partisan on behalf of the Republican Party. Collectively, of course, the movement represents the strongest popular base of the Republican Party. Said one activist, "It's not like a secret that religious conservatives favor the Republican Party."[73] For many election cycles, campaign rallies targeting Christians have had all the elements of a church service or religious revival.[74] Leaders in the movement have had the closest of ties with the Republic Party establishment. Party officials openly acknowledge the role movement leaders play in delivering tens of millions of Christian voters.f[75] And movement leaders openly claim responsibility for building the Party[76] and for helping to deliver electoral victories.[77] Among the leadership there is no disagreement about the task at hand: "The only way to continue with the freedom we possess is to see a national moral revival. We've got to mobilize millions of new voters. Power is measured in this city by one equation: can you deliver the votes?"[78] Since the 1980s, movement leaders have been successful at turning out the Evangelical and, increasingly, the Catholic vote locally and nationally for one party—the Republicans.

The fact is that the movement and its organizations walk a very fine line. Legally these groups are nonpartisan as the tax code defines it. Substantively, though, they are intensely partisan. How they parse this logic is interesting. Dobson, for example, is emphatic about Focus on the Family being nonpartisan, yet he leaves no doubt about what side he and his organization are on.

This ministry has been nonpartisan from the beginning, and it will remain that way. On the other hand, we will continue to address the great moral issues of the day, even when they take us into the political

arena . . . As Christians, I believe we are obligated to defend the principles of morality and righteousness in this representative form of government, which is an expression "of the people, by the people and for
the people." "The people" in this phrase quoted by Abraham Lincoln
certainly includes people of faith. Thus, Focus on the Family will continue to lobby for and defend our fundamental beliefs as long as I am
at the helm of this ministry.[79]

In one particular situation, Dobson targeted six Democratic senators who
were up for election and engaged in negative campaigning. Speaking of the
Democratic leader of the Senate, Dobson summarized: "Let his colleagues
beware . . . especially those representing 'red' states." A senior official with
Focus on the Family Action defended the statement and larger strategy
saying, "Without question, the vast majority of the American people want to
see marriage preserved, and the greatest threat to the institution of marriage
is the federal courts. If a senator votes against marriage, or votes against a
federal judge nominee who will preserve marriage, we believe constituents of
any senator need to know that—and we intend to make that clear to them.
So, in essence, [targeting these Senators] is voter education—it is not partisan politics."[80] Call it what you will, the intent and net effect is partisan
politics. This is only reinforced in those extreme cases when Christian leaders
declare that one cannot be a Christian if they vote for the Democratic nominee
for president or when priests deny communion for Democrats.[81]

A second characteristic is the clear desire and ambition for dominance or
controlling influence in American politics and culture. Few of these organizations or activists deny the pluralism that exists in America and thus few are
so extreme as to publicly call for the demise or elimination of opponents. But
neither do they trust others with political power nor do they seek to share it.
The desire of all groups on the Christian Right is to ensure that public life is
ordered on their terms. In their own words, their intent is to "recapture
America's values," to "win the new civil war."[82] One prominent Presbyterian
pastor declared, "[Christians] didn't start the culture war but by the grace of
God, with the love and gospel of Jesus Christ, through the transformation of
thousands and millions of hearts and lives in this country, dear friends, we are
going to win it."[83]

This desire and ambition is sometimes framed in conventional political
terms. As political consultant, Ralph Reed, once put it, "[Religious conser-
vatives] must do more than 'send a message' to the elites and party leaders.
They must win elections. They must govern. They must pull the levers
of government and turn the wheels of the larger society for the good of the

nation. Politically, people of faith have come of age. They must act the part."[84] Yet this doesn't express the urgency felt by most. "We must win this culture war," one prominent Christian Senator explained. Recalling the motto "In God We Trust," Mr. Brownback asked, "Is it still true? I say it is, and I say we fight."[85] For him and for most of his colleagues, the principal means of doing so is to appoint more conservative judges. In a more pragmatic vein, the goals are more specific. As Pat Robertson once announced to a group of activists: "The Christian Coalition's goal is to gain substantial influence, if not full control, over the Republican Party apparatus in all 50 states."[86]

At times the desire and ambition to have controlling influence in politics and culture extends to demand and threat. The most prominent of the movement's leaders and organizations repeatedly tell their constituencies to demand action in conformity with their wishes. "Demand your senators support efforts to . . ."; "demand senate Republicans spend scheduled Senate floor time in vigorous debate and then have an honest up-or-down vote"; "call U.S. Capitol Switchboard and demand a final vote," "flood the office of congressmen and senators demanding that they . . ."; candidates must understand "in no uncertain terms that America's Christian voters expect and deserve strong moral leadership in government."[87] The main objective is to "send a powerful message to politicians in Washington that they cannot afford to ignore the Christian vote."[88] As one pastor explained, "Real power concedes nothing without demand."[89] These demands reach beyond politics proper to the culture industry as groups threaten to boycott films (such as *Kinsey*), television series (such as NBC's *Book of Daniel*), and companies (such as Disney) for "antifamily content and policies."

At the same time, some of these same leaders go beyond demanding to intimidation and threat. This temptation is greatest not least when the Party establishment fails to conform to the movement's demands and expectations. As Gary Bauer explains, "Social conservatives feel that they are half the Republican coalition and as such their concerns deserve attention."[90] In a letter to the Republican National Committee Chairman, Dobson wrote: "Remember, 43 percent of your votes [in the previous election] came from evangelical Christians. They trusted Republicans to deal with their deepest longings and fears."[91] Elsewhere he warned, "What I'm trying to say is to anyone who will listen, 'Don't ignore the traditional conservative vote that's out there. You do so, as a Republican, at your own peril.' "[92] This is the problem with electoral politics in our time. Politicians cannot get nominated without the support of the grassroots activists, but they cannot get elected and govern without moving to the political center. It is inevitable that politicians who do get elected betray their most ardent supporters by moderating their positions. Needless to say, this comes as a source of terrible frustration to the movement leaders. Movement leaders regularly and probably rightly accuse Republican politicians and officials of "just ignoring those that put them in office." As Dobson complained and then warned after one election, "There's just very, very little to show for what has happened, and I think there's going to be some trouble down the road if they don't get on the ball."[93] The frustration has gotten so deep at times that Dobson has threatened, in effect, to undermine the Republican Party unless it made conservative social issues a higher legislative priority. "If I go," he has said, "I will do everything I can to take as many people with me as possible."[94] As described in the press, Dobson would urge social conservatives to abandon Republicans in November—to stay at home or vote for third parties—with the goal of ending the GOP majority in Congress. "It doesn't take that many votes to do it. You just look how many people are there by just a hair, [who won their last election by] 51 percent to 49 percent, and they have a 10- or 11-vote majority. I told [the House Majority Whip], 'I really hope you guys don't make me try to prove it, because I will.'"[95] A colleague of Dobson's echoed the threat: "If [Republicans leaders] think Ross Perot caused them indigestion, they haven't seen anything yet. If they want to experience what it's like to have three parties—one a pro-life, pro-family party—we're prepared to accommodate them."[96] Threats, sometimes open and sometimes veiled, are not so uncommon.[97]

The Hope Placed in Politics

The hope Christian conservatives place in politics is quite astonishing. Consider some of the things said in this regard. Political action will return "a sense of cultural ownership to Christian citizens nationwide,"[98] "preserve, protect and defend the Judeo-Christian values that made this the greatest country in history,"[99] "begin renewing America's culture,"[100] "save traditional marriage—and the traditional family,"[101] "ensure broadcast decency,"[102] make America "a land of individual liberty, respect for family integrity, public and private virtue, and private enterprise."[103] Among other things, legislative action can "affirm the national relationship with God," and "secure our national interest in the institutions of marriage and family," "our fundamental right as parents to the care, custody, and control of our children," "our God-bestowed right to life," "our god-granted liberties," and "an environment of decency."[104] Voting itself can "take us in the direction of righteousness,[105] and "preserve America as a place that believes in family, faith and freedom."[106] The premise is that "to engage our culture and claim it for Christ, begin[s] with your vote.

Remember, only you can elect your future!"[107] Collectively, the result can be amazing. "The only way to continue with the freedom we possess is to see a national moral revival. We've got to mobilize millions of new voters."[108] A moral revival through the mobilization of voters! This is why elections are regarded as moments of decisive importance. Referring to the 2004 election, James Dobson declared, "We're at a crossroads as a nation. Everything that we care about, a good part of the Judeo-Christian system of values, hangs in the balance [of the presidential election.]"[109] Four years later, Tony Perkins said the same thing: "The future of our children and grandchildren hangs in the balance on Nov. 4. Will they inherit an America based on our Judeo-Christian heritage or will they inherit a secular, godless society where individual responsibility and freedom have disappeared? We are on an even more slippery slope, and we simply cannot afford to shirk our responsibility as citizens.[110] As Rick Scarborough concluded, "we must stay engaged or America is lost."[111] By winning, Christians can, in the word of one activist, "do more than just elect a president. *We seek to heal a nation.*"[112]

America and the Church, Together

What is never lost in the hurt, the fear, the hostility, and the heat of battle is a longing for an America restored. For a minority of Evangelicals and Fundamentalists, restoration means returning to a Christian America. As the late D. James Kennedy has put it, "Our job is to reclaim America for Christ, whatever the cost. . . . As the vice regents of God, we are to exercise godly dominion and influence over our neighborhoods, our schools, our government, our literature and arts, our sports arenas, our entertainment media, our news media, our scientific endeavors—in short, over every aspect and institution of human society."[113] Most conservative Christians, and certainly the more intellectually sophisticated, are not so explicit about making America Christian but rather speak in tones that are more inclusive and civil religious. For these, "America became the greatest nation on earth for one reason and one reason only: because her people served God and lived according to His principles."[114] Thus, "restoring America begins with recapturing the original American vision of a just society, and becoming agents of healing—bringing our nation back to God and rebuilding our moral and spiritual foundations."[115] One Christian politician declared excitedly, "What Congress can accomplish with a Republican President will be incredible. It will be nothing less than a rediscovery of the values that made America a great nation and that have made Americans a good people."[116]

The mythic connection between the Christian faith and America is variously understood by conservative Christians, but the link itself is not doubted. The fate of one has been, is, and will be intimately tied to the fate of the other. The bond is strong because each is, in indefinable ways, constitutive of the other. It is not surprising then, that they are often conflated, such that Christian faith and national identity are fused together in political imagination. This particular alliance has evolved in such a way as to forge a strong connection to the agenda of a political party where the interests of one become wedded to the interests of the other. Republican Party officials and conservative Christian leaders instrumentalize and leverage each other's power to serve shared ends, though it is clear which side has the better deal. This is why conservative Christians are often called the "useful idiots of the Republican party."

It is true that these kinds of alliances are common in history in many, many different settings. One can undoubtedly point to pragmatic benefits in some instances. Yet in this situation, as in those other settings, the close association between faith and the social and political order generates a range of profound concerns and not a few serious problems that will be explored later in this essay.

Change and Continuity in the New Politics of Culture

In politics, nothing is permanent. The winds of political change have been blowing in recent years, especially within the Christian Right. For one, the leadership is changing. Some of its leaders have grown older and are stepping back from active, day-to-day involvement (such as James Dobson and Paul Weyrich). Some have died (such as D. James Kennedy and Jerry Falwell). At the same time, other leaders in the Evangelical movement who are not so openly political in their ministries have become more prominent (Rick Warren and Bill Hybels are cases in point). For another, among the rank and file, there is obvious disappointment and disillusionment set in with what religious involvement in politics has wrought. Thus, it is possible to argue that at the same time the Christian Right acquired and exercised its greatest power—culminating in the 2004 presidential election—this movement also generated greater hostility toward the Christian faith than ever before in the nation's history—more anticlericalism among ordinary Americans and more disaffection among a younger generation of theologically conservative believers.[117] In line with this, there is a political shift leftward, especially among younger Evangelicals who, by 2008, moved enthusiastically to support Barack Obama as president.

Yet, as I noted at the beginning of the chapter, the old Christian Right is far from dead as a movement. New leaders are emerging in prominence.[118] But even as its power fragments, its aging leaders continue to try to influence politics—as James Dobson did through his denunciations of Republicans who were not conservative enough (as with Senator McCain in the 2008 campaign[119]) and Democrats who are hostile to the Judeo-Christian tradition (as with Dobson's accusations against Senator Obama in the same election.)[120] As Jonathan Falwell put it,

> There are lots of people in the media who say that the religious right is dead. The rumors of death are greatly exaggerated. We are very much alive. We are very much moving forward into the future to continue to change our nation to continue to lead our nation back to where it began and to where it came from.[121]

That said, the established Christian Right it is undergoing a crisis and a transformation.

One transformation within politically conservative Christian circles is a shift in emphasis away from politics per se. There is a recognition that politics may not be quite as important as they have thought and that "culture" may be a bigger problem after all. A number of new groups have emerged with this broader agenda, groups such as Legacy[122], The Clapham Group,[123] and Reclaiming the 7 Mountains of Culture.[124] These groups vary considerably in mission and sophistication, but there are clear continuities among their leaders and in the logic between some of these groups and the more established Christian Right. Consider the founding rationale of Reclaiming the 7 Mountains of Culture. It is worth quoting at length.

> In every city of the world, an unseen battle rages for dominion over God's creation and the souls of people. This battle is fought on seven strategic fronts, looming like mountains over the culture to shape and influence its destiny. Over the years the church slowly retreated from its place of influence on these mountains leaving a void now filled with darkness. When we lose our influence we lose the culture and when we lose the culture we fail to advance the kingdom of God. And now a generation stands in desperate need. It's time to fight for them and take back the mountains of influence.
>
> The mountain of government where evil is either restrained or endorsed. The mountain of education where truths or lies about God and His creation are taught. The mountain of media where information is interpreted through the lens of good or evil. The mountain of

arts and entertainment where values and virtue are celebrated or distorted. The mountain of religion where people worship God in spirit and truth or settle for a religious ritual. The mountain of family where either the blessing or a curse is passed on to successive generations. And the one mountain they depend on. The mountain which fuels and funds all the other mountains. The mountain of business where people build for the glory of God or the glory of man. Where resources are consecrated for the kingdom of God or captured for the powers of darkness. Those who lead this mountain control what influences our culture.

The last fifty years we have seen the most rapid moral decline in history. The culture we inherited from our forefathers is disintegrating before our eyes. What kind of world are we leaving for our children and grandchildren?[125]

A more ambitious initiative of this sort is an alliance of Christian organizations concerned with Christian worldview, including Colson's BreakPoint Ministries, the Wilberforce Forum, the Family Research Council, The Truth Project, the Acton Institute, Teen Mania, God's World Publications, Summit Ministries, and the C. S. Lewis Institute. In its launching manifesto, the alliance, which has called itself "The Movement," laid out a strategy for "Restoring the Gospel of the Kingdom and the hope of that Good News to the churches and the public square." According to the author, T. M. Moore, the first premise of an effective social movement is the recognition of the need "to redress some clearly-identified and boldly defined social evil."

They must identify their Enemy—or, the Other—in clear and uncompromising terms, and labor diligently to explicate and demonstrate why it is an evil, where it lurks, what are its harmful effects, and how it may be eradicated. They must declaim against their identified Other and seek to persuade the public and relevant powers concerning the utter necessity of its overthrow and eradication.[126]

Moore identifies the social evil of our times as a secular postmodernism— "The Lie [that] has inundated the unbelieving world and swept into the Church, and as yet not been fully exposed and forcefully evicted."[127] This, he argues, "is an unmitigated evil and must be attacked directly and earnestly if it is to be overthrown." Elsewhere he spoke of the need to "eradicate the Other to the fullest extent of the movement's ability." To this end,

we will need to be willing to name names, point the finger at specific offenders, engage The Lie wherever it has established a base of operations, challenge and expose The Lie in all its forms, demonstrate the many and variegated forms of evil for which The Lie alone is responsible, and patiently and lovingly, point the way beyond The Lie to the basic premise of the Biblical worldview, that God is Truth.[128]

The ultimate aim of The Movement is to be "a catalyst for achieving a watershed moment in history" that includes revival in the churches, renewal in the culture, and "a new Great Awakening" in society. As Moore concludes, "let it be our earnest longing that those who persist in The Lie might be *compelled to admit* that we have indeed, turned their world upside-down for Jesus Christ."[129]

In these new initiatives, one sees again the well-meaning hope to make the world a better place. Though the tactics have expanded to include worldview and culture more broadly, the logic at work—that America has been taken over by secularists, causing harm to America and harm to the church, that it is time to "take back the culture" for Christ through a strategy of acquiring and using power is identical to the longstanding approach of the established Christian Right. The leading edge of such initiatives is still one of negation. To use words and phrases like "enemy," "attack," "drive out," "overthrow," "eradicate the Other," "reclaim their nations for Christ," "take back" influence, "compel," "occupying and influencing [spheres] of power in our nations," "advancing the kingdom of God," and so on, continues to reflect the same language of loss, disappointment, anger, antipathy, resentment, and desire for conquest.[130] This is because the underlying myth that defines their identity, their goals, and their strategy of action has not changed. The myth continues to shape the language, the logic, and the script for their engagement with the culture. Circumstances might change as might the players, but if the myth that underwrites the ideal of Christian engagement does not change, then very little has changed at all.

Chapter Four

THE CHRISTIAN LEFT

L IKE POLITICALLY CONSERVATIVE CHRISTIANS, politically progressive Christians also are defined by and operate within a reading of myth and history. If conservatives are animated by a mythic ideal of the right ordering of society, and thus see modern history as a decline from order to disorder, progressives have always been animated by the myth of equality and community and therefore see history as an ongoing struggle to realize these ideals.

Myth and History

Insight into the nature of progressive politics can be drawn from its origins in the modern West. Clearly one can find many antecedents in history and, not least, in the history of the church. Elements can be found in St. Augustine's *City of God*, the Waldensians of the twelfth century, St. Francis and the Franciscans in the early thirteenth century, and St. Thomas More's sixteenth-century masterpiece *Utopia*, among other places. Yet in its contemporary manifestations, progressive politics—whether liberal or socialist, secular or religious—has taken form and evolved in relation to a particular legacy of the Enlightenment. It is crystallized in the rallying cry of the French Revolution: its threefold ideals of liberty, equality, and fraternity. The key word in the progressive lexicon, and arguably the paramount virtue, is justice. Justice, though, is defined as economic equity—the equality component. Within the contemporary left, there is a tension between the communitarian wing and the social libertarian wing, and the dividing line is far from clear-cut. Over the course of the last two centuries, liberalism has had less to say about "fraternity," though socialism has made this a central part of its agenda. In

contemporary America, most secular progressives define the "liberty" component in terms of individual autonomy and the freedom to choose one's own
lifestyle; that is, in terms of sexual identity and practice, relationships, entertainment, and so on. But religiously oriented progressives, Christians among
them, tend to lean toward the communitarian side of this divide. For these,
liberty is understood largely as liberation; often enough this means freedom
for individuals and communities from poverty caused by economic domination and exploitation of the wealthy. As to community itself (the "fraternity"
component), it is the idea of solidarity among equals—across the boundaries
of race, ethnicity, gender, sexual orientation, and social class. In this light,
the hope of peace is a related virtue among politically progressive Christians,
not incidentally because war, historically, is often waged by the rich and the
privileged as a means of defending or expanding their power, wealth, and
social advantage.

The biblical tradition that Christian progressives appeal to is the prophetic tradition in its condemnation of the wealthy for their abuse of the
poor, the weak, and the marginalized. In the Hebrew Scriptures, God speaks
to Israel through the prophet Isaiah saying, "If you do away with the yoke of
oppression, with the pointing finger and malicious talk, and if you spend
yourselves on behalf of the hungry and satisfy the needs of the oppressed,
then your light will rise in the darkness, and your night will become like the
noonday" (Isa. 58:9–10). Elsewhere he declares, "Woe to those who make
unjust laws, to those who issue oppressive decrees, to deprive the poor of
their rights and withhold justice from the oppressed of my people, making
widows their prey and robbing the fatherless" (Isa. 10:1–2). Likewise, the
prophet Jeremiah rails against those who "do not judge with justice the cause
of the orphan, to make it prosper, and [those who] do not defend the rights
of the needy" (Jer. 5:28). In the Psalms, the writer proclaims, "I know that
the Lord maintains the cause of the needy, and executes justice for the poor"
(Ps. 140:12). And in the Wisdom literature, believers are called to "Speak
out, judge righteously, defend the rights of the poor and needy" (Prov. 31:9).
This is a tradition that extends into the New Testament as well, as Jesus proclaims that the nations will be judged by how they treat "the least of these"
(Matt. 25). So too in the Epistles, believers are told that the sign of pure religion is "to look after orphans and widows in their distress and to keep oneself
from being polluted by the world" (James 1:27). As it is often pointed out,
the number of references to the requirement for justice for the poor is far
greater than any other social issue.

It is not only the prophetic past that provides inspiration for Christians
who are politically progressive; it is also the future. For those on the secular

Left, of course, the "progress" in the word "progressive" derives from a view of history as evolution, advancement, and improvement; in its origin, it was a secularized version of biblical eschatology. Over the centuries, it has played out as the dream of the perfectibility of humankind and the triumph of reason over illusion and suffering. Among Christian progressives, it is the future vision of the *eschaton* itself—the realization of the kingdom of heaven, where justice, peace, equality, and community exist in their ultimate state of perfection—that is the abiding ideal. It is the vision of the *eschaton* that Christian progressives see themselves working hard to realize.

Georges Sorel wrote in 1908 that the thing about a political myth is that it "cannot be refuted, since it is, at bottom, identical with the conviction of a group, being the expression of these convictions in the language of movement."[1] It is only natural, then, that history is recounted in ways that reinforce the mythic ideals of the group. Thus, just as politically conservative Christians are selective in their telling of history (according to the dominant concepts of their myth), progressives are selective as well. For politically progressive Christians, the salient movements of American history are abolition, women's suffrage, the female seminary movement, child labor reform, the programs of social relief in the Social Gospel movement, the peace movement before World War I, desegregation and the civil rights movement, and the war against Vietnam. The heroic figures of this political tradition are exemplars of these struggles—Frederick Douglass, Dorothy Day, Martin Luther King, Mother Teresa, Nelson Mandela, Desmond Tutu, Oscar Romero and so on.

Politically progressive Christianity achieved its apex of visibility and influence in the middle decades of the twentieth century. Most of the major mainline denominations had their social justice ministries that lobbied on behalf of particular public policy in Washington, D.C., as of course did such ecumenical bodies as the National Council of Churches. There were clergy organizations, such as the Clergy Leadership Network, that weighed in on the political issues of the day. Internationally, it was the World Council of Churches that took up the progressive cause around the world. Much the way that the Christian Right is associated with the social conservative agenda of the Republican Party at the end of the twentieth and in the early twenty-first century, these denominations and ecumenical bodies were, in those days, identified closely with left-of-center politics. These bodies also cultivated the presumption that their particular agenda represented *the* Christian voice in public affairs.[2] Among the issues they pursued were civil rights (for), the war in Vietnam (against), public education (for), nuclear proliferation (against), ecological justice (for), and liberation movements generally (for).

Perhaps the strongest manifestation of the Christian Left in these years was outside of the United States in the form of liberation theology and its attending movements of liberation in the Third World, especially in Latin America. Liberation theology shared affinities with black and feminist theologies, but beginning in the 1960s, it was primarily Catholic in its institutional expression. It interpreted (and still does) the Christian faith through the suffering, struggle, and hope of the poor, and the person of Jesus as the liberator of the oppressed.[3] In its more extreme expressions, it privileged orthopraxy or practice rooted in a political interpretation of the Gospels over orthodoxy, or proper belief. In this way it became closely aligned with Marxist ideology and even various communist movements in their call to arms against oppressive regimes around the Third World.

After reaching a height of influence in the 1970s and 1980s, liberation theology declined in popularity and authority, primarily because the Vatican took a consistently hard line against its more radical spokespeople and their positions. In the United States, the Catholic Left lost ground as well, yet continued to pursue progressive policies through groups like NETWORK—A National Catholic Social Justice Lobby.[4]

Mainline Protestant activism in the United States also weakened in visibility and influence. This was in part because the demographic base of the mainline churches declined so precipitously in these years. It is also because the mainline social agenda—including most prominently, civil rights, the war in Vietnam, and women's rights, among others—was realized. Racial problems didn't disappear, of course, but the quest for civil rights had largely succeeded. The war in Vietnam came to an end. Women's rights were acknowledge and embraced as normative. And so on. Their fading significance was partly a function of having achieved so many of their objectives. Even so, the mainline bodies through their Washington Offices (such as the Peace and Justice Ministries of the Episcopal Church, the General Board of Church and Society of the United Methodist Church, the Washington Office of the Evangelical Lutheran Church in America, the Justice and Witness Ministries of the United Church of Christ,[5] and especially their Public Life and Social Policy Ministries) have continued to press a progressive political agenda. Fairly typical of these offices is the "public policy ministry" of the Presbyterian Church, USA.[6] The office

> is the public policy information and advocacy office of the General Assembly of the Presbyterian Church (U.S.A.). Its task is to advocate, and help the church to advocate, the social witness perspectives and policies of the Presbyterian General Assembly. . . . Ministry in Washington

THE CHRISTIAN LEFT | 135

offers a chance to translate the church's deep convictions about justice, peace and freedom from words into reality. The political process is where decisions are made that help or harm people; decisions that help to make the kind of world God intends. . . . The church, if it is to remain true to its biblical roots, theological heritage, and contemporary practice, must not fall silent. It must speak faithfully, truthfully, persuasively, humbly, boldly and urgently.

What Does Scripture Say About Justice? Throughout the Bible, scripture reveals God's will to do justice. The Hebrew prophets continually remind God's people ". . . What does the Lord require of you but to do justice, and to love kindness, and to walk humbly with your God?" (Micah 6:8). In a recent theological perspective, Presbyterian Hunger Committee member the Rev. Rims Barber writes that "We Christians are called to share what we have by the grace of God. . . . So we are called to stand with the people who live at the edges of society, even though this may mean being against the interests of those high up in the social/economic/political pecking order." The prophets give specific warning to those who seek only their own well-being and ignore the well-being of the marginalized and oppressed. Israel's failure to be just and righteous is clearly seen as disobedient to God and the reason for national decay and destruction. Jesus frequently witnessed to the priority of the poor in the reign of God. He challenged the rich young ruler, he sharply criticized the hard-heartedness of religious leaders, and he taught that those who reached out to marginalized persons were serving him (Luke 18:18–25, Matthew 19:16–24 and Luke 10:25–37). In addition, Christ speaks of the accountability of nations to do justice in Matthew 25 and states, "Truly I tell you, just as you did it to one of the least of these who are members of my family, you did it to me."[7]

The progressive voice of the PCUSA is clearly in harmony with the refrain of progressive politics heard across the range of mainline and liberal bodies and the Left more generally. Denominations in this tradition also are in cooperation with the public policy ministries of the umbrella-group the National Council of Churches, its Washington office, and its Justice and Advocacy Commission.[8]

The Resurgence of the Christian Left—Evangelical Progressives

As noted before, for all of the activity of the mainline denominations and representative organizations since the 1980s, these organizations have largely receded from public attention. The endless position taking, policy proposals, and commissions have been mostly ignored by the government, political parties, the media, and the general public. Yet there has been a resurgence of the Christian Left in the early years of the twenty-first century. This movement has strong affinities with the broader "spiritual Left" that includes liberal Jews, Buddhists, Unitarians, and various expressions of new age spirituality, but it remains distinctly Christian.[9] This resurgence is not led by the mainline and liberal bodies but rather by the political activism of progressive Evangelicals. Among the names and organizations associated with this political renewal are Jim Wallis, John Perkins, Sharon Gallagher, Tony Campolo, Ron Sider, Tom Sine, Brian McLaren, Randall Balmer, Sojourners, Evangelicals for Social Action, Call to Renewal, the Evangelical Environmental Network, and Red Letter Christians.[10] The most visible figure of this movement, thus far, has been Wallis.

Evangelicalism never was politically homogeneous, though the organizational and media success of politically conservative Christian groups made it seem so. Yet, like the mainline denominations, the Evangelical Left had also labored for years in obscurity, frustrated by the success of their conservative counterparts. Sojourners has been in existence since 1971. Call to Renewal was founded in 1995. Their political advocacy was also mostly ignored until the Republican presidential win in 2004. It was only then that the Democratic Party, for many decades tone-deaf to faith, recognized that it would not mobilize the American public and win elections until it learned to use the language and grammar of faith that has always informed the values and beliefs of most Americans. The problem was that most Democrats have been uncomfortable using the language of faith. From across the Democratic Party, many called for "soul-searching" and internal reform that would address the so-called God-gap. Sojourners was there to show the way. It had previously published a full-page ad in several newspapers including the *New York Times* on 30 August 2004 that read "God is not a Republican . . . or a Democrat," and another two months later in *USA Today* that read "200 Christian Leaders Condemn a Theology of War." Democratic politicians from the highest to the lowest level, began to catch on. Former President Clinton put it this way, "Political involvement dictated by faith is not the exclusive province of the right wing."[11] Thus, even in the obscurity of a congressional district, Democratic politicians, such as Anthony Weiner, were saying things like, "Instead of recoiling from this word [faith-based] simply because President Bush has co-opted it and bastardized the term, we should seize the opportunity when it presents itself."[12]

The Evangelical Left was finally gaining the platform for which it had long worked. In describing this triumph, Jim Wallis declared, "the monologue is over; a new dialogue has begun."[13] The original monologue between Christianity and politics, however, was by progressives in the mainline and liberal bodies. The resurgence of a progressive voice in Christianity, then, is not new but rather a renewal; a renewal that is weak but perhaps only because it is in its early stages. Compared to the Christian Right, its organizational resources are meager, but it has achieved a platform that it hadn't had for decades. How much traction it will have in popular consciousness remains to be seen.

Harm to America and Its Weakest

Unlike politically conservative Christians, the harm that most concerns religious progressives and the harm they most want to address is the harm done to the weak and disadvantaged of our society and world. Given the mythic importance of equity in the progressive worldview, this is what one would expect. There is, in this renewal, no departure from the liberal and old-fashioned socialist tradition. For religious progressives, the disadvantaged includes women, gays, minorities, immigrants, and the poor but it is the more embracing category of poverty that has animated Evangelical progressives more than anything else. Needless to say, these categories are not mutually exclusive—women and minorities, after all, often bear the disproportionate burden of poverty.

In the words of the Sojourners/Call to Renewal document, "From Poverty to Opportunity: A Covenant for a New America,"

> The Hebrew prophets consistently say that the measure of a nation's righteousness and integrity is how it treats the most vulnerable. And Jesus says the nations will be judged by how they treat "the least of these" (Matthew 25).
>
> As our religious forebears declared that slavery was morally intolerable, we now insist that widespread poverty in the midst of plenty is a moral wrong we refuse to accept any longer. Poverty is the new slavery. It is time to lift up practical policies and practices that help people escape poverty and clearly challenge the increasing wealth gap between rich and poor. The Bible condemns extremes of wealth and poverty. Across the globe, inequality is on the rise. The disproportionate impact of poverty on women and people of color is a further indictment of our society.[14]

As another put it, "We've gone from a war on poverty to a war on the poor."[15] Wallis elaborated these concerns,

There is indeed class warfare raging in this country, but not from those who speak for the poorest Americans. It is the class warfare of tax cuts and budget priorities that make the rich richer while further decimating low- and middle-income families. . . . that inequality is becoming intolerable.

The ongoing costs of the war, combined with tax cuts for the wealthy, have led to a crisis for America's poorest children. Indeed, America's poor were the first casualties of the Iraq war, as U.S. domestic needs were pushed off the political agenda. . . . The consequences of these actions have become a silent war, felt most severely in the poorest parts of the United States, where low-income families are desperately clutching onto the bottom rungs of the failing economy.[16]

The problem of poverty is not spiritually inconsequential for America. As Wallis declared, "God is angry with America and with the world because of the statistics of poverty."[17] As Tony Campolo has written, "I love this country so much that I do not want to see it fall from its pinnacle of well-being into a state of disarray—which it surely will, unless it changes its ways. That's why I choose to critique America from what I believe to be a biblical perspective."[18]

Though concern for the poor and disadvantaged dominates their political agenda, their interests extend to the environment, war, HIV, and immigration among other issues. As Wallis puts it, ". . . we start by subjecting all projects, initiatives, decisions, and policies to new criteria: whether they make justice more possible for all of us and especially for those on the bottom, whether they allow us to live in more harmony with the earth, and whether they increase the participation of all people in decision making. In other words, we must learn to judge our social and economic choices by whether they empower the powerless, protect the earth, and foster true democracy."[19] Not only are new organizations being formed to address these issues—for example the Evangelical Climate Initiative and the Christian Coalition for Immigration Reform—but also leaders are speaking out on these matters.[20]

Harm to the Faith

For all of the diversity one can find among progressives, one of the central catalysts of solidarity over the years has been their hostility to the leaders, organizations, ideology, and agenda of the Christian Right. The intensity of this hostility has tended to wax and wane with the expansion and contraction of influence exercised by the Christian Right. As the visibility and influence of the Christian Right has increased, so has the antipathy of the Christian Left intensified and the negative solidarity they derive from it. The reverse is true as well. The aversion to Christian conservatism, however, is fairly constant.

The hostility is multilayered. For Christian progressives, the Christian Right has harmed the faith by not representing Christianity fairly. In their view, the Christian Right casts its issues narrowly. Jim Wallis, for example, continually asks, "Is Jesus pro-rich? Pro-war? Pro-American? I don't think Jesus' top priorities would have been a capital gains tax cut and the occupation of Iraq. I go city-to-city and people say, 'That's not MY faith, the way it's portrayed in the election or in the media or the way it's invoked in the White House or Congress. I've got a faith too, and that's not it.'" In this light he decries the "seduction" of key leaders of Evangelicalism by the Republican Party.[21] This is an opinion echoed by Tom Sine:

> Seemingly out of nowhere, in the late seventies the religious right appeared and hijacked the evangelical movement. Jerry Falwell, Jimmy Swaggart, Pat Robertson, Tim La Haye, the Moral Majority, the Religious Roundtable, and a host of others took over the evangelical parade and detoured it sharply to the right. It was an intellectual takeover from which American evangelicalism has never recovered.[22]

Randall Balmer elaborates the point, mincing no words. In his view, the evangelical faith has been "hijacked" and "bastardized" by the Christian Right.[23] The effect is a "distortion of the faith" and of "the teachings of Jesus."[24] Their method is "the ruse of selective literalism;" in effect, a process by which "they wrench passages out of context and offer pinched, literalistic interpretations . . . that diminish the scriptures by robbing them of their larger meaning."[25] The preachers of the Christian Right "have led their sheep astray from the gospel of Jesus Christ to the false gospel of neoconservative ideology and into the maw of the Republican Party."[26] By so doing, they have "compromised the faith," turning it into "something less than the best of Christianity."[27] For the Sojourners community, the compromise of the Christian Right has gone so far that their confession of Christ has been "co-opted by militarism and nationalism."[28]

For the Christian Left, the consequences of the Christian Right's distortions and bid for power are seen not only in Christianity but also in American democracy. Again, Balmer speaks directly to this. Their agenda is "misguided, even ruinous to the nation I love."[29] The net effect of their political machinations, he says, "has been a poisoning of public discourse."[30] "By seeking to commandeer and to dominate the conversation, . . . the leaders of the Religious Right have failed to observe even the most basic etiquette of democracy."[31] The Christian Alliance for Progress has made the same observations: "The success of the Religious Right in appropriating the language of Christianity has led many people to become generally wary of religion in the public sphere and of Christianity in particular. The Religious Right has used the language of Christianity to promote an extreme and divisive political agenda that has helped polarize our nation."[32]

Ressentiment

There is deep anger and antipathy among many Christian progressives about this entire state of affairs. "God hates inequality"[33] and America is not only increasingly unequal, but the Christian Right has legitimated these inequalities of power and wealth. As Tom Sine puts it in his book, *Cease Fire*,

> The pro-family folks need a wake-up call. The real threat to our Christian families isn't some sinister elite living in Washington, D.C. The real threat is Christian families unquestioningly buying into the secular aspirations and addictions of the American dream. Christian parents trying to get ahead in their careers and in their upscale living are often among those working the longest hours.[34]

Perhaps there is no clearer expression of hurt and the anger that has resulted than that expressed by Randall Balmer in his book, *Thy Kingdom Come: An Evangelical's Lament*. This is a curious book, for it reflects most of the problems he attributes to the Religious Right. His disdain for the Christian Right leads him to engage in name-calling that is as one-dimensional and dehumanizing as the most extreme voices of the Christian Right, labeling his opponents "right-wing zealots" and "bullies"[35] and their followers "minions,"[36] who together are "intolerant," "vicious," "militaristic," "bloviating," and theocratic.[37] In this regard, his perspective also matches the Manichaeism of the most extreme voices of the Christian Right for there is no shade or nuance in his description of the political realities with which he is wrestling. The Christian Right is monolithic and it is bad. Liberals, by contrast, are good. The sum of his *ressentiment* is found in an anticipatory sense of personal injury that may not measure up to the stories in *Foxe's Book of Martyrs*, but is clearly of formative importance to him. It is worth quoting at length.

I know . . . that when this book appears, the minions of the Religious Right will seek to discredit me, rather than engage the substance of my arguments. The initial wave of criticism, as an old friend who has endured similar attacks reminded me, will be to deny that I am, in fact, an evangelical Christian. When that fails—and I'll put up my credentials as an evangelical against anyone!—the next approach will be some gratuitous personal attack: part of the academic elite, spokesman for the northeastern establishment, misguided liberal, prodigal son, traitor to the faith, or some such. Another evangelical friend with political views similar to mine actually endured a heresy trial.

To take another example, I've been an (unpaid) editor for *Christianity Today*, the signature publication of evangelicalism, for the better part of a decade and have written a dozen articles for them, including a half dozen features and several cover stories. A couple of years ago, the managing editor tried to pressure me into resigning from the masthead because I had agreed to address a group of gay evangelicals and because of a piece I had written challenging Religious Right orthodoxy on the abortion issue. I refused to oblige him by tendering my resignation then, but now, with the appearance of this book, he has the material he needs to force my ouster.

The evangelical subculture, which prizes conformity above all else, doesn't suffer rebels gladly, and it is especially intolerant of anyone with the temerity to challenge the shibboleths of the Religious Right. Despite their putative claims to the faith, the leaders of the Religious Right are vicious toward anyone who refuses to kowtow to their version of orthodoxy, and their machinery of vilification strikes with ruthless, dispassionate efficiency. Longtime friends (and not a few family members) will shuffle uneasily around me and studiously avoid any sort of substantive conversation about the issues I've raised in this book—then quietly strike my name from their Christmas card lists. That's how the evangelical subculture operates. Circle the wagons. Brook no dissent.[38]

In this, Balmer is not alone but representative of many who have been hurt deeply by the lack of grace many times found in the conservative churches and who remain angry about it. The Christian Alliance for Progress, for one, gives vent to that anger on a separate page on its website for members to tell stories of their own hurt. Typical is the comment of one member: "I feel embarrassed and angry that Christianity has been used to divide our country and to promote bigotry and war. I joined this movement to stand up for compassion and justice."[39] From another, "I received physically threatening phone calls, obscene phone calls (from the church building as I found out by using *69 on my phone), and my children were harassed by other children during Sunday School."[40] This hurt spills over into a bitterness rife among religious progressives.[41]

Power, Politics, and Partisanship

The problem, from the progressive point of view, is not just the "dangerous liaison of religion with political power" witnessed in "the almost total identification of the Religious Right with the new Republican majority in Washington."[42] The subtext in all of this and, it would seem, the larger complaint of politically progressive Christians has to do with their own eclipse from the realm of power. They don't have the media organizations and outlets and thus the public visibility of the Christian Right and for decades now, they have not been given credibility or regarded as religiously or politically consequential by the political parties or the American people. They are as certain as their conservative counterparts that they are on the side of good. They also believe that they are smarter and more sophisticated than their conservative counterparts. Yet these things have not translated into either public authority or significance.

What is to be done about this? Given the harm done to the nation and to the Christian faith, the obvious solution is to seize power back from the Right. As Jim Wallis puts it, "For decades the religious right has held the upper hand in religion and politics. This is changing and they must share the stage."[43]

The first order of priority is to take back Christianity from those who would pervert it. The very purpose of the Christian Alliance for Progress is "to reclaim the vocabulary of Christianity from extremists and to restore the morals and values of Christianity."[44] This is in line with Balmer's purposes as well: "As an evangelical Christian, someone who takes the Bible seriously and who believes in the transformative power of Jesus, I want to reclaim the faith from the Religious Right."[45] Wallis agrees. Said he, "It feels sometimes that our faith has been stolen in the public arena. And when your faith is stolen, it's time to take it back."[46] This is a theme he repeats again and again in his writing and public speaking: "We need to take our religion back."[47]

It is the "ruinous" agenda of the Christian Right, as Balmer puts it, that is also the basis for the call of politically progressive Christians to "Tak[e] the Country Back."[48] The Christian Alliance is committed to "use the collective power of our individual members to help shape the political realities in our country and to strive to build a more just and compassionate nation."[49] The ultimate goal, then, is to create a more just world. What this means, of course, is to give appropriate attention to the needs of the poor.[50] But how? Through politics. As the Sojourners community advises, "Vote. The simple act of voting is one of the most empowering actions you can do to create a just and peaceful world."[51] As Wallis himself put it just before the 2008 election, "It is always an act of faith to believe that, in the end, hope will prevail over fear: so pray, and vote."[52]

It does go beyond voting, of course. In the 2008 election, Christian Progressives established a new political action committee, the "Matthew 25 Network." Its premise, of course, was that "people of faith should actively participate in the political process as an important avenue for social change."[53] It was created formally outside of the Democratic Party in order to better target centrist and progressive Evangelicals. As with all PACs, its goals were both to raise money and to mobilize voters. This was why Wallis and Campolo worked to put an "abortion reduction" plank in the Democratic Party platform. As Wallis put it, "There are literally millions of votes at stake."[54]

No one doubts the sincerity of their motives or the high-mindedness of the cause. There is also no doubt that underlying the call to "take back" the faith and the nation is a basic will to power that is not unlike what one finds within the Christian Right. Katha Pollitt, writing in *The Nation*, made precisely this observation. "In this sense," she wrote, "Wallis' evangelicalism is as much a power play as Pat Robertson's. And Wallis is as much a power player. By a remarkable act of providence, God's politics turn out to be curiously tailored to the current crisis of the Democratic Party."[55]

Wallis protests that his agenda is not partisan in nature. God, he repeatedly says, "is neither a Republican nor a Democrat," and therefore parties and candidates should "avoid the exploitation of religion or congregations for partisan political purposes."[56] Pollitt, though, is closer to the truth.[57] The net effect of his work as a consultant and advisor to the Democratic Party, his grassroots activism, and his own writing is a partisanship as Democratic as Dobson's is Republican. This is equally true for other politically progressive Christian organizations. In the lead-up to the 2008 election, for example, Brian McLaren offered an elaborate apology for the Democratic candidate in a series of essays entitled, "Why I'm Voting for Obama, and Why I Hope You Will Too."[58] With the possible exception of abortion, there is little in the actions and writings of the larger Christian Left that would be objectionable to the progressive wing of the Democratic Party.

Wallis and others *do* take issue with the secular Left for not taking religion seriously, "mistakenly dismissing spirituality as irrelevant to social change."[59] Yet, in substance, the perspective they offer is not an alternative to the ideology of the secular left, but a faith-based extension of its discourse; the social movement they want to lead, its popular base. Wallis and others, in effect, provide the voice of the religious Left for a new generation.

As a longstanding activist on the Left, Wallis understands the need for popular support and the legitimacy that public opinion can provide. For him, then, the civil rights movement is the model for social change he believes is necessary.[60] His ideal is to spawn a movement that will create an irresistible "change in the wind." The framework by which change is enacted, however, is the State—its rituals, practices, laws, policies, and procedures. Though animated by a social movement, the dominant vehicle for achieving the goals of justice and peace is politics. For his own part, his goal is to create and lead "a new special interest group"[61] on behalf of the poor.[62]

Civil Religion of the Left

Jim Wallis, among other politically progressive Christians, has rightly complained that the Christian Right is engaged in promoting "civil religion" rather than biblical Christianity. Civil religion is a diffuse amalgamation of religious values that is synthesized with the civic creeds of the nation; in which the life and mission of the church is conflated with the life and mission of the country.[63] American values are, in substance, biblical, prophetic values; American identity is, thus, a vaguely Christian identity. This is particularly rudimentary when politically conservative Christians make public policy around biblical texts, for example, when they cite the book of Leviticus or Romans 1 to justify laws against homosexuality. Wallis puts the problem this way: "You don't say, 'This is a Judeo-Christian country, so we get to win' or 'God spoke to me this morning and I've got the fix for Social Security.' You bring your faith or values or whatever it is that motivates you and mobilizes you to action. You say, 'I want, in the public arena, to make an argument. I've got to persuade my fellow citizens that what I think is best for the common good is indeed best for the common good.'"[64] Yet Wallis and others in the Evangelical Left engage in the identical practice for which they criticize the Christian Right. From *God's Politics*[65]:

- Governmental budgets and tax policies should show compassion for poor families rather than reward the rich. Foreign policies should include fair trade and debt cancellation for the poorest countries. (Matthew 2:34–40, Isaiah 10:1–2)

- Policies should protect the creation rather than serve corporate interests which damage it. (Genesis 2:15, Psalm 24:1)

- Policies in the name of citizens should respect international law and cooperation in responding to global threats rather than in preemptive wars of choice. (Matthew 5:9)

- Government officials should tell the truth in justifying war and in other foreign and domestic policies. (John 8:32)

- National officials should foster change in attitudes and policies which led to the abuse and torture of Iraqi prisoners.

- National officials should drop the dangerous language of righteous empire in the war on terrorism which confuses the roles of God, church, and nation. They should be alert to perceiving evil in our actions rather than only in our enemies. (Matthew 6:33, Proverbs 8:12–13)

- Policies on abortion, capital punishment, euthanasia, weapons of mass destruction, HIV/AIDS—and other pandemics—and genocide around the world should obey the biblical injunction to choose life. (Deuteronomy 30:19)

He performs the same exercise with the prophetic statements of the Hebrew scriptures. For example, he cites Micah 4:1–4 as the standard for American foreign policy. So the conclusion Wallis draws for American policy is that "military solutions are insufficient to bring peace and security," and only when all people on earth "have some share in global security" will they be able to beat their swords into plowshares. For this reason, the United States should not have gone into Iraq, and the architects of the Iraqi policy—then Secretary of Defense Donald Rumsfeld and his deputy, Paul Wolfowitz— should "step aside."[66] He also uses Isaiah 65:20–25 as the standard by which to measure the Federal budget.[67] By this yardstick, he argues, "it is not inappropriate to name the federal budgets now being passed [by the Republicans] as 'unbiblical.'"[68] Wallis explains it this way:

> It's the kind of talk we don't hear much these days in America. But we need it. If the Hebrew prophets were around today, they would surely be preaching about our tax and budget policies that enrich the wealthy

and "make misery for the poor." And I don't think they would have worried much when accused of class warfare.

If biblical prophets like Amos and Isaiah had read the news about what happened to child tax credits for low-income families, for example, they surely would be out screaming on the White House lawn about the justice of God—and be quickly led away by the Secret Service.

Here too, Wallis does not hesitate to become specific. "The [Bush] administration's tax cuts to the wealthiest Americans must be immediately rescinded, and the no-bid contracts to U.S. corporations favored by the Bush administration . . . must be suspended."[69] Wallis even quotes Isaiah in defense of an increase in the minimum wage.[70]

The problem, of course, is that Amos, Micah, Isaiah, and the other prophets were living in a Jewish theocratic setting. The only way that Wallis and others can make these strong statements is to confuse America with Israel and the political dynamics of modern American democracy with the divine laws mandated for ancient Israel. It isn't that the wisdom of scripture is irrelevant for the formation of political values, but one can only make the close associations and specific political judgments Wallis does by turning progressive religion into a civil religion of the Left. It may be a more compassionate civil religion than what one finds in the American mainstream, but it is just a different expression of the same phenomenon, not something different from it. Both Right and Left, then, aspire to a righteous empire. Thus, when he accuses Falwell and Robertson of being "theocrats who desire their religious agenda to be enforced through the power of the state," he has established the criteria by which he and other politically progressive Christians are judged the same.[71]

Ironies

In its commitment to social change through politics and politically oriented social movements, in its conflation of the public with the political, in its own selective use of scripture to justify political interests, and in its confusion of theology with national interests and identity, the Christian Left (not least the Evangelical Left) imitates the Christian Right. The message is obviously different, their organizational scale and popular appeal are different, and their access to media outlets are different, but in their framework, method, and style of engagement, politically progressive Christians are very similar to their politically conservative counterparts.

There is another point of similarity. It is found in their relationship with the party system and the Democratic Party in particular. With all sincerity, they aspire to broaden and deepen the values people bring to the political process. But influence is never unidirectional in any relationship. Given the resources of the Democratic Party and the special interests that drive it, there is little question that progressive Christianity is instrumentalized (or used as a means to an end) by the Democratic Party in its quest for power, just as conservative Christianity has been used for quite some time by the Republican Party. For many years it was profoundly frustrating for Democrats to be out of power. They finally recognized that they could not regain power without accommodating their discourse to the religious beliefs of their constituency. Leading up to the 2004 presidential election, only one of the primary candidates had any staff member whose job was to help the candidate reach out to religious constituencies.[72] But all of that changed. The Party launched a website in the summer of 2005 called "A Word to the Faithful" that was designed to reach out to the religious community.[73] Officials said the website was "dedicated to illustrating how people of faith and Senate Democrats can work together to lift our neighbors up and achieve our common goals."[74] They also created the Faith Working Group in February 2005 as "an avenue to reach out to people of faith across the country."[75] Presidential candidates themselves hired consultants and strategists to advise them on how to appeal to religious voters.[76] The newly revitalized Christian Left has also facilitated the close working relationship. Religious progressives have created consulting firms, such as Common Good Strategies, dedicated solely to helping Democrats "reclaim the debate on faith and values."[77] The range of political advocacy groups in the mainline and liberal denominations has created a hospitable climate as well. So too have new organizations such as "faithfulamerica.org" and Faith in Public Life, founded in early 2007, to strengthen "the effectiveness, collaboration and reach of faith movements" through, among other things, strategic partnerships, a media infrastructure, and a media bureau.[78] In the 2008 election, the election campaign of Barack Obama organized hundreds of house parties, dozens of Christian rock concerts, gatherings of religious leaders, campus visits, and broadcast many television ads in order to mobilize moderate and progressive Evangelicals to get behind Obama. As the *New York Times* put it, this effort was "the most intensive effort yet by a Democratic candidate to reach out to self-identified evangelical or born-again Christians and to try to pry them away from their historical attachment to the Republican Party."[79] In each instance, the language of faith is not viewed by Party officials as the foundation for social justice or peace, but rather as a way to relate rhetorically to the electorate and mobilizing them to vote. "Outreach" is the name Party leaders have used, but power is the end game. The political goals are different but the *realpolitik* is, in essence, identical to the long-standing instrumentalization of the Christian conservative constituency by the Republican Party—control over the power of the State.

Chapter Five

THE NEO-ANABAPTISTS

THERE ARE SEVERAL POINTS of commonality between the Christian Left and the neo-Anabaptists. First, they share a common antipathy to the human and environmental consequences of an unrestrained market economy and, for some, this is a hostility to capitalism itself—its logic, its organizational structures, its implicit moral character. Second, they tend to share a cultural style by virtue of being upper middle class—better educated, more urban and urbane, and more ironic than the average American Christian. Perhaps most importantly, their discourse reflects a mutual contempt for the Christian Right. These points of commonality are so striking that it is sometimes difficult to distinguish their positions. It further complicates matters that groups like Sojourners, and Jim Wallis himself in times past, have integrated Anabaptist themes within their own. And in practice, many of those attracted to the neo-Anabaptist vision vote in the same ways as the Christian Left.

As a group, the neo-Anabaptists number even fewer than the Christian Left. There is a small but very interesting initiative called the Ekklesia Project that gives expression to many of these commitments. There are also a number of intentional communities and missional orders modeled on Anabaptist principles and values, of which the Potter Street Community in Philadelphia is one of the more prominent.[1] To the extent that one can speak of a popular movement composed of a community of these kinds of communities, it is very small.[2] The distinctions that mark this political theology as an alternative to the Christian Right and Left do have practical implications. As an alternative, however, it is mainly known through its intellectual apologias; it plays out more in theology than in practice, more in political sensibilities than in institutional structures. As a set of commitments for engaging the world, however, it is intellectually serious and that is one reason why it has growing appeal among young Christian adults. It provides a credible, even compelling, script for those who find the account offered by Christian conservatives distasteful if not dangerous and the narrative offered by Christian progressives unconvincing and irrelevant.

The main point of difference between the Christian Left and the neo-Anabaptist position is found in their respective views of the State. The former is committed to a strong State and is willing to press it to realize its agenda in law and policy, while the latter keeps its distance from the State, maintaining a basic distrust toward its structure, action, and use of power.

Myth and History

This distinctive commitment of the neo-Anabaptist becomes clear in light of the mythic ideal that animates the neo-Anabaptist: the ideal of true and authentic New Testament Christianity and the primitive church of the apostolic age. This was central to the origins of the Anabaptist movement in the radical Reformation of the sixteenth century; its rejection of the Roman Catholic Church, on the one hand, and the failures of the mainstream Reformation to go far enough, on the other. One visible manifestation of that authenticity was the rejection of infant baptism and, thus, the *rebaptism* of those who had been baptized at birth (hence, *Ana*baptists). Though there were many types of Anabaptists, the Swiss, Dutch, German, Austrian, and Moravian branches all tended to share a radical congregationalism that rejected apostolic succession and much of the hierarchy of traditional ecclesiology. The succession they sought to perpetuate, rather, was the succession of an authentic Christian congregation whose life, order, and practices were inspired by the witness of Christ and the gospels and the social ethics of the Christian church in the apostolic age—living in simplicity, sharing goods in common, caring for the poor and the widowed, seeking reconciliation, and making peace.[3] It is not incidental to the emergence and development of Anabaptism that first-century Christianity took form not only in a way that was independent of the State, but in a political environment that was hostile to the faith. This opposition was and remains centrally important to the Anabaptist identity and its vision of social and political engagement with the world.

Needless to say, the Anabaptist tradition continues in the "peace churches"—tiny denominations such as the Mennonites, the Brethren, the Quakers, the Amish, and the Hutterites. But the *neo*-Anabaptist vision is not necessarily rooted in these denominations; it rather draws from this tradition a model for a genuine Christian witness in the context of the late twentieth and early twenty-first centuries.

Perhaps no one has been more important in the development of the neo-Anabaptist vision and for making it intellectually respectable than the Mennonite theologian, John Howard Yoder. And within his extensive writings, perhaps no book of his was more important than *The Politics of Jesus*, published in 1972. Yoder's work inspired many others; indeed, some of the most talented theological minds of the generation that followed, including Stanley Hauerwas, Nancey Murphy, Richard Hays, Craig A. Carter, James McClendon, and Michael Cartwright. Hauerwas has been especially influential. Hauerwas's theological debt to Karl Barth has given him a much stronger appreciation for liturgy, the Eucharist, and for catholicity than one typically finds in the neo-Anabaptist tradition, which has also helped to establish several important points of commonality with the "radical orthodoxy" of John Milbank, Graham Ward, Catherine Pickstock, and some of their talented younger American allies such as William Cavanaugh, Daniel M. Bell Jr., and Eugene McCarraher. These points of agreement are striking enough and the spirit behind them "catholic" enough to see them as kindred movements that aim, at times, for much the same things and reinforce many of the other's objectives. And, as noted, the vision is beginning to find its way into parish life as expressed in initiatives like The Ekklesia Project.[4]

The Constantinian Error, Past and Present

Though it plays out in ways fundamentally different from the Christian Right and the Christian Left, the commitment of the neo-Anabaptist to changing the world may be as strong as the others. The critical reference point for defining the nature and scope of change and thus Christianity's larger engagement with the world is the life of Jesus and the church that followed in the generations immediately after his ascension. From the neo-Anabaptist perspective, Christians fail to understand Jesus at all if they fail to see him other than as he was: an agent of radical social change. Mary, the mother of Jesus, recognized the social and historical significance of the baby she carried the moment Gabriel brought the news of her conception. In her praise to God she declared:

He has shown strength with his arm.
He has scattered the proud in the imagination of their hearts.

He has put down the mighty from their thrones,
And exalted those of low degree;
He has filled the hungry with good things,
And the rich he has sent away empty. (Luke 1:51–53)

Jesus himself began his public ministry by reading passages from Isaiah 61.

He has anointed me to preach good news to the poor,
He has sent me to proclaim release to the captives;
And recovering of sight to the blind;
To set at liberty the oppressed,
And proclaim the acceptable year of the Lord. (Luke 4:18–19)

It was an audacious claim. Those who heard his message understood that the "acceptable year of the Lord" was the year of jubilee mentioned in Leviticus 25, a Sabbath year when, among other things, all the debts accumulated through the years would be forgiven and slaves would be freed.

In the most rudimentary ways, Christ's life and ministry were a declaration that the present world order would be turned upside down. Within the neo-Anabaptist vision, the obligation to engage the world by his followers would be no less radical.

But, with a few exceptions, the actual record of the church's history is anything but radical. With the conversion of Constantine and then the Edict of Milan in AD 313, came a rapprochement between piety and power that compromised the church's distinctiveness and thus its inimitable witness to the world.[5] The Constantinian error has been fatal in many ways. Rather than challenging the principalities and powers, the people of God became united with the powers; rather than proclaiming the peace, the church embraced an ethic of coercion, power and, thus, violence; rather than resisting the power of the state, the church provided divine legitimation for the state, which has invariably led to the hubris of empire, conquest, and persecution; rather than modeling a new kind of society, the church imitated the social structures of hierarchy and administration; rather than being a servant to the poor and the oppressed, the church has been complicit in wielding economic and political power over the poor and the oppressed.

Constantinianism is a multifaceted heresy that has surfaced and resurfaced throughout history. In late antiquity, Christianity moved from preferential status under Constantine in the early fourth century to the religion of the empire under Theodosius in 391. Augustine himself called on the Roman government in the early fifth century to squash the Donatist movement, which meant that Christians were now legally persecuting other Christians through the power of the state. Constantinianism was reinvented in the Reformation of the sixteenth century. Now it existed on a regional level that laid the groundwork for warfare among various Christian nations (i.e., the Thirty Years' War). The error of Constantine was reinvented yet again in the age of nationalism, even when there was a formal disestablishment of church and state. The archetype of this neo-Constantinianism was the founding of the American republic, where an informal establishment of Christianity became the basis of all of the nation's governing institutions.[6] To the extent that Christians still seek to bring together the witness of the church with the power of the state—as it does with the contemporary Christian Right and Christian Left—it reformulates and perpetuates this ancient heresy. Even when the church distances itself from formal alliances with the political establishment but still operates within civil society, it engages a version of the Constantinian alliance. The reason is that civil society is not a free space independent of the State's coercive and compromising reach. The State has permeated civil society to such an extent that the two are mostly indistinguishable. Indeed, the State has effectively co-opted any efforts in education, science and technology, human welfare, and the professions to effectively prohibit them from acting contrary to the State's interests.

As the Radical Orthodox theologians have helped to show, the Constantinian error now even extends beyond the State to the way the church has established alliances with all the dominant institutions of late modernity, most importantly the complex amalgam of institutions that comprise global capitalism. The reason this is important is that we now live at a time when the power of the state has declined relative to the market and in this context, international capitalism and the technological innovation that drives it have become every bit as oppressive as the state.[7] How is capitalism oppressive? Beyond the obvious failure to provide adequately for the needs of the poor and disadvantaged, its more significant problems derive from its success.[8] In short, when it is working well, capitalism deforms and corrupts human desire, turning it into the insatiable appetite for more and more. Augustine was right in his observations that desire and the continual renewal of desire is part of our nature as human beings. The problem is that our desires continue to fall on objects that distract us from our chief desire and the longing for which we were made: the desire for God. Absent God, all other desire, by necessity, will fail to fully satisfy us. Under the conditions of modern capitalism, prosperity and consumption become ends in themselves and, thus, the source of idolatry. The net effect, as Eugene McCarraher puts it, is that "American capitalism cheapens life, denatures liberty, and perverts our happiness. Capitalism, I submit to you, is the political economy of the culture of death, and the business corporation is its bogus ecclesial vehicle."[9] The coercive power of modern capitalism resides in the fact that it has no common ends, only a "coincidence of individual ends," and in the absence of an objective idea of the common good, all that remains is power in pursuit of profit. This power is manifested most clearly in the manipulation of desire through marketing and the inequitable and often exploitative power exercised by corporate management over workers. The Constantinian error here is that American Christianity has whole-heartedly and uncritically embraced its logic and practices to its own detriment and the detriment of the world it seeks to serve.

For the neo-Anabaptists, it is within the logic of the Constantinian error, though in its varied manifestations, that we understand the injury the church has done to itself.[10] The problem today is that the American church is caught up in a dual allegiance to both Christ and the political economy of liberal democracy and consumer capitalism. Loyalty to this political economy is nothing less than idolatry. It signals that the church has fallen away from grace and is now under submission to "a yoke of slavery."[11]

The consequences have been disastrous. In the case of American Catholicism, for example, "Catholics of the professional and managerial classes have been in the vanguard of the American *aggiornamento* and they now set the tone for much of the Catholic Church in the United States. Their participation in the national culture of expertise, consumption, and therapeutic spirituality marks the triumph of a new American Catholic religious culture: a Starbucks Catholicism embodied in a Church Mellow."[12] Protestantism has fared no better.[13] In Hauerwas's view, it is not surprising that "God is killing Protestantism and perhaps Christianity in America and we deserve it."[14] Overall, Michael Budde summarizes, "few people inside the churches seem eager to admit it, but in matters of human allegiance, loyalty, and priorities, Christianity is a nearly complete, unabashed failure. . . . The twentieth century provides too many examples of Christian failure to consider any other conclusion."[15] The most egregious harm is done by conservative theologians—Protestant and Catholic—who continue to justify the Constantinian project, misleading the church along the way. "What is to be done?" McCarraher asks.

> First, we must demolish unrelentingly the illusions promulgated by [Michael] Novak, [Jean Bethke] Elshtain, [George] Weigel, [Richard John] Neuhaus, and other embedded Christian intellectuals. Whether ignorant or heedless of American hubris, they sanitize their accounts of the imperial order; pervert the critical intelligence of Christian

faith; and bivouac in the discursive parameters drawn by the corporate regime. Stale and obscurantist, their rendering unto Official Sources merits rebuke and inattention. It's time for regime change among Christian intellectuals.[16]

Radical Christology, the Church, and the Powers

In the neo-Anabaptist view, the only hope for the church to properly engage the world is to recognize anew the messianic identity and mission of Jesus Christ. His incarnation was the beginning of a new moral, spiritual, and political order that would restructure the social relations among the people of God. It would be a new form of human community leading a new way of life. To declare the lordship of Christ, then, is not just to see his relevance for how the church should engage the world, but his centrality for that task; his life, death, and resurrection is not just illustrative for the church's relation to the world, but normative, the final standard that defines the church's existence and by which the church should act. The statement, "Jesus Christ is Lord," Yoder once observed, is not a statement about inner piety or intellect or ideas but about the nature and structure of the cosmos.[17]

What was the nature and meaning of his lordship? To begin, Jesus endured suffering as one who was innocent. The cross—the reality and the symbol of suffering—was the culmination of the life of one who being equal with the Father became man, who selflessly served the needs of others, who tolerated the insults, envy, hatred, and torture of his adversaries and yet who also loved and prayed for his enemies, and who finally bore the sins of the world. He had the power to resist his fate but willingly sacrificed himself as the Lamb of God. The way of the "suffering servant," then, is not only the way into the Kingdom of God, it was the essence of the Kingdom.[18] As he told the disciples who were quarrelling over who was the greatest, "the greatest among you should be like the youngest, and the one who rules like the one who serves."[19]

The new humanity he modeled also entailed a rejection of coercion and violence. In the setting of first-century Palestine, the temptation to join with the zealot insurgency in their resistance to Roman rule was ever present. Some of his disciples wondered if he were aligned with them. Yet Jesus consistently resisted the temptation of force. His pacifism was reaffirmed in word and action throughout his ministry, but not least in the hour of his greatest danger. At his arrest, he rebuked the disciple who struck the servant of the high priest, saying, "all who draw the sword will die by the sword. Do you think that I cannot call on my Father and he will at once send me more than twelve legions of angels?"[20]

Not least, Jesus modeled an alternative relationship with the reigning powers of the day. For Yoder, this was hinted by the way Jesus responded to the second of the three temptations he faced from Satan recounted in Luke 3:21–24. The temptation was political in nature: the offer to rule over the whole world if he only submitted to the Tempter. In another context, he stated plainly that one should "render unto Caesar what is Caesar's; and render unto God what is God's." The temptation to exercise political power was always present and, in each case, he rejected it. More importantly, Jesus challenged and overcame "the powers."

The concept of "principalities and powers" bears some further reflection because of its importance to the neo-Anabaptist tradition.[21] The concept refers to the institutional or systemic patterns of thought, behavior, and relationship that govern our lives and the spiritual realm that animates them. They were originally part of the created order and as such, were good. They were intended to mediate the creative purposes of God in the world, but like us they are now fallen. Rather than reflecting truth, they became adversaries of the truth. Rather than serving the aim of human flourishing, they came to dominate, coerce, and enslave humankind by claiming for themselves absolute power. They are "the rulers of this age" (1 Cor. 2:6). The power they wield is, at its source and in its consequences, demonic in character. Yet at this point one finds a paradox, for even in their fallen state, the powers function to maintain order in society. In this task the powers have their own mandate that still operates within God's permissive will. Even in the fallen world, as Hendrikus Berkhof explained, "they still undergird human life and society and preserve them from chaos. But by holding the world together, they hold it away from God, not close to Him."[22] The powers do give unity and direction to individual and social life, yet in this unity and direction, they also separate people from the true God. "They let us believe that we have found the meaning of existence, whereas they really estrange us from true meaning."[23]

Take government, for example. In the context of the fallen world, the ends of government become distorted and its authority is corrupted. The result is an institution that has become an end in itself and thus an idol that both seduces and enslaves through its power. In its claims to freedom, peace and justice, it promulgates a false theology of redemption to the world. It is false not only because it offers itself and its best ideals as a substitute for God but also because its ideals can only be realized through force and the appeal to force. And yet God still permits human government to exist and, in existing, it functions to restrain human evil.[24]

Even so, as Yoder argues, if God "is going to save man in his humanity, the Powers cannot simply be destroyed or set aside or ignored. Their sovereignty must be broken. This is what Jesus did, concretely and historically, by living among men a genuinely free and human existence. This life brought him, as any genuinely human existence will bring any man, to the cross."[25] As he puts it elsewhere, "the triumphant affirmation of the New Testament is that Jesus Christ by His cross, resurrection, ascension, and the pouring out of His Spirit, has triumphed over the powers."[26]

What does Christ's life and witness mean for the people of God? As Berkhof puts it, with Christ,

> a new force has made its entry on the stage of salvation history: the church. . . . The very existence of the church, in which Gentiles and Jews. . . . live together in Christ's fellowship, is itself a proclamation, a sign, a token to the Powers that their unbroken dominion has come to an end. . . . All resistance and every attack against the gods of this age will be unfruitful unless the church herself is resistance and attack, unless she demonstrates in her life and fellowship how men can live freed from the Powers.[27]

If Christ has overcome the powers, then the task of the church is to proclaim it and to live it out. This task certainly finds expression in the personal life of the believer but for the neo-Anabaptist, its primary expression is collective. It is as an alternative community that manifests a new form of social relations. Ecclesiology, then, is the form by which engagement with the world takes place.[28]

Individually and collectively, discipleship entails a sharing in Christ's indiscriminant, sacrificial love but especially on behalf of those in need, subordinating one's own interests on behalf of others, and dying to the false gratifications of the world. As the body of Christ, the church is called to share in a life that culminates in the cross. But the cross is not just a personal problem. For Jesus, the cross was a political punishment. When believers are truly imitating Christ, their very existence, not to mention their actions, will be perceived as a threat to the reigning powers. When the church is the church, it will suffer the condescension and hostility of the world for its social and political nonconformity. When that happens, the community of faith should endure it, as Christ did; without defense, without retribution, with active forgiveness.

Implied in this is the commitment to nonviolence. For neo-Anabaptists, pacifism is the fundamental mark of Christian discipleship and the central ethical teaching of the gospel.[29] This traces back to the very character of

Christ himself. Because the love of God, demonstrated through the life and death of Christ, is noncoercive, discipleship also requires a renunciation of violence and a posture of nonresistance to those who do evil. Such an ethical ideal is utterly counter-intuitive by the ways of the world and impossible to live by through one's own wisdom and strength. Yet, as Yoder argues, the impossible ideal becomes possible through the work of Christ and the power of the Holy Spirit.[30]

This is not just a response to the question of war. Anabaptists, of course, are perhaps best known historically for their pacifism in wartime. Yet war is not the central problematic but violence itself—broadly defined. This is why the state figures so prominently within the Anabaptist imagination. The state is the locus of self-legitimating violence and its very existence is defined by the exercise (or the threat of exercise) of coercion. Its power is always manifestly or latently coercive. As such it has the authority to compel citizens against their will and to wage war against other nations.

Pacifism in wartime, then, is symbolic of a more general ethical orientation toward the "principalities and powers." The commitment to nonviolence is paramount; the ethical mandate is always to resist coercion, whether from the state or the market. This also explains why it is that the Anabaptist tradition is foundationally committed to the "free-church" model of voluntary association. The freedom to choose is a demonstration of the absence of coercion. Thus, "the true church is the *free* church."[31]

This is also why neo-Anabaptist writers never state but strongly imply that a true Christian must avoid certain vocations. For some, like Yoder, working for the State is itself potentially problematic. As Yoder puts it, "the function exercised by government is not the function to be exercised by Christians;" "the functions the government did actually ask of its citizens did not include participation in bearing the sword of government;" and "[scripture calls] on the disciples of Jesus to renounce participation in the interplay of egoisms which this world calls 'vengeance' or 'justice.'"[32] Hauerwas is sympathetic to this argument, up to a point. "I maintain that Christians must withdraw their support from a 'civic republicanism' only when that form (as well as any other form) of government and society resorts to violence in order to maintain internal order and external security. At that point and that point alone Christians must withhold their involvement with the state."[33] In a more popular articulation of this matter, Shane Claiborne puts it this way: "How do we run the world as Christians? This question would echo throughout the centuries in questions like, how do I run this profit-driven corporation as a Christian? How can we make culture more Christian? How would a responsible Christian run this war? But Jesus taught that his followers—or even the son of God!—should not attempt to 'run the world.'"[34] In the case of the military, Claiborne is explicit: "It appears as though we are encouraging folks to leave the military," he writes, "that's because we are."[35]

The danger of leadership in any government or corporation is the risk of being complicit in the violence of the powers. The danger of being in positions of political or corporate leadership is twofold. First, leadership in these contexts puts one in a position of power and that power inherently compromises the commitment to noncoercion and it also violates the religious and moral obligation of subordination. Lessons repeated through the Gospels were that Christ's disciples were "to reject governmental domination over others as unworthy of the disciple's calling of servanthood."[36] Following Christ and his example means that the believer should "accept powerlessness."[37] As Yoder explained, "The political novelty that God brings into the world is a community of those who serve instead of ruling, who suffer instead of inflicting suffering, whose fellowship crosses social lines instead of reinforcing them." In sum, the very idea of coercive rule over others is contrary to what it means to be a believer. In these instances, according to Hauerwas, "what is required for Christians is not withdrawal but a sense of selective service and the ability to set priorities. This means that at times and in some circumstances Christians will find it impossible to participate in government, in aspects of the economy, or in the educational system. Yet such determinations can be made only by developing the skills of discrimination fostered in and through the church."[38]

The Church and the World; the Church in the World

Implied in neo-Anabaptist theology and social criticism is a strong antithesis between Christian revelation and the wisdom of the world; between the church and the dominant culture. This is a predisposition shared with the theological movement of Radical Orthodoxy. Yet, where Yoder was trying to lead theology and the church to an anti-Constantinian self-understanding and thus to a recognition of the future of the church in a post-Christian world, recent theological efforts have attempted to go beyond this to a critique of all the cultural forms of secular modernity. The aim, here, is to lead theology and the church to a genuinely *postsecular* self-understanding.

The more basic theological conviction that informs and contextualizes this ethical orientation is a perspective that makes a sharp dichotomy between the church and the world. Following Yoder, Hauerwas, and others, as the church is understood eschatologically, so is the world. The present *aion houtos* or world "is characterized by sin and centered on man; [whereas] the coming *aion* is the redemptive reality which entered history in an ultimate way in Christ."[39] In a more dramatic articulation, Yoder claims that the "world signifies . . . not creation or nature or the universe but rather the fallen form of the same, no longer conformed to the creative intent . . . Over against this 'world' the church is visible; identified by baptism, discipline, morality, and martyrdom."[40] As to the present world order, it has no independent ontological status or homogeneous character but "is at the same time chaos and a kingdom," "a demonic blend of order and revolt."[41] Against this is the "otherness" of the church, a community "called to be now what the world is called to be ultimately. . . . a foretaste of the peace for which the world was made."[42] It follows, then, that in lived-history the people of God are to be "resident aliens," a "Christian colony," an "alien" people," defined by its own purposes and the practices of baptism, servanthood, forgiveness, and the love of enemies.

The central calling of the church is to be a worshipping community. It is in the preaching of the Word, in the observance of sacrament, and in the practice of praise that the church achieves its highest purpose. Its main task day-to-day and year-to-year is the formation of disciples who are capable of participating fully in the life of the church. In this context, ethics—both individual and social—is not about believing the right values or applying the right principles but of obedience to the command to follow Jesus—bearing one's cross, loving and serving as Christ did, and being subordinate as Christ was.

Taking this line of reasoning further, all of the neo-Anabaptists emphasize in their own way that the community of faith is its own *polis*.[43] William Cavanaugh puts it this way: "The earthly city is not a true *res publica* because there can be no justice and no common weal where God is not truly worshipped." For this reason, he writes, "it is the Church . . . which is the true politics."[44] Citizenship in the church is true citizenship, one that trumps loyalties in the world. It creates an alternative space in the world and an alternative set of practices against which the world is judged and beckoned. As Hauerwas and Willimon put it, "The church doesn't have a social strategy, the church *is* a social strategy."[45] The church does not have a social ethic, it is a social ethic.[46]

A strong view of the church, then, stands in sharp contrast to a strong view of a corrupted world. This opposition is as central to the neo-Anabaptist view of redemptive history as it was to the Anabaptists of the sixteenth century. What animates this sharp dualism is both the desire to be all that God calls the church to be and the fear that the church will somehow be contaminated by worldliness and complicit in its corruption.

There is a separatist impulse at work here. Within the neo-Anabaptist conversation there is some dispute over *how* separatist it should be. Hauerwas doesn't want people to withdraw from the world as much as he wants people to *be* Christian in it.[47] What this means is left unclear. Younger voices, however, contend that Hauerwas is not nearly sectarian enough. For example, Robert Brimlow states: "My difficulty with Hauerwas is precisely the opposite of most of his critics: he is not quite sectarian enough."[48] As he explains,

> we need to reflect upon Hauerwas' contention that we ought to continue our involvement in social and political affairs and at least raise troubling questions about the extent of our involvement and how that is consistent with our call to be church. And it is important to examine Hauerwas in particular because his theology is otherwise so good that it is crucial for us to understand where he goes wrong and why sectarianism is required for the church.[49]

But wherever neo-Anabaptists come out on this, they all contend that "sectarianism" does not mean that a turning inward will have no outward effect. Indeed, the church is "an instrument of social change" in history and yet only indirectly.[50] The first task of the church, the neo-Anabaptist theologians often say, is to *be* the church. Efficacy, influence, and change are never the ends that define its engagement with the world. "The church will be most effective," Yoder argued, "where it abandons effectiveness and intelligence for the foolish weakness of the cross in which are the wisdom and the power of God."[51] Yet the Christian community exists in large part to serve the world and is, at the same time, "the primary social structure through which the gospel works to change other structures."[52]

Politicization

In a paradoxical way, the dominant language and thus the primary frame of reference for the neo-Anabaptist view of how the church is to engage the world is similar to the Christian Right and the Christian Left. That language and framework is, in a word, politics. Christian ethics comes down to "the politics of Jesus." Jesus himself was a "political figure" and the "model of radical political action."[53] "Christianity is mostly a matter of politics"[54] and thus "the Christian community . . . is a political reality."[55] This is because true Christianity is an expression of "the politics of the cross."[56] It is not a great leap, therefore, toward seeing "liturgy as a political act."[57] In the end, "the church's politics is our salvation."[58] As with the Christian Right and Christian Left, the neo-Anabaptists make no distinction between the public and the political. Indeed, Cavanaugh argues that many efforts to distinguish the public from the political fail because so much of the public is subsumed by the state—its laws, policies, and other instrumentalities.

Yoder goes so far as to argue that the only suffering that has spiritual meaning is political suffering. This is the true meaning of the cross that Christ endured and that those who seek to imitate him must endure as well. "The believer's cross," he argues, "must be, like his Lord's, the price of his social nonconformity."[59] Elsewhere, he explains, "The cross of Calvary was not a difficult family situation, not a frustration of visions of personal fulfillment, a crushing debt or a nagging in-law; it was the political, legally to be expected result of a moral clash with the powers ruling his society. . . . only if their suffering be innocent, and a result of the evil will of their adversaries, may it be understood as meaningful before God."[60] The contention is extraordinary, for it demonstrates the reach of politicization in some neo-Anabaptist thinking. Though the Christian Right and Left may politicize "the cross," even they do not make the sufferings that follow social nonconformity the exclusive way in which Christians meaningfully suffer.

At this point it should be clear that neo-Anabaptists fundamentally redefine the nature of politics and political action.[61] Insofar as the church refuses to operate according to the rules of reigning powers but according to the requirements of biblical obedience, the politics of Christian faith is rightly seen as a "negative intervention" against the dominant powers and their processes of social change.[62] This intervention is negative in the sense that its very existence is a judgment against power structures that are, after the Fall, corrupt by their very nature. The challenge Jesus made to the legitimacy of the ruling authorities of his day were so politically relevant that they put him to death for it.

The problem is that language is never neutral, and its use, consciously or unconsciously, is never innocent. Even though the nature of politics and political action in the church is an inversion of the prevailing powers of the present age, *the language of politics* still provides the meaning for the public witness of the church. In a context in which traditional pragmatic definitions of politics prevail, it is a bit naïve to imagine one can use the word so promiscuously and be free of those traditional and pragmatic meanings. The use of the language of politics is a bid to translate social marginality into social relevance. The problem is that this language comes with all sorts of baggage and it cannot rid itself of this baggage.

The language of politics also provides the structure for the public witness of the church. For one, the active opposition to the powers (to war, globalization, and the like) is ultimately oriented toward changing political, military, and economic policy. Thus, even when the intervention is motivated by a desire to realize God's peace and justice, the framework of operation is still a politics of *this* world. In some respects, neo-Anabaptists politicize their engagement with the world even more than the Right and the Left because they cast their oppositions to the State, global capitalism and other powers in eschatological terms. To literally demonize such powers as the State and the market as they do means that they draw much of their identity and purpose in the here and now through their cosmic struggle with them. Where the identity of the Christian Right is forged largely through their opposition to secularism and secularists, where the identity of the Christian Left derives from their opposition to the Right, the collective identity of the neo-Anabaptists comes through their dissent from the State and the larger political economy and culture of late modernity. Their identity *depends* on the State and other powers being corrupt and the more unambiguously corrupt they are, the clearer the identity and mission of the church. It is, as my colleague Charles Mathewes has put it, a passive-aggressive ecclesiology. The church depends on its status as a minority community in opposition to a dominant structure in order to be effective in its criticism of the injustices of democratic capitalism.[63]

Against the World

This may partly explain why it is that the tone and character of their critique of the world and the church is, in its parts and in its sum, so relentlessly negative. Again, one does find affirmations of the poor and victims of oppression and affirmations of an eschatological church, but little else beyond.

In the writings of the neo-Anabaptist theologians, there is little good in the world that deserves praise and no beauty that generates wonder and appreciation. As to the church, there is much to admire about it as a theological abstraction or, say, as it could be or yet will be. But of the church as it exists in the here and now of history, there is little to admire except in the work of a few exemplary Christians such as Martin Luther King, Mother Teresa, Oscar Romero, Dorothy Day, and their followers. The majority of American Christians and the churches they attend, by contrast, are mostly corrupted by neo-Constantinianism and/or an unthinking rapprochement with global capitalism. The failure of the church is everywhere visible. Hauerwas gives voice to this: though clearly a Christian, Reinhold Niebuhr's account of our knowledge of God is, "little more than a pale theism," his God, a "reflection of ourselves."[64] Richard John Neuhaus's Christianity is at best "politically irrelevant, but at worse is politically immoral."[65] Jerry Falwell "is an idolater when it comes to America."[66] George W. Bush's faith "is the Christian faith of Alcoholics Anonymous."[67] It is no surprise that whether Roman Catholic or Southern Baptist, "the church is always tempted to imitate the habits of those in power."[68] Thus, of the world we live in today, "Christians owe it to themselves and their neighbors to confess that such disorder is but a reflection of the failure of the churches to be faithful."[69] It is no wonder, as previously noted, that "God is killing Protestantism and perhaps Christianity in America."[70] We Christians, Hauerwas contends, clearly do deserve it. The neo-Anabaptists claim their message is prophetic but in its net effect (that is, in what people both inside and outside of the tradition hear), it is overwhelmingly a message of anger, disparagement, and negation. Christianity in America, as it is believed and lived by most believers, is just not Christian enough.

Even at the popular level, the leading message is often one of persistent negation as well. For example, the occasional PAPA Festival is a gathering of neo-Anabaptist communities who come together under the name, "People Against Poverty and Apathy." After many years, the organizers recognized the problem of being known for what they are against but have struggled to find a consensus about what they could be for as reflected in their name.[71] These themes are captured as well by a "liturgy of resistance" advocated by Shane Claiborne.

> With governments that kill . . . we will not comply.
> With the theology of empire . . . we will not comply.
> With the business of militarism . . . we will not comply.
> With the hoarding of riches . . . we will not comply.
> With the dissemination of fear . . . we will not comply.
> But today we pledge our allegiance
> to the kingdom of God . . . we pledge allegiance.
> To the peace that is not like Rome's . . . we pledge allegiance.
> To the Gospel of enemy love . . . we pledge allegiance.
> To the poor and the broken . . . we pledge allegiance.[72]

The pietist and perfectionist tendencies in the Anabaptist tradition are, in large part, the source of their separatist tendencies. (Not sharing in either, this is an important point at which the radical orthodox parts company with the neo-Anabaptist.) But is separatism the same as sectarianism? This argument has been made repeatedly; most forcefully in the contemporary period within the perspective of "Christian realism" given voice by the Niebuhr brothers, H. Richard and Reinhold, but also in the arguments of James Gustafson.[73] Their claim was that Yoder and the neo-Anabaptists articulated a strategy of withdrawal, tribalism, and, therefore, political irrelevance. This accusation, of course, was rejected unequivocally by Yoder when he was alive and is mostly rejected today.[74] The very word "sectarian," the neo-Anabaptists contend, presupposes an acceptance of the standards of the dominant culture. The church, then, only withdraws from responsibility as the world understands it. By existing as an alternative humanity living a different way of life, it constitutes a fundamental challenge to the ways of the world. This kind of lived-proclamation, they argue, does not constitute withdrawal but rather is its primary and most effective form of political responsibility.[75] As Hauerwas puts it, "Rather than disavowing politics, the pacifist must be the most political of animals exactly because politics understood as the process of discovering the good we have in common is the only alternative to violence."[76]

Whether separatism is sectarian or not as theologians define it is not the most important point. (In its net sociological effect, it probably is.) What is more interesting and significant is the character of this separatism. Clearly one sees the continuity of the neo-Anabaptists with the historic Anabaptist tradition, but the particular ways that neo-Anabaptists use the language of politics, their ideological affinities with certain secular movements in late modernity, and their relentless hostility to all that is not God and his ideal church, distinguish neo-Anabaptism as something new; a political theology that reinforces rather than contradicts the discourse of negation so ubiquitous in our late modern political culture.

Chapter Six

ILLUSION, IRONY, AND TRAGEDY

T HE FEAR EXPERIENCED and the injury borne by Christians of all commitments are not rooted in misapprehension but have a basis in the
historical realities of our time. For one, the forces of secularity in contemporary America, within such institutions as higher education, public education,
the news media, advertising, and popular entertainment, *are* very powerful
and their agenda (deliberately or not) *is* fundamentally at odds with traditional Christian morality and spirituality. Whatever positive contributions
one may find in it, much of this secularity *is* a solvent on settled convictions
and ways of life. What remains of a traditional culture, therefore, *is* threatened with extinction, and Christian conservatives are right to worry about
the effects of this on their descendants. It is also true that among various
Christian groups, the Christian Right has held disproportionate political
power since the early 1980s. Their concerns *are* narrowly conceived and do
not at all represent the spectrum of Christian conviction. One result of this is
that the interests and concerns of Christian progressives *have* been eclipsed.
Christian progressives are right to be alarmed and distressed by this situation. By the same token, their fear of a Christian community in America
unthinkingly assimilated to the worst aspects of consumer culture and complicit in the perpetuation of a Constantinian alliance with the secular State
and consumer capitalism is undoubtedly well grounded. The effectiveness of
the church as "salt" and "light" *is* certainly compromised by those alliances,
especially when they proceed without any consideration for the standards of
Scripture and the tradition. The neo-Anabaptists are right to be uneasy with
the present situation. Because the fear experienced is real and the injury borne
is deeply felt, it is not surprising that these Christians want to do something
about it.

What they all do, as we have seen, is to politicize their concerns. This is not all they do but it tends to be the strategy of choice for collective and public engagement. Though there are always changes in the political landscape, the propensity of certain Christian organizations and their leadership to politicize their engagement with the world is not likely to diminish any time soon.[1] For all of the leading voices in Christianity up to now—and in their own way—politics has come to provide the language for thinking about the problems they see. To use Charles Taylor's helpful concept, politics has become a "social imagery" that defines the horizon of understanding and the parameters for action. Myth and history provide narrative context but in each of the three dominant perspectives on the church's engagement with the culture, politics is the way in which social life and its problems are imagined and it provides the framework for how Christians envision solutions to those problems. This is especially true for the largest factions, the Christian Right and the Christian Left, but it is even true for the neo-Anabaptists, whose own compelling but unusual approach is an inversion of the model embraced by the conservatives and progressives. Politics is always and everywhere the framework.

Most people think that what matters is the ideological direction of one's politics. Are you conservative? Are you liberal? These differences occupy most of our attention and argument. What is never challenged is the proclivity to think of the Christian faith and its engagement with the culture around it in political terms. This proclivity today has been both ubiquitous and unquestioned for a long time. Precisely because culture is always most powerful when it is most taken for granted, it brings into relief just how powerful a force politicization is in our time. For all, the public has been conflated with the political. Despite their wide ideological and theological differences, then, Christians have been assimilated to the deeper movements of our culture in remarkably similar ways.

But there is another way in which Christians in America have assimilated the dominant political culture. As I argue in Chapter 2 of this essay, contemporary political culture in America is marked by a *ressentiment* manifested by a narrative of injury and, in turn, a discourse of negation toward all those they perceive to be to blame. Though each expresses this *ressentiment* differently, in different degrees and to different ends, it is present in all of these factions. It is especially prominent, of course, among Christian conservatives, which may be why they have been so effective over the years in mobilizing their rank and file to political action. *Ressentiment* is also centrally present among Christian progressives and it is clearly a major source of their new solidarity and the motive behind their recent assertiveness in Democratic party politics. Both the Right and the Left ground their positions in biblical authority and they both appeal to democratic ideals and practices to justify their actions. But the *ressentiment* that marks the way they operate makes it clear that a crucial part of what motivates them is a will to dominate. The neo-Anabaptists are different in this regard. It is true that they too participate fully in the discourse of negation but domination is not their intent.

The Public Witness of the Church is a Political Witness

It is not an exaggeration to conclude that the public witness of the church today has become a political witness; the public identity of the church is its political identity. In this sense, Hauerwas and Willimon were right when they declared that "Christianity is mostly a matter of politics;"[2] just not in the way that they want it to be.

The fact is that most of the resources and energies of Christians of all traditions go into things *other* than politics—education, social service, spiritual development, and the like.[3] The prominent nature of the Christian community's political witness is in part due to the growth of public affairs associations. Their number and prominence grew quite dramatically since the early 1960s.[4] American Christianity's political witness is also in part due to the increase in media coverage over the last several decades.[5] Not least, of course, are the highly visible ways in which Christians have politicized conflict on a variety of cultural issues. This along with voter registration drives, voter guides, and sermons from across the ideological spectrum organized to mobilize the faithful go far toward eclipsing any public representation of other faith-based ministry.[6] This has had an inevitable effect not only on how Christianity is perceived by non-Christians, but also on Christian leaders and the laity. As contradictory as the intentions and directions of various actors may be, in the end, the Christian Right and Left and the neo-Anabaptists operate with an understanding of the good society through the prism of politics.

But this begs the question, "so what?" Why is this a problem?

Illusion

For the time being we can leave the neo-Anabaptists out of the discussion, for the way they engage politics is quite different from the Right and Left. Their strategy poses other problems we will address later in this chapter and in subsequent chapters. The question "so what?" is most poignantly addressed to the Christian Right and the Christian Left because they operate within the framework of the political establishment in the same ways as the major special interest groups. Here, there are significant problems.

To see these problems one must first recognize the critical distinction and relationship between "democracy" and "the state." Most people assume that the state is subsumed by democracy; that it is the means by which democratic governance occurs. Yet for the better part of the last century, many of the most insightful political and social theorists—including Max Weber, Lewis Mumford, Robert Michels, Michel Crozier, Reinhard Bendix, and Jacques Ellul—have insisted that there is an important distinction between the two, that they are decoupled in important ways and, most importantly, the relationship between them is at odds.

The general perspective of these theorists is that in the modern world, democracy and the state are two different entities that overlap with one another in some ways, but in the end, they each operate according to their own imperatives. Democracy resides in an elected political class and its relation to citizens. This relationship is bound together by a ritual act of popular will that serves the interest of political legitimacy. The state, by contrast, is where the real power resides. The state is a massive, relatively autonomous bureaucratic organization whose purpose is to administer innumerable discrete tasks that make the regime function. Decisions made are filtered through numerous, often-unrelated bureaus staffed by professionals who have their own autonomous (and nondemocratic) decision-making authority. The tasks the state undertakes may be influenced by ideals or values provided by the political class, but those tasks do not embody those ideals. Rather, the tasks that define the actions of the state are administrative in nature and the highest aim is always efficiency.

The importance of specialists in politics is not restricted to governance but it extends into the core rituals and practices of democratic processes—not least of which is the challenge of getting elected. Here too political experts are involved at every level shaping the terms by which candidates present themselves, the positions they take on issues, and so on.

There are two critical implications of this situation. The first is that the state is not subject to electoral will. What this means is that political participation—both for politicians and citizens—is less about the expression of their sovereignty over the state than it is a surrender of their will to various political experts and technicians and the rules they have established. As Jacques Ellul noted long ago, that submission may be accompanied by great devotion to the cause, great prestige from being part of a group, and a great mystique surrounding the personalities who lead, but these are mainly "bromides for the conscience" that distract one from the reality of how much authenticity and freedom of judgment one has actually lost in the bargain.[7] He undoubtedly overstates the case, as he often did, but the contention is more correct than not. In the end, popular sovereignty means less than we might hope. In this light, democracy is led by the bureaucratic necessities of the state arguably even more than it leads and directs the state.

The second implication is that there are no political solutions to the problems most people care about. Politics can provide a platform for dissent and procedures for establishing public order and, as just noted, the state can address administrative problems. This is what it is designed to accomplish, but this only happens through accommodation, compromise, and conciliation. The state can also address some of the legal and administrative aspects of these problems and in this way either help or hinder the resolution of value-based problems. Laws that prohibit discrimination against minorities are one important illustration of the constructive influence of the state. And while politics can only do so much, it is also true that bad politics can do truly horrific things. These are all good reasons to be involved in the work of creating and maintaining good government. The issue is really one of the appropriate expectations one should have of the state and its instrumentalities.

What the state cannot do is provide fully satisfying solutions to the problem of values in our society. There are no comprehensive political solutions to the deterioration of "family values," the desire for equity, or the challenge of achieving consensus and solidarity in a cultural context of fragmentation and polarization. There are no real political solutions to the absence of decency or the spread of vulgarity. But because the state is a clumsy instrument and finally rooted in coercion, it will always fail to adequately or directly address the human elements of these problems; the elements that make them poignant in the first place. As a rule, when the state does become involved in such matters, its actions can often create more problems through unintended consequences, not fewer.

At best, the state's role addressing human problems is partial and limited. It is not nearly as influential as the expectations most people have of it. It is true that laws are not neutral. They do reflect values. But laws cannot generate values, or instill values, or settle the conflict over values. The belief that the state could help us care more for the poor and the elderly, slow the disintegration of traditional values, generate respect among different groups, or create civic pride, is mostly illusory. It imputes far too much capacity to the state and to the political process.

Irony

Values cannot be achieved politically because politics is invariably about power—not only power, but finally about power. *For politics to be about more than power, it depends on a realm that is independent of the political sphere*. It depends on moral criteria, institutionalized and practiced in the social order, that are autonomous from the realm of politics.[8] The problem is that the impulse toward politicization extends to the politicization of values. This means that the autonomy of moral criteria on which a higher practice of politics depends is increasingly lost. Today, most of the ideals and values that are discussed in public have acquired political content and connotation. Fairness? Equity? Justice? Liberty? These have come to have little or no meaning outside of the realm of politics. The other ideals and values that are discussed in public have been largely reduced to instruments for one side or another in the quest for power. Decency, morality, hope, marriage, family, and children are important values but they have become political slogans.[9] The irony, of course, is that no group in American society has done more to politicize values over the last half century, and therefore undermine their renewal, than Christians—both on the Right (since the early 1980s) and on the Left (during the 1960s and 1970s). Both sides are implicated and remain implicated today.

The deeper irony, though, is that in the Christian faith, one has the possibility of relatively autonomous institutions and practices that could—in both judgment and affirmation—be a source of ideals and values capable of elevating politics to more than the quest for power. But the consequence of the whole-hearted and uncritical embrace of politics by Christians has been, *in effect*, to reduce Christian faith to a political ideology and various Christian denominations and para-church organizations to special interest groups.[10] The political engagement of the various Christian groups is certainly legal, but in ways that are undoubtedly unintended, it has also been counterproductive of the ends to which they aspire.

A final irony has to do with the idea of political responsibility. Christians are urged to vote and become involved in politics as an expression of their civic duty and public responsibility. This is a credible argument and good advice up to a point. Yet in our day, given the size of the state and the expectations that people place on it to solve so many problems, politics can also be a way of saying, in effect, that the problems should be solved by others besides myself and by institutions other than the church. It is, after all, much easier to vote for a politician who champions child welfare than to adopt a baby born in poverty, to vote for a referendum that would expand health care benefits for seniors than to care for an elderly and infirmed parent, and to rally for racial harmony than to get to know someone of a different race than yours. True responsibility invariably costs. Political participation, then, can and often does amount to an avoidance of responsibility.

. . . And Tragedy

With the conflation of the history and identity of America with the life and mission of the church (for the Right and the Left), there is a fundamental distortion of theological truth and historical reality. Such a distortion is commonplace in the history of the church and when it occurs, it invariably leads to consequences that are ambivalent at best. With the reduction of the public to the political and the subsequent politicization of so much of human experience, there is an accommodation to the spirit of the age that has made politics the dominant witness of the church to the world. And then there is Christianity's embrace of certain key characteristics of contemporary political culture, a culture that privileges injury and grievance, valorizes speech-acts of negation, and legitimates the will to power. There is variation throughout the Christian community, of course, and yet the loudest public voices are all implicated in this in distinct ways. The problem, though, is especially acute for Christian conservatives.

This last point bears more reflection. To be sure, there is significant spiritual vitality in Christianity in all of its communities, not least within Evangelicalism and Fundamentalism. At the same time, key leaders and factions within American Christianity have cultivated collective identities that are constituted in distinct ways by a sense of injury to the faith and to America itself. The histories from which this narrative are drawn are always selective and sometimes just plain wrong, though, as I have argued, the injuries sustained are not a complete fiction. There is a basis in fact for the claims made by each of these groups. Yet an identity rooted in resentment and hostility is an inherently weak identity precisely because it is established negatively, by accentuating the boundaries between insiders and outsiders and the wrongs done by those outsiders.

Christian leaders, para-church organizations and denominations did not create this political culture, at least not by themselves. These patterns of understanding and engagement are, rather, fixed deeply in the larger structure of contemporary political culture. For example, both established political parties, as David Brooks observed, depend on the culture war for their internal cohesion. The extremists in the parties, he writes, tell themselves that their enemies are so vicious they have to be vicious too. They rationalize their behavior by insisting that circumstances have forced them to shelve their integrity for the good of the country. They imagine that once they have achieved victory through pulverizing rhetoric they will return to the moderate and nuanced sensibilities they think they still possess. But the experience of DeLay and the net-root DeLays in the Democratic Party amply demonstrates that means determine ends. Hyper-partisans may have started with subtle beliefs, but their beliefs led them to partisanship and their partisanship led to malice and malice made them extremist, and pretty soon they were no longer the same people.[11]

The problem is that many prominent Christian leaders and Christian organizations in America have been at the corrupting center of this kind of tribalism, Christian conservatives most prominently. Christians may not have created this tapestry but they are certainly a fabric within it.

What is even more striking than the negational character of this political culture is the absence of robust and constructive affirmations. Vibrant cultures make space for leisure, philosophical reflection, scientific and intellectual mastery, and artistic and literary expression, among other things.[12] Within the larger Christian community in America, one can find such vitality in pockets here and there. Yet where they do exist, they are eclipsed by the greater prominence and vast resources of the political activists and their organizations. What is more, there are few if any places in the pronouncements and actions of the Christian Right or the Christian Left (none that I could find) where these gifts are acknowledged, affirmed, or celebrated. What this means is that rather than being defined by its cultural achievements, its intellectual and artistic vitality, its service to the needs of others, Christianity is defined to the outside world by its rhetoric of resentment and the ambitions of a will in opposition to others.

The neo-Anabaptists are not greatly different in this regard. By no means do they hold or cultivate abhorrence toward life itself. They are anything but Stoics. Nor do they dislike people or nature. It is the social world and its institutions around them that are the problem. *In effect*, theirs is a world-hating theology. It is not impossible but it is rare, all the same, to find among any of its most prominent theologians or its popularizers, any affirmation of good in the social world and any acknowledgement of beauty in creation or truth shared in common with those outside of the church. Rare too are expressions in their public discourse of delight, joy, or pleasure with anything in creation. Their targets are different from those of the Christian Right, but their dominant witness is also a witness of negation, and their language can be as hard and aggressive as that of the Christian Right. Thus, they offer little alternative to the world they critique except the existence of the church itself. This is fine as far as it goes, but its silence toward every affirmation except doxology and Eucharist means that the neo-Anabaptists have little to say to those outside of their own particular (and very small) community besides judgment.

To suffer is one thing; how one bears that suffering is quite another. Among all factions within contemporary American Christianity, one can readily find an anger and resentment about what suffering they do endure. We know, of course, that bitterness can provide its own consolations. For one, it creates a gratifying sense of being winners and on the right side of history. Indeed, one cannot deny that prophetic judgment is a part of the biblical narrative and the tradition of God's people, but is the Kingdom of God to be known predominantly by its negations?

To the extent that collective identity rooted in *ressentiment* has been culti-vated and then nurtured through a message of negation toward "the other," many of the most prominent Christian leaders and organizations in America have fashioned an identity and witness for the church that is, to say the least, antithetical to its highest calling. The political options taken by the Chris-tian Right, the Christian Left, and the neo-Anabaptists are perfectly legal, of course, but that doesn't mean that the way many of them engage their poli-tics is either salutary or constructive. Not least, it creates a dense fog through which it is difficult to recognize each other as fellow human beings and impossible to recognize the good that still is in the world.

The tragedy is that in the name of resisting the internal deterioration of faith and the corruption of the world around them, many Christians—and Christian conservatives most significantly—unwittingly embrace some of the most corrosive aspects of the cultural disintegration they decry. By nur-turing its resentments, sustaining them through a discourse of negation toward outsiders, and in cases, pursuing their will to power, they become functional Nietzscheans, participating in the very cultural breakdown they so ardently strive to resist.

Chapter Seven

RETHINKING POWER: THEOLOGICAL REFLECTIONS

IN 1908 GEORGES SOREL wrote that myths in politics are "a model to which [people] can compare existing society in order to estimate the amount of good and evil it contains." Therefore, they "are not descriptions of things, but expressions of a determination to act."[1] In this light, political myths can be seen as a source of moral energy and enthusiasm—they motivate, they inspire, and they enflame passions to create and even to destroy. Part of what is so powerful about a political myth, according to Sorel, is that "people who are living in this world of 'myths,' are secure from all refutation."[2] What intensifies the power of political myths is the fact that they are often infused with ultimate meaning; and among people of faith, they are often conflated with the ideals of the coming kingdom. This fact makes political myths combustible—as much of a problem as it is a potential for good—for the way they invariably provide other-worldly justifications for this-worldly actions. What, after all, are the concrete actions that our myths justify? We know from history that these actions can either be terrifying in their destructive capacity or salutary, reasonable, wholesome, and beneficial in their creative potential.

The infusion of myth with ultimate meaning is problematic on its own terms but it is especially so in a context where there are competing myths. It is a dilemma made all the more difficult by the fact that the three competing myths discussed here, and the political theologies that derive from them, are all held passionately by people of the same faith community. As such they become the basis of some measure of exclusion and division in the church, especially to the degree that they are embraced uncritically. In the end, the proponents of all three perspectives are able to produce elaborate and sophisticated theological justifications for such division and yet it is for precisely that reason that one should pause to reflect on how much meaning one should impute to politics, political myths, and political ideology in the first place. The fact that politics is pursued today in ways that not only comport (variously) with but also give expression to the nihilism of the dominant culture, provides even more reason to pause and reflect.

Homo Potens

I begin with what appears to be a simple contradiction. When we think of faith, we think of "the hope in things unseen." Faith in God is "other-worldly" in that it looks beyond the practical realm of human affairs to the mysteries of God, his being, and his purposes. By contrast, when we think of power, we think of the harsh, demanding, nitty-gritty forces of human affairs. It is "this-worldly" and its workings are anything but mysterious or transcendent but cold, hard, pragmatic, brutalizing—nearly always unpleasant, except for those who have it. Yet in the story of the people of God through history and their engagement with the culture in which they are placed, power is an important subtext—ever present, always essential. How people engage the world is at least implicitly a question of how they relate to power. Why is this? Why is power inextricable from human experience, and not least, from the experience of those whose life-world orients them to a world beyond the present?

The reason is that power is inherent to our nature as human beings and is part and parcel of human experience.[3] I come to this broad conclusion from the scholarly insights of philosophical anthropology. Human beings have a peculiar relationship to nature and the natural world—one of indeterminacy, an indeterminacy so great that it threatens our very existence. Other species in the animal kingdom have a highly developed instinctual apparatus to direct their actions to ensure their survival. The species *homo sapiens* is, by comparison, "instinctually deprived" and must develop patterns of thinking and acting on their own that will make survival both possible and sustainable. In other words, human beings are, within the boundaries of their biology, "self-determining" and in this way they must make a difference in nature, expending energy to shape nature to make it possible to manage the insecurities and dangers endemic to human existence. That energy expended and that difference made in nature is the most essential expression of power.[4]

Needless to say, power is not just an expression of the relationship of human beings to nature but of human beings to each other. Human beings are constituted and continually formed by the relationships we have with others. And yet human beings have differing capacities to act in the world and to influence the environment around them. It is for this reason that interdependency is built into human experience. We need each other and the abilities and talents everyone brings to make survival possible. But this fact means that power is inherently asymmetrical. Some one, some group, some institutions will always have more capacity to act than others and some one, some group, and some institution will always have a greater capacity to acquire resources than others. Indeed, part of their power is the capacity—at least the potential—to deprive others of the ability to act or accumulate. Cumulatively, this means that human relations are inherently power relations. Power saturates all of social reality and unless a person lives in complete and utter isolation from others and the things they provide, it is impossible to remove oneself from the complex dynamics of power and what power provides. Power, in short, is inherently relational, interactive, dynamically shared, and contentious, and it plays out at every level of society—not just among individuals but among social groups, institutions, and local and national communities.

The most obvious expressions of power are behavioral in nature and we see this through action in the spheres of economics and politics. Power can manifest itself in abusive ways in these spheres, but when it does it is not because power is strong, but because it is relatively ineffective in its cultural manifestations. In other words, power is far more strongly and efficiently demonstrated when it is exercised symbolically and culturally. This is what political scientists call "soft" power as opposed to the "hard" power rooted in the technologies of force. The power that inheres in culture is the capacity to define what is real in all the ways that reality presses against us. What is truth? What is knowledge and legitimate science? What are the goods worth having in life and the ideals worth sacrificing for? What is a family? Legitimate sexuality? Friendship? What is moral behavior? Just action? And by the same token, what is inappropriate and unacceptable behavior and what is abhorrent? The power to define these things, to name them, and to describe their purpose is power of the first order for it portrays the natural and social world in ways that predispose some action versus others. Yet here too, power is asymmetrical. The capacity to define reality varies extensively and those individuals and institutions that have more engage in a kind of "symbolic violence" (or forms of coercion that are effected without physical force) against those who have less.[5] The ultimate expression of this symbolic violence is to so thoroughly define a situation that dissent or opposition becomes unimaginable.

What is power then? Power is not a substance or a property but a facility that is exercised in relation to others as well as, of course, to the natural world. This facility manifests itself through individuals, through social groups of every size, shape and kind, through social structures (the "powers" of which Berkhof speaks)[6], and through our own subjectivity. It is within *every* institution, and not just the institutions of government or market. It is through power that worlds are created—the larger cultures of which we are a part and our own personal worlds shared with those closest to us. Precisely because human beings are by nature social in constitution and habits of life, everyone possesses at least some power and participates in the distribution of varying expressions of power. Power, then, is inescapable. This is not to say that all things significant are related to power or that all things are reducible to power. It is to say that power is ubiquitous. In other words, against the contentions of Nietzsche and Foucault, power and violence have no ontology. Power is not the essence or grounding of social being. It is not, therefore, the only factor to consider in human affairs. Yet it is always a factor that is present. Its use—for good or ill—is a function of the cultural assumptions and narratives through which it is legitimated and exercised. It cannot be evaded or transcended.

Three further observations about power in brief:

The first observation is that power tends to become an end in itself. There are many reasons why power grows and why people want to keep it but mostly it is because of the material, social, and symbolic advantages that accompany it. Studies have shown that even voluntary organizations protect their organizational interests against the interests and needs of the very members they are supposed to serve.[7]

The second observation is that because it is inherently relational and asymmetrical, power always generates its own resistances. It is not something that is exercised exclusively by the mighty against the vulnerable and defenseless with the latter always complying. Even the weak possess the power to challenge, subvert, destabilize, and oppose. It may not be easy and it may even be costly, but the power to act is always present within the relations of power itself.

The third observation is that power always seems to carry with it unintended consequences. For one, the exercise of power is always hard to undo. It tends to act back on those who have it and use it. Thus, when it is objectified in law or institutional practices, it is difficult to reverse, even when the effects are known to be ineffective or harmful. Power is mastery of a sort but it is also self-limitation, what Herbert Rosinski calls "counterpower."[8] Anthropologically speaking, the purpose of the human struggle for power is for human beings to free [themselves] from the multiple bonds of nature. . . . Yet in the very act of freeing himself from these primeval bonds, man sets up new forces whose effect is to threaten his new-found freedom from a totally new angle. The very qualities that enabled him to raise himself so radically above his fellow animals carry within them the threat of a new and even more fateful bondage.[9]

Nowhere is this contradiction more present than in the technologies of power. In the earliest years of human history, the dominant form of power was simply the physical exertions of the human body. In hunting, gathering, and farming, in the work of artisans, and in the acts of protecting oneself and one's community from the ravages of nature, of animals, or of banditry and war, the primary if not only form of energy available to do these tasks was the muscular strength of the body. Of course, human history can be told as a chronicle of the ever more complex and controlling technologies invented to shape nature and the course of human affairs. Such a chronicle shows that the more power we have at our disposal, the more we are distant from its actual workings and the less able we are to control its effects. Once technologies—whether military, economic, managerial, or therapeutic—are established, they have a life and logic of their own that will act back on those who consent to use them.[10]

Theology and Power

These reflections on human beings as *homo potens* may seem a digression from the main argument and yet a survey of contemporary theological discourse reveals that they have not been adequately considered for their implications for political theology. For our purposes, this reflection helps to establish a context or baseline for an alternative view of power, politics, and, more broadly, the Christian engagement with the world.

The utility begins to become clear in reference to the neo-Anabaptist theology of church and society, whose influence in the American context has grown so in recent years. By understanding the nature of power—its ubiquity, its inherent relationality, its inherent asymmetry, and the unintended consequences that nearly always follow its exercise—we see the limitations of and problems generated by the neo-Anabaptist theology of power and politics. It is important to acknowledge at the outset that there is subtlety, nuance, and range in the theological positions of neo-Anabaptism for which a hurried summary cannot do justice. For all of the boldness of their polemic there is also a sophistication that makes it difficult to pin down exactly what pacifism means and what their commitment to pacifism entails. Yoder and Hauerwas, for example, both acknowledge a variety of pacifisms, and motives for pacifism and that power is present in human affairs. Hauerwas and Willimon, in particular, acknowledge that Christians are in a fight.[11] Nor does it mean that Christians disengage from politics.[12] According to Hauerwas, pacifism is the only faithful posture for Christians.[13] Their concern is mainly with violence and coercion and with the principalities and powers that embrace these as strategies of action—whether it be capitalism (since "capitalism is, after all, the ultimate form of deconstruction"),[14] the state ("for the power of the flag is, by necessity, violent"),[15] or pluralism (and its subtle "repressiveness").[16] As Robert Brimlow has written, "Our response to the call of discipleship not only threatens the powers of the world but positively and publicly overthrows them."[17]

In its popular rendering, however, one major thrust of the neo-Anabaptist view is that the mark of true discipleship is to "accept powerlessness."[18] The problem is that on the face of it, "powerlessness" presupposes a truncated theory of power. *Only by narrowing an understanding of power to political or economic power can one imagine giving up power and becoming "powerless."* Against this truncated view, anthropology helps us see that short of living in complete isolation from the world and independent of its resources, the church and its faithful are implicated in nearly every way in the exercise, exchange, and contest of power. Consider the church's relation to the "principalities and powers." Even in a situation where Christians are self-employed, grow their own vegetables, use a wood stove to heat their homes, and send their children to Christian schools, they are still likely to own a car, have electricity, own books, hold small positions in mutual funds, and pay taxes. All of these represent complicity with the structures of power that rule the present age; all of these acts serve to perpetuate those structures. Consider too the church as social organization. Linguistically, the neo-Anabaptists have a preference for speaking of the church as a "fellowship," a "community," and a "gathering" and as such it forms a voluntary society free of coercion. Craig Carter describes it this way:

> The voluntary nature of the community rules out coercion and makes freedom integral to the nature of the community. For Yoder, the distinction between the church and the world allows for the freedom of non-confession, which in turn allows for the freedom of confession. The kind of leadership to be exercised in this community must be different from that exercised in a community based on coercion, such

as the state or the Constantinian church. Servant leadership and voluntary confession are the marks of the community founded by Jesus and are the distinguishing marks of the New Testament doctrine of the church. Only within this kind of community is fellowship based upon love actually possible.[19]

The church certainly is community, fellowship, and gathering, but it is also an institution, and institutions, by their very nature, possess power and exercise power. The church exercises a power within its own social organization in ways that are both symbolic and practical; ideational and material. It does this through the formation of the young, who do not voluntarily choose to become members; through the ongoing education and discipline of its members; and in the distribution of its collective resources. The church also exercises influence in the larger culture. Even in acts of civil disobedience Christians wield an inner-worldly power that may not be violent but is manifestly coercive. Such action cannot help but have pragmatic effects on the distribution and relations of power. With no desire to be cheeky, it is fair to observe that the very theologians and pastors who champion powerlessness have disproportionate life-chances (through salary, status, health care, and opportunities) and symbolic capital that provide them disproportionate material and discursive power. By virtue of their vocation and station, they themselves perpetuate asymmetries in power.

One could go on with other examples, but the point is now obvious: every grammar and every narrative is an imposition; every source of inequality in power is a source of intimidation and force; even love itself has force—for it draws and compels people in ways that they may not desire in themselves. Thus, as long as the church is constituted by human beings and is a human institution, it will participate in the structures of power at work in the world and will exercise a power that is spiritually and ethically ambiguous at best. The perfectionist impulse within the neo-Anabaptist tradition (or any other pietist confessions) is, this side of heaven, fundamentally misleading. Any effort to draw a sharp line between the church and the world cannot help but result in failure. That line is far less distinct than many in the pietistic traditions hope or believe, not least as it bears on matters of power. Simply by virtue of the church's being constituted by human beings, there are dynamics that the church and the world share. The strong, hermetic distinction between church and world made by many neo-Anabaptists is, then, often overdrawn, exaggerated, and false. As it bears on the matter of power, "powerlessness" is a fiction. Even in the political and economic realm, "powerlessness" can only be relative.

What has been argued from anthropology can be argued more straight-forwardly from theology: to be made in the image of God and to be charged with the task of working in and cultivating, preserving, and protecting the creation, is to possess power. The creation mandate, then, is a mandate to use that power in the world in ways that reflect God's intentions. With the Fall, however, the divine nature and potential of human power was com-promised. While Christ's life, death, and resurrection does fundamentally alter the relationship of believers to the "powers" and to power itself, in the time while believers wait for the *eschaton*, power is inherently tainted and its use inherently compromising of the standards to which Christ beckons.

What this means is that faithful Christian witness is fated to exist in the tension between the historical and the transcendent; between the social real-ities that press on human existence and the spiritual and ethical requirements of the gospel; between the morality of the society in which Christian believers live and the will of God. These oppositions are a fact of existence for the church and each Christian believer and they pull in conflicting directions— one toward the necessities of survival and the other toward the perfect will of God. There is no place of equilibrium between these oppositions and no sat-isfying resolutions. In this world, the church can never be in repose. The tension is not lessened by the fact that there are unavoidable ambiguities that inhere in the application of biblical promises, values, and ideals to everyday life. Nor is it lessened by the fact that the love required of the Christian is unlivable, except in flawed approximation.

This is a tension that faith communities throughout history, consciously or unconsciously, have sought to lessen. In our own time, most believers have sought to reduce the tension through denying the opposition between reve-lation and the order of the world. Both theological conservatives and theolog-ical progressives have done this by "Christianizing" their very different ideals of the social order; the former by uncritically associating revelation with tra-ditional social practices and the latter by relativizing revelation in confor-mity to liberal-modernist social practices. Still other believers (mainly the neo-Anabaptist world and other pietists) recognize the tensions but have sought to lessen them by distancing themselves from them. Each of these three postures toward the world becomes the measure of true faithfulness, which is why conservatives, progressives, and pietists all hold the suspicion that the others are not really true Christians. Yet the call "to be in the world but not of it" is a call to abide in the will and purposes of God in the present world disorder with integrity, and the only way to reach for that integrity is to recognize the tension and to reside within it knowing that failure is inevitable, forgiveness is ever available, and the work of the Holy Spirit to transform and sanctify our efforts is always inscrutably at work.

The church is, first and foremost, a worshipping community whose life centers on the word of God. As such it is an *altera civitas*, yet one not so clearly distinct from the rest of the world as some would have it. The reason is that it is also a human institution and its members are part of overlapping communities of relationship and as such—individually and collectively, symbolically, structurally, and spiritually—it possesses power in the world. The question for the church, then, is not about choosing between power and powerlessness but rather, to the extent that it has space to do so, *how will the church and its people use the power that they have*. How will it engage the world around it and of which it is a part?

Toward a Postpolitical Witness in the World: Two Essential Tasks

To acknowledge the inherent and endlessly complex intermingling of Christian practice and worldly power, to acknowledge the inescapable tensions that are present for the church operating faithfully in the world, and to acknowledge the unavoidable failure that awaits even the most faithful Christians who seek to obediently witness to the good news of Christ's kingdom does not mean that they accept things as they are. It certainly does not mean that the Religious Right or Left has an appropriate relationship to power. It does mean believers must press ahead to find or, perhaps better put, rediscover a better relationship to power and the powers. It also means, from the outset, that Christians must operate with as much grace and forgiveness as possible because failure to use power rightly is, as I say, unavoidable.

More will be said about a constructive relationship between power and Christian practice, but before getting there, it is important to lay out two essential tasks. There may be other charges to dispatch as well but these two very practical tasks are prerequisite to moving constructively toward a postpolitical Christian witness.

The first task is to disentangle the life and identity of the church from the life and identity of American society. The neo-Anabaptists are right about the problems that attend the close association of the two. As it applies to the Constantinian associations of the church with the nation-state and political economy, their criticisms are mostly correct and little more needs to be added. For conservatives and progressives alike, Christianity far too comfortably legitimates the dominant political ideologies and far too uncritically justifies the prevailing macroeconomic structures and practices of our time. What is wrong with their critique is that it doesn't go far enough, for the moral life and everyday social practices of the church are also far too entwined with the prevailing normative assumptions of American culture. Courtship and marriage, the formation and education of children, the mutual relationships and obligations between the individual and community, vocation, leadership, consumption, leisure, "retirement" and the use of time in the final chapters of life—on these and other matters, Christianity has uncritically assimilated to the dominant ways of life in a manner dubious at the least. Even more, these assimilations arguably compromise the fundamental integrity of its witness to the world.

Be that as it may, the way in which Christians assimilate to the political culture is just an extension of its assimilation to all of culture and the ways of life it lays down as normal. Its lack of critical distance and reflection about politics is an extension of its failure to critically reflect about the rest of the world they inhabit. In the case of politics and political culture, the Christian community has indeed linked its own future to the success of certain political myths, ideologies, and agendas. Though leaders on the Right and on the Left may plausibly deny that this is a problem for themselves, the realities of this linkage for the movements they lead are sociologically undeniable. To be sure, it would be impossible to completely disentangle the church from any society in which it is found. Christians, like all human beings, are constituted by the particularities of their time and culture, and it is only natural that they should identify with their communities and nation. But on all fronts, the merging of faith and politics/culture is deeply problematic. It is time for a disentangling.

The second task is for the church and for Christian believers to decouple the "public" from the "political." Politics is always a crude simplification of public life and the common good is always more than its political expression. As we have seen, the expectations that people place on politics are unrealistic for most of the problems we face today are not resolvable through politics. That, however, is not the most serious problem. Far more grave is the way politicization has delimited the imaginative horizon through which the church and Christian believers think about engaging the world and the range of possibilities within which they actually act. Politics is just one way to engage the world and, arguably, not the highest, best, most effective, nor most humane way to do so. This does not mean that Christians shouldn't "vote their values" or be active in political affairs. It is essential, however, to demythologize politics, to see politics for what it is and what it can and cannot do and not place on it unrealistic expectations. It cannot realize the various mythic ideals that inspire different Christian communities, it cannot even reduce the tension that exists between the concrete realities of everyday life and the moral and spiritual ideals of the Kingdom of God. At best, politics can make life in this world a little more just and thus a little more bearable.

Indeed, precisely because the dominant public witness of the church is a political witness, often of the crudest, most manipulative, and arrogant kind, there are good reasons to keep politics at arm's length. Put differently, it would be salutary for the church and its leadership to remain silent for a season until it learns how to engage politics and even talk politics in ways that are non-Nietzschean.

To decouple the public from the political will open up other options for engaging the world and addressing its problems in ways that do not require the state, the law, or a political party. There are innumerable opportunities not only in art, education, the care for the environment, and the provision of relief for the widow, orphaned, and sick, but in the market itself to engage the world for the better. Efforts in these directions could entail significant outlays of time, money, and moral commitment, but the consequences for the common good would be extraordinary. To decouple the public from the political will not necessarily address the problem of the will to power and the belligerent ways in which it is pursued. There are those who would approach culture in the same way that they approach politics[20] and, if they have their way, their efforts will be as ruinous to culture as they have been to politics. But the will to power is a problem of a different order. The task of decoupling the public from the political is a challenge first of the imagination and then of practice. Such a task, if successful, would isolate the coercive power wielded by the state thereby opening up other options, making other types of power imaginable.

Some argue that what we need is a redefinition of politics, one that is more capacious and capable of absorbing actions, ideas, and initiatives that are independent of the State. The idea here is to reclaim or restore a "proper" understanding of the political. Such efforts would, in principle, accomplish the same end as I am describing here. This position is certainly worthy of serious debate but as a sociologist who is attentive to the power of institutions, I am inclined to think that all such efforts will be swallowed up by the current ways in which politics is thought of and used. It is why I continue to think that it is important to separate the public from the political and to think of new ways of thinking and speaking and acting in public that are not merely political.

All in all, these tasks and the problems they seek to address are massive, but it is difficult to imagine that progress can be made toward achieving a better understanding of power and a better engagement with the world until these two tasks are addressed. They create the conditions through which other ways of thinking and acting publicly are possible.

Jesus and "Social" Power

If the question is not about choosing between power and powerlessness, then how will the church and the people of God use the power that they have? Christology is the heart of any method for thinking about the church and its engagement with the world and so the starting point is Jesus Christ, the first-born of the New Creation, the living embodiment of the new Kingdom.

First, a caveat: what follows here is neither a systematic nor a comprehensive study of Jesus and power. Beyond a few passing comments, it will not address the question of the spiritual power—the power of sin in the world and in people's lives and the power of Christ to triumph over sin. Neither will it address the important but often tedious relationship between Christian faith and the power of government and of civil society. All of these issues have been explored and commented on before with great insight by numerous biblical scholars and theologians.

The concern here is narrower. Operating with the wider, postpolitical understanding of power on which we have been reflecting, my interest is to review the core teachings of Jesus as they bear on the matter of "social power" or "relational power," the power one finds in ordinary life. It is exercised every day in primary social relationships, within the relationships of family, neighborhood, and work in all of the institutions that surround us in daily life and therefore it is far more common to people than political power. Political power, for most, impinges concretely on everyday life but it tends to be experienced as an abstraction. Not so with social power. For those individuals, communities, and institutions that aspire to follow Christ and his teachings, what are the most vital lessons to be learned about the use of this kind of power?[21]

Much of the gospel story, of course, can be read as a commentary on Christ's relationship to power and "the powers" generally. Consider the period of Christ's temptations in the wilderness at the start of his ministry. Here Satan offered to Jesus "all the kingdoms of the world and their splendor" (Matt. 4:8). Satan's implicit claim was that he possessed a ruling authority in and over the world. The biblical narrative makes clear that the scope and time of Satan's power were limited by God's sovereignty, and yet within those parameters he declared that power in the world was his to wield. Importantly,

Jesus did not take issue with this claim. Indeed, Christ himself called the evil one "the prince of this world" (John 12:31; 16:11). This is a description that Paul, in his letter to the Corinthians, asserts as well, describing Satan as "the god of this world" (2 Cor. 4:4). It is also an account affirmed by John's first letter where he declares, "that the whole world is under the control of the evil one" (1 John 5:19.)

If this reading is right then the spirit that animates worldly power—whether held by individuals, social groups, communities, institutions, or social structures—naturally tends toward manipulation, domination, and control. Rooted in the deceptions of misdirected desire, it is a power that in its most coarse expressions would exploit, subjugate, and even enslave. Within a fallen humanity, then, all power is tainted, infected by the same tendencies toward self-aggrandizing domination. The natural disposition of all human power is to its abuse.[22]

It is this power and the spirit that animates it whose sovereignty Christ came to break.[23] Paul writes that it was through the cross that Christ "disarmed the principalities and powers and made a public example of them, triumphing over them in him" (Col. 2:13–15). Through his suffering, death, and resurrection, Christ laid bare the illusions on which worldly power was based. The most basic of these illusions was that the distorted realities of this world are ultimate realities and the powers by which they are established and legitimated are there by right and cannot and should not be challenged. Another way to put this is that the principalities and powers posit an ontology of necessity—that reality is what it is and it cannot be changed. It goes even further when it makes necessity a virtue, claiming, in effect, that reality is as it should be and therefore should not be changed. But the incarnation of God through Christ changed all of that. His birth was *the* world-historical event that ruptured the established structures of power—spiritual, cultural, social, and political—and inaugurated a new reality for humankind. Through his very life, he exposed the true nature of these powers as forces inimical to God's purposes in creation. In his crucifixion, Christ disarmed all forms of worldly power and in his resurrection, he triumphed over them and by so doing, made it possible for those who believe to be liberated from them and to participate in the reality of his kingdom.

He could only accomplish this extraordinary feat by embodying and exercising a fundamentally different kind of social power. What were its distinctive features? There were at least four characteristics.

First, his power was derived from his complete intimacy with and submission to his Father. In John's Gospel, Christ declared, "For I have not spoken on my own authority, but the Father who sent me has himself given me a commandment—what to say and what to speak. . . . What I say, therefore, I say as the Father has told me" (John 12:49–50). In this, he pursued his Father's will in his Father's way: "the Son can do nothing of his own accord, but only what he sees the Father doing. For whatever the Father does, that the Son does likewise. . . . I can do nothing on my own. . . . I seek not my own will but the will of him who sent me" (John 5:19, 30). And again, "I do nothing on my own authority, but speak just as the Father taught me." "I speak of what I have seen with my Father" (John 8:28, 38). "The words that I say to you I do not speak on my own authority, but the Father who dwells in me does his works" (John 14:10). Paul himself reflects on Christ's "reverent submission" and how Christ "learned obedience from what he suffered" (Heb. 5:7–8). Christ's intimacy with and submission to his Father was demonstrated in his response to the temptations he faced in the wilderness.[24] All three temptations sought to entice him to assert his own authority; what was rightfully his but in ways that were not according to his Father's will. He was weak, his strength diminished from having fasted forty days and nights. He was not a stoic but acknowledged his hunger. In such unimaginable vulnerability, it must have been supremely tempting to demonstrate that he was the Son of God by turning stone into bread, by calling on the angels to miraculously save him, and by taking the kingdoms of this world for his own. We know from the feeding of the five thousand later in his ministry, that he actually possessed and used these powers; but to have yielded to these temptations would have been to use his power at the wrong time, in the wrong way, and for the wrong purposes.[25] He would have been acting on his own authority and not his Father's. Christ abided in his Father's love, depended on him, and trusted him. It was in submission to his Father that he rejected each temptation, instructing Satan from Scripture not to "put the Lord God to the test" and to "worship the Lord your God and serve him only" (Matt. 4:1–10). As commentator Alfred Plummer notes, Christ "refuses to work a miracle which God has not willed, in order to effect what God has willed."[26] Thus, it was because he yielded his own will to his Father's in this circumstance and through his whole life and death that "all authority in heaven and on earth" was given to him (Matt. 28:18).

A second characteristic of the social power exercised by Christ was his rejection of status and reputation and the privilege that accompanies them. Paul summarizes this point concisely in his letter to the Philippians. Christ, he writes,

> being in very nature God, did not consider equality with God something to be grasped, but made himself nothing, taking the very nature

of a servant, being made in human likeness. And being found in appearance as a man, he humbled himself and became obedient to death—even death on a cross!" (Phil. 2:6)

One way to begin to understand the significance of this passage is through the dynamics of power in everyday life. To be sure, wealth and political will are important sources of power but in social life, these are no more important than status, the good opinion of others. Reputational capital, as argued in Essay I, is a form of symbolic power, and people are every bit as much, if not more acquisitive, protective, and ruthless about it as they are about wealth. One can have wealth and political connections but will be quite alone and less effective without the high regard of others, what we call status or prestige. One of the most common practices of rich and poor alike is to use whatever wealth is available to improve social standing, through the consumption of goods that carry status. This is why it is essential to see the dynamics of status and prestige as part of the "principalities and powers" of which both Christ and Paul speak.

This was, in large part, what Jesus self-consciously repudiated in his rejection of worldly power. Not only did the second person of the Trinity voluntarily bear the humility of becoming a man, but as a man, he took on the nature of a servant. At no time was this more poignantly symbolized and demonstrated than when he washed his disciples' feet. As recorded in John's Gospel, he did this knowing at the time fully who he was, "that he had come from God and was going back to God" (John 13:3). In his humanity, Christ clearly understood the indignity of the act. He was aware of the status degradations he was submitting himself to and the loss of social standing and reputation that he endured by doing so. The disciples did as well, which is why Simon Peter protested even the suggestion that his Lord would wash his feet. How could the Messiah do something so demeaning? Yet he embraced these humiliations fully and gladly, never using the power he had to burnish his reputation. And he took it further. As Paul wrote to the Philippians, Christ endured an even more degrading loss of social regard when, though innocent, he submitted to the kind of torture and death reserved for common criminals.

Those degradations he endured willingly because of his love for fallen humanity and for his creation more broadly. This is the third characteristic of Christ's power and the most often noted. Compassion defines the power of his kingdom more than anything else. It was the source, the means, and the end of his power. In principle, the power of love can sound vague and trite, but it took practical form in his everyday service to others. In his own words Christ declared that "even the Son of Man came not to be served but to serve, and to give his life as a ransom for many" (Mark 10:45). We know that there is a way of giving of oneself that is self-conscious, manipulative, and self-serving, but his was rooted in a compassion for real persons—and not just an abstract idea of humanity—that was self-effacing and even self-forgetful.

In the passage from Philippians quoted above, the phrase "made himself nothing" (from the English Standard Version), does not do justice to the text. Other translations come closer by translating it "emptying himself." This is one of the key passages to the doctrine of *kenosis*, a metaphysical puzzle about the nature of God and the interrelationship of the three parts of the Trinity. One need not go into these theological mysteries to see that whatever else it may mean, a plain reading of the text leads to a description of Christ as one who poured himself out on behalf of others.

In this regard, the most obvious illustration is Christ's sacrificial suffering and death. This is true, of course, but focusing on this exclusively obscures the self-emptying love that took place in the course of his day-to-day ministry where the costs could be measured in the time, attention, effort, and resources he gave to address the needs of others—caring concretely for those who were fearful, hungry and thirsty, poor, humiliated, despised, demon-possessed, discriminated against, confused, blind, sick, paralyzed, diseased, and dying. Rather than grasping for position for himself in various social relationships or seeking to defend his own security and privilege, he indiscriminately gave of himself that which was most fundamental to his own giftedness and vocation.

It is not incidental to his compassion that both the healing and teaching aspects of Christ's ministry were integrated. The authority that animated both and the purposes to which they were oriented were joined together in ways that brought about the integrated restoration of mind, body, and spirit—new understanding, renewed health, and reconciliation with God. As David Prior observes, "His power in healing was not to show power over people but to release them for greater effectiveness—as a servant by his actions seeks to enable his master to be better equipped for his daily life."[27] The compassion that defined his power was concrete, specific, and substantial, and it came from the core of his own gifts and calling.

A fourth characteristic of the social power exercised by Christ was the noncoercive way in which he dealt with those outside of the community of faith. The starting point is that Christ made his kingdom available to all. Though he had particular compassion for the social outcast, the rule of his kingdom was offered without prejudice to everyone: men, women, young, old, servant, master, slave, freeman, Jew, Samaritan, Gentile. Christ made himself a slave to *all*—and the benefits of his ministry were for the good of everybody.

His power vis-à-vis Jews and non-Jews alike was noncoercive. His dealings with the Samaritans is instructive here. Samaritans were an ethnic minority and religious hybrid who had tangled roots within the twelve tribes but who were also outside of the mainstream beliefs and ritual practices of Judaism. To the Jews at the time of Jesus, Samaritans were socially, religiously, and racially inferior; second-class citizens at best. Merely associating with Samaritans was socially contaminating. This helps to explain why, in John 8:28, when the religious leaders sought to denigrate Jesus, they accused him of being a Samaritan. Yet Christ's disposition toward the Samaritans was always one of blessing. There was the parable of the "good Samaritan" (Luke 10:30–37), the one grateful leper of the ten he healed (Luke 17:12–19), and the Samaritan woman at the well (John 4:7–26). And then there is the instance of the Samaritan village that rejected him simply because he was a Jew (Luke 9:51–56). His disciples James and John were furious and wanted to retaliate. In their anger they asked, "Lord, do you want us to tell fire to come down from heaven and consume them?" Christ, in response, simply "turned and rebuked them, and they went to another village."[28] James and John had not yet learned the nature of God's power in his new kingdom. Violence, coercion, and revenge were never legitimate means for bringing about God's purposes. As Jesus taught in the Sermon on the Mount, "Do not resist an evil person. If someone strikes you on the right cheek, turn to him the other also." And also, "love your enemies and pray for those who persecute you" (Matt. 5:39, 44). This was a sentiment reinforced by Peter, who exhorted believers not to repay evil for evil or abuse for abuse, but to repay evil with a blessing (1 Pet. 3:9).

His relationship vis-à-vis the pagans he encountered in his life and ministry—the Roman rulers, soldiers, and other functionaries—was also one of unequivocal blessing. He blessed the centurion by healing his paralytic servant (as told in Matt. 8 and Luke 7), he blessed the ruler (mentioned in Matt. 9) by raising his daughter from the dead, he blessed the "official" (recounted in John 4) by healing his sick son, he blessed the despised Zacchaeus by sharing dinner with him (as told in Luke 19). Even at the time of Jesus's arrest, he healed the soldier Malchus, whose ear had been cut off by one of his disciples (Luke 22). Even through his imprisonment, derision, and torture (recounted in Matt. 27, Luke 23, Mark 15, and John 19), he didn't condemn, judge, or strike back, but rather blessed by asking his Father to forgive those who were to kill him.

In the present world disorder, some types of coercion are probably inevitable. Even for the Christian, coercion is unavoidable because at times it is necessary, as, say in the defense of the defenseless; a means to achieve a lesser of various evils. But even then it cannot be justified "in the name of Jesus" or put forward as "the Christian way" because force and coercion are not a part of and cannot bring about the kingdom of God.

Conclusion

One of the consequences of framing discussions of power in political terms is that it removes the discussion from the power that operates in everyday life. It is perhaps an unintentional strategy of avoidance of what most people deal with day in and day out. Discussions of political power focus attention on those people and structures with whom the average person has little to do. The "kingdoms of this world" referred to in Luke 4:5 include politics and economics, of course, but they also include every sphere of social authority and influence that form the dominant realities of everyday life for most people.

The Son of God was the new Adam. He was both the actual presence and the harbinger of a new kingdom. Everything about his life, his teaching, and his death was a demonstration of a different kind of power—not just in relation to the spiritual realm and not just in relation to the ruling political authorities, but in the ordinary social dynamics of everyday life. It operated in complete obedience to God the Father, it repudiated the symbolic trappings of elitism, it manifested compassion concretely out of calling and vocation, and it served the good of all and not just the good of the community of faith. In short, in contrast to the kingdoms of this world, his kingdom manifests the power to bless, unburden, serve, heal, mend, restore, and liberate.

What follows is clear: as ones who accept his invitation into his kingdom, Christians must follow him. As Christ said, "If anyone would come after me, let him deny himself and take up his cross and follow me (Matt. 16:24).

What does this mean for Christians who want to engage the world for good? In our day, Christians have not only embraced strategies that are incapable of bringing about the ends to which they aspire, they have also embraced strategies that are deeply problematic, shortsighted, and at times, profoundly corrupted. If the flourishing of Christian faith and its cultures depends on a model of power that derives from Christ's life and teaching, what does this look like in practice? This is the question that I will explore more fully in Essay III.

Essay III

TOWARD A NEW CITY COMMONS: REFLECTIONS ON A THEOLOGY OF FAITHFUL PRESENCE

Chapter One

THE CHALLENGE OF FAITHFULNESS

FOR CHRISTIAN BELIEVERS, the call to faithfulness is a call to live in fellowship and integrity with the person and witness of Jesus Christ. There is a timeless character to this call that evokes qualities of life and spirit that are recognizable throughout history and across cultural boundaries. But this does not mean that faithfulness is a state of abstract piety floating above the multifaceted and compromising realities of daily life in actual situations. St. Paul, in Acts 13:36, refers to King David having "served God's purpose *in his own generation.*" This suggests, of course, that faithfulness works itself out in the context of complex social, political, economic, and cultural forces that prevail at a particular time and place. The circumstances and character of any particular historical moment vary considerably, of course, and thus the challenges that Christian believers face will vary. To face up to the challenge of integrity and faithfulness in our generation, then, requires that Christians understand the unique and evolving character of our times.

The Temper of Our Times

By the start of the twenty-first century, American society had established itself as the first hyperpower in world history. What is called globalization is a complicated and multidimensional development, but there are ways in which one can rightly say that globalization was and remains in many respects Americanization writ large. American products, technology, and popular culture remain nearly ubiquitous around the world as are the financial, political, and military structures that make this possible. There is no question that challenges to American hegemony are already present. Internally, there is the challenge that emanates from its own faltering credit markets, growing debt, looming inflation, and weakened currency relative to the global economy. Externally, the greatest economic challenges are coming from China and India, and politically the challenge of the Middle East is only growing. There is also no question that a largely unilateralist foreign policy during the Iraq War did much to weaken America's reputation in the world. In the long term, all of these challenges will have enormous consequences. That said, even now—in every sphere of human affairs and in nations and societies everywhere—America remains a dominating presence and influence in the world.

Yet the character of American civilization is a bundle of contradictions, containing both vitality and lassitude, energy and exhaustion. For example, despite its ups and downs, American capitalism remains fairly robust, and its growth over many decades has brought unprecedented freedom, wealth, and mobility to people. But a consumer mentality has moved out of the marketplace to become a dominant cultural logic, transforming inherited frameworks of moral meaning and social obligation. Likewise, American democracy has a rich legacy and the political idealism at its core remains vibrant in the hearts and minds of its citizens. As it has expanded its reach, American democracy has drawn more and more people into the political process, empowering them with tools of self-governance. Yet democratization has also spilled out of the realm of politics and into the realm of aesthetics and morality with the consequence of flattening out ethical and artistic distinctions, challenging our ability to make coherent moral judgments. Not least, the achievements of technology have been stunning, but even as these innovations have improved the quality of life, they also have delivered new forms of violence and oppression. One could go on. In each instance, we see great vitality in the functioning of different social institutions—the market, the polity, intellectual life, technology, and so on—and yet the culture that infuses them is in considerable disarray. American political culture continues to be fragmented and relatively polarized, its commercial and entertainment culture is gradually more tasteless and vulgar, its technological culture is ethically incapable of keeping up with the pace of innovation, and its moral and intellectual culture is evermore disjointed, incoherent, relativistic and superficial. It is not surprising that the attitudes and opinions of ordinary Americans reflect these kinds of contradictions: average Americans are committed and hopeful yet they are also strongly distrustful of the major institutions and their leaders, dubious about the future of the nation, and often confused about their own nature and purpose in this life.

There is more to say about the temper of our times, and yet it is appropriate to pause for a moment and reflect on the significance of what has been said thus far. If the context for faithfulness has changed, then it means that the challenge *to* faithfulness—that is, the challenges that faithfulness must address—has changed as well. How do the categories used by most Christians size up the challenge?

Among most theological conservatives, the main challenge presented by the modern world has been secularity. Their solution, therefore, is a "resacralization" of society—bringing God back into all spheres of social activity. Among most theological and political progressives, the primary challenge has long been one of inequality, a problem that has grown global over the last two centuries as the disparities of wealth and power in capitalism have grown and internationalized. For progressives, then, the solution is a redistribution of wealth and power with a preference for the poor and needy. Among many neo-Anabaptists, the most significant challenge of our time is the violence and coercion built into the polity of liberal democracy and consumerism of global capitalism. Their solution, then, is the peace-living *koinonia* of the church-based community.

All of these theological and political communities in their own way understand important parts of the puzzle of the contemporary world. All of these challenges are correctly identified as problems and they are all at least partially correct about the solutions. Where they are mistaken is in assuming, explicitly or implicitly, that the challenge they see is *the* defining one, in effect, trumping all others. On reflection, it is arguable that there is not one single challenge to Christianity that eclipses all others in importance. There are many challenges that have different effects on different communities within Christianity at different times. The multiplicity of challenges and the dizzying complexity of their causes are largely what make the modern world so confounding. Yet even in their totality—that is, drawing from the most important insights from each way of thinking about the modern world—the problems they explicate seem to miss the mark. If this is true, engaging the world with integrity in our time requires a rethinking of the particular challenges to authentic Christian witness that derive from this historical moment.

Though important efforts have been made, Christian theology has yet to systematically articulate a thorough critique of the modern world. That task is enormous—it would take many talented scholars many years to achieve it. And yet there are two elements of this task that require immediate, even if abbreviated, attention. I refer here to the important matters of "difference" and "dissolution." On the surface, the problem of difference bears on how Christians engage the world outside of their own community, while the problem of dissolution bears on the nature of Christian witness. In reality, these problems are interrelated and mutually reinforcing and together they represent challenges that Christian believers have not adequately acknowledged, the dynamics of which Christians have not understood well and, thus, whose implications Christians have not worked through. Coming to terms with both of these, then, is central to the questions at hand—what does the renewal of the church look like in our time and what does this mean for its engagement with the culture?

THE CHALLENGE OF DIFFERENCE

On the face of it, the challenge of difference is straightforward: how do we think about and relate to those who are different from us and to a world that is not our world?[1] The simplicity of this question, however, masks issues of profound historical, theological, sociological, and psychological significance.

The challenge of difference is rooted in the ever-present, indeed unavoidable realities of modern pluralism. Pluralism in its most basic expression is nothing more than the simultaneous presence of multiple cultures and those who inhabit those cultures. For most of human history, communities and societies existed in relative isolation and thus were insulated from exogenous social and cultural influences. The operative word here is "relative" because pluralism, in fact, has existed for millennia all around the world. As the locus for commerce and migration, ancient cities and trade routes were the meeting places of a remarkable diversity of people and cultures, representing a wide range of geographic, ethnic, religious, and social variation. Most people, however, did not live in cities or along trade routes but were based in agricultural communities that tended to be very small in the number of people and limited in their geographic reach.

Yet beginning with the age of modern exploration, followed by Western industrialization and urbanization and, most recently, the powerful forces of globalization, pluralism has emerged as one of the defining features of the contemporary world order. Pluralism has become so prominent in part because of the extraordinary growth of cities, in both their size and in their number. The majority of people in the world now live in and around cities. Yet global urbanization has occurred simultaneously with the stunning growth in technologies of transportation, not only making travel easier but rapidly increasing the mix of cultures regionally and internationally. Perhaps more significant than urbanization and travel has been the growth of communications technologies—television, newspapers, film, and the Internet—and with it, the massive flow of information. These technologies and the concomitant flow of communication and information make it impossible to avoid the plurality of cultures. All of this together means that instead of just a small minority of any given society coming into sustained contact with the differences represented by competing cultures, now the vast majority does— indeed, *the majority is constituted by precisely those differences.* Under the conditions of modernity and late modernity, then, the incidence of pluralism has increased massively, which means that average people experience it more frequently and more intensely than ever before in human history.

Part of what makes contemporary pluralism interesting is the way it is presently configured. In most times and places in human history, pluralism was the exception to the rule; where it existed, it operated within the framework of a strong dominant culture. If one were a part of a minority community, one understood the governing assumptions, conventions, and practices of social life and learned how to operate within them. Because of the relatively insular nature of social life, whether in the majority or the minority, one could be convinced of the superiority of one's own beliefs and ways of life and never really have to seriously face up to the claims of another's. Even through the modern period, diversity existed within a dominant culture. In nineteenth-century America, Catholics and Jews had to learn how to survive in an overpoweringly Protestant culture, and through most of the twentieth century, Jews, secularists, Buddhists, Hindus, and Muslims have had to learn how to survive in a predominantly Christian culture.

But pluralism today—at least in America—exists without a dominant culture, at least not one of overwhelming credibility or one that is beyond challenge. This doesn't mean that there isn't the effort to establish a dominant culture. This, after all, is what the "culture war" in America has been about—a contest for cultural ascendancy and the capacity to enforce conformity. Neither does it mean that in some important quarters of social life, a particular culture will not have an upper hand over others. In elite realms of cultural production (for example, the world of academia), a certain kind of narrow secularity prevails. The playing field, then, is far from even. Yet from all that we can tell, social systems seem to require some basic consensus to survive. In our time, those agreements tend to be minimal at best. To imagine any unanimity beyond these minimal agreements, one that would give expression to extensive and multilayered understandings of the world and our purpose in it, is implausible. For the foreseeable future, the likelihood that any one culture could become dominant in the ways that Protestantism and Christianity did in the past is not great. An irresolvable and unstable pluralism—the collision and conflict of competing cultures—is and will remain a fundamental and perhaps permanent feature of the contemporary social order, both here in America and in the world.

If this is true, then the implications of this fact are quite significant. Perhaps the most obvious implication this presents is in the objective reality of dissimilarity—that is, the observable differences in dress, food, languages, beliefs, moral commitments, ways of organizing social relationships, and habits of daily life. These have generated social, legal, and political conflicts for over three centuries. Though the genius of modern democracy has been to provide a legal and political framework for managing these differences that has been more or less adequate to the task, the solutions have not been fully satisfying to anyone. For this reason, the legal and political debate surrounding the just management of plurality will continue well into the future.

As contentious and preoccupying as these social and political conflicts are, the challenge of difference is every bit as consequential in the perceptions and experiences of ordinary people. No one has gone further in untangling the complex social and psychological dilemma this creates than Peter Berger. In Berger's view, the credibility of one's beliefs depends on certain social conditions that reinforce those beliefs. It is not just the benefit of living around other people who affirm the same beliefs as yours; it is the language, the symbols, and the social practices all woven into everyday life that underline and buttress those beliefs. These social conditions comprise what Berger famously calls "plausibility structures." For Berger, "there is a direct relation between the cohesion of institutions and the subjective cohesiveness of beliefs, values and worldviews."[2] It is true that there are religious virtuosi who maintain strong beliefs on their own with little or no social support but these individuals are rare. Most of us, however, need the reinforcement that social institutions provide to believe coherently and live with integrity. There is a sociological truth, then, to the statement *extra ecclesiam nulla salus*; that "there is no salvation outside of the church." Strong and coherent beliefs require strong institutions enveloping those who aspire to believe. These are the conditions that turn belief into settled convictions. And when social conditions are unstable or when the cohesion of social life is fragmented, then the consistency and intelligibility of belief is undermined.

By these lights, modern pluralism not only represents a multiplicity of ways of perceiving and comprehending the world but also a multiplicity of plausibility structures that make those perceptions credible in the first place. Put another way, fragmentation not only occurs among worldviews, but in the social structures that support those worldviews. The number and variety of cultural systems mean that the social conditions supporting any particular belief system are necessarily weaker. Belief is certainly possible, but it is necessarily different. The confidence borne from beliefs that are taken for granted typically gives way to belief plagued by ambivalence and uncertainty. The uncertainty is not a matter of insufficient will or deficient commitment but a natural social psychological reaction to weakened plausibility structures. In such circumstances, one is no longer enveloped by a unified and integrated normative universe but confronted by multiple and fragmented perspectives, any or all of which may seem, on their own terms, eminently credible. This social situation obligates one to choose, but once the choice is made—given the ubiquitous presence of alternatives in a market culture oriented toward consumer choice—one must reaffirm that choice again and again. These are social conditions that make faithfulness difficult and faithlessness almost natural.[3]

Another way to describe the dilemma for religious faith is that pluralism creates social conditions in which God is no longer an inevitability.[4] While it is possible to believe in God, one has to work much harder at it because the framework of belief is no longer present to sustain it. The presumption of God and of his active presence in the world cannot be easily sustained because the most important symbols of social, economic, political, and aesthetic life no longer point to him. God is simply less obvious than he once was, and for most no longer obvious at all—quite the opposite.

This dynamic plays out every bit as much for those in the Christian faith as for anyone else. While it is possible to be a faithful Christian believer, it requires an act of will much greater than in the past because the reminders of God's love or his judgment or of his purposes in daily experience—all of those things that reinforced belief—may not have disappeared but they have receded from shared public life. Consider, for example, "God-talk." In a predominantly religious culture it is relatively easy to integrate the language of faith into the discourse of everyday life—commerce, education, civic life, and so forth. But in a culture that is characterized by the simultaneous presence and interaction of different linguistic communities, this kind of speech becomes less probable because it is indecipherable to those outside of the community of faith. Thus, as the Christian community has lost its prominence in American public life and the culture has pluralized, the grammar of Christian faith has become more strange and arcane, less natural and more foreign, spoken awkwardly if at all. To be sure, "God-talk" is certainly possible within the framework of the church, but outside religious community it has little or no resonance at all.

Pluralism creates other pressures on religious belief as well. Over time, pluralism can foster a syncretism in which competing cultures influence, adapt, or assimilate to each other. Through ongoing interaction, the hard edges of each are softened, accommodations are made, and the sources and expressions of various cultures and cultural traditions mix together. At times the result is something new, but at the very least the particular traditions that made up the pluralistic combination evolve within themselves and become something different than what they were before. Catholicism is different because of its encounter with Protestantism. Evangelicalism is different because of its encounter with Judaism. Christianity is different because of its encounter with secularism. Syncretism is something that occurs in degrees, and while in theory it may not be inevitable, the pressures toward at least some assimilation are enormous. Even in a situation of cultural conflict, where leaders of competing cultural traditions strive to preserve the distinctiveness and continuity of their faith, adaptations can and do occur. Over the last two centuries, Protestantism, Catholicism, liberalism, fundamentalism, and Evangelicalism have all been thus affected.

In sum, the challenge of difference that is rooted in modern pluralism plays out on many levels. First, pluralism has incalculable effects on the collective identity of the tradition of belief itself. As Christianity has moved from being the dominant culture-shaping influence to just one among many, its historic role as defender of social order has dissolved. As we have seen in Essay II, many Christian leaders continue to aspire to play a role, but in playing it they will be viewed (and are viewed) as much as a danger to the social order as a support. Pluralism, then, changes the public identity of the church, both in how it understands itself and in how it is perceived. Second, pluralism inevitably changes the content of belief and practice. To the extent that Christian believers and the church as a whole engage the world, it will experience the pressures of assimilation to the world. Try as it may, those pressures are difficult if not impossible to resist, and even in resisting, the church can assume the character and content of the world around it. (This also was a lesson of Essay II.) Third, pluralism certainly undermines the possibility of belief but even more significantly, it undermines the *character* of belief—that is, *how* one believes. Even for ordinary people, belief requires a conscious awareness and a deliberateness that is unfamiliar to past generations. As the structures of belief have weakened, so has the self-assurance of belief. There is little if anything one can take for granted about the faith any longer.

THE CHALLENGE OF DISSOLUTION

A second formidable challenge to faithfulness is the challenge of dissolution. By dissolution, I refer to the deconstruction of the most basic assumptions about reality. There are different ways of telling this story but, in light of the argument of the present essay, perhaps the most interesting is the one framed by George Steiner in his reflections about the changing meaning of words in the modern world. In his book *Real Presences*, Steiner argues that, in the most rudimentary way, our civilization—and the communities and traditions of which it is comprised—is above all else a civilization of the word. Everything from values and laws and all social relations to our conception of history and God and personal identity "are inseparable from verbalization and from functions of value intimately inwoven in discourse and syntax."[5] A human being is a "language animal," a being "in whom the isolating privilege of speech . . . is definitional."[6] All of this, of course, is commonplace. What is less obvious is the implicit trust that underlies the language of our civilization. "There would be no history as we know it," Steiner contended, "no religion, metaphysics, politics or aesthetics as we have lived them, without an initial act of trust. . . . This instauration of trust . . . is that between word and world."[7]

His argument is not that there is a strict correspondence between words and the realities that make up human experience. After all, words notoriously fail to adequately express, describe, and explain the depths and complexities of love, beauty, knowledge, and sensation. Critics are right to observe that we abuse and demean reality when we ask words to stand in lieu of or be a substitute for the phenomenon itself. But this is not the issue. Rather, his point is that our civilization is based on the confidence or presumption that such a correspondence exists; that the world and our being in it are articulable; "that the raw material of existentiality has its analogue in the structure of narrative." "Truth," as Steiner put it, "in so far as it was deemed accessible to the limited means of mortal supposition, was answerability to the meaning of the world."[8]

The modern world, by its very nature, questions if not negates the trust that connects human discourse and the "reality" of the world. In its mildest expressions, it questions the adequacy of language to make the world intelligible. In its more aggressive expressions, however, it fosters a doubt that what is said has anything to do with what exists "out there." Indeed, it is an aggressive form of dissolution that we see most prominently and pervasively today in both intellectual discourse and popular culture.

The problem is this: when the objectified and shared meaning of words is undermined, when we no longer have confidence that words signify what we thought they signified, then it is possible to impute any meaning to words one desires. And if words can mean anything, then they have no intrinsic meaning or at least no possibility of a common meaning. They only mean what we say they mean. There are no fixed points of reference. What is more, there is no authority that can be appealed to in order to definitively establish the meaning of words or to adjudicate which meaning is more truthful or better than another. God? Nature? Science? Democracy? Tradition? None of these sources of authority can be trusted because each one exists under the same questioning gaze—they too are words that have been emptied of meaning. None make any sense outside of their own specific discourse. The confidence we might have once had that they signify what they had once signified has also been undermined and so it is that they too lead us to the same subjectivist cul-de-sac. God? It is possible to fill this word up with any content that we desire and so we have. So it is with meaning we give to our lives. Because meaning in life is constituted by words it is possible, within the framework of our circumstances, to fill it up with the meaning we choose. We can interpret or construct a story about it in any number of ways. But by the same token, we have no capacity to determine whether the interpretations we produce or the stories we tell or the decisions we make are right or good. Nor do we have any way to determine whether any choice we make will make any difference. Thus, in the contemporary world we have the capacity to question everything but little ability to affirm anything beyond our own personal whims and possessive interests.

In a culture in which the covenant between signified and signifier, word and world is broken, words are emptied of meaning. The forces of dissolution, then, lead us to a place of absence, a place where we can never be confident of what is real, what is true, what is good; a place where we are always left wondering if *nothing* in particular is real or true or good. Indeed, in the social world, the only thing that is irrefutable, the only thing left to connect words to the world, are will and power—that is, a will to power rooted in desires and judgments that have no justification but are their own measure of moral worth and significance. Steiner is not alone in seeing this rupture between word and world as a genuine revolution in the history of the human spirit.

What are the causes of this profound change?

In part, the roots of dissolution are intellectual. The Enlightenment's own quest for certainty resulted not in the discovery of new certainties but rather in a pervasive and astringent skepticism that questions all, suspects all, distrusts and disbelieves all. Even in the early decades of the seventeenth century, the great poet John Donne wrote presciently of this new age, "New philosophy calls all in doubt."[9] Marx and Freud made titanic contributions to the project of modern skepticism. Marx, of course, challenged the given-ness of the social order and its structure of inequality; Freud challenged the relationship of morality, consciousness, and personality and the very nature of and borders between psychopathology and mental health. These were only starting points. The project has been advanced and refined through a number of intellectual fashions over the years—from existentialism to poststructuralism and from postmodernism to pragmatism. As it has evolved, it has disseminated through many fields in the academy. At its core is a misgiving, a doubt, a suspicion about the trustworthiness of language to connect reliably and consistently with reality. Thus, in the field of literature such skepticism has come to reject the finality of the text or the authority of the author. In law it has come to repudiate the immutability of constitutions and declarations and the legitimacy of law itself. In history it has come to deny the immutability of past events and the credibility of the accounts surrounding them, and in science it questions the given-ness of basic scientific facts and the methods for establishing those facts. Such skepticism presents a formidable challenge to all of the core ideals of the traditional liberal arts and their objects of inquiry. Underneath these passing fashions is an enduring skepticism that constitutes a new epoch in the history of ideas and scholarship, especially in the humanities, one that may end but now has no end in sight.

But here a qualification: it would be unfair to construe all of modern skepticism negatively. There have been innumerable myths rooted in either history or tradition or folklore or collective lunacy that have needed debunking. Every bit as important have been the pretensions of power in the modern world that have needed demystifying and discrediting. The problem is that skepticism took a dissolutionist turn at the point at which it offered nothing ameliorative, but rather pursued doubt for its own sake; because it could not see anything beyond itself.

Nietzsche, it is often acknowledged, was the first to understand radical skepticism of this kind and its portentous implications for the Western world. He also did more than his share to encourage the process along. Ever since Nietzsche, intellectuals have been grappling with the meaning of this rupture, and among the scholars who are most celebrated are those who have seen the implications most clearly. But radical skepticism leading to radical nihilism is, of course, rare. Apart from a few celebrity nihilists and a few disaffected graduate students, there are actually few consistent relativists or committed postmodernists for the simple reason that it is not livable. Dissolution is always a matter of degrees and yet, even in its approximations, it is highly toxic. In spite of the highly abstruse and self-contradictory nature of this intellectual discourse, it has had a large influence outside of the ivory tower, not least through the credentialing of emerging elites and their placement in the culture-forming institutions of American society.

But it is not only radical skeptics and their students who contend with consequences of dissolution. More and more it is the person on the street who faces the challenge of dissolution. It is not because they are reading the French deconstructionists but rather because the social conditions of the contemporary world reinforce the cultural logic that forms this break in trust. Simply to live under these social conditions is to have one's consciousness shaped in similar ways.

One of those social conditions, as I've already argued, is pluralism. By its very nature, pluralism juxtaposes culture, each with its own definition of words or perspectives on the meaning of words. God, love, family, faith, courage, loyalty—the entire lexicon of signs, gestures, utterances, speech acts, ideals, and beliefs—mean different things within different social and cultural contexts. Confidence in the meaning of words cannot help but be undermined. We cannot be sure that words mean what they once meant or that words are understood as we intend. In that doubt, a gap emerges between speaker and word spoken, between word spoken and the word as it is understood by those who hear it. Authority and truth are weakened.

Of even greater significance are the social conditions created by the new communications technologies of the past half-century. Attention is always given to the latest innovation, and yet the "most recent" advance is only the latest part of a larger revolution in the history of communications, which has unfolded piecemeal and has run from the telegraph and radio to the television, to video technology, fax machines, video games, the Internet, cell-phone technology, and so on. Cumulatively these electronic media represent an epoch-defining transition, perhaps only the third revolution in communication in human history, the first being the invention of writing in the axial age civilizations, the second being the invention of movable type in the sixteenth century Europe. Each revolution transformed the way in which people perceived, related to, and organized the world around them.[10]

These electronic media have transformed the nature of consciousness and culture as well. For those who study contemporary media, such problems are well known. Consider four of the most important. First, these media transform time and space by radically "compressing them," transforming the objective qualities of space and time by accelerating or eliding spatial and temporal distances.[11] In brief, time is shortened and space is shrunken to the point where they almost disappear—as when we witness events simultaneously with others around the world through the television or communicate with people from great distances in the same time through a telephone or through the Internet.[12] Through these technologies, people halfway around the globe are as proximate as people in the next room. Second, electronic media such as the radio, television, and Internet compartmentalize the world and place its parts together in incoherent ways, as when a news report on a famine in Africa is followed by an advertisement offering pharmaceutical help for erectile dysfunction, which is then followed by the latest results of the NCAA basketball tournament in Charlotte, North Carolina; the stock market news from New York, London, Frankfurt, and Tokyo; a murder trial in Los Angeles; a trailer for a new coming-of-age movie; and so on. The format of the newspaper also compartmentalizes this way with no overarching narrative structure, but the new electronic media does it more seamlessly, rapidly, and intensely. The fictional and the real, the comical and the serious, the insignificant and the significant, all blend together flattening out the distinctions among them. The net effect is that all content is trivialized. Third, because radio, television, the Internet, and the like are so driven by commercial interests, entertainment becomes the primary format for representing experience. Though the appeals are different, the pressures are every bit as great for the evening news as for prime-time drama, and for televised worship services as for a sporting event. Here too, distinctions in content are mashed together and flattened out. Needless to say, entertainment also contributes to the trivialization of meaningful content. Since the goal is to generate positive approval from as large an audience as possible, content has to be driven by the audience's changing wishes and inclinations. Fourth, these media in their various ways create an illusion of intimacy with actors, politicians, talk show hosts, sports celebrities, and strangers with whom we do business because we share the same conversational space. The information shared is, by its nature, both extremely public but deeply private as well.

Altogether these media foster a reality that exists primarily if not only within the surfaces of sensory awareness and understanding. This is a world constituted by image, representation, simulation, and illusion. This is, of course, a highly engineered reality that distances us from our natural surroundings and the immediacy of primary relationships. It is a simulated reality that, in many ways, supersedes lived reality. Indeed, as it is often noted, there is a radical uncertainty about the reality presented by and experienced through these media for the difference between image and presence, simulated and lived, represented and embodied, doesn't disappear but it does significantly dissolve. The fact that these media are also a sales media guided by the competitiveness of business interests means that there are powerful institutional and historical forces at work to make resistance to their effects nearly impossible. As one observer put it, the off-button doesn't really work.[13]

In sum, consciousness is never independent of the social reality in which it is embedded; worldview never transcends the environment that surrounds it. An environment that is constituted by surface images and simulations and that is fragmented and flattened out cannot help but undermine the reality to which Christian belief and faith point. The words we use simply fail to have the same kind of traction they once did. In such a context, it is difficult to imagine that there is a spiritual reality more real than the material world we live in. Neither is such an environment conducive to depth in reflection, relationships, or commitments. It is difficult to discover the quality of intimacy in a friendship or in love that is nurtured through time and attentiveness to the subtleties of need, memory, joy, and hurt. So too, it is difficult to forge moral commitments capable of enduring the vagaries of hardship, boredom, failure, and even triumph. A world created by these technologies may not occlude depth in these ways but it will war against it.

In their net effect, this ongoing and intensifying revolution in communications creates conditions that dissolve the trust we have that words spoken refer reliably to a reality "out there." Here too, by their very nature, these technologies empty words of meaning. They are every bit as much, if not more, a solvent than the most mordant skepticism of radical deconstruction. Whatever good they provide—which is substantial—they too lead to a place of absence, a place where we cannot be confident of what is real, good, or true.

Christians are not above the effects of this historical rupture. Some intuitively resist its force and pressure and effects but many (probably more) innocently embrace it. This historical reality envelops them and it effects their perception and ways of relating to the world nearly as much as anyone else. As we will soon discuss, Christian institutions also perpetuate it in many ways.

INTO NEW TERRITORY

Though we live in times of breathtaking change, the lines of continuity between past and present can be traced. Not all things are new and yet it is important not to underestimate the significance of the change on us. There are key aspects of contemporary life that take us into radically new territory; into a social and cultural landscape that has very few recognizable features from cultures, societies, or civilizations past.

The challenge of difference and the challenge of dissolution are not new. They are both longstanding fixtures of the modern world. Yet they are also challenges that have been intensifying and evolving. It is critical to note that their effect is primarily manifested not as problems that can be seen, objectified, analyzed, and responded to but as a complex array of assumptions so deeply taken for granted that they cannot be fully grasped much less questioned. Culture is most powerful, as I have argued, when it is perceived as self-evident. In this way, the structures of culture form the structures of consciousness and shape the implicit understandings of what is good, worthy, appropriate, right, wrong, abhorrent, and evil. It is in this way that the dilemma of difference and dissolution play out in contemporary America. As these new structural conditions have become fixed in modern social life, they come to fundamentally change the character of the world around us, of reality as we perceive it, and of life as we experience it.

What does all of this amount to? Difference and dissolution have their positive aspects, as I have noted. Yet there is also an underside, perhaps the most challenging of which is that they present conditions advantageous for the development of nihilism—genial and otherwise. I define nihilism as autonomous desire and unfettered will legitimated by the ideology and practice of choice. I don't want to be misunderstood here. The power of self-determination is, of course, our reigning definition of freedom, and such freedom can indeed be liberating. For many, and not least the poor and disadvantaged and oppressed minorities, such freedoms are rare and cherished, and one can only hope that they will expand. The problem, then, is not with the freedom of will as such but rather its autonomy from any higher value.

The power of will first becomes nihilistic at the point at which it becomes absolute; when it submits to no authority higher than itself; that is, when impulse and desire become their own moral gauge and when it is guided by no other ends than its own exercise. The nature of pluralism, as I have argued here, creates conditions in which one is required to choose. The dynamics of dissolution are that it dissolves all reality, all meaningful authority, and all meaningful moral purposes but will. In America, nihilism of this kind tends to foster a culture of banality that is manifested as self-indulgence, acquisition for its own sake, and empty spectacle that makes so much of popular culture and consumer culture trivial.

We indeed find ourselves in territory that is less and less familiar. It is often said that, although many vestiges remain, American culture has become post-Christian culture. This is certainly true, but a statement like this is almost trite, for it fundamentally understates the changes that have taken place in late modernity. It may be more accurate to say that we are witnesses to and participants in a cultural transformation that radically challenges and deconstructs, if not inverts, the ontological and moral substructure of inherited social institutions, inherited conventions of everyday social life, and the inherited frameworks of understanding and experience. How this transformation will turn out is anyone's guess, but it is essential to come to terms with both the enormity and complexity of the change and to face its implications squarely, for it means that the context in which faithfulness is pursued today is quite different from anything seen before.

Chapter Two

Old Cultural Wineskins

I F SINCERITY WERE THE same thing as faithfulness, then all would be well, for Christians, as a rule, are nothing if not sincere—not least in their desire to be "faithful in their own generation." But if I am even partially correct about the nature and profundity of the changes of late modernity, then against these sincerity could never be enough by itself. At least a fragment of wisdom would be required as well. At the deepest levels of experience, the changes that have brought about the challenge of difference and dissolution go right to the core of the ability of Christians to live out their faith with integrity. In this way, it goes to the core of their witness in the world. How is faithfulness possible in a world such as ours? And what might be a way forward?

To address these questions it is first necessary to reconsider the dominant models through which faithfulness has been conceptualized and pursued. Some of what I describe will be familiar. Yet precisely because the social and cultural landscape has been changing, with new players innovating familiar roles, it is worth sorting through anew the leading ways of thinking about faithfulness in our time. This will also help clear the ground for thinking through a possible alternative course.

Three Paradigms of Engagement: "Defensive Against," "Relevance To," and "Purity From"

The three political theologies discussed in Essay II are, in fact, the leading public edge of more complex paradigms of cultural engagement that I call "defensive against," "relevance to," and "purity from." In using this phrase, "paradigms of cultural engagement," I do not mean to propose anything as ambitious and inclusive as a formal conceptual model, akin to the one proposed by H. Richard Niebuhr in his masterwork, *Christ and Culture*. I merely refer to relatively different understandings of the world, ways of being in the world, and ways of relating to the world. These are, in short, different ways of thinking about and pursuing faithfulness in the world. The word "paradigm," then, may be too strong, for each one is defined more by tendencies and priorities rather than by mutually exclusive qualities and consistent commitments. Each paradigm, then, is at best a general orientation that anticipates exceptions, qualifications, and some blending with the other two. And unlike Niebuhr's typology, which was designed as a conceptual construct that could be applied to many situations in history, these paradigms primarily apply to the historically specific circumstances of Christianity in contemporary North America.

DEFENSIVE AGAINST

Theological and political conservatism are often linked in a model of cultural engagement that seeks to create a defensive enclave that is set against the world. This "defensive against" paradigm has long been embraced by Protestant Fundamentalists and mainstream Evangelicals, though it has also become a strategy in recent decades for many conservative Catholics. For Christians operating within this paradigm, their objective has always been, first and foremost, to retain the distinctiveness of Christian orthodoxy and orthopraxy within the larger world. Against the challenges of late modernity, this has not been easy not least because their proprietarian relationship to American culture has obligated them to preserve the nation as well as their faith. The defensive nature of this paradigm is rooted in the massive nature of the assault of secular modernity. Conservatives of all confessions have been angry about their loss of prominence, as well as anxious, on guard, and self-protective in ways that have created walls between themselves and the outside world. Since the late nineteenth century, they have pursued this ideal by constructing a complex empire of parallel institutions—in music, education, media, law, and the like—that functions as a parallel universe to the secular world.[1]

Even while pursuing this, the leaders of the conservative churches, denominations, and para-church organizations have held out the hope that they could "hold the ground against apostasy" and even win back the larger culture to a situation where Christianity would regain its place of privilege. Its implicit strategy for accomplishing this has been twofold: first to evangelize unbelievers, calling for the nation to repent and come back to the faith;

second to launch a direct and frontal attack against the enemies of the Christian faith and worldview. One hand has been open and offering the good news of the gospel (even if only as "life insurance"), while the other hand has been tightened into a fist ready to fight—which is, of course, precisely what they have done, one issue after the other right through the century: temperance, creation and evolution, communism, prayer and Bible reading in the public schools, pornography, abortion, feminism and the traditional family, vulgarity in the arts and entertainment, and homosexuality and gay rights.

Those who embrace the "defensive against" paradigm continue to believe, by and large, that the main problem in the world is secularization; if only God could be re-enshrined in the social order, they assume, the culture would be restored. The church (in its diversity) would regain its standing in society, the family and local community would recover its Christian character, and the leading spheres of social life—including law and government, social welfare and reform, hospitals, education, and the like—would again be influenced by the categories and codes of Christian moral understanding.

RELEVANCE TO

Historically, the "relevance to" paradigm of engagement was embraced by theological liberalism. Yet more recently it is a paradigm of engagement embraced by Evangelicals in the "seeker-church" movement and by more progressive Evangelicals in the "emerging church" movement, and such new initiatives as Catalyst, the Fermi Project, and other kindred organizations.

Unlike those who prioritize distinctiveness though self-conscious continuity with Christian orthodoxy of the past, those in the "relevance to" paradigm make a priority of being connected to the pressing issues of the day. The leadership of theological liberalism long believed that the only way to remain relevant was to resymbolize Christianity in ways that more or less reflected the epistemological and moral assumptions of romantic modernism. It was in this way that the mainline denominations in Protestantism and the progressive factions within Catholicism made their peace with the institutions and expressions of secular life through the better part of the twentieth century. And yet theological liberalism, like its conservative counterpart, was also bound by a proprietarian relationship toward American culture, though in ways that were more ethical than spiritual, more oriented toward social amelioration than theological purity. Indeed, from the end of the nineteenth century and beyond the middle of the twentieth, those Christians operating in this paradigm were relevant to the most contentious issues of the moment— child labor, the labor movement, Communism, the war in Vietnam, and above all, the civil rights movement. At present, old-fashioned liberals continue to hold the view that corporate capitalism is the heart of the problem with the modern world not just for the savage inequalities it creates but for the ways in which capitalism despoils the environment, disturbs local economies, harms local communities, and distorts human values.[2] If only the appropriate ethical restraints could be imposed on the self-aggrandizing interests of corporate leaders and the profiteering of their corporations, the world would be a better place.

This paradigm of engagement plays out in slightly different ways for centrist and progressive Evangelicals. There are two points worth emphasizing. First, while there is no apparent departure from classical Evangelical orthodoxy, the truth and integrity of faith is mostly assumed to take care of itself. It is for this reason that their emphasis is less on the defense of the faith than on being relevant and connected to contemporary culture. In the seeker-church movement the emphasis away from the use and explication of creedal confession is obvious, since the whole point is to focus on the "felt-needs" of the person in the pew—especially the felt-needs of nonbelievers. The rationale is that the church and its main service are evangelistic in nature. Because nonbelievers simply cannot penetrate the arcana of historic Christianity, the felt-needs of people become the point of entry into conversation with them. The emphasis away from creedal confession in the emerging church movement is similar, but the point of entry has moved from identifying with people's felt-needs to the need for the church to resonate better with the world around it. Here the focus becomes something called "missionality" by which all people are brought into orthodoxy as it comes into conversation with what they already believe. So the focus is not on conformity with a given creed but on the emergence of an ever-evolving creed, and church is the locale of this emergence, wherever it may be. As with liberation theologies, a priority is given to praxis and from praxis emerges a conversation with the creeds of the church. Thus, Brian McLaren argues that his approach "celebrates orthodox doctrine-in-practice, and it comes not to bury doctrinal distinctives but rather to put them in their marginal place."[3] "A generous orthodoxy," he explains, "is an emerging orthodoxy, never complete until we arrive at our final home in God."[4]

The passion among these Evangelicals, then, is to speak into contemporary culture; to be as relevant as possible to the people and issues of our time. This leads to the second point, which is that the main point of reference in defining itself as a movement and its main focus of critique is not contemporary culture but the established church. As one mega-church pastor put it, "People think of the church as a draconian thing of the past, with big towers and iron gates and frocked people who do weird things and speak a language no one understands. We get the message out that we are relevant."[5]

Within the newer initiatives among young Evangelicals, conferences such as Catalyst and Q, or organizations such as the Fermi Project, and the like, these dynamics are very much in play. There is an acute sense that the established church and its forms of witness are no longer speaking to the culture; that they are "out of date," "old-fashioned," and "out of tune with the real-world choices, challenges and lifestyles they face."[6] Thus, the Fermi Project sponsored research on teenagers and young adults and found that Christianity has an image problem. Christians are supposed to represent Christ to the world. But according to the latest report card, something has gone terribly wrong. Using descriptions like "hypocritical," "insensitive," and "judgmental," young Americans share an impression of Christians that's nothing short of . . . unChristian.[7]

This is cause for great alarm. It is not just that Christians are irrelevant to the culture, but they are vilified by the culture. It is for this reason that many of their leaders insist that "something has to change—we as a church have got to figure out how to do this differently!"[8] This has been the motivation behind a discussion around "rebranding Christianity."[9] The ultimate goal, as the Catalyst website describes it, is "to stir the fires of faith in the next generation of leadership . . ., to tap into the God-created void in young leaders that hungers for real truth and real meaning in life by calling them to an all-out, sold-out passion for Christ."[10] "We want to equip them to engage with those around them and be seen as relevant to their peers yet separate in Who guides them."[11] The quest is for something more authentic and "real" to the moment. Indeed, this yearning for something different is the foundation of their solidarity; it is what holds this group together. But what is that "something different" that they propose? The answer is vague by design. What is not provided is any new theological content for the simple reason that "this has been divisive in the past."[12] Rather, what they offer is a process that is slickly packaged and aggressively marketed for a fee, in which young Christian leaders have access to conversations and talks given by celebrity Christian and non-Christian leaders about various areas and issues in the culture.[13] One cannot emphasize enough how "celebrity" and "spectacle" permeate these initiatives. In the end, it is the process and the presentation that matter. Thus, in answer to the question of how to better relate to the larger culture, one of the leaders, Gabe Lyons, puts it this way: "Well we just need to be there. For too long we've left the culture. We just need to be part of the culture, to be friends, to be thoughtful Christians, [to be] aware of the issues that are at stake and just going for it."[14] In the end, these initiatives, while well-intended and rooted in a deep longing, take their cue from the culture around them, and offer little clarity for the confusion of the times.

PURITY FROM

Those who operate within the "purity from" paradigm of cultural engagement are similar to those who operate within the "defensive against" paradigm in their desire to preserve the historical truths of Christian faith. Yet unlike the latter, they take the view that there is very little that can be done for the world because, in its fallen state, the world is irredeemable this side of Christ's return. The church itself has been compromised by its complicity with the world's sinfulness. The central task of the true church, then, is to extricate itself from the contaminating forces of the world and by so doing, return to its authentic witness.

In light of the foregoing argument, this paradigm is most obviously embraced by the neo-Anabaptist theologians and clergy but they also share an odd affinity with separatist factions in the traditionalist Catholic community, in some conservative Evangelical denominations (such as the "truly-reformed" in the Presbyterian Church in America or the Orthodox Presbyterian Church), and among most Pentecostals. While these Christians would not share much in common with neo-Anabaptists politically or in terms of social class, they tend to operate with a "two kingdoms" view of church and the world that also moves them to increasingly withdraw into their own communities with less and less interest in any engagement with the larger world. It is also in the "purity from" paradigm where one would locate those ecumenical gestures in Christianity toward a "new monasticism." This is an inchoate movement that identifies itself by a number of commitments, among them, a commitment to "relocation to the abandoned places of Empire," "sharing economic resources with fellow community members and the needy among us," "geographical proximity to community members who share a common rule of life," "nurturing common life among members of intentional community," and "a commitment to a contemplative life."[15]

What concerns those operating within the "purity from" paradigm, then, varies widely by tradition. Pentecostals and many Evangelicals tend to be concerned about sexual sin, while neo-Anabaptists worry about the violence built into modern capitalism and the structures of political power that defend it. Whatever the case, their identity depends on a logic of "us-against-them," a logic that is, for all practical purposes, separatist, even if not sectarian.[16] Thus, even when they are out in society, say, serving the needs of the poor, these communities exist as enclaves of righteousness. This subliminal ideal of the church as a utopian enclave is partly reinforced by an anti-institutional view of the church. To recognize the church in its institutional manifestations would force one to see the line between the church and the world as blurred. At the same time, this subliminal ideal of the church is reinforced by elements of perfectionism in traditional pietism. In the case of the neo-Anabaptists, "biblical perfectionism affirms not a simple possibility of achieving love in history, but a crucial possibility of participating in the victory of Christ over the effects of sin in the world."[17] Not being burdened by the neo-Constantinian obligations to support the established regime, the church has no other obligation other than to be itself. The strategy of engagement within the "purity from" paradigm is, in its net effect—and ironically, a certain kind of disengagement.

IN SUM

Needless to say, each of these here is sketched out in rough form, and the distinctions are useful at best in describing relatively different tendencies in the way Christians think about how to be faithful in the world. They become more interesting, however, in how they frame the problem of difference and dissolution.

Responding to the Challenge of Difference

Up to the present, how the church has dealt with the challenge of difference has largely been an unconscious function of its implicit theory of cultural engagement. The positions it takes follow naturally from its vision of faithfulness.

Within the "defensive against" paradigm, difference is always seen as "danger," or at least a potential threat. The "other" who embodies that difference is a stranger and is construed as either a potential ally (through conversion) or as an enemy. Pluralism has been massively threatening, and in the face of it the elaborate structure of parallel institutions these Christians created has functioned as a network of plausibility structures that have allowed them to live in a pluralistic world without really participating in it. Today, the difference represented by pluralism might be a necessary evil but it would be acceptable only to the extent that the conservatives operating in this paradigm determined the limits and expressions of that difference. This is what is significant about the term "Judeo-Christian." It represents a range of acceptable difference that conservatives now defend. Jews may represent the "other" to some Christians but today they are not regarded as so different as to constitute a threat. In fact, just the opposite—(conservative) Jews and Christians share enough in common religiously and culturally as to be allies on certain social and political issues.

Within the "relevance to" paradigm, maintaining the distinctive character of Christianity has not been and is not the uppermost priority and so the point was and remains to downplay any difference between themselves and the "other." In the context of the racial politics of the mid-twentieth century, this made complete sense. Racism was rooted in the perception of fundamental difference and not only was the perception completely wrong, but it was the cause of sin against fellow human beings. To combat racism, difference had to be obliterated. On this issue, there was no real other, no *essential* difference, because underneath our skin, we are really all the same. The same could be said about gender and sexual orientation. The only difference that was unacceptable was the difference created by those who sought to maintain their distinctive religious identity for they, in fact, were the most racist (and sexist and homophobic) people of all. The problem was that the cultural logic that led theological liberals to a correct position on race had become the defining cultural logic of the "relevance to" paradigm as a whole. By the late 1960s, progressives were left in creed and practice with less and less that resembled anything like historic Christianity. While progressive Evangelicals who operate in this paradigm are different from the old liberals, they too are eager to play down difference (i.e., most significantly on the issue of homosexuality); to reduce the potential tension and conflict between themselves as Christians and all those who are not. They are upset by the image of Christianity as old-fashioned and out-of-date, insensitive and judgmental, and they are keen to do something about it.

Finally, Christians operating in the "purity from" paradigm of cultural engagement tend to construe difference as "darkness." Thus, the only justifiable strategy is to separate from darkness as a community of light. Rather than developing parallel institutions within the Christian world as a means of preserving their distinctiveness, the church itself is considered the only legitimate structure for safeguarding the faith, and the activity within the church is viewed as the core expression of that faith. Needless to say, "darkness" is deepened in a post-Christian context, which may be why pietism in the form of Pentecostalism, neo-Anabaptism, and the new lay ecumenical monasticism may be enjoying a rebirth.

Responding to the Challenge of Dissolution

What about the challenge of dissolution? Once again, what I mean by dissolution is the negation of the trust that connects human discourse to the "reality" of the world. Any understanding of what is real, true, good, and right depends on a covenant between the words spoken and the reality to which they refer. But this covenant has been broken, and the result is an emptying of words of their inherited meaning. In the context of the Christian tradition, the challenge of dissolution plays out most pointedly in relation to a particular word, the "Word of God," and the creedal confessions and understandings that emanate from it. Needless to say, for over a century there have been extraordinary pressures undermining the confidence that Scripture in particular, and by extension, the historic creeds, the articles of faith, and the truth of a Christian understanding generally, have any bearing at all on the world as it is or the daily lives of believers. Christians of all communities have aspired in different ways to resist these pressures but with curious and often self-defeating effects.

Historically, theological liberalism in the "relevance to" paradigm resisted the separation of word and world simply by renegotiating the meaning of the Word in ways that were more plausible to modern secular circumstances. Of course, skepticism toward the creed has long been a defining characteristic in this tradition of theological understanding, manifesting itself in the range of theologies of immanence from process theology to the liberation theologies that have been so important to the Black, Latin American, and feminist communities. The motive for this in part was as a means of retaining the efficacy of Christianity's ethical code to address problems in the world. Christian dogma may no longer be plausible, they reasoned, but the ethics of love would always be relevant, always have traction against the problems we face in society.

Progressive Evangelicals today do not share the liberal proclivity of skepticism toward historical belief yet they are similar in their desire to apply their faith to important problems in society—issues such as global warming, famine and drought in Africa, the sex slave trade, conflict diamonds, immigration, and so on. In this, they certainly do not deny the historical faith but they do tend to downplay the creedal aspect of the faith in favor of its ethical ideals. The purpose, as it was within liberalism, is to achieve relevance through the language and effectiveness of ethical practices. Rick Warren, pastor and author of *The Purpose-Driven Life*, expresses this sentiment concisely in a statement he has often repeated:

> I'm looking for a second reformation. The first reformation of the church 500 years ago was about beliefs. This one is going to be about behavior. The first one was about creeds. This one is going to be about deeds. It is not going to be about what the church believes, but about what the church is doing.[18]

Within the Evangelical world, this may not be a turn away from orthodoxy but it does signal a dramatic shift in emphasis, one that will have profound, even if unintended consequences in succeeding generations.

Conservatives in the "defensive against" paradigm are the most interesting in their response to the challenge of dissolution. On the one hand, they
have sought to resist the erosion of the truth-claims of Christianity by attack-
ing the world's efforts to undermine the integrity of the Word of God. The
authenticity of Christian faith and witness has long been defined by the
strong affirmations they make about the Bible and their defense of its authority (i.e., from "The Fundamentals" in the early twentieth century to "The
Truth Project" in the early twenty-first century). And yet those who operate
in this paradigm have lacked a certain critical awareness about the nature of
the modern world they live in, assuming that its technologies of communication are culturally neutral and without their own side effects. As a consequence, those in the "defensive against" paradigm unwittingly engage in
practices that contribute to the very thing they want to resist. Indeed, the
appetite among Evangelicals and Fundamentalists for all of the new innovations in communication technology has been, from the invention of radio,
voracious. In April 1995, *Christianity Today* ran a cover story called "Cyber
Shock," that insisted that "new ways of thinking must be developed for the
church to keep pace in the information age."[19] Evangelicals probably did not
need the encouragement, since no religious movement has ever exploited
these technologies more fully than they. All aspects of religious life have been
encompassed by these technologies—evangelism, spiritual counseling, education, bible study, and worship. As one advertisement for a Bible
study software put it, "You're only a mouse click away from deepening your
spiritual walk."[20]

There is no question that much good has come to the community of faith
from what is made available through these technologies. At the same time,
all of the faith-based work that comes through these technologies bends to fit
the technology's requirements, fostering a reality that exists and operates
primarily on the surfaces of sensory perception. Here no less than in its
secular use, reality becomes constituted by the ephemera of image, representation, and simulation. Pseudo-intimacy with well-known personalities provides the primary form and style of communication for a population hungry
for significance. Here too the message is fragmented, creating a context in
which the distinctions between simulated and lived realities are largely dissolved. And because these media are used as a sales media within the Christian marketplace, this material is packaged in the same way as any other
consumer goods in the marketplace are promoted, offering sensational
appeals but making no demands and providing no accountability. How much
spiritual fruit actually comes from the frenetic symbolism created by these
media is debatable, but there is no question that in all of these ways, these

technologies unwittingly weaken the connective tissue "between word and world."

Finally, instead of fighting, Christians in the "purity from" paradigm seek to resist the dissolution of trust between word and world by simply retreating from all that would undermine the integrity of the gospel and the practices that enact it. In the Pentecostal tradition, they pursue authenticity through a traditional pietism that tends to shun the world. Because they are populists, they are oriented toward faith in ways that resemble mainstream Evangelicalism and thus use the new communications technologies in church life and ministry with little awareness or concern for their unintended consequences. Among the neo-Anabaptists and new monastics, however, authenticity is defined as incarnation—the unity of belief and practice. Yet they interpret incarnation in a particular way. Incarnation is something that happens in the disciplines of the Christian life—especially in the corporate disciplines of Eucharist, the liturgy, the observance of holy days, and the like. The individual disciplines of prayer, silence, fasting, tithing, biblical study, and so on are equally important. As we will see in Chapter 4, however, they ignore the implications of the incarnation in the vocations of ordinary Christians in the workaday world. So far as I can tell, this is not an oversight. Among some, it is a deliberate strategy rooted in the conviction that authentic Christian witness exists primarily if not only in the community of Christian believers when they are together in worship and fellowship.

The Need for an Alternative Way

In sum, all three paradigms capture something important to the experience, life, identity, and witness of the church. The concern to be "relevant to" the world, "defensive against" the world, and "pure from" the world all, in certain ways, speaks to authentic biblical concerns. Yet the desire to be "relevant to" the world has come at the cost of abandoning distinctiveness. The desire to be "defensive against" the world is rooted in a desire to retain distinctiveness, but this has been manifested in ways that are, on the one hand, aggressive and confrontational and, on the other, culturally trivial and inconsequential. Finally, the desire to be "pure from" the world has entailed a disengagement and withdrawal from active presence in huge areas of social life. All want to engage the world faithfully, yet all pursue that end in ways that minimize the inherent tension that comes with being ones who are called to be "in the world but not of it."

My point is not that these paradigms of engagement are equally problematic, but rather that none seems to be a fully adequate way of making sense of or pursuing faithfulness in our world. This inadequacy becomes especially apparent in light of the historical and sociological processes that have brought about the challenges of difference and dissolution. Separately and together, these changes in the social organization of modern life challenge Christian faith to its core. *Both undercut the capacity to believe, and to believe coherently, thoroughly, effectively.* In the process, one—the fact of difference through an intensifying pluralism—distorts our views of those outside the community of faith and the social, cultural, and political space we share with them, fundamentally challenging the identity of the church as well as the content and character of belief. The other—the process of dissolution—undermines our capacity to incarnate Christian faith within all of life.

And so the questions continue to press on us: How can one be authentically Christian in circumstances that, by their very nature, undermine the credibility and coherence of faith? What is an authentically biblical way of existing within a pluralistic world in which Christianity will never be anything other than one culture among others? How should the Christian think about the "other"? How is a faithfulness that gives full expression of the gifts of the entire body of Christ for the benefit of the church and the common good possible? What does it mean for the believer to be faithful in this generation?

The late modern world is deeply confounding, and its spiritual consolations are few. Like everyone else, Christians are hungry for authenticity, coherence, and depth, and yet the ways these are pursued fail to respond fully to those longings. The need for an alternative vision that is at least a little more adequate to the temper of our times is palpable.

Chapter Three

THE GROUNDWORK FOR AN ALTERNATIVE WAY

IN A MILIEU WHERE the church and its people are so quickly and roundly criticized for their shortcomings, it is easy to overlook a central theological truth; that is, that however inadequate or pitiful the church may seem at times (and may, in fact, be), where the scripture is proclaimed, the sacraments administered, and the people of God continue to seek to follow God in word and deed, God is at work; the Holy Spirit is still very much active. This is not just an abstract article of faith but a reality that we can see all around us if we have the eyes to see it: a ministry in Harrisburg, Pennsylvania, that provides long-term housing and mental health services for indigent adults; an ecumenical project that provides job-search assistance and training for refugees and immigrants; a mission that provides the medicine to cure leprosy in over 25,000 people a year; a Christian environmental program based in Sante Fe that buys thousands of acres of rain forest to protect it from development and destruction; a ministry based in Iowa that has drilled dozens of wells in the poorest villages in Haiti; a ministry to AIDs patients in Annapolis, Maryland; a Christian group in Columbus, Mississippi, that provides homes for abused and orphaned children; a Christian agency based in Memphis that conducts literacy training in prisons; an organization that continues to distribute tens of millions of Bibles in dozens of languages every year; and a ministry based in Colorado Springs with 3,000 staff and 27,000 volunteers committed to sharing the gospel with teenagers. These are initiatives of monumental courage, sacrifice, and fidelity, and the list of undertakings like these is long indeed.

So if the gospel is being proclaimed and lived in such remarkable ways, what is there to complain about? What precisely is the problem?

The problem is that these initiatives represent just a fraction of the potential within the church to bear witness to the love, grace, mercy, and truth of Christ. The people of God, individually and collectively, are called to give expression to the redemptive work of God in all of their lives. As we've seen, the challenges to this calling in our time are formidable to say the least. *What has been missing is a leadership that comprehends the nature of these challenges and offers a vision of formation adequate to the task of discipling the church and its members for a time such as ours.* By misreading the nature of the times and by focusing so much energy and resources on politics, those who have claimed the mantle of leadership have fixed attention on secondary and tertiary problems and false solutions. By admonishing Christian lay people for not, in effect, being Christian enough, they shift responsibility for their own failures onto those that they lead.

On Formation—Preliminary Reflections on the "Great Commission"

When you distill it to its simplest expression, a "vision of formation" referred to above is nothing more and nothing less than the pursuit of the "Great Commission." It is the task of "making disciples," of being conformed to the image of Christ. If there is an alternative way forward besides the "defensive against," "relevance to," and "purity from" paradigms of cultural engagement, this is the starting point. But how do we understand the task of formation?

In some parts of the Christian community, the great commission is understood as evangelism *tout court* and thus, once converted, the work of sanctification is in God's hands—spiritual growth is assumed to be a natural process guided by the Holy Spirit. Formation, in short, will happen as an expected outgrowth of conversion. In other parts of the Christian community, formation is understood as learning to practice the spiritual disciplines, such as participating in regular worship, engaging in daily prayer and scripture reading, regular tithing and periodic fasting, and enjoying periods of quiet and solitude.

Both evangelism and the practice of spiritual disciplines are, of course, central to the Christian life, but Scripture suggests that there is more to formation than these things. In Christ's own words, making disciples entails "teaching them to observe all things that [he] commanded [them]." (Matt. 28:19–20). Likewise, St. Paul describes the mature Christian in his letter to the new believers in Colossae as those who would be "filled with the knowledge of his will in all spiritual wisdom and understanding, so as to walk in a manner worthy of the Lord, fully pleasing to him, bearing fruit in every good work and increasing in the knowledge of God" (Col. 1:9–10). Formation—the task of making disciples—is oriented toward the cultivation of faithfulness in the totality of life. To this end, St. Paul and St. Timothy "proclaimed [Christ], admonishing and teaching everyone with all wisdom, so that we may present everyone complete in Christ" (Col. 1:28). St. Paul writes that he toiled and struggled at this task. Making disciples or formation, then, requires intentionality and it entails the hard work of teaching, training, and cautioning believers with wisdom in the ways of Christ so that they are fit for any calling and any service to him.

The problem for Christians—to restate the broader issue once more—is not that their faith is weak or inadequate. In contemporary America, Christians have faith in God and, by and large, they believe and hold fast to the central truths of the Christian tradition. But while they have faith, *they have also been formed by the larger post-Christian culture*, a culture whose habits of life less and less resemble anything like the vision of human flourishing provided by the life of Christ and witness of scripture. The problem, in other words, is that Christians have not been formed "in all wisdom" that they might rise to the demands of faithfulness in a time such as ours, "bearing fruit in every good work."

The Church as Culture and Community—The Enactments of Shalom

To achieve a formation that seeks the renewal of all of life presupposes a culture that in fact expresses and embodies the renewal of all of life. If, for whatever reason, the culture of a local parish and the larger Christian communion of which it is a part does not express and embody a vision of renewal and restoration that extends to all of life then it will be impossible to "make disciples" capable of doing the same in every part of their lives. *In formation, it is the culture and the community that gives shape and expression to it that is the key.*[1] Healthy formation is impossible without a healthy culture embedded within the warp and woof of community.

This has always been the case, but it is especially important in a context where the plausibility structures that make belief credible and consistent are so weakened. Community is no longer "natural" under the conditions of late modernity, and so it will require an intentionality that is unfamiliar and perhaps uncomfortable to most Christians and most churches.

Besides intentionality, what are the hallmarks of this community? The vision of this community—the hope for which it longs and the ideals to which it strives—is the vision of shalom. It is a vision of order and harmony, fruitfulness and abundance, wholeness, beauty, joy, and well-being. For the Christian, this was God's intention in creation and it is his promise for the new heaven and the new earth.

In this light, the entire biblical narrative centers around the shalom God intended and that he will, one day, restore. The details of the story, however, focus on the Fall, its consequences, and finally God's response to it. Idolatry, covetousness, envy, pride, vanity, deceit, hatred, and murder, the perversion of justice, political oppression, exclusion, division, and inequality all shattered and despoiled the shalom of God. Again and again, God's judgment was against those who worked against this reality.

> Woe to those who devise wickedness and work evil on their beds! . . . They covet fields and seize them, and houses, and take them away; they oppress a man and his house, a man and his inheritance. (Mic. 2:1–2)

> Woe to the wicked! It shall be ill with him, for what his hands have dealt out shall be done to him. (Isa. 3:11)

> Woe to those who call evil good and good evil, who put darkness for light and light for darkness! . . . who acquit the guilty for a bribe, and deprive the innocent of his right! (Isa. 5:20, 23)

> Woe to those who decree iniquitous decrees, and the writer who keeps writing oppression, to turn aside the needy from justice and to rob the poor of my people of their rights, that the widows may be their spoil, and that they may make the fatherless their prey! (Isa. 10:1–2)

> I will pronounce my judgments on my people because of their wickedness in forsaking me, in burning incense to other gods and in worshiping what their hands have made. (Jer. 1:16)

And yet God is not merely opposed to those who seek to undermine his shalom, but is active in defense of its victims.

> Lord, you hear the desire of the afflicted; you will strengthen their heart; you will incline your ear to do justice to the fatherless and the oppressed, so that man who is of the earth may strike terror no more. (Ps. 1:17–18)

The Lord is a stronghold for the oppressed, a stronghold in times of trouble. (Ps. 9:9)

Because the poor are plundered, because the needy groan, "I will now arise," says the Lord; "I will place him in the safety for which he longs." (Ps. 12:5)

It will be a sign and a witness to the Lord of hosts, in the land of Egypt. When they cry to the Lord because of oppressors, he will send them a savior and defender, and deliver them. (Isa. 19:20)

Implied in the biblical law laying out the rights of the poor, the orphan, the widow, and the stranger is the fact that all of them lack a protector who can stand up on their behalf. They do not have a next of kin to intercede for them and so the law intervenes in this way. And the guarantor is God himself.[2] To this end, he beckons his people to co-labor with him in establishing shalom.

Give justice to the weak and the fatherless; maintain the right of the afflicted and the destitute. (Ps. 82:3)

Wash yourselves; make yourselves clean; remove the evil of your deeds from before my eyes; learn to do good; seek justice, correct oppression; bring justice to the fatherless, plead the widow's cause. (Isa. 1:16–17)

For if you truly amend your ways and your deeds, if you truly execute justice one with another, if you do not oppress the sojourner, the fatherless, or the widow, or shed innocent blood in this place, and if you do not go after other gods to your own harm, then I will let you dwell in this place, in the land that I gave of old to your fathers forever. (Jer. 7:5–7)

He has told you, O man, what is good; and what does the Lord require of you but to do justice, and to love kindness, and to walk humbly with your God. (Mic. 6:8)

In the most momentous event in history, God became incarnate in Christ, not only to model shalom (by forgiving the sinner, feeding the hungry, healing the sick and infirm, raising the dead, loving the outsider, and caring for all in need) but, as St. Paul writes, to be "our shalom"[3] (Eph. 2:14). The kingdom of God—the shalom of God—was at hand.

And so until God brings forth the new heaven and the new earth, he calls believers, individuals and as a community, to conform to Christ and embody within every part of their lives, the shalom of God. Time and again, St. Paul calls Christians to "shalom" (I Cor. 7:15), to "follow after the things which make for shalom " (Rom. 14:19), to "live in shalom and the God of love and shalom will be with you" (II Cor. 13:11) for He is "the Lord of shalom" (II Thess. 3:16). *In this Christians are to live toward the well-being of others, not just to those within the community of faith, but to all.*

Such a rendering of biblical history is simple perhaps to the point of being commonplace, even platitudinous. Yet to look closely, it raises more questions than it answers. The most obvious question is what does this mean practically? How does it look for Christian believers in their various circumstances and walks of life? This is a question I will pick up in another chapter. For now, there is a more immediate question concerning context: how does a community that longs for this shalom relate to the world around it?

Tensions with the World

As I mentioned toward the end of Essay II, a tension exists for the Christian community, a community caught in the unavoidable pull between history and revelation; between the conditions of social life in any particular epoch and the call of God on the church.[4] It is easy to imagine this tension as either merely psychological and therefore individual or else theological and therefore cognitive and abstract. These are certainly implicated, but on their own, they do not fully capture the complexity of the situation. The Christian community is a linguistic community that speaks simultaneously not just through its ideas but also through its institutions—and there the tension is reflected in an unavoidable tangle of words, grammars, assumptions, dispositions, theories, practices, and social organizations. Needless to say, sorting this all out in ways that provide a clear line of distinction is humanly impossible. This is an awkward way to put it but it is not just the "wheat and tares" of souls that are mixed together in inseparable ways, but the wheat and tares of culture—in all of the ways just mentioned—that are in many instances impossible to distinguish as well.

This tension is inevitable and irresolvable and living with it is finally unsatisfying. It is, however, the only option for the church and its people. Scripture does offer a way to think about it however. In an important reflection on the relationship of church and culture in 1 Peter, Miraslov Volf unpacks the tension as experienced by the early church.[5] On the one hand, he argues, the dominant metaphor of the church in 1 Peter is that of "alien." Christians are "aliens and strangers in the world" (1 Pet. 1:1, 2:11), and for this reason, they are a "chosen race, a royal priesthood, a holy nation" (1 Pet. 2:9). In its beliefs, values, ideals, and institutions, then, the church is distinct from the larger society in which it is found. By virtue of the new birth, Christians are not what they used to be nor do they live as they used to live. On the other hand, 1 Peter instructs its readers to accommodate to existing social realities. "Be subject for the Lord's sake to every human institution" (1 Pet. 2:13–17). And this pertains to the realm of politics (emperors and governors), economics (servants, slaves, and masters), and the household (husbands and wives). Both of these instructions are present in the text: accommodation to existing social realities and calling them into question by being different.

But rather than confusion, the contradiction is constructive. The purpose of Christian existence as a whole is to "proclaim the mighty acts of him who called you out of darkness into his marvelous light" (1 Pet. 2:9). To this end, Christians should conduct themselves "honorably among the Gentiles . . . so that they may see your honorable deeds and glorify God when he comes to judge" (1 Pet. 2:12). In short, as Volf puts it, "Christian difference is . . . not an insertion of something new into the old from the outside, but a bursting out of the new precisely within the proper space of the old."[6]

Affirmation and Antithesis

Let me unpack this contradiction by proposing that Christians are called to relate to the world within a dialectic of affirmation and antithesis.[7]

The first moment in the dialectic is affirmation. Theologically, affirmation must be the starting point because the story of life begins with God's creative initiative and the affirmation he declares on it at each moment of creation—of earth, vegetation, light, animals, and man and woman. "And God saw everything that he had made and behold, it was very good" (Gen. 1:31). And he blessed it, calling the earth, all living creatures, and humans themselves to bring forth life. The significance of affirmation as the first moment in the dialectic is accentuated in a larger public culture defined, in large part, by negation. As we have seen, the public witness of Christianity has for too long, shared in, contributed to, and deepened the negational character of this culture.

Affirmation is based on the recognition that culture and culture-making have their own validity before God that is not nullified by the fall. It isn't just that the social order is preserved because the rule of sin is restrained, in the old Calvinist formulation, but that goodness, beauty, and truth remain in this fallen creation. Even in the context of late modernity, suffused as it is by failed ideologies, false idolatries, and distorted ideas of community, joy, and love, one can still find much good. Life still has significance and worth.

What is more, people of every creed and no creed have talents and abilities, possess knowledge, wisdom, and inventiveness, and hold standards of goodness, truth, justice, morality, and beauty that are, in relative degree, in harmony with God's will and purposes. These are all gifts of grace that are lavished on people whether Christian or not. To be sure, there is a paradox here that perplexes many Christians. On the one hand, nonbelievers oftentimes possess more of these gifts than believers. On the other hand, because of the universality of the fall, believers often prove to be unwise, unloving, ungracious, ignorant, foolish, and craven. Indeed, more than any Christian would like to admit, believers themselves are often found indifferent to and even derisive of expressions of truth, demonstrations of justice, acts of nobility, and manifestations of beauty outside of the church. Thus, even where wisdom and morality, justice and beauty exist in fragments or in corrupted form, the believer should recognize these as qualities that, in Christ, find their complete and perfect expression.[8] The qualities nonbelievers possess as well as the accomplishments they achieve may not be righteous in an eschatological sense, but they should be celebrated all the same because they are gifts of God's grace.

There is more . . .

As a backdrop to all of this, there is a natural life originating in creation and a natural order in things that can be understood, developed, and enjoyed. The dazzling processes of growth in a tree or a bug or a newborn baby, the intricacies of molecular biology, the stunning ordered-complexity of mathematics, and the underlying logic of music all speak of an order that God has created and that has not been effaced by the fall, that people can discover and take pleasure in as well.[9] These things too, Christians should neither dismiss nor disparage but rather be grateful for and be delighted by because they are gifts of God's grace meant for their benefit and the benefit of all.

In sum, there is a world that God created that is shared in common by believers and nonbelievers alike. In the classical Christian view, the goodness of creation is fundamentally and ubiquitously marred by sin but it is not negated by sin. It may be fractured, incomplete, and corrupted, but his goodness remains in it. The gifts of God's grace are spread abundantly among the just and unjust in ways that support and enhance the lives of all. As it is in the world that God has given, so it is in the world that his creatures fashion. This work is also typically pursued in common with those outside the community of faith. The task of world-making has a validity of its own because it is work that God ordained to humankind at creation. Since all are created in his image, world-making is an expression of our divine nature. Though what we produce is fundamentally flawed at its best, it always possesses the potential and can, in fact, serve the good of all. It too is a place of grace.

It is important to emphasize that the realm of "common grace" is, by no means, a neutral space. It is *God's* grace after all—it emanates from him and its purpose is to give him glory. To make strong and active affirmations about the present world, then, in no way implies the autonomy of knowledge, morality, desire, justice, or beauty. The idea that there are common or objective standards for these things independent of the created order is an illusion. In the contemporary world, neutrality is the pretence of all secular establishments; a myth concealed by its hegemony. All human reasoning and understanding, all human morality, and all human visions of beauty are rooted in the particularity of tradition, narrative, and community and the only question is to what degree do they conform to the *nomos* of the kingdom of God. This does not mean that there are no points of contact or overlap and no points of common cause in the pursuit of beauty, justice, peace, and well-being between the Christian community and others.[10] There are many, in fact, but those points require careful discernment that never concedes the radical alternative offered by the gospel.

It is also important to underscore that while the activity of culture-making has validity before God, this work is not, strictly speaking, redemptive or salvific in character. Where Christians participate in the work of world-building[11] they are not, in any precise sense of the phrase, "building the kingdom of God." This side of heaven, the culture cannot become the kingdom of God, nor will all the work of Christians in the culture evolve into or bring about his kingdom. The establishment of his kingdom in eternity is an act of divine sovereignty alone and it will only be set in place at the final consummation at the end of time. It is only then that "swords will be beaten into plowshares and . . . spears into pruning hooks"; only then will "the wolf . . . dwell with the lamb, and the leopard . . . with the kid"; and only then will "the earth . . . be full of the knowledge of the Lord, as the waters cover the sea."[12] Perhaps it will be that God will transform works of faith in this world into something incorruptible but here again, it is God's doing and not ours.

For Christians to regard the work of culture in any literal sense as "kingdom-building" this side of heaven is to begin with an assumption that tends to lead to one version or another of the Constantinian project, in which the objective is for Christians to "take over" the culture, fashioning all of the world in the image of the church or at least in accord with its values. Typically, this assumption leads to the dualism in which the culture either declares Jesus as Lord or it doesn't. Christians are either "winning" the culture or "losing" it, "advancing the kingdom" or "retreating," which is why all versions of the Constantinian approach to culture tend to lean either toward triumphalism or despair, depending on the relative success or failure of Christians in these spheres. This is why it is always dangerous to aspire to a "Christian culture" or, by extension, a Christian government, a Christian political party, a Christian business, and the like.

In this respect, the neo-Anabaptists and radical Orthodox theologians are exactly correct in their critique of the Constantinian predispositions in most of Western Christianity. But they go too far to suggest that the lives and work of Christians in the world have no spiritual significance outside of the explicit enactments of church life. Of this more will be said in a later chapter. For now Christians of many traditions can agree with the words of the Westminster Shorter Catechism when it declares that the chief end in life—in all of life—is "to glorify God and enjoy Him forever." When his rule is established in the hearts, minds, and souls of believers, and in their daily lives and sphere of influence, God is indeed present and he is glorified.

Indeed, insofar as Christians acknowledge the rule of God in all aspects of their lives, their engagement with the world proclaims the shalom to come. Such work may not bring about the kingdom, but it is an embodiment of the values of the coming kingdom and is, thus, a foretaste of the coming kingdom. Even while believers wait for their salvation, the net effect of such work will be a contribution not only to the good of the Christian community but to the flourishing of all.

Let me finally stress that any good that is generated by Christians is *only* the net effect of caring for something more than the good created. *If there are benevolent consequences of our engagement with the world, in other words, it is precisely because it is **not** rooted in a desire to change the world for the better but rather because it is an expression of a desire to honor the creator of all goodness, beauty, and truth, a manifestation of our loving obedience to God, and a fulfillment of God's command to love our neighbor.*

It is clear at this point that the very source of affirmation—its motive, its logic, and its *telos*—contains the second moment in the dialectic: antithesis. Antithesis is rooted in a recognition of the totality of the fall. In this light, all human effort falls short of its intended potential, all human aspirations exist under judgment, and all human achievement is measured by the standards of the coming kingdom. In the present historical context, this means that Christians recognize that all social organizations exist as parodies of eschatological hope. And so it is that the city is a poor imitation of heavenly community;[13] the modern state, a deformed version of the *ecclesia*;[14] the market, a distortion of consummation; modern entertainment, a caricature of joy; schooling, a misrepresentation of true formation; liberalism, a crass simulacrum of freedom; and the sovereignty we accord to the self, a parody of God himself. As these institutions and ideals become ends in themselves, they become the objects of idolatry. The shalom of God—which is to say, the presence of God himself—is the antithesis to all such imitations. Always and everywhere he relativizes the pretensions of all social institutions to power, fellowship, joy, freedom, and authority. Always and everywhere his presence declares that human endeavor is never the final word.

For this reason, however much Christians may be able to affirm in the world, the church is always a "community of resistance." Such a phrase can sound adversarial in a dreamy and idealistic way, but it contains a challenge that is difficult to imagine, much less realize. It is a challenge to think through resistance in an institutional way. The power of individual will is weak by comparison to the power of institutions. Institutions can only be effectively challenged by alternatives that are also institutionalized—either alternatives that are developed within existing institutions or alternatives that are altogether new. First and foremost, of course, this means that the church itself must model its alternative both symbolically (e.g., through the Eucharist) and in actuality, that is, in the conduct of body life. But every bit as important, the church, as it exists within the wide range of individual vocations in every sphere of social life (commerce, philanthropy, education, etc.), must be present in the world in ways that work toward the *constructive* subversion of all frameworks of social life that are incompatible with the shalom for which we were made and to which we are called. As a natural expression of its passion to honor God in all things and to love our neighbor as ourselves, the church and its people will challenge all structures that dishonor God, dehumanize people, and neglect or do harm to the creation.

In our present historical circumstances, this means that the church and its people must stand in a position of critical resistance to late modernity and its dominant institutions and carriers; institutions like modern capitalism, liberalism, social theory, health care, urban planning, architecture, art, moral formation, family, and so on. But here again, let me emphasize that antithesis is not simply negational. Subversion is not nihilistic but creative and constructive. Thus, the church—as a community, within individual vocations, and through both existing and alternative social institutions—stands antithetical to modernity and its dominant institutions in order to offer an alternative vision and direction for them. Antithesis, then, does not require a stance that is antimodern or premodern but rather a commitment to the modern world in that it envisions it differently. Such a task begins with a critical assessment of the metaphysical, epistemological, and anthropological assumptions that undergird modern institutions and ideologies. But the objective is to retrieve the good to which modern institutions and ideas implicitly or explicitly aspire; to oppose those ideals and structures that undermine human flourishing, and to offer constructive alternatives for the realization of a better way.

Nowhere is the task of critical resistance more urgent than in the church itself for the ways that it too has accommodated to the spirit of the late modern age. St. Peter is right to say, "judgment begins with the household of God" (1 Pet. 4:17). Antithesis, then, means that the church's own structures and its own engagement with the world must be continually scrutinized. Here especially, critical resistance must always be creative and constructive; guided by devotion to the beloved community.

Returning to Formation

There is a strong tendency, especially within the pietistic branches of Protestantism, to see formation or, if you will, "the great commission" as a new and different work for the people of God in history; that redemption is of a different nature than creation. It is absolutely true that the incarnation of God in Christ, his life, his suffering, his death and resurrection represent a radical rupture in human history. This is the *euangelion,* the "good news," and to proclaim it and live out its meaning is a calling for all believers. But this rupture in human history does not represent a departure in God's purposes. Indeed, redemption through Christ represents a reaffirmation of the creation mandate, not its annulment. When people are saved by God through faith in Christ they are not only being saved from their sins, they are saved in order to resume the tasks mandated at creation, the task of caring for and cultivating a world that honors God and reflects his character and glory. God indeed forgives people of their sin. As they are formed into disciples, more and more conforming to the image of Christ, they are liberated from the corrupting and oppressive power of sin, healed and renewed to the end that they might love God and enjoy him forever. As we will see, this has enormous implications for every aspect of their lives—their work, leisure, family life, civic duties, and so on.

Beyond the worship of God and the proclamation of his word, the central ministry of the church is one of formation; of making disciples. Making disciples, however, is not just one more program—it is not Sunday School, a Wednesday night prayer meeting, or a new book one must read. Formation is about learning to live the alternative reality of the kingdom of God within the present world order faithfully. Formation, then, is fundamentally about changing lives. It is the church's task of teaching, admonishing, and encouraging believers over the course of their lives in order to present them "as complete in Christ," "fit for any calling." At the foundation of this task, of course, are the fundamental preparations of the catechesis—instruction into central truths of Christian belief, the development of the spiritual disciplines, and the observance of basic sacraments. It will also include teaching a new language rooted in Scripture that is at the heart of the story of creation, redemption, and consummation. Words such as covenant, grace, gift, sin, mercy, forgiveness, love, hope, blessing, the flesh, glory, creation, resurrection, sacrament, and the like must be learned anew in part by understanding the significance of the language and narrative of faith within the context of the social, political, and cultural realities of one's own time. As Walter Brueggemann has put it, Christians must renounce the dominant script of the world and embrace the alternative script that is rooted in the Bible and enacted through the tradition of the church.[15] This task, however, presupposes that Christians are capable of discerning the difference between the two scripts. Making disciples, in other words, means that the people of God will learn to live with and reflect in life the dialectical tension of affirmation and antithesis.

The task of formation at any time, but not least one that is adequate to a time such as ours, is not an easy task. It requires wisdom, discernment, hard work, and the active guidance of the Holy Spirit in it all. Yet when a vision for the renewal of all things is embodied in the church—when reflected in a coherent and common *weltanschauung*, when expressed in a communal narrative that forms the church's collective memory and identity, when shared in rituals that define a common practice, when enacted in lives that are models of faithfulness in vocation in the world, and when expressed in relationships within which one finds encouragement and accountability—the formation of disciples fit for any calling and any service will unfold as a natural expression of its common life.

Toward an Alternative Way Forward—Faithful Presence Within

The groundwork having been laid, it is now time to turn directly to a possible alternative way of understanding the renewal of the church and its engagement with the culture. Over against the "Defensive Against," "Relevance To" and "Purity From" paradigms, I would offer an alternative: "Faithful Presence Within."

Chapter Four

Toward a Theology of Faithful Presence

Reality, I have claimed, is a problem in our late modern world. As I argued in Chapter 1 of this essay, words now seem to fail us. Language no longer reliably connects us to the world around us. We no longer completely trust words to be answerable to the world.

Presence and Place

This has curious implications for our experience of presence and place. For millennia of human history, body and location were inextricably connected to experience. The worship of God, the cultivation of friendship, the conduct of business, and the expression of anger and hostility, the pursuit of romantic affection, the experience of the natural world all presupposed physical presence. The expressions on the face, the gestures of the hands, the body's mien, touch itself—by their nature, worked together to limit, expand, and shape communication and relationship. Place mattered no less. The towering reaches of a cathedral, the foreboding form of a fortress, the warmth and intimacy of a home or hostel, the beauty and power of the ocean or landscape, for example, were all inwoven with the experience within these places.

Both physical presence and place continue to matter to us, but neither matters as much as they once did. We are, of course, present in time, but less and less present by virtue of our physical presence. For example, when one can communicate with anyone at anytime from anywhere and to anywhere—whether through a cell phone, the Internet, or some other technology—presence and place simply matter less. They matter less to the cultivation and maintenance of relationships and less to the work we do. We are, in a sense, released from the gravitational pull that presence and place once necessitated for both relationship and labor.

What is more, when the physical places we inhabit—whether homes, offices, gyms, shopping malls, interstate highways, airports, parking lots, cities—look alike, place seems to matter even less. What was distinctive about a place etiolates into space and we end up with what James Kunstler has called "a geography of nowhere"—where every place looks like no place in particular.[1]

The development of new technologies of information and communication are clearly one of the sources of this cultural change. In a time such as ours, more and more of us inhabit our relationship to the world—at least increasingly so—through these technologies. Whether work, friendship, romance, rivalry, hostility, the natural world, or specific places in the world—all can be and indeed are increasingly mediated through programming. Consciousness, experience, identity, physical presence, and the landscape around us, in short, are disembodied *through* these technologies.[2]

The weakening significance of presence and place is but one way in which what we take as reality has dissolved. Like most things in the world, there is ambivalence about this turn of circumstances. There are ways that the technological changes that have brought this about can be and are liberating and empowering. But they are not without cost, for in their net cultural effect, they can also be profoundly disorienting and, in ways, deeply incapacitating. As it bears on faith, the weakening significance of presence and place brought about by the broken trust between word and world cuts to the very core of what it means to believe—the reality of what we believe and the implications of our belief for how we engage the world we live in.

God Spoke . . .

In the creation narrative, we learn of a different relationship between word and world.

God said . . . and so it was.

We read this nine times in the opening chapter of the Bible. Whether light, the heavens, the stars, the seas, the earth, plants and trees, living creatures of all kinds, or man and woman, God *spoke them into being* and in so doing, demonstrated a relationship of trust between the words spoken and world as it came to be. There was no dissolution here.

The witness of the psalmist echoes the point:

The word of the Lord holds true,
and all his work endures.
. . . The Lord's word made the heavens,

All *the host of heaven was made at his command.*
... Let the whole world fear the Lord
and all men on earth stand in awe of him.
For he spoke, and it was;
He commanded, and it stood firm.
(Ps. 33:4, 6, 8–9)

With the incarnation, we have the most dramatic demonstration in history of the trustworthiness of God's word in the world:

The Word became flesh and dwelt among us,
and we saw his glory, such glory as befits the Father's only Son,
full of grace and truth. (John 1:14)

What was true of Christ's birth was true in his life. Jesus spoke with authority and his words were true. As he and his disciples sailed across the Sea of Galilee, he *"rebuked the wind and the turbulent waters.* The storm subsided and all was calm. . . . In fear and astonishment they said to one another, 'Who can this be? *He gives his orders to wind and waves, and they obey him'"* (Luke 8:24–25). Not just in the spectacular events of his life, but in the daily work of his ministry, "he drove the spirits out *with a word* and healed all who were sick" (Matt. 8:16). The people who witnessed his extraordinary deeds exclaimed, *"What is there in this man's words?"* (Luke 4:36).

Needless to say, for the Christian, the incarnation is not only a manifestation of the reality of God and the trust they can put in his word, but also the most breathtaking demonstration in history of the reality of God's love for his creation and his intention to make all things new. Christ himself announced, "you have already been *cleansed by the word that I spoke to you*" (John 15:3). St. Peter affirms this truth when he declares, "You have been born anew, not of mortal parentage but of immortal, *through the living and enduring word of God.* For . . . *the word of the Lord endures for evermore*" (1 Pet. 1: 23–25). And even after Christ's ascension, the Father sent the Holy Spirit, a Counselor who teaches us all things and who "will *be with us* forever" (John 14: 14–16, 26). The Holy Spirit, then, is the divine agent to bring about the new creation.

The Central Argument of This Essay

God, then, does not speak through empty abstractions or endless circumlocutions. Rather, in every instance, God's word was enacted and enacted in a particular place and time in history. In all, presence and place mattered decisively. Nowhere is this more evident than in the incarnation.

Word and world, then, come together not so much because words describe the world accurately or because words correspond to reality. Rather, word and world come together through the word's enactments—both *the fact* that God's word is always enacted but also in *the way* his word is enacted.

This, in short, is the foundation of a theology of faithful presence. It can be summarized in two essential lessons for our time. The first is that *incarnation is the only adequate reply to the challenges of dissolution; the erosion of trust between word and world and the problems that attend it.* From this follows the second: *it is the way the Word became incarnate in Jesus Christ and the purposes to which the incarnation was directed that are the only adequate reply to challenge of difference.* For the Christian, if there is a possibility for human flourishing in a world such as ours, it begins when God's word of love becomes flesh in us, is embodied in us, is enacted through us and in doing so, a trust is forged between the word spoken and the reality to which it speaks; to the words we speak and the realities to which we, the church, point. In all, presence and place matter decisively.

This summation is rather compressed and requires some unpacking.

God's Faithful Presence

The very character of God and the heart of his Word is that God is fully and faithfully present to us. On the face of it, faithful presence suggests proximity, but it is much more than this. His faithful presence is an expression of commitment marked by at least four attributes.

First, God's faithful presence implies that *he pursues us.* Though estranged through indifference or rebellion, God still seeks us out. His people are "*chosen* out of all the peoples on the face of the earth to be his people, his treasured possession" (Deut. 7:6). In the words of the prophet, Jeremiah, God declares, "Yea, I have loved you with an everlasting love: therefore *with loving-kindness have I drawn you*" (Jer. 31:3). Likewise, the Lord, speaking through Isaiah, says, "*I have called you* by your name; you are mine" (Isa. 43:1). And then, out of his love for the world, "*He sent His only son*" (John 3:16). The Son of God himself bids all that labor and are heavy laden to "*come*" for he will give them rest (Matt. 11:28). He plans a feast and invites all to come (Luke 14:16–24). And Christ reiterates the ancient covenant that defies the pretensions of human will—that we didn't choose God but rather God has chosen us (John 15:16). In all, it is God who initiates; it is he who in love persists in following after us. As J. R. R. Tolkien puts it,

As the hound follows the hare, never ceasing in its running, ever drawing nearer in the chase, with unhurrying and steady pace, so does God follow the fleeing soul by his divine grace. And though in sin or in human love, away from God it seeks to hide itself, divine grace follows after, unwearyingly follows ever after, till the soul feels its pressure forcing it to turn to him alone in that never ending pursuit.[3]

A second attribute of God's faithful presence is his *identification with us*. As the psalmist wrote, "For He knows our frame; He remembers that we are dust" (Ps. 103:14). Indeed, God knows our joys, our hopes, our needs, and our longings, as well as our cowardice, our failures, our betrayals, and our sufferings. Yet more than this God, through Christ, took them on himself— experienced them and became like us, though without sin. He was, after all, "born in the likeness of men" (Phil. 2:7). It was out of an understanding grounded in direct presence that he had compassion for those who were hungry (Matt. 15:32) and those who were blind and infirm (Matt. 20:29–34).

A third attribute of his faithful presence is found in *the life he offers*. This was his intent from the beginning, as demonstrated by the shalom he created in Eden. Even after the fall, he made a covenant with Abraham with the promise of the whole land of Canaan (Gen. 17:3). His plans are "to prosper [us] and not to harm [us], plans to give [us] hope and a future" (Jer. 29:11). This is consistent with his nature. As the psalmist put it, the Lord "is the fountain of life; in [his] light we see light" (Ps. 36:9). The fulfillment of this promise came with the incarnation of God in Christ, for "in him was life, and the life was the light of men" (John 1:4). As Christ himself put it, "I have come that they may have life, and have it to the full" (John 10:10). Indeed, he declares of himself to be "the bread of life"; and that those who come to him will never go hungry and those who believe will never go thirsty (John 6:35). The life that God offers is marked by goodness, peace, truth, beauty, joy, fruitfulness . . . the shalom of flourishing. "The whole creation has been groaning" for the time when it will be "liberated from its bondage to corruption into the liberty of the glory of the children of God" (Rom. 8:21–22).

Finally—and inextricably intertwined with the preceding—the life he offers is only made possible by his *sacrificial love*. "The Lord prepared a sacrifice" (Zeph. 1:7), "a sacrifice of atonement" (Rom. 3:25); indeed, "the atoning sacrifice for our sins, and not only for ours but also for the sins of the whole world" (1 John 2:1). God put himself in our place, taking on the punishment that was rightly ours, and through this suffering he reconciles himself to us and "we are made holy" (Heb. 10:10). As John wrote, "This is love: not that we loved God, but that he loved us and sent his Son as an atoning sacrifice for our sins" (1 John 4:10).

Pursuit, identification, the offer of life through sacrificial love—this is what God's faithful presence means. It is a quality of commitment that is active, not passive; intentional, not accidental; covenantal, not contractual. In the life of Christ we see how it entailed his complete attention. It was wholehearted, not half-hearted; focused and purposeful, nothing desultory about it. His very name, Immanuel, signifies all of this—"God with us"—in our presence (Matt. 1:23).

And the point of God's active and committed presence, of course, has always been to restore our relationship with him. This, of course, is the meaning of the Eucharist. God's coming to us, his becoming flesh and blood like us, and his atoning sacrifice for us are manifested in the bread and wine that is fed to us. His faithful presence is manifested in the body that was broken and the blood that was shed for the remission of sins. In the Eucharist, we not only have a backward-looking remembrance of what God accomplished long ago but we have a celebration of the start of God's restoration in the life, death, and resurrection of Christ.[4] In the Eucharist, Christians celebrate the in-breaking of the new creation within the framework of the old; the kingdom that is to come within the present.

Two points that are implicit need to be made explicit here. The first point is that in this drama, *we are the "other."* Though we are irreducibly different from him and, in our sin, irreducibly estranged from him, he does not regard us as either "danger" or "darkness." We neither threaten him nor diminish him in any way. The second point is that though he is all powerful, he pursues us, identifies with us, and offers us life through his sacrifice not because he needs us to do something for him but simply because he loves us and desires intimacy with all his creation. In other words, he does not use his power instrumentally in ways that force us against our will.

Toward a Theology of Faithful Presence

How does this bear on the larger argument? A theology of faithful presence is a theology of engagement in and with the world around us. It is a theology of commitment, a theology of promise. It is disarmingly simple in concept yet in its implications it provides a challenge, at points, to all of the dominant paradigms of cultural engagement in the church.

At root, a theology of faithful presence begins with an acknowledgement of God's faithful presence to us and that his call upon us is that we be faithfully present to him in return. This is the foundation, the logic, the paradigm.

We are present to God as a worshipping community; fully present through participation in the sacraments, collective adoration, repentance, contemplation, intercession, devotion, and service. In that context, we are present to him through the disciplines of individual devotion—prayer, meditation, fasting, study, simplicity, and solitude, among others. In this, Christians acknowledge that there is no other God before us; that our wills are his, and that in all of life, his kingdom has indeed come.

We, as Christians, are fully present to him as he is to us—not for what we get out of it or what he can do for us but simply because he is God and worthy of our adoration. As he does not pursue us for instrumental purposes, so we do not pursue him for instrumental purposes. As our creator and redeemer, our highest aim is to be in his presence; worshipping and enjoying him forever.

Only by being fully present to God as a worshipping community and as adoring followers can we be faithfully present in the world. This plays out in three critically important ways.

. . . TO EACH OTHER

First, faithful presence means that we are to be fully present to each other within the community of faith and fully present to those who are not. Whether within the community of believers or among those outside the church, we imitate our creator and redeemer: we pursue each other, identify with each other, and direct our lives toward the flourishing of each other through sacrificial love.

On the face of it, the argument, as it applies to the body of Christ, would not seem controversial. In truth, of course, this is far from the common practice for which we would hope. Indeed, if the history of the church provides any indication, this will be an impossible challenge to meet. The divisions within the Christian community along lines of social class, ethnicity, and race remain very deep, and the divisions that fall along denominational or confessional lines are as tribally factional as they have ever been. If Christians cannot extend grace through faithful presence, within the body of believers, they will not be able to extend grace to those outside. Though Christians affirm the principle of unity, the issue here is how practice will ever conform to the truths so widely affirmed.

Rather the difficult part for most is what it means to be faithfully present to those outside the community of faith. But here scripture makes it clear that the burden is precisely the same—we are to pursue others, identify with others, and labor toward the fullness of others through sacrificial love. In the laws prescribing holiness in the book of Leviticus, it reads:

> When a stranger sojourns with you in your land, do him no wrong. You shall treat the stranger who sojourns with you as the native among you, and you shall love him as yourself, for you were strangers in the land of Egypt: I am the LORD your God. (Lev. 19:33–34)

We are not only to do no wrong to those outside of our community but are to actively love the stranger as we love ourselves. In this passage, the better translation of "as yourself" (*kamocha*) is "for he is like you" and of "love" is "caring and tender concern."[5] The reason is that we too were aliens once—ones outside the community—yet this is how God treated us. This point is reiterated in Deuteronomy 10:18–19, where it states emphatically that God loves the stranger and Israel should do the same for the Israelites too were strangers in Egypt.[6]

Christ himself echoed the very point, making our treatment of strangers a measure of righteousness:

> Then the King will say to those on his right, "Come, you who are blessed by my Father; take your inheritance, the kingdom prepared for you since the creation of the world. For I was hungry and you gave me something to eat, I was thirsty and you gave me something to drink, I was a stranger and you invited me in, I needed clothes and you clothed me, I was sick and you looked after me, I was in prison and you came to visit me." Then the righteous will answer him, "Lord, when did we see you hungry and feed you, or thirsty and give you something to drink? When did we see you a stranger and invite you in, or needing clothes and clothe you? When did we see you sick or in prison and go to visit you?" The King will reply, "I tell you the truth, whatever you did for one of the least of these brothers of mine, you did for me." (Matt. 25:34–40)

To welcome the stranger—those outside of the community of faith—is to welcome Christ. Believer or nonbeliever, attractive or unattractive, admirable or disreputable, upstanding or vile—the stranger is marked by the image of God. And so St. Paul also exhorted believers in this way. "Keep on loving each other as brothers," he said. "Do not forget to entertain strangers, for by so doing some people have entertained angels without knowing it. Remember those in prison as if you were their fellow prisoners, and those who are mistreated as if you yourselves were suffering" (Heb. 13: 1–3). And elsewhere, he declared, "We who are strong ought to bear with the failings of the weak and not to please ourselves. Each of us should please his neighbor for his good, to build him up. For even Christ did not please himself" (Rom. 15: 1–3).

Scripture does not teach that the stranger is not strange to us or that the differences among us are somehow insignificant. But however different, the stranger or the "other" represents neither metaphysical danger nor darkness. When one's life is "hidden in Christ," the existence of the other neither threatens nor diminishes.

Importantly, this calling not only places a burden on us as individuals, in acts of personal benevolence toward those among whom we live and work. It also requires that we be faithfully present in all of these ways through the institutions we live in—the church first and foremost, but other institutions of which we are a part as well. Here too, individually and collectively, we direct ourselves toward the flourishing of others through actions and structures that embody sacrificial love.

. . . TO OUR TASKS

Second, faithful presence requires that Christians be fully present and committed to their tasks. What does this mean in light of the paradoxical teaching of Genesis on the nature of work? On the one hand, God placed Adam in the Garden to work in it, and in so doing, Adam was obedient to his creator. Even more, the work gave expression to his divine nature. And yet as a result of Adam's disobedience, labor also became a punishment for sin. "Cursed is the ground because of you! In toil shall you eat its yield all the days of your life" (Gen. 3:17–19). We must labor to sustain ourselves and more often than not, our labor is difficult, stressful, tedious, monotonous, and wearisome. The paradox is what it is and those who emphasize the dignity of work over the instrumentality of work or the instrumentality of work over the dignity of work are missing the irresolvable tension that exists in Scripture.

Yet St. Paul's instruction about work in Colossians offers a way through the tension. "Whatever you do, work at it with all your heart, as working for the Lord, not for men" (Col. 3:22–24). What we do certainly would include our jobs, but the reality is that our tasks are many, and they range far beyond paid labor. They involve our work as parents, students, volunteers, citizens, and the like. But in the many capacities in which we operate, St. Paul's instruction is that we pursue our tasks with all of our hearts. This not only suggests that we give our full attention to those tasks but that we pursue excellence in them. Here too, what is required is a commitment defined by pursuit, identification, and sacrificial love that gives life.

But the key to the passage is the phrase "as working for the Lord." When our tasks are done before God, they have their own integrity apart from anything else they might accomplish, for the labor itself brings honor to God. What is more, if we perform our tasks "as working for the Lord," we will want to pursue them with all the skill, care, and quality we can bring. At the same time, when we engage our tasks "as working for the Lord," there is a built-in safeguard against work—whatever it is—becoming a source of idolatry. Needless to say, in our world, our tasks often do become godlike in the ways we sacrifice family, health, friendship, and church on their behalf, and nowhere does this happen more than in the higher echelons of business and the professions. But as I say, faithful presence requires that there be no other gods before him. To engage our tasks before the Lord, we see our labors as a means by which we honor God and pursue obedience to him.

. . . WITHIN OUR SPHERES OF INFLUENCE

Third, faithful presence in the world means that Christians are fully present and committed in their spheres of social influence, whatever they may be: their families, neighborhoods, voluntary activities, and places of work. As I argued in Essay II, power is a given of social life. Christians will wield it in relationships and in the institutions and organizations of which they are a part. The question we face is how will we use whatever power we have. Needless to say, it is critically important that power not be exercised thoughtlessly, in passive conformity to the ways of the world. It is useful, in this regard to keep in mind that against the omnipotence of God, all human power is relativized and all instrumental agendas are held to account. Where power is exercised, therefore, it must conform to the way of Jesus: rooted in intimacy with the Father, rejecting the privileges of status, oriented by a self-giving compassion for the needs of others, and not only noncoercive toward those outside of the community of faith, but committed indiscriminately to the good of all.[7]

What this means is that where and to the extent we are able, faithful presence commits us to do what we can to create conditions in the structures of social life we inhabit that are conducive to the flourishing of all.

Following the argument of the last chapter, faithful presence in our spheres of influence does not imply passive conformity to the established structures. Rather, within the dialectic between affirmation and antithesis, faithful presence means a constructive resistance that seeks new patterns of social organization that challenge, undermine, and otherwise diminish oppression, injustice, enmity, and corruption and, in turn, encourage harmony, fruitfulness and abundance, wholeness, beauty, joy, security, and well-being. In the normal course of social life, the challenge and alternative that faithful presence entails is not so much a direct opposition through a contest of power but, as Miraslov Volf puts it, a "bursting out" of an alternative within the proper space of the old.[8] This does not, by any means, preclude direct prophetic opposition to established structures, but rather makes such opposition a last resort. Instead, prophetic witness becomes the net effect of a lived-vision of the shalom of God within every place and every sphere where Christians are present.

Points of Contention

So what? Is there anything exceptional being said here? After all, few Christians would doubt the foundational reality of God's presence through the incarnation and through the abiding presence of the Holy Spirit. Though harder to realize in daily life than many would admit, at least *in theory* few believers would doubt our need to be fully present to God in return. Likewise, though Christians sometimes behave abominably toward each other, in principle, most Christians would agree about the need for unity in the church. But there, consensus seems to end. On the matter of work and social influence, the issue becomes rather contentious.

In the "relevance to" paradigm, the primary strategy of engagement is adaptation for the purposes of making authentic connections to the people and events of the contemporary world. Thus, there is no real distinctive perspective or practice among old-fashioned liberals or within the emerging church beyond maintaining high standards of ethical behavior. This is no minor commitment in today's world, but in this there is nothing distinctively Christian.

In the "defensive against" paradigm, it is the Evangelicals and Fundamentalists who have fashioned a somewhat unique approach to these issues. The backdrop for their approach is the dualism created by the division between public (and secular) and private (and religious) life inherent to the modern world. As we know, this dualism is both embedded within social institutions and legitimated by political philosophy and they mutually reinforce each other in powerful ways. Though in theory Evangelicals and Fundamentalists believe God is sovereign in all of life, in practice their traditions of pietism actually reinforce this dualism. All of this has resulted in a peculiar approach to faith and vocation. For generations of faithful Evangelicals and Fundamentalists, vocation in the secular world was at best a necessary evil. To the extent that work had "kingdom significance," it was as a platform for evangelism. The mark of true piety for a committed believer whether in skilled or manual labor or in the realms of business, law, education, public policy, and social welfare, was to lead a Bible study and evangelize their associates in their place of work. In this paradigm, work was instrumentalized—it was regarded as simply a means to spiritual ends.

Thus, if one achieved some distinction for the quality of one's work in any field or for reason of an accomplishment, its significance was primarily because celebrity brought attention and credibility to the gospel. As Eric Liddell's father says to him in the film *Chariots of Fire*, "What the world needs right now is a muscular Christian—to make them sit up and take notice!" "Run in God's name and let the world stand back in wonder!" Likewise, if one achieved any disproportionate influence in a sphere of life or work, this had significance primarily as a bulwark against the tide of secularism or liberalism. Phyllis Schafly's Miss America crown; Jimmy Carter's and George Bush Jr.'s presidencies; and Clarence Thomas's Supreme Court appointment; Joe Gibbs's and Tom Landry's achievements as football coaches; Orel Herschiser's, Payne Stewart's, and George Foreman's achievements as professional atheletes were and are significant primarily to the extent that they leveraged their achievement toward the end of resisting the slide toward secularity. This is certainly how C. S. Lewis, Charles Williams, and J. R. R. Tolkein are regarded by Evangelicals and Fundamentalists as well; their appointments at Oxford (in Williams's case, Oxford University Press) were significant because they provided a unique platform for defending Christianity. Their achievements in poetry, literary criticism, and philology are unknown, or if known, uncelebrated or ignored. In short, for Evangelicals and Fundamentalists, tasks in the world have little if any significance of their own but are instrumentalized on behalf of narrow spiritual ends. So too, influence in one or another social sphere has little if any significance except as it is instrumentalized on behalf of other social and political agendas.

In the "purity from" paradigm, it is the neo-Anabaptists who are the most distinctive of all. The neo-Anabaptist perspective has not been elaborated extensively, but where commentary exists, there is little ambiguity as to where they stand. The baseline of this view is an affirmation of the incarnational impulse, particularly in the context of church life and its direct ministries of mercy. But there it stops. Work and social life outside the church have little or no significance beyond their function to provide for one's needs.

As to work, the idea that humankind is invited to be a cocreator with God is simply wrong. As Stanley Hauerwas argues, "The good news of the creation account is that God completed his creation and that mankind needs to do nothing more to see to its perfection. That is exactly why God could call it good and rest—and more importantly invite us to rest within his completed, good creation."[9] For Hauerwas, humankind is only God's representative and a "representative is not a cocreator. A representative does not 'share by his work in the activity of the creator,' but instead reflects what that activity has already accomplished."[10] Work, then, is not a way to provide fulfillment or "[play] a role in God's continuing creation, but rather . . . the way we earn our living."[11] Robert Brimlow writing for the Ekklesia Project makes the point even more strongly, saying, "The fact that we must work to survive does not express our dignity; it expresses our fallen nature and sinfulness."[12]

The idea that the tasks one has in life—but especially one's job—can be construed as a "vocation" or "calling" is not only rejected by the neo-Anabaptists, but treated at times with remarkable contempt; their hostility to other believers with different views, unrestrained. Brimlow calls the view that work is a calling "apologetic nonsense," "foolishness," and "a bit of flatulence from theology's attempt at relevance." Its net effect is "to cheapen the gospel."[13] In a critique of Pope John Paul II's encyclical *Laborem Exercens (On Human Work)*, Hauerwas argues that his effort to renew a sense of dignity to common work not only fails but "underwrites our already overwhelming temptation to attribute too much significance to our individual efforts."[14] John Paul II's suggestion that Christ's occupation as a carpenter itself elevates work to a higher status is "ludicrous," "nothing less than an embarrassment from someone who ought to know better."[15] Critics also contend that "capitalism has so changed the nature of work today that we should not give work a spiritual decoration by designating it as a vocation. Work, at most, is a necessity of survival."[16] As Brimlow argues,

> there really is no distinction between serving fast unhealthy food to nameless clientele and serving the unhealthy appetites of fat-cat clients; nor in laboring to produce overpriced footwear for spoiled American consumers and designing luxury cars for the fantasies of the wealthy. No distinction other than salary and prestige: a whore is a whore whether for ten dollars or ten thousand. Most of our jobs are intrinsically the same: variations on themes of exploitation, catering to greed and promoting the greater comfort of the already comfortable.[17]

Rather, the idea of vocation is proper to various roles within the church.[18] As Gary Badcock explains, being a firefighter is a job, but being a church deacon is a vocation.[19]

Likewise, the idea that through our various spheres of social influence our work can contribute to the common good is also rejected. Brimlow contends that the "common good" is nothing more than "wealth generation," and thus to pursue it means that "the poor . . . become better market capitalists." This is a dubious "good," and it is hardly "shared in common."[20]

The neo-Anabaptist view of work and Christian presence in the world has important and, perhaps, unintended consequences. As a matter of theological conviction, the neo-Anabaptists cannot offer a constructive theology of work or art or commerce. Fair enough. But they also fail to offer any wisdom or encouragement or grace to believers who have to work (let alone *want* to work!) outside the church for a living. Their silence on the matter declares that the daily labor (and thus much of the lives) of most believers has little or no spiritual meaning outside of their activity in the church; in effect, that God does not care what they do as long as it is not immoral; that the day-to-day concerns of most believers do not merit the attention of church's leaders. There is an implicit elitism here that stratifies those who work in the church and those who work for a living outside the church. Clearly it is better to work in the church. This point is reinforced by the fact that the modern heroes of the faith invoked again and again—Mother Teresa, Oscar Romero, Dorothy Day, and so forth—were and are those whose lives are encompassed by the church.

There is also an implicit gnosticism within the neo-Anabaptist perspective. By not providing a theology of work, of vocation, of the arts, commerce, scholarship, and so on, the neo-Anabaptists offer a disembodied theology to the average person. What people do with their bodies and minds through most of their waking hours has no real meaning. The implication is that labor is dirty and therefore the bodies that engage in labor—the bodies that *must* engage in labor to survive, to provide for children to survive—are dirty as well. Once again, the world-hating impulse in the "purity from" perspective comes into sharp relief: there is no good in the world that can be affirmed (that is, outside the church), no beauty acknowledged (beside the beauty of holiness), no delight in anything that is not the church.

What is more, the absence of any affirmation of work of any kind—indeed the condemnation of efforts to infuse work with meaning—also underwrites the old pietistic dualism that separates the world of the sacred (church life) from the world of the profane (the world of work). Their ecclesiology is different from what we find in Evangelicalism and Fundamentalism, but the dualism they embrace is of the same fabric. Ironically, by its very commitments, such theology goes a long way toward underwriting modernity's nightmare of disenchantment described by Max Weber, where "the ultimate and most sublime values have retreated from public life either into the transcendental realm of mystic life or into the brotherliness of direct and personal human relations."[21]

Conclusion

The context is key. I have argued that in our world today, less and less ties word and world together other than will and power. In fact, the will to dominate, which I describe in Essay II, is only the most obvious expression of the dominance of will itself. In this situation, the will is ever seeking its own aspirations, fulfillment, and pleasure. Its appetites are limitless but they are made plausible all the same by a culture of apparent limitless consumer choice. But its commitments last only so long as its desires are satisfied.

Against this, I have argued that there is a different foundation for reality and thus a different kind of binding commitment symbolized most powerfully in the incarnation. The incarnation represents an alternative way by which word and world come together. It is in the incarnation and the particular way the Word became incarnate in Jesus Christ that we find the only adequate reply to challenges of dissolution and difference. If, indeed, there is a hope or an imaginable prospect for human flourishing in the contemporary world, it begins when the Word of shalom becomes flesh in us and is enacted through us toward those with whom we live, in the tasks we are given, and in the spheres of influence in which we operate. When the Word of all flourishing—defined by the love of Christ—becomes flesh in us, in our relations with others, within the tasks we are given, and within our sphere of influence—absence gives way to presence, and the word we speak to each other and to the world becomes authentic and trustworthy. This is the heart of a theology of faithful presence.[22]

In our day, the personal and even psychological implications are profound. The very nature of modern life is its fragmentation and segmentation into multiple constellations of experience, knowledge, and relationships with each constellation grounded in a specific social and institutional realm of a person's life.[23] Under such conditions, we experience a fragmentation of consciousness—what someone has recently called, "continuous partial attention." This fragmentation is often reinforced by a world of hyperkinetic activity marked by unrelenting interruption and distraction. On the one hand, such conditions foster a technical mastery that prizes speed and agility, and facility with multiple tasks—for example, using e-mail, I-M, the cell phone, the iPod, all the while eating lunch, holding a conversation, or listening to a lecture. But on the other hand, these very same conditions undermine our capacity for silence, depth of thinking, and focused attention. In other words, the context of contemporary life, by its very nature, cultivates a kind of absence in the experience of "being elsewhere." Faithful presence resists such conditions and the frame of mind it cultivates.

But what does a theology of faithful presence call for?

Against the limitless horizon of a will that is ever seeking its own fulfill-ment and pleasure, faithful presence calls believers to yield their will to God and to nurture and cultivate the world where God has placed them. "Be im-itators of God," St. Paul writes in his letter to the Ephesians, "and live a life of love, just as Christ loved us and gave himself up for us as a fragrant offering and sacrifice to God" (Eph. 5:1).

I would suggest that a theology of faithful presence first calls Christians to attend to the people and places that they experience directly. It is not that believers should be disconnected from, or avoid responsibility for, people and places across the globe. Far from it. Christians are called to "go into all the world," after all and to carry the good news in word and deed that God's kingdom has come. But with that said, the call of faithful presence gives priority to what is right in front of us—the community, the neighborhood, and the city, and the people of which these are constituted. For most, this will mean a preference for stability, locality, and particularity of place and its needs. It is here, through the joys, sufferings, hopes, disappointments, con-cerns, desires, and worries of the people with whom we are in long-term and close relation—family, neighbors, coworkers, and community—where we find our authenticity as a body and as believers. It is here where we learn forgiveness and humility, practice kindness, hospitality, and charity, grow in patience and wisdom, and become clothed in compassion, gentleness, and joy. This is the crucible within which Christian holiness is forged. This is the context within which shalom is enacted.

In our tasks, the call of faithful presence implies a certain modesty that gives priority to substance over style; the enduring over the ephemeral, depth over breadth, and quality, skill, and excellence over slick packaging or "high production values." It would encourage ambition, but the instrumentalities of ambition are always subservient to the requirements of humility and charity.

Even if our tasks in this world do not have "ultimate significance," that does not mean that the tasks we perform have no spiritual significance.[24] To be sure, sin pervades work and, in our own day, capitalism transforms the nature of work in ways that can be profoundly dehumanizing. But this does not negate the dignity that comes from tasks well done or the good done for neighbor and stranger alike. Indeed, when our various tasks are done in ways that acknowledge God, God is present and he is glorified. Such tasks may not be redeeming, but they can provide a foretaste of the coming kingdom. What can be said of tasks generally can be said, for example, about specific profes-sions. To manage a business in a way that grows out of a biblical view of relationships, community, and human dignity before God has divine significance, irrespective of what else might be done from this platform. Policy pursued and law practiced in light of the justice of God is a witness to the right ordering of human affairs. Inquiry, scholarship, and learning with an awareness of the goodness of God's created order is a discovery of what is truly higher in higher education. And, not least, reflecting the beauty of God's creation in art or music is nothing less than an act of worship. In short, fidelity to the highest practices of vocation before God is consecrated and itself transformational in its effects.

As to our spheres of influence, a theology of faithful presence obligates us to do what we are able, under the sovereignty of God, to shape the patterns of life and work and relationship—that is, the institutions of which our lives are constituted—toward a shalom that seeks the welfare not only of those of the household of God but of all. That power will be wielded is inevitable. But the *means of influence* and the *ends of influence* must conform to the exercise of power modeled by Christ.[25]

Thus, when the Word of life is enacted within the whole body of Christ in all of its members through an engagement that is individual, corporate, and institutional, not only does the word become flesh, but an entire lexicon and grammar becomes flesh in a living narrative that unfolds in the body of Christ; a narrative that points to God's redemptive purposes. It is authentic because it is enacted and finally persuasive because it reflects and reveals the shalom of God.

Chapter Five

THE BURDEN OF LEADERSHIP: A THEOLOGY
OF FAITHFUL PRESENCE IN PRACTICE

W HAT DOES A THEOLOGY of faithful presence look like in practice? Or, perhaps better put, how does the enactment of faithful presence take shape in everyday life? I'll approach this in parts if only to help sharpen the progression of my thinking about this challenge.

Though it might seem odd at first, I would suggest that a useful point of entry to the question of faithful presence in practice is a discussion of leadership. Why this is so will become apparent in short order, but only after clearing away some of the brush and debris surrounding the concept of leadership itself.

Part One: The Question of Leadership

Leadership is, in part, a set of practices surrounding the legitimate use of gifts, resources, position, and therefore influence (or relational power). But leadership is not simply one half of a dichotomy that divides the world between leaders and followers. Nor is leadership a one-dimensional or "zero-sum" property, which is to say it does not operate on a single continuum where more influence for one person or group will mean less for another. The fact is, our lives are constituted by multiple spheres of activity and relationship—not just one—and, in each of these, we have varying kinds and evolving degrees of influence. The relationships and influence we have within our families are of a different nature and capacity than what we have in our neighborhoods, or the town or city in which we live, and the relationships and influence we have in the places where we volunteer are different from those in the organizations in which we work. And within each of these spheres of activity we have different kinds of influence. It is our influence within the range of spheres of activity and relationship that defines the leadership we exercise. In short, everyone exercises leadership to varying degrees, for we all exercise relative influence in the wide variety of contexts in which we live.

By the same logic, we are all also followers in a sense, for even where we exercise leadership, we are held to account—we follow the dictates, needs, and standards of others. We are answerable to our spouses, children, and parents, to our neighbors, to employers, and to those for whom we volunteer. Even the most powerful are held to account: politicians are accountable to their constituencies; lawyers are accountable to their clients and firms; physicians are accountable to their peers, professional associations, and their patients; middle managers are accountable to senior managers; CEOs of corporations are accountable to their boards of trustees, stockholders, and employees; and all are held to account by the ethical codes of their profession. Leadership depends on a trust between those who lead and all those to whom the leader is answerable, so that when trust is violated or undermined by incompetence, leadership loses its legitimacy. To be sure, failure to be held accountable is one definition of corruption, and in a world where there is any justice, corruption will lead to a person's removal from leadership.

Leadership, then, like power, is relative. With that said, I do not want to imply naively that social influence does not operate on an absolute basis as well. Obviously, some people have more influence than others and a small number have incalculably more influence than the majority. Likewise, there are some who have next to nothing by way of life-chances or influence, and the disparities between the most influential and the least can be deplorable. My main point is that a simple dichotomous view that divides people into leaders and followers either with influence or without it is, like the concept of power itself, mostly useless, for it does not describe the reality of the world or our lives in it. Leadership, then, is an issue not for the clergy alone, nor for the "rich," the "powerful," or the "talented." Everyone is implicated in the obligations of leadership. In varying degrees and varying ways, all Christians bear this burden.

"GO INTO ALL THE WORLD"

With all of this in mind, let me offer a slight twist to the words of "the great commission." Jesus calls his followers to "go into all the world" (Mark 16:15). This, of course, has long been interpreted geographically—the call of missionaries to go to faraway places to proclaim the good news and to make disciples.[1] But the great commission can also be interpreted in terms of social structure. The church is to go into all realms of social life: in volunteer and paid labor—skilled and unskilled labor, the crafts, engineering, commerce, art, law, architecture, teaching, health care, and service. Indeed, the church should be *sending people out* in these realms—not only discipling those in these fields by providing the theological resources to form them well, but in fact mentoring and providing financial support for young adults who are gifted and called into these vocations. When the church does not send people out to these realms and when it does not provide the theologies that make sense of work and engagement in these realms, the church fails to fulfill the charge to "go into all the world."

The shalom that God offers even extends to realms of life and human experience that seem rarified and out of reach. To be obedient to Christ's instruction to "go into all the world," then, will inevitably result in some who will exercise varying degrees of leadership in these different spheres of life. Some will even operate in or close to the "center" of institutions of social, cultural, and political life. As such they will have disproportionate privilege, access, and influence that the majority of people simply don't have.

The pursuit of faithful presence in all spheres of life, then, will have social consequences. To acknowledge and to encourage this is not elitist, as some might say, but rather an obedience to Christ's directive to "go into all the world."

But on this matter, one should be very clear: this reality invariably places believers and the Church in dubious territory. Put differently, leadership may be relative, but the dangers of the abuse of power are universal and at all levels of its exercise. To the extent someone is in a position of influence, they are vulnerable to the misuse of their position. Indeed, stories of the misuse of position and influence by parents, teachers, coaches, employers, politicians, lawyers, professors, and so on are commonplace. To be sure, most Christians appropriately balk at the very mention of the word "elitism," but to adequately address it one must have a clearer understanding of the dynamics of status that underwrite it.

ELITISM AND THE PROBLEM OF STATUS

Status is a profoundly noxious subject matter, for on its face, it is intrinsically repugnant to Christian faith and witness. Yet it is part of the hard reality of the world in which the contemporary church operates and seeks to be faithfully present. The subtle and often disorienting dynamics of status are at the root of the unwritten rules by which our culture operates and, to the extent that they live in the world, Christians cannot live isolated from or untouched by its effects.

Status can be defined as social approval or disapproval and it is organized according to an often rigid, even if unformalized and unspoken, hierarchical system of ranking.[2] One can think of it as a form of capital but, in this case, it is a "symbolic capital." It is a form of "currency," but one distinct from wealth in very important ways. First, status is measured not by quantity but by quality. The more rare a distinction, the greater the prestige associated with it. Think of aristocratic titles, or awards of distinction, or election into a highly selective club or organization. Second, status does not transfer easily to others. Wealth can be passed on to children and power can be passed on to colleagues or cronies, but how can one pass on a good reputation? Likewise, status cannot easily be acquired by either wealth or power. One can buy the symbols of status, such as a college degree from a diploma mill or a large home in a wealthy neighborhood, but one cannot purchase the esteem of others or force people to have a good opinion of oneself. These factors all point to one of the key purposes of status orders—to protect the privileged by providing a resource not easily acquired nor taken by others. High status groups carefully restrict access into their circle and their benefits, otherwise, the status they possess would be diluted and their social power lessened. Another way to put this is to say that *the social dynamics of status are really fundamentally about the dynamics of exclusion.* This is, of course, why—at least on the face of it—it is so pernicious and antithetical to the gospel.[3]

Needless to say, this is a highly complex symbolic economy, the rules of which are not written down. Moreover, this economy is actually a myriad of economies localized to particular fields of social life. For example, the unspoken rules, hidden conventions, and tacit standards of excellence that make up the landscape of prestige journalism, high-end academia, corporate boardrooms, and the arts establishment (among so many other fields) all vary. Access into these fields of social life requires knowledge, experience, and accomplishment particular to these fields—which again demonstrates why status, unlike money, is not easily transferable.

The dangers are apparent. The most obvious danger is the temptation that Christians who are in positions of leadership will act in a way that is elitist. They will misuse their position to exclude others for the sake of exclusion or to protect their own power and vested interests for no other reason than to aggrandize power and privilege. Just as dangerous are the pressures of duplicity. Because Christianity has lost status in the institutional centers of the modern world, those believers who work and live in the higher echelons of culture, politics, business, and finance are under great pressure to carefully "manage their identities" in part by hiding this discrediting information about themselves. In this case, the consequence of disclosure is to be excluded themselves. The temptation to be deceptive or dishonest about one's faith in these circles is enormous.

FACING THE PARADOX

To the extent that Christians exercise leadership, then, they face an unavoidable paradox between pursuing faithful presence and the social consequences of achievement; between leadership and an elitism that all too often comes with it. The paradox is that all Christians are called to a life of humility, of placing others' interests ahead of their own, of attending to the needs of "the least among us." Yet leadership inevitably puts all in relative positions of influence and advantage. There is no way around this paradox and it is especially acute the more social influence one has.

The paradox can be seen in the witness of Christ, who reserved his harshest criticisms for the elites of his day—the Scribes, Pharisees, and Sadducees. These were cultural elites who had the privilege of education, position, even relative wealth. Christ called them on their misuse of position and power, calling them, among other things, "hypocrites," "whitewashed tombs . . . full of dead men's bones and everything unclean" (Matt. 23:27). On the face of it, one might conclude that Christ was disdainful of all those with position and rank. Yet, to establish his church among the Gentiles, he chose Paul, a man of incredible privilege, to lead. Paul was a Jew and a rabbi of high pedigree, from a wealthy trading city, born into privilege with all the advantages of Roman citizenship and trained by Gamaliel, one of the most brilliant educators of that day.[4] All of his intellectual gifts and training were brought to bear in his new service to the kingdom, yet with the full recognition that his knowledge, credentials, and elite networks were *skybala*—garbage, street filth, dung (Phil. 3:8). Christ himself was a rabbi with superior knowledge, wisdom, and authority, but he "did not consider equality with God something to be grasped" (Phil. 2:6).

What this tells us is that though the association between leadership and elitism is strong, elitism is not inherent to leadership. Though the pretensions of influence and authority are ever present, and the opportunities for hubris are everywhere, there is a different way modeled on the leadership of Jesus who rejected status and its privileges.

Though I have elaborated on this "different way" in Essay II,[5] let me reiterate a few of the key points. The practice of leadership for the Christian is sacrificial in character. The quality of commitment implied in faithful presence invariably imposes costs. To enact a vision of human flourishing based in the qualities of life that Jesus modeled will invariably challenge the given structures of the social order. In this light, there is no true leadership without putting at risk one's time, wealth, reputation, and position. In a related way, the practice of leadership is selfless in character. As Christ said, "You know that those who are considered rulers of the Gentiles lord it over them, and their great ones exercise authority over them. But it shall not be so among you. But whoever would be great among you must be your servant, and whoever would be first among you must be slave of all" (Mark 10:42–45). This he demonstrated innumerable times but one of the most poignant was his washing of the disciples' feet. The beginning of that passage notes that Christ "knew that the Father had put all things under his power, and that he had come from God and was returning to God" and so it was with this knowledge that "he got up from the meal . . . wrapped a towel around his waist . . . and began to wash his disciples' feet, drying them with the towel that was wrapped around him" (John 13:3–5). The reason that leadership is sacrificial and selfless is because its practice is an expression of "power under submission."[6] The gifts, resources, and influence one stewards are not one's own to use as one wishes but rather they belong to God: they exist under his authority, and believers are held to account for how they steward them.

In short, faithful presence in practice is the exercise of leadership in all spheres and all levels of life and activity. It represents a quality of commitment oriented to the fruitfulness, wholeness, and well-being of all. It is, therefore, the opposite of elitism and the domination it implies.

It is also the antithesis of celebrity, a model of leadership that many Christians in prominent positions have a very difficult time resisting. Celebrity is, in effect, based on an inflated brilliance, accomplishment, or spirituality generated and perpetuated by publicity. It is an artifice and, therefore, a type of fraud. Where it once served power and patrons, in our own day it mainly serves itself and its pecuniary interests. Celebrity must, of necessity, draw attention to itself. In American Christianity, the relentless pressure to raise funds within churches and para-church organizations reinforces the pressure toward celebrity, with an endless flow of direct mail, advertising, and ghostwritten sermons, speeches, articles, editorials, and so on. These pressures are difficult to resist even for those who, by instinct, might find celebrity either tasteless or problematic. The reason is that celebrity is not just a certain kind of status one achieves but it is also a powerful institution the entire structure of which is oriented toward burnishing a leader's image and projecting his or her visibility. The justification one often hears is that more people are reached in this way, yet there are often financial interests at stake for the celebrity leader and his or her organization, and these can either obscure or undermine the ends of outreach.

And so, whether leadership is expressed within the dynamics of celebrity or outright arrogance rooted in a sense of superiority, such leadership is artificial, unbiblical, organizationally unhealthy, inherently corrupting, and all too common in the Christian world—especially in the United States. Christianity needs to rediscover an alternative.

Part Two: Faithful Presence as Covenantal Commitment

This may seem like mere throat-clearing, but what has been said thus far is, rather, central to the question at hand. Before more can be said of a practical nature here, let me make a caveat: volumes could and should be written to address the questions surrounding practical application. It is essential to address this question through further biblical and theological reflections. Every bit as important are stories from individuals, organizations, and churches that are creatively practicing faithful presence, whether by instinct or by conscious design. For all that could be said, my purposes here are modest; to be suggestive rather than comprehensive.

I have argued that faithful presence is a theology of commitment and promise. The commitment is "covenantal." It is a binding obligation manifested in the relationships we have, in the work we do, and in the social worlds we inhabit, and it is all oriented toward the flourishing of the world around us. Consider the analogy of marriage. As with marriage, one is bound by oath to live for the benefit of one's spouse. It is not a coincidence that one of the central metaphors of scripture is that of marriage. In the creation narrative, God institutes marriage as a gift to humanity.[7] It is not only the bond of unity between man and woman but a sign and symbol of his covenant with humanity; with all creation. In their hope for the renewal of the covenant, the prophets often describe God, or the coming messiah, as a bridegroom taking Israel as his spouse or bride (Jer. 2:2; Isa. 54:4–8).[8] "I will betroth you to me forever," Hosea writes. "I will betroth you in righteousness and justice, in love and compassion. I will betroth you in faithfulness, and you will acknowledge the Lord" (Hos. 2:16–24). In a similar way, Jesus repeatedly called himself the bridegroom and his followers, a virgin, a bride, or the espoused,[9] and St. Paul elaborates on this theme repeatedly in his epistles.[10] Scripture, of course, concludes with a description of the final consummation, "the marriage feast of the Lamb," which marks the beginning of the new creation—"a new heaven and a new earth" (Rev. 19:9, 21:9; 22:1). The point of this covenantal commitment—the ends to which it is all directed—is the shalom of God, the flourishing of his creation.

The covenantal character of marriage is not identical to the commitment required in the practice of faithful presence but it is akin to it. It is an image of presence and of proximity or nearness. The central question in such a relationship is what does love require?

This understanding of covenant and covenantal relationship is not only seen through the metaphor of marriage, it is also the origin of the idea of justice itself. As Nicholas Wolterstorff has demonstrated, the modern ideal of justice has roots far deeper than the secular Enlightenment. It is, in fact, rooted in Jewish and Christian sources that understood justice not as the claims that could be made by an aggrieved party (as it is in contemporary rights language) but rather in the obligations we owe to all those who are aggrieved and in need.[11]

. . . TOWARD FAITH, HOPE, AND LOVE

What, then, are the obligations of faithful presence? What are the contours of flourishing toward which the Christian community should strive? If the *means* by which this faithful presence is enacted is through pursuit, identification, and the offering of shalom through sacrifice, what does the offering of shalom comprise? The answer I offer here is certainly not exhaustive, but I would suggest that the concrete manifestations of the shalom offered centrally include faith, hope, and love, for where these are present, so is joy.[12]

Faith, hope, and love? It is both natural and essential for Christians to understand these practices in the traditional terms of personal piety—the individual's faith in God, the hope of one's own resurrection, and the personal love of God and neighbor. Clearly, these practices also extend to the faith shared, the hope claimed, and the love expressed by the whole body of Christ together in worship and in acts of mercy. These are, of course, central to Christian experience and witness. For this reason it would always be mistaken to diminish the importance of the individual or collective expression of these spiritual virtues. At the same time, it is important not to limit their understanding to personal experience alone or to their specifically Christian meaning. Faith, hope, and love have a broader character as well, for they speak to basic human needs shared throughout the human community.

Faith, of course, speaks to the fundamental need for meaning. Without at least a partial belief in our own significance, the significance of what we do, and the significance of life, we are left with a cynicism that tends to be contemptuous of others, derisive toward the good, and blind toward all that is beautiful and blessed. Hope speaks to the fundamental need for purpose. Without a commitment to ideals that transcend the self and that direct life beyond self-interest, one is left with a despair that is not only joyless but also is indifferent toward need and thus incapable of addressing need. Hope is also intimately tied to beauty for it is images of beauty and loveliness that inspire imagination and thus expand the horizons of human possibility. Love is even more encompassing than faith and hope. Love is certainly about the elemental need for intimacy, affection, and the bonds of belonging without which one is left alienated and estranged from others and one's environment. But love is also about grace, mercy, and justice, without which we are left with malice and humiliation, cruelty and coercion, and injury and injustice.

The practice of faithful presence, then, generates relationships and institutions that are fundamentally covenantal in character, the ends of which are the fostering of meaning, purpose, truth, beauty, belonging, and fairness—not just for Christians but for everyone. Christians in these relationships and institutions, of course, will find a freedom to appropriate the particularity of their Christian faith and flourish accordingly. People of other faiths and no faith will enjoy the same freedom, and in these contexts will find places of grace and beauty in all of their expressions. Here they will also discover that their lives matter and their work makes a difference; that they belong to a community in which they are valued and treated with fairness, respect, and compassion.

Many Christians would undoubtedly object to this broader understanding of faith, hope, and love and, even more, object to creating common space in which those outside of the Christian community can also appropriate meaning, purpose, beauty, and belonging. Why should their commitment to the world go beyond trying to persuade nonbelievers to convert in order to attain heaven? Beyond being a good in its own right, there are at least two reasons why Christians must move in this direction. The first is a political reason: Christians cannot demand for themselves what they would deny others. A right for one is a right for another and a responsibility for all. A right for a Christian is a right for a Jew is a right for a Humanist is a right for a Muslim is a right for a Buddhist, and so on.[13] The second is a cultural reason: the very plausibility and persuasiveness of the Christian faith depend on a cultural context in which meaning, purpose, beauty, and belonging are possible. The viability of Christian faith and the possibility of sharing that faith depend on a social environment in which faith—any faith—is plausible.

Needless to say, much of the late modern world is antithetical to the ideals and practices of faith, hope, and love—and not just the particular

Christian understanding and observances of them. Nihilism may not be all-pervasive but it is endemic to the late modern world. It is most apparent, of course, in the violence and empty spectacle of large swaths of popular culture. But it is also built into a social order whose dominating logic, symbols, language, and metaphors give expression to market utility (as well as other forms of instrumentalism). This is what is meant by the idea of a "market society," where the logic, language, and ideals of rational and free exchange based on a calculation of costs and benefits spill out of the economy proper and into the entire culture thus shaping every sphere of social life. It isn't just the world of commerce, strictly speaking, or even the business of entertainment, sports, and the media, that operate on market principles. But in a market society, the means and ends of popular and higher education, law, art, and religious institutions are increasingly organized along market principles as well. In the case of the mega-churches or the seeker church movement in Evangelicalism, the embrace of a market rationale is the deliberate foundation of its strategy. In a market society, private life is similarly affected. Even friendship, intimacy, parenting, career, and the organization of everyday life, not to mention life-planning, are organized less according to ethical principles or spiritual ideals and obligations and more according to the principle of maximizing benefits and minimizing costs. This kind of autonomous instrumentality is also fundamentally nihilistic.

It is not surprising, then, that for all the good that remains in the world and that we continue to create, there is much in the late modern world that generates meaninglessness, ugliness, estrangement, heartlessness, and outright cruelty. Ironically, this also explains the fierce reaction of fundamentalisms both at home and abroad, for fundamentalism is not so much a resurgence of traditional[14] religion but, rather, a reaction to the very discontents the contemporary world generates. Yet fundamentalism is also nihilistic because its identity is established, in the most primordial way, negatively—in reaction to the cultural deprivations of the late modern world. The proof of its nihilism is its failure to offer any creative achievements or constructive proposals for the everyday problems that trouble most people. Is it any wonder that fundamentalisms tend to contribute to estrangement and cruelty?

It is against the invasive nihilism of the late modern world and the cultural logics that produce them, then, that we see the significance of faithful presence in practice. The covenantal commitment at the root of faithful presence cultivates faith, hope, and love, and as such, it radically challenges the cultural foundations of much of the late modern world. Put differently, the practices of faithful presence represent an assault on the worldliness of this present age. However, as I have argued throughout, this assault does not manifest itself as mere negation of nihilism. If this were the primary expression of this challenge it would be, in its means and method, of a fabric with the nihilism it seeks to repudiate. It would simply be one more negation. Rather, the primary nature of the assault is, as I have argued, more of a bursting out of new creation from within it. To the extent that Christians have any influence and exercise leadership in whatever sphere of life they inhabit, to that extent Christians have a covenantal obligation to actively and concretely realize faith, hope, and love in all that these ideals mean.

Part Three: Faithful Presence as Practice

But what would this entail? Take as a starting point, the world of work and the institutions of business and commerce in particular. The first challenge is simply to recognize that employees and customers have a greater intrinsic value than their tangible contribution as economic actors. In this light, the challenge is to conceptualize the relationship of employer to employee or the relationship between business and customer in terms that go beyond mere contract to that of covenant. What do employers owe to their employees besides a payment for services? What do businesses owe customers besides a product or service for a fee? Such a reconceptualization would fundamentally change the established terms of market relations and, in turn, profoundly humanize the work environment.

Further, in the visual arts, literature, and music, the first challenge is to simply demonstrate a commitment to excellence in aesthetics (the theory of art) and in the production of artifacts of art generally. I say this is first because such a commitment among Christians generally has been weak over the past century, and among Protestants all but absent. The obligation among artists who are Christians is, among other things, to demonstrate in ways that are imaginative and compelling that materiality is not enough for a proper understanding of human experience; that there is durability and permanence as well as eternal qualities that exist beyond what we see on the surface of life. In this, they must show a depth and complexity to people and the world that defy the one- or two-dimensional existence of modern life. In the process, it is possible to symbolically portray possibilities of beauty and fullness we have not yet imagined. In architecture and urban planning, the challenge is to create spaces that go beyond mere efficient functioning to places that respond to our deepest needs for safety, sociality, and human scale–living; places that retain or encourage the development of the distinctive imprint of individual design and craft.[15] In the news media and in academia, the challenge begins by creating resources and space for the pursuit of knowledge and understanding that are protected from the enormous pressures of partisan politics (which makes knowledge a tool in the quest for power) and commercial interest (in which the worth of knowledge is gauged by its market value). This creates a context in which genuine inquiry is possible and thus truths about the world we live in are possible. In public discourse, the challenge is not to stifle robust debate, but rather to make sure that it is real debate. The first obligation for Christians is to listen carefully to opponents and if they are not willing to do so, then Christians should simply be silent. To engage in a war of words is to engage in a symbolic violence that is fundamentally at odds with the gospel. And too often, on such hot button issues as poverty, abortion, race relations, and homosexuality, the poor, children, minorities, and gays are used as weapons in ideological warfare. This too is an expression of instrumentalization.[16]

In all, the practice of faithful presence generates relationships and institutions that are covenantal. These create space that fosters meaning, purpose, and belonging and by so doing, these relationships and institutions resist an instrumentalization endemic to the modern world that tends to reduce the value of people and the worth of creation to mere utility, whether utility is oriented toward market efficiency, expanding power, or personal fulfillment. To use gifts, resources, and influence in ways that do not translate immediately or perhaps ever into utility may seem extravagant. In our day, such commitment cannot be justified on economic or political grounds for it cannot measure up to contemporary standards of efficiency or efficacy. Yet to provide for the physical, aesthetic, intellectual, and social health of the community is a good in its own right and it is part and parcel of the covenant that believers have with the people that God has placed in their lives and the social and physical world in which God has placed them.

A Few Vignettes . . .

Consider a few vignettes of the practice of "faithful presence within."

. . . An automotive company in the Southeast has organized its business model on the basis of a rethinking of capitalism. Instead of running the business purely on the model of exchange and contract, this company actually operates along the lines mentioned above, on the premise of covenant; its core question being: "what do we owe our customers and our employees?" The result is a very different way of doing business. Consider one way it has benefited customers: seeing that the profit margins of inner-city dealerships (which tended to serve lower income and minority populations) were higher than the suburban dealerships (which served a better educated and wealthier clientele), the company fixed prices for cars in the inner-city dealerships at a level that brought in a much lower profit margin than the suburban dealerships. But at these lower pricing levels, the company has generated a much greater volume of business than ever; more too than any of its competitors. As to employees, the leadership recognized that lower-level wage earners would not have the same life chances as management, so the business established a scholarship fund that pays the college tuition of all children of the company. The cost of the program is high, though the benefit to the business is the loyalty of its employees. In both situations, the guiding question has been, what does it mean to do good to the vulnerable? These are just two illustrations of the many innovations that have emerged from this business model.

. . . An art gallery in northwest Washington, D.C., operating from the premise that people with the greatest need had the greatest need for beauty, sponsored thirty D.C. artists to paint and sculpt scenes from Anacostia, the area of the nation's capital most stigmatized by poverty and violence. The art show was previewed on the streets of Anacostia and later exhibited in Washington's Union Station. Officials claimed that it was the most successful exhibit ever held in the station, with over 1.5 million viewers of the collection. The beauty, history, and humanness of those long forgotten was honored and celebrated.

. . . A not-for-profit housing corporation in central Michigan came into existence on the basis of the belief that all people deserve safe, clean, affordable housing. Its corporate values include the conviction that all persons are created in God's image and exist in the light of his love and, for this reason, all who are served are to be treated with respect and equality; that housing should be designed to complement surrounding architectural character, affirming personal dignity, beauty, and inspiring neighborhood pride; that human and financial resources should be administered conscientiously and with integrity; and for its own staff, a commitment to education and professional growth that will promote effectiveness and personal fulfillment. Since its inception, the corporation has repaired, constructed, or reconstructed nearly five hundred housing units. At present, they serve over 2,500 families annually in need of emergency shelter services, permanent rental housing, or home ownership opportunities.

. . . A medical doctor has conducted years of research into strategies that humanize and bring meaning to long-term care for debilitating illnesses and, in the process, she has become a public champion for palliative care in the medical profession, which often wants to look away when it reaches the limits. She has begun three palliative care and geriatric programs training health-care professionals in advanced illness care.

. . . A business in Kansas City was restructured on the basis of a different view of human nature. Abandoning the notion that people should be "managed," the leadership team was restructured around the concept of "mentoring." Mentoring makes sense when work is a calling rather than a career, performed with colleagues rather than employees, and the focus is profession as much as production. In this way, mentoring instills a code for life—as it ought to be, is, can be, and will be—including work. Work, in this model, has become a source of meaning that has transformed all associated with the company.

. . . Three college classmates from a large state university started a magazine that showcased "signs of life in music, film, and culture." Avoiding the aesthetic and moral squalor often depicted in rock 'n' roll magazines, the magazine celebrated musical quality and promoted cultural products that ennobled the human spirit. It has grown to having today over 100,000 subscribers—the third-largest music magazine in the United States—and has been repeatedly nominated for the top national magazine award. When the magazine was faced recently with declining advertising revenue, loyal subscribers who valued its unique voice contributed over $220,000 to a "save the magazine" campaign.

. . . A supercomputer genius and high tech entrepreneur launched his technological breakthrough in the entertainment industry by providing extreme computing solutions for CGI and VFX applications. The company is using the profits to establish a film and cultural renewal fund in order to invest in projects that foster human flourishing and the common good.

. . . A group of business leaders in Houston generated the funds to establish a private, faith-based school in the most poverty- and crime-ridden part of the city. The school exclusively serves children from low-income families with a program designed to provide them the educational, spiritual, social, and practical resources they need in life. Partnering with FORGE for Families, the school reaches out to address the needs of the families as well by providing counseling, life-skills training, an anti-addiction program, and the like. In its own words, the school "exists to promote human flourishing among Houston's poorest families."

. . . And last, not least, is a woman who rang up and bagged groceries and whose sphere of influence was only six square feet. Every day she greeted her customers with genuine enthusiasm, remembering customers' names and asking about their families. She would end every conversation by saying that she was going to pray for their family. Over time, this caused problems, for people wanted to get in her aisle, which resulted in large lines. People would wait, though, because they enjoyed being with her, encouraged just by her presence. At her funeral, years after she retired, the church was packed to standing-room-only capacity, and she was eulogized again and again by people whom she had encouraged for years.

These are only a few of the innovative ways in which Christians are practicing "faithful presence within" and, in so doing, living and working toward the well-being of others.[17] Much more could be said about how in each of these situations, the material conditions and institutional circumstances were addressed in ways that responded to the complex array of need of those served. The point of recounting them is not to be exhaustive, of course, but to be illustrative of the ways in which Christians use the space they live in toward the flourishing of others. They are less a blueprint to be applied than a catalyst for thinking about other imaginative possibilities for the transformation of culture in business, the arts, medicine, housing, and the like.

Part Four: The Burden of Leadership

The burden of leadership—and thus the task for the church and all Christians—in every generation is to "seek first the Kingdom of God and His righteousness"; to seek to integrate the very order of the heavens within our personal lives and relationships, our families, our work and leisure, and our communities. God's Kingdom, of course, is not political in character but spiritual, moral, relational, vocational, and environmental (including the social milieu). In this way Christians proclaim the good news, that the light and life of heaven itself is available to everyone through the person of Jesus. The practice of faithful presence, then, is the incarnation of a kind of leadership that realizes in the relationships we have, in the tasks we undertake, and within the actual places (both physical and social) we inhabit, the shalom that comes from God and that is God in the person of Jesus Christ.

Another and perhaps simpler way of saying this is that *the burden of shalom falls to leaders*. Thus, the obligations of shalom fall to *all of us* to the extent that we wield any influence at all. Because "in Christ we who are many form one body, and each member belongs to all the others," this burden is borne by and through the whole church and in turn within every sphere of human activity.[18] It goes without saying that in every sphere of life, the greater the influence we have, the greater the burden we bear.

Overlapping Networks in Common Cause

It is important to emphasize that this is a burden borne by every Christian individually, but it is also a responsibility to be realized institutionally. In each occupation, vocation, or profession, leaders need to look for opportunities to form networks and mobilize resources including symbolic capital, financial capital, social capital, and administrative capital in common purposes. This was part of the lesson of the vignettes recounted above. Such initiatives would need to take shape over specific concerns and in specific spheres of life. In each, Christians will have to be attentive to and operate within the dynamics of center and periphery. The tension-laden and potentially compromising realities of power will be in play. In the way such initiatives are pursued and in their net effect, however, Christians and the church as a whole would be creating structures that incarnate blessing, beauty, meaningfulness, and purpose not just for the benefit of believers but for the good of all.

This institutional aspect to faithful presence is not optional but rather of essential importance. Without addressing the material conditions and social institutions of daily life, one ends up with the same individualism and idealism that so fatally undermine Christian life and witness at present. This means that it will inevitably permeate elite networks, status systems, and the larger cultural economy with a different vision and way of life.

In all of this, the church—local parishes, consortiums of congregations, and denominational bodies, among others—is of central importance here. As the locus of worship and formation it should not only be the catalyst for the active cultivation of these networks but also the connective tissue among overlapping networks. The church discovers in this a vital manifestation of its call to "go into all the world proclaiming the good news."

Let me be clear. What is required here is not a new ministry or a new program. Thinking of ways to instantiate a vision of human flourishing in the wide range of circumstances and spheres of social life (and thus, of ways to be public without being narrowly political) will take creative thinking, imagination, and hard work. Learning to move outside of the dominant individualist, idealist, and pragmatist assumptions may be impossible for many.[19] This is not the work of a three-step, six-month plan. Nor is it a new strategy at all but a mode of individual and collective being. What I am suggesting again is a new paradigm of being the church in the late modern world. The institutional aspect of faithful presence means that Christians and the church are settling in for the duration.

The Christian tradition has a long history of doing precisely this work in everything from the patronage of the arts and the establishment of schools and universities to the creation of hospitals and institutions that care for the poor and the needy. These were all institutions that practiced faithful presence. The church and Christians everywhere must do this again in ways appropriate to the times. Indeed, there are intellectual, economic, and managerial resources available within the church and among Christians to make a profound difference in every sphere of life—the social welfare of the needy, the environment, education, the arts, academia, business, community formation and urban life, and so on; and at every order of magnitude—the local, the regional, the national, and the international. This will invariably mean collaboration, networking, mutual dependence, and institution-building. At times Christians will go it alone and at times they will partner with those of other faiths and none. But it all should be oriented toward enhancing the well-being of all.

Efficacy

In the most practical terms, the measure of the efficacy of such engagement is found in the many ways vitality finds expression. Do individuals and communities grow in health, knowledge, wisdom, prosperity, freedom, and generosity? Of special concern are the least privileged and those who are most disadvantaged. Do they benefit in tangible ways, gaining a range of advantages that enhance their lives that they did not have before? Are the tasks we undertake done well and do they contribute to the good of others? And do the specific social milieus and physical surroundings where we live and work become more beautiful, more civil, and more just?

What is achievable? It will vary of course in time and circumstance. Certainly one should be careful not to confuse shalom (this side of the veil) with material excess, where desire is never satisfied and one never has enough. Nor should it be confused with the absence of physical defects or the elimination of all suffering. Shalom comes with an awareness of life's goodness, an experience of "plenitude," and therein, joy. Thus, with shalom, there can be abundance even in the absence of affluence, joy even in the absence of cheerfulness, harmony even in the absence of agreement, and health even in the absence of a cure. Against those theologians who argue that the common good is a fiction,[20] living toward the well-being of others in these ways will make constructive and incremental differences for others, for the community and the city in every sphere of life.

One can find in the history of Catholicism, Protestantism, and Orthodoxy heroic expressions of faithful presence. Such an orientation, then, is not without historical precedence. Even today, there are organizations, businesses, social initiatives, and ministries that give expression to faithful presence in several realms of social life. There are Christians today who have been yearning for something different, who recognize intuitively that the older paradigms of engagement are fundamentally flawed and are discovering an alternative that looks something like what I have described here. In the context of contemporary Christianity in North America, the paradigm "faithful presence within" represents an alternative to the "defensive against," "relevance to," and "purity from" paradigms; and the more closely one looks, the more one realizes just how quietly radical this alternative actually is.

Chapter Six

TOWARD A NEW CITY COMMONS

W E ARE NOW at the point where we can begin working through the implications of a theology and practice of faithful presence. To start off, it would be good to run through a few highlights of the argument to this point.

I note in Essay I that Christians have long had a healthy desire to change the world for the better, a desire with roots in sound biblical and theological reasoning. In the past, however, they have done so with mixed effect. Even in a context of a revisionist history that would highlight all of the instances of hypocrisy and harm, overwhelmingly and in the quiet ways that history never records, the consequences of this engagement have been wholesome, courageous, constructive, and life-giving. At other times, of course, the outcomes have been less than salubrious, even if unintentionally so. And it would be dishonest to history not to acknowledge the instances, sadly not so infrequent, of those efforts that have been outright stupid, heartless, cruel, craven, and depraved. But noble intentions abound, and it is fair to say that Christians today are no less well intentioned and no less motivated to do good than in times past.

The first problem is that the implicit social theory that guides so much of their efforts is deeply flawed. Christians from many different traditions tend to believe that cultures are shaped from the cumulative values and beliefs that reside in the hearts and minds of ordinary people. The means and ends of world-changing, they argue, are to change the hearts and minds of enough people that the social order will finally come to reflect the values and beliefs that they hold. This is why Christians often pursue social change through evangelism (and conversion), civic renewal through populist social movements, and democratic political action (where every vote reflects values). The evidence of history and sociology demonstrates that this theory of culture and cultural change is simply wrong and for this reason, every initiative based on this perspective will fail to achieve the goals it hopes to meet. This is not to say that the hearts and minds of ordinary people are unimportant. To the contrary. Rather, the hearts and minds of ordinary people are only relatively insignificant if the goal is to change cultures at their deepest levels.

Against this view, I have argued that cultural change at its most profound level occurs through dense networks of elites operating in common purpose within institutions at the high-prestige centers of cultural production. In light of this, the cultural economy of contemporary Christianity has been strongest, in the main, where cultural leverage is weakest—on the social periphery rather than the cultural center and in tastes that run to the lower-middle and middle brow rather than the high brow. The idea that significant numbers of Christians are operating in "the halls of power" in ways that are thoughtful and strategic, then, is simply ludicrous. What is more, for all the vitality it still manifests, Christianity in North America and the West more generally is a weak culture; weak insofar as it is fragmented in its core beliefs and organization, without a coherent collective identity and mission, and often divided within itself, often with unabated hostility. Thus, for all the talk of world-changing and all of the good intentions that motivate it, the Christian community is not, on the whole, remotely close to a position where it could actually change the world in any significant way. This does not mean that Christians don't have important influence in interpersonal settings or in local cultures—they can and do—but typically when Christians speak of world-changing, their sights are considerably more ambitious. They want to change societies and civilizations. It is this ambition that is not even distantly linked to realistic strategies or positions capable of achieving those ambitions.

Were Christians to be in a position to exert enduring cultural influence, the results would likely be disastrous or perhaps mostly so. The reason, I argue in Essay II, is that world-changing implies power and the implicit theories of power that have long guided their exercise of power are also deeply problematic. First, the working theory of power is still influenced by Constantinian tendencies toward conquest and domination. As we have seen, these tendencies play out among Christian progressives as well as among Christian conservatives: though guided differently by powerful mythic narratives, most Christians cannot imagine power in any other way than toward what finally leads to political domination. Thus, it is not surprising that, in conformity to the spirit of the modern age, Christians conceive of power as *political* power. Christians, like most modern people, have politicized every aspect of public life and private life as well—from church/state issues, education, the media, entertainment and the arts, and the environment to family values, sexuality, and parenting. In this, they mistakenly imagine that to pass a referendum, elect a candidate, pass a law, or change a policy is to change culture. In truth they probably know better, but in terms of the amount of energy expended and money spent, the net effect is a view much like this. While Christian activists (conservative and progressive) have been fairly influential in the political sphere at different times in recent decades, they have embraced a means to power that seethes with resentment, anger, and bitterness for the injury they believe they have suffered. The public and political culture of contemporary Christianity have become defined by such negations. There is nothing illegal about any of this, of course. Christians believe that they have a legitimate right to participate in the democratic process and they are, of course, right. The problem resides with the political culture they not only embrace but have helped to create. The tragic irony is that in the name of resisting the dark nihilisms of the modern age, Christians—in their will to power and the *ressentiment* that fuels it—perpetuate that nihilism. In so doing, Christians undermine the message of the very gospel they cherish and desire to advance.

Finally, I argued in the present essay, the political agendas of the Christian Right, Christian Left, and the neo-Anabaptists are just the leading edge of larger paradigms of cultural engagement that I call, respectively, "defensive against," "relevance to," and "purity from." Each of these paradigms operates with different understandings of what it is that most needs changing within the contemporary world. Within the "defensive against," the problem is secularization; for those in the "relevance to," the main problem is the exploitation of people and the environment rooted in modern capitalism; and within the "purity from," it is varied, but for the most intellectually robust faction the central problem is found in the violence and other deformities of power rooted in the modern state and market. All three understandings of what is most challenging if not destructive in the modern world have a great deal of merit. At the same time, the ground has shifted in ways that most Christians have not recognized or come to terms with. As serious and problematic as secularization, exploitation, and violence are, the challenges of "difference" and "dissolution" discussed earlier in this essay go to the core of what it means to be a Christian in the first place. Until Christians come to terms with these matters, they cannot begin to coherently or effectively address the other matters.

Toward a New City Commons

So how should Christians engage the world?

For one, it should be clear at this point that good intentions are not enough to engage the world well. The potential for stupidity, irrationality, cruelty, and harm is just as high today as it has ever been in the past. God save us from Christians who are well-intentioned, but not wise!

As to a strategy for engaging the world, perhaps there is no single model for all times and places. I don't know enough to even speculate. But in the twenty-first century, there is a growing recognition that the old models of engagement no longer work, if they ever did. If I am right about the challenges of difference and dissolution, there is no way the old models could ever be sufficient to address the challenges of the present age. What is more, there is a yearning for a different way, especially among the young; a way that has integrity with the historic truths of the faith and the witness of the Spirit and that is adequate to the challenges of the present moment.

In opposition to the "defensive against," "relevance to," and "purity from" paradigms, then, I have suggested a model of engagement called "faithful presence within." Its foundation is a theology of faithful presence, a theology I have only sketched in the most simple and unsophisticated of terms. What does this model of engagement look like? Let me offer a picture from the book of the prophet Jeremiah.

> Thus says the Lord of hosts, the God of Israel, to all the exiles whom I have sent into exile from Jerusalem to Babylon: Build houses and live in them; plant gardens and eat their produce.
>
> Take wives and have sons and daughters; take wives for your sons, and give your daughters in marriage, that they may bear sons and daughters; multiply there and do not decrease. But seek the welfare of the city where I have sent you into exile, and pray to the Lord on its behalf, for in its welfare you will find your welfare. (Jer. 29:4–7)

One hears this passage quoted from time to time but typically not with reference to the context, a context that is critical to a more complete understanding of the text and its contemporary implications.

In 588 BC, the armies of Nebuchadnezzar conquered Jerusalem. His strategy of subjugation included confiscating much of the collective wealth from the temple and forcefully deporting the vast majority of Jews, including their leadership—the king and queen mother, priests, local officials, and the most skilled craftsmen—back to Babylon, nearly a thousand miles away.[1] The Israelites did not understand what God was doing. One of the reasons was that several prominent figures in the community had prophesied the imminent deliverance of the Jews from their captivity, their return to Judea, and the restoration of Jerusalem. One such prophet, Hananiah, predicted it would happen within two years. But Jeremiah had a different word. This part of the text was written by Jeremiah, who was still in Jerusalem, as a letter to the refugees to help them make sense, theologically and historically, of their exile.

The premise of Jeremiah's message was that the exiles would be in Babylon for several generations—at least seventy years, a time period that included not only the reign of Nebuchadnezzar but of his son and grandson (Jer. 25:11; 27:7; 29:10). The Israelites would simply need to come to terms with this fact. It was toward this end that Jeremiah counseled his community not to be nostalgic for the past, for the past could not be recovered. Nor did he advise them to plan for insurrection, for there was no promise of their restoration in Jerusalem, at least not any time soon. Nor yet was the community's survival tied to the remnant that remained in Jerusalem (Jer. 24:5–10). For Jeremiah, exile did not mean that God had abandoned Israel. Rather, exile was the place where God was at work. God's purposes with Israel, in other words, were served by the Babylonian invasion. God, as the text repeats, "sent" them into exile. Indeed, Jeremiah contends that Nebuchadnezzar was, in some sense, God's servant (Jer. 27:6). For this reason, his counsel was for them to settle in for the long term: "build," "plant," "marry," "have children," "take wives for your sons, and give your daughters in marriage that they also may bear sons and daughters." Exile would clearly last long beyond the present generation.

Jeremiah's guidance was even more counterintuitive than it might first seem. If God's purposes really were being realized through these circumstances, then the welfare of the Babylonian conquerors was linked to their own welfare. To this end, Jeremiah instructs the Jews in exile to "seek the welfare" of their captors, to pray for the very people who destroyed their homeland, for the welfare of the exiles and the captors were bound together. As they pursued the shalom of Babylon, God would provide shalom for his people.

Clearly it would have been justifiable for the Jews to be hostile to their captors. It also would have been natural enough for them to withdraw from engaging the world around them. By the same token, it would have been easy for them to simply assimilate with the culture that surrounded them. Any of these three options made sense in human terms. But God was calling them to something different—not to be defensive against, isolated from, or absorbed into the dominant culture, but to be faithfully present within it. On the face of it, this was not a posture of radical and prophetic challenge to the powers that be, but neither was it a passive acceptance of the established order. The people of Israel were being called to enter the culture in which they were placed *as God's people*—reflecting in their daily practices their distinct identity as those chosen by God. He was calling them to maintain their distinctiveness as a community but in ways that served the common good.

It is not surprising that Jeremiah was viewed as something of a traitor to the cause of Israel for conveying this view, but his point—and God's message to the Jews—was that God was present to them and at work with them *in the context of exile* and in this context, faithfulness meant being a blessing to the world in which they were placed.

What does this passage mean for us? Though it is quite possible that this portrayal from Jeremiah is not applicable to Christians in all times and all places, I do believe this is a word for our time. The story of Jeremiah 29 comports well with what we learn from St. Peter, who with so many others speaks of Christians as "exiles in the world" (1:1, 2:11) encouraging us to "live [our] lives as strangers here in reverent fear" (1:17). God is at work in our own place of exile, and the welfare of those with whom we share a world is tied to our own welfare. In this light, St. Peter encourages believers repeatedly to be "eager to do good" (3:17) and for each person to "use whatever gift he has received to serve others, faithfully administering God's grace in its various forms" (4:10). This understanding also comports with other New Testament admonitions to "never tire of doing right" (II Thess. 3:13), to "let your magnanimity be manifest to all" (Phil. 4:5), and to "look to each other's interest and not merely to your own" (Phil. 2:4). As Paul writes elsewhere, "Now to each one the manifestation of the Spirit is given for the common good" (1 Cor. 12:7). All of this is in keeping with the instruction that the people of God are to be committed to the welfare of the cities in which they reside in exile, even when the city is indifferent, hostile, or ungrateful.

This is an older wisdom, but in the situation in which Christians find themselves today, it holds the markings of a new paradigm. A theology of faithful presence calls Christians to enact the shalom of God in the circumstances in which God has placed them and to actively seek it on behalf of others. This is a vision for the entire church. It is a burden for the entire laity in all the tasks they undertake, in all vocations—ordinary and extraordinary, "common" and rarified—and in all walks of life with whatever resources they have available to them. In God's eyes, it is faithful presence that matters. As I have argued repeatedly in this essay, faithful presence has implications that go far beyond individual engagement with the world. It also goes far beyond an engagement of "values," "worldviews," or "artifacts." The enactments of shalom need to extend into the institutions of which all Christians are a part and, as they are able, into the formation of new institutions within every sphere of life.

A premise of this view is a recognition that Christians share a world with others and that they must contribute to its overall flourishing. This imperative is captured by the image of a "new city commons." What is "new" in the new city commons? Against the dominant liberal modernist notion that the public sphere is constituted by a diversity of autonomous and unencumbered individuals, in this view there is a recognition that public diversity—whose focal metaphor is the city—is also defined collectively by multiple traditions and communities. Needless to say, some of these are very different from, if not hostile to, the community of Christian believers. But even when there is disagreement, tension, and conflict, there is also a recognition that there are common goods that communities of Christians, drawing on the resources of their tradition, must still hold up, pursue, work at, foster, and practice.[2] *In short, commitment to the new city commons is a commitment of the community of faith to the highest ideals and practices of human flourishing in a pluralistic world.*

The Church in Tension . . .

The account in the book of Jeremiah makes it clear that God, in his own timing, will eventually bring about the restoration of Jerusalem. So too, for Christians, restoration in the New Jerusalem will come one day. Until then, however, there are tensions that the church must not only live with, but deliberately and actively cultivate.

WITH ITSELF

One cluster of tensions it must cultivate is within itself—tensions that naturally arise from a desire to do good, on the one hand, and its own worst proclivities in pursuing that good, on the other.

The first of these plays out in the Constantinian temptation discussed at length in these essays. Though I don't want to beat a dead horse, the issue of power is so critically important that it is worth revisiting one last time.

Consider the matter in this way: a young leader in the emerging church movement recently made the case that Christians "must redeem entire cultures, not only personal souls."[3] It is difficult to know what this might mean practically, but the phrase is interesting, for it is a new iteration of an old way of speaking about the world and the way the church should engage it.

I call attention to this because I have argued throughout this treatise that we need a new language for how the church engages the culture. It is essential, in my view, to abandon altogether talk of "redeeming the culture," "advancing the kingdom," "building the kingdom," "transforming the world," "reclaiming the culture," "reforming the culture," and "changing the world." Christians need to leave such language behind them because it carries too much weight. It implies conquest, take-over, or dominion, which in my view is precisely what God does not call us to pursue—at least not in any conventional, twentieth- or twenty-first-century way of understanding these terms.

Two of the three leading political theologies in the church today are rooted in such language. The third political theology is, ironically, just as beholden to this language, for its frame of reference and its defining characteristic is the rejection of Constantinian forms of engagement. The very nature of the third political theology, in other words, is the mirror opposite of the first two—it opposes all forms of Constantinianism while being dependent on it for its self-understanding.

The ideal is to shift to a *post*-Constantinian engagement, which means a way of engaging the world that neither seeks domination nor defines identity and witness over against domination. For most, this will mean coming to terms with the past. Christians must recognize that though it clearly benefited in many fundamental and extraordinary ways from people of faith and the good ideals of the Christian tradition, America was never, in any theologically serious way, a Christian nation, nor the West a Christian civilization. Neither will they ever become so in the future. The goal for Christians, then, is not and never has been to "take back the culture" or to "take over the culture" or to "win the culture wars" or to "save Western civilization." Ours is now, emphatically, a post-Christian culture, and the community of Christian believers are now, more than ever—spiritually speaking—exiles in a land of exile. Christians, as with the Israelites in Jeremiah's account, must come to terms with this exile.

It isn't just the Constantinian temptation the church must repudiate but, more significantly, the orientation toward power that underwrites it. The proclivity toward domination and toward the politicization of everything leads Christianity today to bizarre turns; turns that, in my view, transform much of the Christian public witness into the very opposite of the witness Christianity is supposed to offer.

A vision of the new city commons, rooted in a theology of faithful presence, certainly leads to a repudiation of *ressentiment* that defines so much of Christianity's contemporary public witness. Yet it also leads to a postpolitical view of power. It is not likely to happen, but *it may be that the healthiest course of action for Christians, on this count, is to be silent for a season and learn how to enact their faith in public through acts of shalom rather than to try again to represent it publicly through law, policy, and political mobilization.* This would not mean civic privatism but rather a season to learn how to engage the world in public differently and better.

There is another tension with which the church must come to terms. This one arises from its passion for truth and the way such passions tend to justify internal factionalizing. Unfortunately, schism seems to be part and parcel of Christianity, and, Christians being who they are, this is not likely to change any time soon. Put differently, the problem of difference is an inescapable feature of its own identity and witness.[4]

There are two important implications of this. The first implication is that *a vision of the new city commons rooted in a theology of faithful presence would lead believers to hold many of these differences lightly.* It is important to remember that Christianity—in its beliefs and practices—is defined from the center out. This is not to say that particularities on the periphery don't matter—they do: they give social life complexity and personal life richness, and in so many respects we are defined by these particularities. But those particularities on the periphery matter less in a context of exile on at least two fronts. They matter less on the issue of formation and they matter less on the issue of public engagement. In the context of exile, and on these two matters, many of the schisms that have divided the church over time have become functionally irrelevant. This would include the great schism of the sixteenth century that divided Protestants and Catholics. It would include the divisions between the Western Church and Eastern Church as well. Within the confessions of historic Christian faith— and on the matters of formation and engagement—the particularities on the margins of faith really do matter less. Unity around the core beliefs and practices of Christian faith can only serve the larger purposes of making disciples, on the one hand, and serving the common good, on the other.

The second implication is simply this: where differences remain there is the challenge to demonstrate love toward the other. Clearly, if Christians cannot extend grace and love through faithful presence within the body of believers, they certainly will not be able to extend grace to those outside.

WITH THE WORLD

The second cluster of tensions the church must cultivate is with the world. As I argued earlier in this essay, the church must live within a dialectic of affirmation and antithesis. This means, among other things, that for all the good that can be embraced in the world today, the pursuit of the new city commons unfolds with a full awareness and critique of the profoundly dehumanizing trends and movements of our time and the way in which the "principalities and powers" animate, institutionalize, and legitimate these destructive tendencies. I would certainly include here such forces that create conflict and violence over scarce resources in the far reaches of the world, often in the name of peace; the underside of technological innovation that instrumentalizes human beings, even while the technologies themselves claim to improve conditions for human life; and the processes in the economy and in society that undermine the bonds of family, friendship, and community, often in the name of personal freedom. I would include dispositions that continue to denigrate persons simply by virtue of their social class, skin color, ethnic background, nationality, mental or physical capability, age, beliefs, gender, and so on. I would also include realities closer to home: the ideologies that predispose people to measure human worth and to find personal significance in material possessions, in appearance, in minor celebrity, or career success, or the cultural forces that orient people to find emotional stability and even serenity through various medications—prescribed, licit, or illicit. Perhaps even more profound, though far less obvious, are the destructive tendencies that emanate from the forces of dissolution. The weightlessness that attends experience and all manner of speech in the late modern world weighs heavily on Christians and non-Christians alike, but for the Christian, it undermines the very reality of belief and witness. One could go on, for the sources of bondage in the world are myriad. The good news is that the shalom of God not only exposes them for what they are but also offers a radical alternative grounded in the hope of the new creation.

Christians must cultivate tension with the world by affirming the centrality of the church itself and the parish or local congregation in particular. The church is God's gift to his people and part of what makes it a strategic gift in our time is that it is a community and an institution. Constituted by powerful ideals, truths, and narratives, patterns of behavior and relationship, social organization, and a wide range of resources, institutions are a social reality that are larger than the sum total of individuals who make them up. Only within strong communities can one find the relational means to sustain the difficulties endemic to life in the modern world. Only within strong institutions can one find the resources to resist its destructive influences and pressures.

Nowhere is this more important than in the task of formation. As a community and an institution, the church is a plausibility structure and the only one with the resources capable of offering an alternative formation to that offered by popular culture. What I am arguing simply reiterates points made earlier: the depth and stability of formation are directly tied to the depth and stability of the social and cultural environment in which it takes place. Formation into a vision of human flourishing requires an environment that embodies continuity, historical memory, rituals marking seasons of life, intergenerational interdependence, and most important of all, common worship. Absent these things, new Christians will have no idea where to begin their walk of faith no matter how many books they are given. Families certainly cannot do this work for their children on their own, for the family has become a weak institution over against, say, the institutions of popular culture. As a rule, young people in the early stages of a job or career cannot figure out their formation by themselves either. At all levels, formation into a vision of human flourishing requires intentionality and the social, economic, intellectual, and cultural resources of a healthy, mutually dependent, and worshipping community provided for Christians by the church.

Thus when the theologians in radical orthodoxy and in the neo-Anabaptist communities speak of the church as a *polis* or *altera civitas*, marked by a distinct narrative recounted in distinct practices, a distinct *telos* whose form and substance is defined by the coming kingdom, and the presence of the Spirit at work among believers through Word and sacrament,[5] they are gesturing in precisely this direction, and their instincts are exactly right. By the same token, observers who contend that the anti-institutional trends that signal an exodus from congregational life are a healthy development—a sign of a new "revolutionary" expression of Christianity—are profoundly misguided. The reason is that such trends are rooted, in fact, in a consumer logic that makes individual choice central and the self sovereign.[6] Niche ecclesiology makes possible churches designed for different needs and interests. As one advocate put it, "Growing numbers . . . are piecing together spiritual elements they deem worthwhile, constituting millions of personalized 'church' experiences."[7] In the end, church is one more consumer choice for Christian believers; not much different in character from any other consumer choice. Such trends are less an expression of "revolutionary Christianity" than of modern individualism and consumerism, the effect of which will undermine the only structures capable of constructively resisting the worst of contemporary culture.

In the context of exile, the tensions between affirmation and antithesis are not only essential, but they are healthy and it is critically important that they be cultivated. Without them, the church merely assimilates into the dominant culture. Yet how to live within this tension is as important as the tension itself. On this count, as Donald Flow has put it, accommodation must always be critical and resistance must always be humble. Thus, if the church has any contribution to make to a new city commons, it will depend on its sustaining these tensions in these ways. The discernment this task will require goes far beyond what any individual, however wise, can provide. Here too, the church is of decisive importance.

A Sketch from Mathetes

The pursuit of a new city commons, grounded in a theology of faithful presence, is not unprecedented by any means. This way of living and engaging the world enjoys a long tradition in the church, particularly at the points in which Christian communities flourished. One picture of this is given to us in the apologetic literature of the second and third century, a literature aimed to defend Christianity from the wide-ranging and often outrageous accusations brought against it. This particular description is found in a famous letter written by an unknown "disciple of the apostles" to Diognetus, in all likelihood, the tutor of Marcus Aurelius. Though clearly romanticized, the letter nevertheless provides an ideal picture of how Christian believers relate or aspire to relate to the world.

> Christians are distinguished from other men neither by country, nor language, nor the customs which they observe. For they neither inhabit cities of their own, nor employ a peculiar form of speech, nor lead a life which is marked out by any singularity. The course of conduct which they follow has not been devised by any speculation or deliberation of inquisitive men; nor do they, like some, proclaim themselves the advocates of any merely human doctrines. But, inhabiting Greek as well as barbarian cities . . . and following the customs of the natives in respect to clothing, food, and the rest of their ordinary conduct, they display to us their wonderful and confessedly striking method of life. They dwell in their own countries, but simply as sojourners. As citizens, they share in all things with others, and yet endure all things as if foreigners. Every foreign land is to them as their native country, and every land of their birth as a land of strangers. They marry, as do all [others]; they beget children; but they do not destroy their offspring. They have a common table, but not a common bed. They are in the flesh, but they do not live after the flesh. They pass their days on earth but they are citizens of heaven. They obey the prescribed laws, and at the same time surpass the laws by their lives. They love all men, and are persecuted by all. They are unknown and

condemned; they are put to death, and restored to life. They are poor, yet make many rich; they are in lack of all things, and yet abound in all; they are dishonored, and yet in their very dishonor are glorified. They are evil spoken of, and yet are justified; they are reviled, and bless; they are insulted, and repay the insult with honor; they do good, yet are punished as evil doers.

Needless to say, this is hardly a comprehensive picture of what the church should look like today. The setting is obviously different in our day, and thus the challenges are different but the sensibility about how the church should engage the world is the same. The church will not flourish in itself nor serve well the common good if it isolates itself from the larger culture, fails to understand its nature and inner logic, and is incapable of working within it—critically affirming and strengthening its healthy qualities and humbly criticizing and subverting its most destructive tendencies.

To Change the World

Will engaging the world in the way discussed here change the world?

This, I believe, is the wrong question. The question is wrong in part because it is based on the dubious assumption that the world, and thus history, can be controlled and managed. This idea continues to be championed by some of the most prominent leaders in American Christianity. The logic that follows is dangerous indeed: once we have determined the right course of history, everything is subordinate to it—nearly any action can be justified if it helps to put the society on course and keeps it going in the right direction. As the logic goes, the world is ours to engineer so long as these efforts are in keeping with our overall objectives of history. By this logic, our actions are justified only by the outcomes they promise to bring about.

The question is wrong because, for Christians, it makes the primary subservient to the secondary. By making a certain understanding of the good in society the objective, the source of the good—God himself and the intimacy he offers—becomes nothing more than a tool to be used to achieve that objective. When this happens, righteousness can quickly become cruelty and justice can rapidly turn into injustice. Indeed, history is filled with the bloody consequences of this logic and the logic is very much present, even if implicit, on all sides and in all factions of the ongoing culture war.

To be sure, Christianity is not, first and foremost, about establishing righteousness or creating good values or securing justice or making peace in the world. Don't get me wrong: these are goods we should care about and pursue with great passion. But for Christians, these are all secondary to the primary good of God himself and the primary task of worshipping him and honoring him in all they do.

This, I would insist, is not a cheap pietism. The fact is that Christ's victory over the principalities and powers was a victory over the power of oppressive institutions—the sense that reality is what it is, that all is as it should be, that the ways of the world are established and cannot be changed; that the rules by which the world operates are ones we must accept and not challenge. We are not bound by the "necessities" of history and society but are free from them. He broke their sovereignty and, as a result, all things are possible. It is this reality that frees all Christians to actively, creatively, and constructively seek the good in their relationships, in their tasks, in their spheres of influence, and in their cities.

Against the present realities of our historical moment, it is impossible to say what can actually be accomplished. There are intractable uncertainties that cannot be avoided. Certainly Christians, at their best, will neither create a perfect world nor one that is altogether new; but by enacting shalom and seeking it on behalf of all others through the practice of faithful presence, it is possible, just possible, that they will help to make the world a little bit better.

NOTES

Essay I

CHAPTER I

1. An illustration of this can be found in an essay by Frederica Mathewes-Green, "Loving the Storm-Drenched," *Christianity Today* 50, no. 3 (March 2006): 36. In sum, she argues that "we can no more change the culture than we can the weather. Fortunately, we've got more important things to do." Using a different metaphor, she writes, "[Culture] is the battering weather conditions that people, harassed and helpless, endure. We are sent out into the storm like a St. Bernard with a keg around our neck, to comfort, reach, and rescue those who are thirsting, most of all, for Jesus Christ." But even Mathewes-Green recognizes that "we can do some things to help improve ongoing conditions."

2. The Christian book market speaks to the strong therapeutic demand of many Christian believers for techniques for managing relationships, dealing with problem emotions, growing older, deepening personal spirituality, and the like. Against the frustrations of changing the world, many today are merely satisfied if they can change themselves. See J. D. Hunter, *American Evangelicalism: Conservative Religion and the Quandary of Modernity* (New Brunswick, N.J.: Rutgers University Press, 1983).

3. Presbyterians for Renewal, www.pfrenewal.org.

4. "Policy for Action—The Episcopal Public Policy Network," www.episcopalchurch.org/eppn.

5. "Policies and Procedures of the Evangelical Lutheran Church in America for Addressing Social Concerns," www.elca.org/socialstatements/procedures.

6. See John L. Carr, "Good News for a Broken World: What's New? What's Broken?," 13 February 2006, www.usccb.org/sdwp (accessed on 21 October 2009). Local priests echo this view. Father Roger Landry of the Diocese of Fall River, Massachusetts, for example, wrote in an editorial that "In every generation, Jesus has called on his disciples to transform society." *The Anchor* (10 August 2007).

7. From the Helixx website, http://www.helixxgroup.com/2006_Centurions_Program_Info.pdf (accessed on 7 October 2009).

8. These takes are found in the following sources: Chuck Colson, "Learning to Think Christianly," www.breakpoint.org (accessed on 17 September 2003); Campus Crusade for Christ International human resources page, www.ccci.org/hr/hq/ (accessed on 5 October 2004); Focus on the Family Institute purpose statement, www.focusinstitute .org/AboutUs.asp (accessed on 5 October 2004); Legionaries of Christ home page, www .legionariesofchrist.org/eng/articulos/articulo.phtml?lc=id-5968_se-90_ca-255_te-193 (accessed on 5 October 2004); Regnum Christi home page, www.regnumchristi.org/ english/articulos/articulo.phtml?se=20&;ca=59&te=10&id=6265 (accessed on 5 October 2004); Pinnacle Forum America home page, www.pinnacleforum.com/ (accessed on 5 October 2004); The Trinity Forum home page, www.ttf.org/index/about/ (accessed on 21 October 2009); Christ for the Nations Institute home page, www.cfni.org/ institute.asp (accessed on 5 October 2004); Summit Ministries home page, www .summit.org/about/ (accessed on 5 October 2004); Aftershock home page, aftershock .wumpus.org/ (accessed on 5 October 2004, site no longer available); Promise Keepers home page, www.promisekeepers.org/conf/venu/confvenu28.htm (accessed on 5 October 2004); John Hagee Ministries website, www.jhm.org/print-partnership.asp (accessed on 11 April 2007); Indiana Wesleyan University home page, www.indwes.edu/about/ mission_statement.htm (accessed on 5 October 2004); Bethel University home page, www.bethel.edu/about-bu.html (accessed on 5 October 2004); Abilene Christian University home page, www.acu.edu/events/changetheworld/home.html (accessed on 5 October 2004).

CHAPTER 2

1. This is precisely the definition given by the pollster George Barna: "Culture is the accumulation of behaviors and beliefs that characterize a group of people. It is comprised of the attitudes, symbols, language, rewards, expectations, customs, and values that define the experience and context of those people." See George Barna, *Revolution: Finding Vibrant Faith beyond the Walls of the Sanctuary* (Wheaton, Ill.: Tyndale House, 2005), 108.

2. Charles Colson and Nancy Pearcey, *How Now Shall We Live?* (Wheaton, Ill.: Tyndale House, 1999), 14–15, 297. Another defined it this way: A worldview is "any ideology, philosophy, theology, movement or religion that provides an overarching approach to understanding God, the world, and man's relations to God and the world." David Noebel, *Understanding the Times: The Religious Worldviews of Our Day and the Search for Truth* (Eugene, Ore.: Harvest House, 1994), 8.

3. Colson and Pearcey, *How Now Shall We Live?* 17.

4. Colson and Pearcey, *How Now Shall We Live?* 13.

5. Colson and Pearcey, *How Now Shall We Live?* 17. Emphasis added.

6. Chuck Colson, "Learning to Think Christianly," www.breakpoint.org (accessed on 17 September 2003). Colson put his money where his mouth was and, in 2004, he launched "The Centurions Program," a ministry "designed to develop and equip an ongoing fellowship of Christian men and women who will be trained . . . to restore our culture by effectively thinking, teaching, and advocating the Christian worldview as applied to all of life." Helixx Web site, www.helixxgroup.com/2006_Centurions_Program_ Info.pdf (accessed on 7 October 2009).

7. All of these statements are taken from Colson and Pearcey, *How Now Shall We Live?* 92–93.

8. Colson and Pearcey, *How Now Shall We Live?* 90.

9. Colson and Pearcey, *How Now Shall We Live?* 90.

10. Colson and Pearcey, *How Now Shall We Live?* 308.

11. Colson and Pearcey, *How Now Shall We Live?* 294.

12. Colson and Pearcey, *How Now Shall We Live?* 308.

13. Colson and Pearcey, *How Now Shall We Live?* 414.

14. Colson and Pearcey, *How Now Shall We Live?* 32. Italics added.

15. Robert P. George, "Danger and Opportunity: A Plea to Catholics," *First Things*, 6 August 2007, www.firstthings.com/onthesquare/2007/08/danger-and-opportunity-a-plea- (accessed on 7 October 2009).

16. Carl Anderson, *A Civilization of Love* (San Francisco: Harper One, 2008), 5.

17. See www.discoverchrist.com, a website selling Christian apparel. The larger argument from which this phrase was selected reads:

> At Discoverchrist.com we pride ourselves not only on offering quality Christian t shirts and apparel, but also trying to make a difference in the world. We believe Christians should be a witness to the world everywhere they go, and wearing our t shirts will do just that. We believe that our t shirts are walking billboards proclaiming the living word of God. Lives can change by experiencing the truth through the visual impact and expressions our t shirts contain. Religious t shirts and hats can change the world one life at a time. (www.discoverchrist.com, accessed on 5 October 2004)

18. From the Center for Cultural Renewal, www.cfacr.org (accessed on 6 October 2004).

19. From Robert E. Quinn, *Change the World: How Ordinary People Can Achieve Extraordinary Results* (San Francisco: Jossey-Bass, 2000). Quinn provides eight steps that will allow "each of us [to] access and apply the power that lies within us in ways that will change our world for the better." (product description)

20. See the Worldview Academy Web site, www.worldview.org/ (accessed on 18 May 2007).

21. From Focus on the Family's The Truth Project informative Web site, www.thetruthproject.org/whatistruthproject/ (accessed on 18 May 2007).

22. As cited in Alf J. Mapp Jr., *Thomas Jefferson: Passionate Pilgrim* (Lanham, Md.: Madison Books, 1991), 266.

23. Boice, "One Nation under God," 30.

24. Taken from a direct mail invitation and brochure dated 16 August 1995, Campus Crusade for Christ International.

25. Bill Bright, "How You Can Introduce Others to Christ," http://powertochange.com/experience/55-plus/ (accessed on 7 October 2009). Also quoted in "Transferable Concepts—How You Can Introduce Others to Christ—You Can Change Your World," www.transferableconcepts.com/transconcepts/english/introduce_others/ (accessed on 5 October 2004, no longer available).

26. See, for example, John Hagee's website, www.jhm.org/print-partnership.asp (accessed on 11 April 2007), where it states: "Our Salt Covenant with you is: we are

absolutely committed to change America and the world by being obedient to the Great Commission, to win the lost to Christ, to take America and the world back to the God of our fathers and, in addition, to continually pray for our partners."

27. David V. Edling, "Cultural Renewal: The Church's Responsibility," www.peacemaker .net/site/apps/nlnet/content3.aspx?c=aqKFLTOBIpH&;b=1084267&content_id= {9AE93038–38B7–4DEB–95B7–5E084597598A}&notoc=1 (accessed on 7 October 2009).

28. "UNIV: 25 Years with John Paul II," from the information office of Opus Dei on the Internet, www.opusdei.org/art.php?w=32&;p=6534 (accessed on 5 October 2004).

29. "UNIV: 25 Years with John Paul II."

30. Fr. Robert J. Carr, "Live the Faith, Change the World," Catholic Online 2004, www.catholic.org (accessed on 5 October 2004).

31. The webpage of Adore Christ for Peace, www.acfp2000.com/main.htm (accessed on 5 October 2004).

32. Billy Graham, "The Moral Weight of Leadership," *New York Times*, 17 March 1998.

33. Taken from Os Guinness, *The American Hour* (New York: Free Press, 1992), 399.

34. An example of this logic was found on the Family Research Council webpage in a question and answer format entitled "Why Should I Care about Judges and Judicial Nominations?" www.frc.org/ (accessed on 28 April 2005):

Q—Why should pro-family citizens care about the appointment of judges?
A—Many of the negative changes in American society over recent decades have been imposed by judges. The removal of prayer from public schools, the creation of a nationwide "right" to abortion, and the legalization of same-sex "marriage" in Massachusetts were all decisions imposed by activist judges, without considering the will of the people and their elected representatives.
Q—What do you mean by "activist" judges?
A—"Activist" judges are judges who impose their own policy preferences in their decisions. Judges are only supposed to interpret the law, not rewrite it. Legislatures, elected by the people, write laws, and the executive branch of government (headed by an elected official) is responsible for enforcing them. Activist judges effectively take away your right to affect policy by your vote.
Q—How have activist judges abused their power?
A—Judges are abusing their power if they read *into* the Constitution principles that are not declared by the plain language *of* the Constitution. For example, the First Amendment says, "Congress shall make no law respecting an establishment of religion." But nowhere does it say that there should be a strict "separation of church and state" at all levels of government, barring any acknowledgment of God. The decision legalizing abortion was based on the "right to privacy"—but no such right is declared in the Constitution.

35. From the Center for American Cultural Renewal, www.cfacr.org (accessed on 6 October 2004).

36. From the Center for American Cultural Renewal, www.cfacr.org (accessed on October 2004).

37. Tom Minnery, *Why You Can't Stay Silent: The Biblical Mandate to Shape Our Culture* (Wheaton, Ill.: Tyndale House, 2001), 58.

38. Minnery, *Why You Can't Stay Silent*, 58.

39. Lines added by Samuel Johnson to Goldsmith's "The Traveler" (Line 429). Found in John J. Richetti's *The Cambridge History of English literature, 1660–1780* (Cambridge: Cambridge University Press, 2005), 290.

40. The observation was made by Senator William Armstrong of Colorado.

41. Quoted in an interview with John Hockenberry, *DayOne*, ABC News, 21 September 1995. Emphasis added. Transcript available at The Transcript Company, www.transcripts.tv (accessed on 22 October 2009).

42. "Dem's Charges 'Pathetic' DeLay Says," www.NewsMax.com (accessed on 5 May 2000).

43. Tom Delay, "Rediscovering Our American Values: The Real State of the Union" (Heritage Lecture #654, Heritage Foundation, 1 February 2000).

44. The NAE's fiftieth anniversary convention in 1992 produced a press release entitled "NAE Inaugurates Prayer and Voter Registration Campaign," 3 March 1992. All quotes in this paragraph are taken from this statement. In the years since, the NAE's policy positions have evolved and its overall sophistication increased, but its basic working model for engaging public life remains the same.

45. Jim Wallis, *The Soul of Politics* (New York: New Press, 1995), xiii.

46. "The Cry for Renewal," *Sojourners* (29 May 1995).

47. Don Eberly, "Compassionate Conservatism: Voluntary Associations and the Remoralization of America" (address, Heritage Foundation, 8 November 1999).

48. Eberly, "Compassionate Conservatism."

49. Don Eberly, ed., *Building a Healthy Culture: Strategies for an American Renaissance* (Indianapolis, Ind.: Hudson Institute, 2001), product description.

50. Don Eberly, "Renewing American Culture," *American Outlook* (Winter, 1999): 50.

51. Don Eberly, *The Soul of Civil Society: Voluntary Association and the Public Vale of Moral Habits* (Lanham, Md.: Lexington Books, 2002), 43.

52. From the "Mission Statement" of Renew our Culture, an affiliate of The Civil Society Project, n.d.

53. Colson and Pearcey, *How Now Shall We Live?* 295.

54. "Brownback, Pitts Host Cultural Renewal Forum," press release of Senator Sam Brownback (13 April 1999), http://brownback.senate.gov/pressapp/record.cfm?id= 175697 (accessed on 6 October 2004).

55. "Brownback, Pitts Host Cultural Renewal Forum."

56. "Brownback, Pitts Host Cultural Renewal Forum." Emphasis added. They go on to affirm the commonplace view that, "We must aim to change hearts and minds as much as we seek to change laws."

57. From a newsletter written by Sam Brownback and Joe Lieberman, honorary cochairs, introducing their "new, non-partisan public initiative," Renew Our Culture (August 1999).

58. Colson and Pearcey, *How Now Shall We Live?* 37.

CHAPTER 3

1. See Roger Finke and Rodney Stark, *The Churching of America, 1776–2005: Winners and Losers in Our Religious Economy* (New Brunswick, N.J.: Rutgers University Press, 2005).

2. See *American Piety in the 21st Century: New Insights into the Depth and Complexity of Religion in the United States—Selected Findings from the Baylor Religion Survey* (Waco, Tex.: Baylor Institute for Studies of Religion and the Department of Sociology at Baylor University, 2006). The data from this survey shows that 45 percent of all white Evangelicals attended church once a week or more compared to 24 percent of all mainline Protestants.

3. According to the *Baylor Religion Survey*, 42 percent of all white Evangelicals read the Bible weekly or more compared to 16 percent of the mainline; and 67 percent of all Evangelicals pray weekly or more compared to 44 percent of the mainliners.

4. From "Faith-Based Funding Backed, But Church-State Doubts Abound: Religion in American Life" (survey report, Pew Research Center for the People & the Press, 10 April 2001), 1–4. See also: Pew Forum on Religion & Public Life, *The American Religious Landscape and Politics, 2004* (Washington, D.C.: Pew Research Center, 2004), 37.

5. David Hollinger, *Science, Jews, and Secular Culture* (Princeton, N.J.: Princeton University Press, 1996).

6. For an insightful and controversial accounting of how this cultural transformation has taken place, see Marshall Kirk and Hunter Madson, *After the Ball: How America Will Conquer Its Fear and Hatred of Gays in the 90s* (New York: Penguin, 1989).

7. Frank Newport, "Third of Americans Say Evidence Has Supported Darwin's Evolution Theory: Almost Half of Americans Believe God Created Humans 10,000 Years Ago," *Gallup Poll News Service*, www.gallup.com/poll/14107/Third-Americans-Say-Evidence-Has-Supported-Darwins-Evolution-Theory.aspx (accessed on 7 October 2009).

8. From *The American Religious Landscape and Politics, 2004*, 27. See also Lydia Saad, "Americans Closely Divided Into Pro-Choice and Pro-Life Camps: Pro-Life Side More Attentive to Supreme Court Appointments," *Gallup Poll News Service*, www.gallup.com/poll/content/print.aspx?ci=16297 (accessed on 12 May 2005, no longer available).

9. From the back cover of James Montgomery Boice, ed., *Transforming our World: A Call to Action* (Portland, Ore.: Multnomah Press, 1988). Emphasis added.

10. Charles Colson, "Reclaiming Occupied Territory," *Breakpoint Worldview: A Christian Perspective on Today's News and Trends* (October 2004): 28. Emphasis added.

11. Jim Nelson Black, *America Adrift* (Fort Lauderdale, Fla.: Coral Ridge Ministries, 2002), 73.

12. Tom Minnery, *Why You Can't Stay Silent: The Biblical Mandate to Shape Our Culture* (Wheaton, Ill.: Tyndale House, 2001), xiv. Emphasis added.

13. Black, *America Adrift*, 22. Emphasis added.

14. "The Wilberforce Forum: A Center for Christian Worldview Thinking," (brochure, n.d.). Emphasis added.

15. Del Tackett, "What's a Worldview Anyway?" *Focus on the Family Magazine* (2 November 2004). Republished online at www.thetruthproject.org/about/culturefocus/A000000048.cfm (accessed on 7 October 2009). Emphasis added.

16. See the Truth Project, www.thetruthproject.org/about/culturefocus/A000000118.cfm/. Dobson elaborates this point in an online solicitation from Focus on the Family (accessed on 10 March 2006):

Everyday, it is more and more difficult to live out our faith in every area of our lives. This fact is reflected in a recent study by the Barna Research Group which revealed a stunning statistic: only 9% of professing Christians have a biblical worldview. Because of this, today's believers live very similarly to non-believers. A personal sense of significance is rarely experienced, we spend our money and time on things that fail to satisfy and we begin to wonder what life's ultimate purpose really is. We are, in short, losing our bearings as a people and a nation.

To help counter this slide within the Body of Christ, Focus on the Family's "The Truth Project" is a DVD-based small group curriculum designed to equip believers with a comprehensive biblical worldview. Taught by Dr. Del Tackett, President of Focus on the Family Institute, this home study is the starting point for looking at life from a biblical perspective. Each lesson discusses in great detail the relevance and importance of living the Christian worldview in daily life.

17. The Truth Project, www.thetruthproject.org/about/culturefocus/A000000 118.cfm/.

18. In Hegel's formulation, there is perfect beauty, moral freedom, and spiritual bliss within the Absolute. In time and space, however, that harmonious perfection is not apparent but rather manifests itself as an impulse and a logically necessary process (through thesis, antithesis, and synthesis) by which the ethical, aesthetic, and religious rationally contend in their variety, and progress toward ever more rational expressions. The Absolute, then, is a living, vital reality, manifesting itself in human experience, guided, if you will, toward the fulfillment of its own divine purpose. Ethics and faith as historical realities are, then, necessary products of the self-explication of the Absolute. Few, least of all Christians, would embrace Hegel's optimistic contentions, but as we argue in the text, the specifics have been eclipsed by the success of the general proposition; that ideas are what really matter.

19. Charles Colson and Nancy Pearcey, *How Now Shall We Live?* (Wheaton, Ill.: Tyndale House, 1999), 17. Emphasis added.

20. Nancy Pearcey, *Total Truth: Liberating Christianity from Its Cultural Captivity* (Wheaton, Ill.: Crossway, 2004), 247.

21. Colson and Pearcey, *How Now Shall We Live?* 237–44.

22. Colson and Pearcey, *How Now Shall We Live?* 17.

23. In a similar idealistic vein, Black claims that "The ideas of Emerson, Marx, Nietzsche, Freud, and Darwin would shake the foundations of faith for millions." *America Adrift*, 28. This may be true but it is not because that many Christians actually read these writers!

24. There is a vast literature on the individualistic nature of American Protestantism and American religion more generally. See, for example, Sidney E. Ahlstrom, *A Religious History of the American People* (New Haven, Conn: Yale University Press, 1975); Robert N. Bellah et al., *Habits of the Heart* (Berkeley: University of California Press, 1985); as well as Bellah's *The Broken Covenant* (New York: Seabury, 1976); Sacvan Bercovitch, *The Puritan Origins of the American Self* (New Haven, Conn.: Yale University Press, 1975); Peter L. Berger, *The Sacred Canopy* (New York: Anchor, 1969); Nathan O. Hatch, *The Democratization of American Christianity* (New Haven, Conn.: Yale University Press, 1989); Will Herberg, *Protestant–Catholic–Jews* (New York: Doubleday, 1960); James Davison Hunter, *American Evangelicalism: Conservative Religion and the Quandary of Modernity* (New Brunswick, N.J.: Rutgers, 1983); James Davison Hunter, *Evangelicalism: The Coming Generation* (Chicago: University of Chicago Press, 1987); George M. Marsden,

Fundamentalism and American Culture (New York: Oxford University Press, 1980); Mark A. Noll, *A History of Christianity in the United States and Canada* (Grand Rapids, Mich.: Eerdmans, 1992); A. James Reichley, *Religion In American Public Life* (Washington, D.C.: Brookings Institution, 1985); Christian Smith, with Melinda Lundquist Denton, *Soul Searching: the Religious and Spiritual Lives of American Teenagers* (New York: Oxford University Press, 2005); Christian Smith, with Michael Emerson, *Divided by Faith: Evangelical Religion and the Problem of Race in America* (New York: Oxford University Press, 2000); Christian Smith, *American Evangelicalism: Embattled and Thriving* (Chicago: University of Chicago Press, 1998); George M. Thomas, *Revivalism and Cultural Change* (Chicago: University of Chicago Press, 1989); Robert Wuthnow, *The Restructuring of American Religion* (Princeton, N.J.: Princeton University Press, 1988); and Alan Wolfe, *The Transformation of American Religion* (New York: Free Press, 2003).

25. It includes beliefs, values, ideas, and images, but it is first and foremost materiality—concrete stuff. See Andy Crouch, "The Horizons of the Possible," Catalyst, www.catalystspace.com/content/read/the_horizons_of_the_possible/.

26. See Andy Crouch, *Culture Making: Rediscovering Our Creative Calling* (Downers Grove, Ill., IVP Books, 2008), 67.

27. See Crouch, *Culture Making*, 25.

28. The definitive statement on cultural materialism was written by Marvin Harris, *The Rise of Anthropological Theory: A History of Theories of Culture*, updated edition (Walnut Creek, Calif.: Altamira, 2001); and *Cultural Materialism: The Struggle for a Science of Culture*, updated edition (Walnut Creek, Calif.: Altamira, 2001). As a full-fledged theory of culture and a self-conscious method for analyzing it, cultural materialism is very different from the perspective Crouch offers. At the level of assumptions and priorities, it has several of the affinities noted here.

29. Crouch, *Culture Making*, 10. Emphasis added.

30. Crouch, *Culture Making*, 24.

31. Crouch, *Culture Making*, 38.

32. Crouch, *Culture Making*, 220. See also page 190.

33. Crouch, *Culture Making*, 67.

34. See the interview with Crouch in the Intervarsity web magazine, *Student Soul* (19 January 2007), www.intervarsity.org/studentsoul/item/andy-crouch.

35. Crouch, *Culture Making*, 239.

36. Crouch, *Culture Making*, 190.

37. Crouch, *Culture Making*, 220. Emphasis added.

38. Crouch, *Culture Making*, 191.

CHAPTER 4

1. The perspective taken here draws heavily from the works of Max Weber, Emile Durkheim, Georg Simmel, Antonio Gramsci, Peter Berger, Pierre Bourdieu, and Michel Foucault, among others.

2. Pierre Bourdieu, *Outline of a Theory of Practice* (Cambridge: Cambridge University Press, 1977), 78.

3. This is the fundamental point of Peter L. Berger and Thomas Luckmann, *The Social Construction of Reality* (New York: Anchor-Doubleday, 1966); now an accepted axiom of social theory.

4. The amount of symbolic integration in the cultural sphere can vary as well—cultural activity could be centralized and more or less coordinated; it could also be decentralized with cultural organizations openly competing.

5. Thomas Carlyle, "On Heroes, Hero-Worship, and the Heroic in History," ClassicAuthors.net, www.underthesun.cc/Classics/Carlyle/HEROWORSHIP/HEROWORSHIP6.html (accessed on 6 April 2005).

6. Carlyle, "On Heroes, Hero-Worship, and the Heroic in History."

7. Consider at some length Carlyle's breath-taking account of Luther's appearance at the Diet of Worms on 17 April 1521. This event, Carlyle declares,

> may be considered as the greatest scene in Modern European History; the point, indeed, from which the whole subsequent history of civilization takes its rise. After multiplied negotiations, disputations, it had come to this. The young Emperor Charles the Fifth, with all the Princes of Germany, Papal nuncios, dignitaries spiritual and temporal, are assembled there: Luther is to appear and answer for himself, whether he will recant or not. The world's pomp and power sits there on this hand: on that, stands up for God's Truth, one man, the poor miner Hans Luther's Son. Friends had reminded him of Huss, advised him not to go; he would not be advised. A large company of friends rode out to meet him, with still more earnest warnings; he answered, "Were there as many Devils in Worms as there are roof-tiles, I would on." The people, on the morrow, as he went to the Hall of the Diet, crowded the windows and house-tops, some of them calling out to him, in solemn words, not to recant: "Whosoever denieth me before men!" they cried to him—as in a kind of solemn petition and adjuration. Was it not in reality our petition too, the petition of the whole world, lying in dark bondage of soul? . . . Luther did not desert us. His speech, of two hours, distinguished itself by its respectful, wise and honest tone; submissive to whatsoever could lawfully claim submission, not submissive to any more than that. His writings, he said, were partly his own, partly derived from the Word of God. As to what was his own, human infirmity entered into it; unguarded anger, blindness, many things doubtless which it were a blessing for him could he abolish altogether. But as to what stood on sound truth and the Word of God, he could not recant it. How could he? "Confute me," he concluded, "by proofs of Scripture, or else by plain just arguments: I cannot recant otherwise. For it is neither safe nor prudent to do aught against conscience. Here stand I; I can do no other: God assist me!"—It is, as we say, the greatest moment in the Modern History of Men. English Puritanism, England and its Parliaments, Americas, and vast work these two centuries; French Revolution, Europe and its work everywhere at present: the germ of it all lay there: had Luther in that moment done other, it had all been otherwise! The European World was asking him: Am I to sink ever lower into falsehood, stagnant putrescence, loathsome accursed death; or, with whatever paroxysm, to cast the falsehoods out of me, and be cured and live?

8. On key regional differences, for example, see Joel Garreau, *The Nine Nations of North America* (New York: Avon, 1999).

9. John Maynard Keynes, *The General Theory of Employment, Interest, and Money* (New York: Harcourt, Brace and Co., 1960), 383.

10. Theda Skocpol, *States and Social Revolutions* (Cambridge: Cambridge University Press, 1979), 287. In Skocpol's argument, the intentional maneuverings of elites are only one part of a larger set of dynamics that include structural forces of international and world-historical scope.

11. This idea is drawn from Robert Wuthnow's masterful work, *Communities of Discourse* (Cambridge, Mass.: Harvard University Press, 1989).

12. It was my mentor, Peter Berger, who first taught me this lesson.

13. Quoted in an interview with John Hockenberry, *Day One*, ABC News, 21 September 1995.

14. These insights are inspired and confirmed by Philip Rieff, "Toward a Theory of Culture," in *The Feeling Intellect*, ed. Johnathan B. Imber (Chicago: University of Chicago Press, 1990), 325f.

CHAPTER 5

1. Robert Wilken, *The Christians as the Romans Saw Them* (New Haven, Conn.: Yale University Press, 1984), 13.

2. Wilken, *The Christians as the Romans Saw Them*, 31.

3. "So long as the Christians were considered to be a group within Judaism—since they shared the same scriptures and many of the historic and conceptual traditions—the Roman authorities were only occasionally active in repression of the Christian movement." Howard Clark Kee, *Christianity: A Social and Cultural History* (New York: Macmillan, 1991), 72.

4. Philip A. Harland, "Connections with Elites in the World of the Early Christians," in *Handbook of Early Christianity: Social Science Approaches*, ed. Anthony J. Blasi, Jean Duhaime, and Paul-Andre Turcotte (Walnut Creek, Calif.: Alta Mira Press), 389–92.

5. Werner Jaeger, *Early Christianity and Greek Paideia* (Cambridge, Mass.: Harvard University Press, 1961).

6. Jaeger, *Early Christianity and Greek Paideia*, 6–7.

7. Jaeger, *Early Christianity and Greek Paideia*.

8. W. H. C. Frend, *The Early Church* (Minneapolis, Minn.: Augsburg/Fortress, 1982), 75.

9. Harland, "Connections with Elites in the World of the Early Christians," 394.

10. Joseph M. Bryant, "The Sect-Church Dynamic and Christian Expansion in the Roman Empire: Persecution, Penitential Discipline, and Schism in Sociological Perspective," *The British Journal of Sociology* 44, no. 2. (June 1993), 328; Harland, "Connections with Elites in the World of the Early Christians," 398.

11. See: W. A. Jurgens, ed., *The Faith of the Early Fathers*, vol. 1 (Collegeville, Minn.: The Liturgical Press, 1970); Kenneth Scott Latourette, *A History of Christianity* (New York: Harper and Brothers, 1953); Geoffrey Dunn, *Tertullian* (New York: Routledge Taylor and Francis Group, 2004); Susan Weingarten, *The Saint's Saint: Hagiography and Geography in Jerome* (Leiden, The Netherlands: Brill, 2005); Anthony Meredith, *Gregory of Nyssa* (New York: Routledge, 1999); Kurt Aland, *A History of Christianity: From the Beginnings to the Threshold of Reformation*, vol. 1, trans. James L. Schaaf (Philadelphia: Fortress Press, 1985); John Ferguson, *Clement of Alexandria* (New York: Twayne, 1974); and Khaled Anatolios, *Athanasius* (New York: Routledge, 2004).

12. As Kee writes, the body of writings that emerged from this transition period of Christianity has come to be called by scholars as the writings of the apostolic fathers, who in the period from about 100 to the middle of the second century were giving intellectual and organizational leadership to Christianity and doing so with a claim of continuity that reached back through the apostles to Jesus. These preserved works include the First and Second Letters of Clement; letters of Ignatius (bishop of Antioch) to several Greek and Roman churches; a letter of Polycarp (bishop of Smyrna in Asia Minor); an allegorical treatise, the Shepherd of Hermas; the Letter of Barnabas . . . ; the story of the Martyrdom of Polycarp (Kee, *Christianity: A Social and Cultural History*, 55).

13. Kee, *Christianity: A Social and Cultural History*, 93–94.

14. Frend, *The Early Church*.

15. Frend, *The Early Church,* 90.

16. Wilken, *The Christians as the Romans Saw Them*, 199.

17. Wilken, *The Christians as the Romans Saw Them*, 200.

18. As Peter Brown put it, it was through *paideia* that power was "rendered dignified" and "naturalized"; in a word, legitimated. *Authority and the Sacred: Aspects of the Christianisation of the Roman World* (Cambridge: Cambridge University Press, 1995), 39–40.

19. Peter Brown, *Power and Persuasion in Late Antiquity: Towards a Christian Empire* (Madison: University of Wisconsin Press), 62.

20. Brown, *Power and Persuasion in Late Antiquity*, 69–70.

21. Brown, *Power and Persuasion in Late Antiquity*, 119.

22. Brown, *Power and Persuasion in Late Antiquity*, 105; cf. Frend, *The Early Church*, 107.

23. Brown, *Power and Persuasion in Late Antiquity*, 123.

24. Brown, *Power and Persuasion in Late Antiquity*, 76.

25. Brown, *Power and Persuasion in Late Antiquity*, 119.

26. Brown, *Power and Persuasion in Late Antiquity*, 136.

27. Brown, *Power and Persuasion in Late Antiquity*, 91.

28. Brown, *Power and Persuasion in Late Antiquity*, 152.

29. Brown, *Power and Persuasion in Late Antiquity*, 94.

30. Brown, *Power and Persuasion in Late Antiquity*, 96.

31. Brown, *Power and Persuasion in Late Antiquity*, 100.

32. In particular, Brown mentions that "the civic ideal off *euergesia*, the ancient search for personal fame through well-publicized giving" was blatantly practiced. *Power and Persuasion in Late Antiquity*, 95.

33. Brown, *Power and Persuasion in Late Antiquity*, 101–2.

34. Emperor Julian, *Epistle to Pagan High Priests*.

35. Thomas F. Mathews, *The Clash of Gods: A Reinterpretation of Early Christian Art* (Princeton, N.J.: Princeton University Press, 2003), 6–8.

36. Richard Fletcher, *The Barbarian Conversion: From Paganism to Christianity* (New York: Henry Holt and Company, 1997), 50.

37. See Fletcher, *The Barbarian Conversion*, 87.

38. Pierre Riche, *Education and Culture in the Barbarian West* (Columbia: University of South Carolina Press, 1978), 328, 330–31.

39. Riche, *Education and Culture in the Barbarian West*, 321.

40. Fletcher, *The Barbarian Conversion*, 130.

41. As Fletcher writes:

> Early medieval missionaries were firm believers in the "trickle-down effect." The most easily identifiable and consistently pursued element of strategy was the missionaries' choice to work from the top downwards. If you can convert the directing elite then those who are subject to its direction will follow the lead given. Such was the hope, and it was frequently realized. . . . Some types of barbarian kingship or chieftainship commanded more exemplary or coercive power than others; individual ruling families could grow more, or less, powerful over time. But in general evangelists from Patrick onwards found it convenient and effective to work with or through the directing secular forces in the societies they strove to Christianize. (*The Barbarian Conversion*, 236)

42. Fletcher, *The Barbarian Conversion*, 174.

43. Fletcher provides an interesting portrait of the resources needed to run a church. *The Barbarian Conversion*, 459–61.

44. Fletcher, *The Barbarian Conversion*, 237.

45. Fletcher, *The Barbarian Conversion*, 516, 518.

46. Fletcher, *The Barbarian Conversion*, 154, 155, 160, 161, 166, 455.

47. David Harry Miller, "Sacral Kingship, Biblical Kingship, and the Elevation of Pepin the Short," in *Religion, Culture, and Society in the Early Middle Ages*, eds. Thomas F. X. Noble and John J. Contreni (Kalamazoo: Medieval Institute Publications, Western Michigan University, 1987), 131–54.

48. Miller, "Sacral Kingship, Biblical Kingship, and the Elevation of Pepin the Short," 131.

49. Jane L. Nelson, "Kingship and Empire in the Carolingian World," in *Carolingian Culture: Emulation and Innovation*, ed. Rosamond McKitterick (Cambridge: Cambridge University Press, 1994), 52.

50. Many scholars argue that Alcuin was likely a Benedictine monk, though the fact is disputed.

51. E. J. B. Gaskoin quoted in *The Catholic Encyclopedia*, vol. 1 (New York: Robert Appleton, 1907), www.newadvent.org/cathen/01276a.htm (accessed on 8 October 2009).

52. Giles Brown, "Introduction: The Carolingian Renaissance," in *Carolingian Culture: Emulation and Innovation*, ed. Rosamond McKitterick (Cambridge: Cambridge University Press, 1994), 30–31.

53. Brown, "Introduction: The Carolingian Renaissance," 34.

54. Brown, "Introduction: The Carolingian Renaissance," 17–21.

55. George Henderson, "Emulation and Invention in Carolingian Art," in *Carolingian Culture: Emulation and Innovation*, ed. Rosamond McKitterick (Cambridge: Cambridge University Press, 1994), 248–73.

56. See Rosamond McKitterick, *The Carolingians and the Written Word* (Cambridge: Cambridge University Press, 1989).

57. Rosamond McKitterick, "Script and Book Production," in *Carolingian Culture: Emulation and Innovation*, ed. Rosamond McKitterick (Cambridge: Cambridge University Press, 1994), 244.

58. Brown, "Introduction: The Carolingian Renaissance," 25.

59. Brown, "Introduction: The Carolingian Renaissance," 25.

60. Robert Wuthnow, *Communities of Discourse* (Cambridge, Mass.: Harvard University Press, 1989), 55–56.

61. As Steven Ozment observes, the distractions were so intense that it wasn't until 1530, when Charles V called the Diet of Augsburg, that he was able to attend to the religious issues at the center of this protest movement. *The Age of Reform 1250–1550: An Intellectual and Religious History of Late Medieval and Reformation Europe* (New Haven, Conn.: Yale University Press, 1980), 256.

62. Ozment, *The Age of Reform 1250–1550*, 232.

63. See Erasmus, *The Praise of Folly*. From Christian Classics Ethereal Library Online, www.ccel.org/ccel/erasmus/folly.toc.html (accessed on 20 October 2009).

64. Alister E. McGrath, *The Intellectual Origins of the European Reformation* (Oxford: Blackwell, 1987), 65. In *The Age of Reform 1250–1550*, Ozment qualifies this contention this way:

> Scholars have argued that without humanism the Reformation could not have succeeded, and it is certainly difficult to imagine the Reformation occurring without the knowledge of languages, the critical handling of sources, the satirical attacks on clerics and scholastics, and the new national feeling that a generation of humanists provided. On the other hand, the long-term success of the humanists owed something to the Reformation. In Protestant schools and universities classical culture found a permanent home. The humanist curriculum, with its stress on languages and history, became a lasting model for the arts curriculum. (316–17)

65. Peter Burke, *A Social History of Knowledge* (Cambridge, U.K.: Polity Press, 2000), 36.

66. Ozment, *The Age of Reform 1250–1550*, 232.

67. For example, Phillip Schaff, *History of the Christian Church*, 3rd ed. (Peabody, Mass.: Hendrickson Press, 1996).

68. Beza was not of noble birth but was from a very prosperous and prominent family from Vezelay, France, that was well familiar with court life. This knowledge proved invaluable for the cause of French Protestantism.

69. Gillian Lewis, "The Geneva Academy," in *Calvinism in Europe, 1540–1620*, ed. Andrew Pettegree, Alastair Duke, and Gillian Lewis (Cambridge: Cambridge University Press, 1994), 35–63.

70. Quoted in Graeme Murdock, *Beyond Calvin: The Intellectual, Political, and Cultural World of Europe's Reformed Churches* (Houndsmills, U.K.: Palgrave Macmillan, 2004). It is said that between 1555 and 1570, the Geneva Academy trained over two hundred pastors for the ministry.

71. Burke, *A Social History of Knowledge*, 38.

72. See, for example, Guido Marnef, "The Changing Face of Calvinism in Antwerp, 1558–1585," in Pettegree, Duke, and Lewis, *Calvinism in Europe*, 143–59.

73. Murdock, *Beyond Calvin*, 2.

74. Ole Peter Grell, "Merchants and Ministers: The Foundations of International Capitalism" in Pettegree, Duke, and Lewis, *Calvinism in Europe*, 254–73.

75. Quoted in Murdock, *Beyond Calvin*, 34.

76. According to John Man, between 1518 and 1525 Luther published approximately 2,100,000 copies of his sermons and tracts. In John Man, *Gutenberg: How One Man Remade the World with Words* (New York: John Wiley & Sons, 2002).

77. Wuthnow, *Communities of Discourse*, 2–3.

78. The worst of it was in the St. Bartholomew's Day Massacre of 1572, which sparked a wave of violence that lasted from August to October of that year. Estimates range from 10,000 to 100,000 people slaughtered in Paris and other major cities throughout France. See the *Oxford Encyclopedia of World History*, Oxford University Press, 1998, p. 585.

79. The power of the Church, wedded as it was to imperial power, was terrifying. It not only sought to destroy Luther and to burn all of his books, but to punish in a like manner, those who assisted Luther in any way. As it was written in the Edict:

> "We have declared and hereby forever declare by this edict that the said Martin Luther is to be considered an estranged member, rotten and cut off from the body of our Holy Mother Church. He is an obstinate, schismatic heretic, and we want him to be considered as such by all of you.
>
> For this reason we forbid anyone from this time forward to dare, either by words or by deeds, to receive, defend, sustain, or favor the said Martin Luther. On the contrary, we want him to be apprehended and punished as a notorious heretic, as he deserves, to be brought personally before us, or to be securely guarded until those who have captured him inform us, whereupon we will order the appropriate manner of proceeding against the said Luther. Those who will help in his capture will be rewarded generously for their good work.
>
> As for his accomplices, those who help or favor the said Martin in whatever manner or who show obstinacy in their perversity, not receiving absolution from the pope for the evils they have committed, we will also proceed against them and will take all of their goods and belongings, movable and fixed, with the help either of the judges in the area in which they reside or of our parliaments and councils at Malines or in other cities in which these events are made known. Action will be taken according to the desire of the accusers or of our fiscal procurators, but always according to the constitution and the laws, whether canon, civil, or divine, written against those who commit heresy or the crime of *lèse majesté*. These laws will be applied regardless of person, degree, or privilege if anyone does not obey our edict in every manner.

See www.crivoice.org/creededictworms.html. (accessed on 20 October 2009)

80. Alastair Duke, "Perspectives on European Calvinism," in Pettegree, Duke, and Lewis, *Calvinism in Europe*, 8.

81. See the wonderful study by Catherine Randall in her book *Building Codes: The Aesthetics of Calvinism in Early Modern Europe* (Philadelphia: University of Pennsylvania Press, 1999).

82. Frank Lambert, "The Great Awakening as Artifact: George Whitefield and the Construction of Intercolonial Revival, 1739–1745," *Church History* 60, no. 2 (June 1991): 230.

83. Michael J. Crawford, "The Origins of the Eighteenth-Century Evangelical Revival: England and New England Compared," *The Journal of British Studies* 26, no. 4 (October 1987): 371.

84. Lambert, "The Great Awakening as Artifact," 223.

85. See Susan O'Brian, "A Transatlantic Community of Saints: The Great Awakening and the First Evangelical Network, 1735–1755," *The American Historical Review* 91, no. 4 (October 1986): 811–32.

86. See O'Brian, "A Transatlantic Community of Saints," 817.

87. See O'Brian, "A Transatlantic Community of Saints," 813. As Lambert put it, "The result was . . . a 'general' awakening that gathered up local or 'particular' awakenings into a cohesive revival." See Frank Lambert, *Inventing the "Great Awakening"* (Princeton, N.J.: Princeton University Press, 1999), 85.

88. See O'Brian, "A Transatlantic Community of Saints," 828–29.

89. Roger Anstey argues in "A Re-Interpretation of the Abolition of the British Slave Trade, 1806–1807," *The English Historical Review* 87 (1972): 311.

90. And yet the convergence of these cultural alliances manifested themselves politically in an alliance between the Evangelicals and Whigs. Though they held very different worldviews, they did find common ground in their conceptions of liberty, hierarchy, *noblese oblige*, and the like. See Abraham Kriegel, "A Convergence of Ethics: Saints and Whigs in British Antislavery," *The Journal of British Studies* 26 (1987): 423–50.

91. Stephen was married to Wilberforce's sister, Sarah.

92. This summary of the Enlightenment draws extensively from Robert Wuthnow, *Communities of Discourse: Ideology and Social Structure in the Reformation, the Enlightenment, and European Socialism* (Cambridge, Mass.: Harvard University Press, 1989). See Part 2.

93. See, for example, Robert Darnton, *The Forbidden Best-Sellers of Prerevolutionary France* (New York: W. W. Norton, 1995); and *The Corpus of Clandestine Literature in France, 1769–1789* (New York: W. W. Norton, 1995).

94. Wuthnow, *Communities of Discourse*, 364.

95. Wuthnow, *Communities of Discourse*, 364.

96. Alvin Gouldner, *Against Fragmentation: The Origins of Marxism and the Sociology of Intellectuals* (Oxford: Oxford University Press, 1985), 4.

97. Wuthnow, *Communities of Discourse*, 364.

98. Alvin Gouldner, *Against Fragmentation: The Origins of Marxism and the Sociology of Intellectuals* (Oxford: Oxford University Press, 1985), 14.

99. Wuthnow, *Communities of Discourse*, 563.

100. Wuthnow, *Communities of Discourse*, 383.

101. Lenin goes on to say, "I perceived concretely where the secret of using our enemy lay, how to compel those who had opposed communism to build it, how to build communism with the bricks which the capitalists had chosen to hurl against us! We have no other bricks! And so, we must compel the bourgeois experts, under the leadership of the proletariat, to build up our edifice with these bricks." V. I. Lenin, "Achievements and Difficulties of the Soviet Government," in *Collected Works*, 4th ed., vol. 29 (Moscow: Progress Publishers, 1972), 55–88. marxists.org/archive/lenin/works/1919/mar/x01.htm.

102. Darwin himself was a descendent of the very prosperous and famous Darwin-Wedgewood family. His success came partially because of his education at Edinburgh

and Cambridge and the networks of scientists and patrons in those places. The central event of his career, the voyage of the *Beagle*, would never have taken place without the resources of Captain Robert Fitzroy, who provided the boat, the crew, and the funds for research. Darwin, at the age of twenty-two, simply came along as a gentleman's companion to Fitzroy but, as an amateur naturalist, he took full advantage of the five-year voyage. His reputation was established and expanded through his connections with the Geological Society of London, The Zoological Society, the Royal Society (of London for the Improvement of Natural Knowledge), and the British Association for the Advancement of Science.

103. Even Nietzsche—the original postmodern philosopher—was not just a lonely explorer on the frontiers of thought. He studied at Liepzig with the preeminent philologists of the time, who sponsored him for a chair at age twenty-four. His most influential connection was the composer Richard Wagner. Wagner had been given literally unlimited patronage by Lugwig, the king of Bavaria (to the point where he was able even to construct a theater of his own design in Bayreuth). Thus, by becoming a personal disciple of Wagner, Nietzsche was guaranteed a high public profile. Still, Nietzsche would have died in obscurity had it not been for the networks cultivated by his sister, Elizabeth. She was a central part of the literary and political life of Germany from Bismark to Hitler—so important as the high priestess of the "Nietzsche cult," that her name was proposed to the Swedish Academy for the Nobel Prize in Literature on three occasions (1908, 1913, and 1923). Hitler himself attended her funeral and laid a laurel wreath on her coffin. Even Nietzsche's posthumous influence is directly tied to the political capital his work enjoyed among the Nazis and the financial capital provided by the German Count Kessler and the wealthy Swedish banker Ernest Thiel (who loved Nietzsche because his writings had "released him" from the taboos of Swedish society). Thiel not only translated many of Nietzsche's books into Swedish, but in 1908 he granted a huge endowment to the Nietzsche archives, which allowed Nietzsche's sister Elizabeth to disseminate his writings on a massive scale.

104. The success of literary modernism in the early twentieth century had much to do with the patronage of Harriet Shaw Weaver. This wealthy British patron gave James Joyce over one million dollars between 1917 and 1941 (roughly 3 million in today's dollars); she supported Ezra Pound and D. H. Lawrence financially as well. In a similar way, Scofield Thayer and James Sibly Watson, another affluent Briton, provided the financial capital to fund *The Dial*, the organ of literary modernism (together they provided the 2002 equivalent of $800,000 per year to sustain the publication). Though its circulation was only 10,000, *The Dial* was critically important to sustaining this literary movement. It was here, for example, that T. S. Eliot's *The Wasteland* and other seminal literary works were published.

105. In the world of art, there is no question that contemporary art would not be what it is without the vast resources of Peggy Guggenheim. Her first "hobby" museum, Guggenheim jeune (London), showed Wassily Kandinsky in the United Kingdom for the first time. And Art of This Century (NYC) was singly crucial to the early career of Jackson Pollock. Guggenheim financially supported Pollock for a year leading up to his debut one-man show. The making of the avant-garde in America was almost single-handedly brought about by the financial resources and networking of Alfred Stieglitz, whose "291" gallery became a place not just of exhibition for the avant-garde, but a

place to meet, discuss, and become inspired. He became the first patron to vigorously promote Matisse, Cezanne, Picasso, and Rodin in America, and then his coterie of prominent American artists became known as the "Stieglitz Circle."

106. The coming together of financial and intellectual capital in common purpose also accounts for the astonishing success of humanistic Marxism in the middle to late twentieth century. Its home was The Institute for Social Research based in Frankfurt, Germany. It was made possible by the funding of Hermann Weil, the owner of an international grain and food company, who agreed to finance the building and its equipment entirely, provide an endowment of 3.5 million marks and a yearly grant of 120,000 marks. Though only started in 1924, by 1928, the institute's library consisted of 37,000 volumes, 340 scholarly journals, and 37 German and foreign newspapers, and it was used by 5,000 people annually. The facility had eighteen offices for ten permanent academic members and a handful of staff members. There were, in addition, eight to ten research associates who were paid on a short-term basis for specific publications or projects. Between 1933 and 1944, the institute provided support at one level or another for 130 émigré academics and 116 doctoral students and 14 postdoctoral students.

107. See Christian Smith, *The Secular Revolution* (Berkeley: University of California Press, 2003).

CHAPTER 6

1. Laura Nash, *Believers in Business* (Nashville, Tenn.: Thomas Nelson, 1994).

2. This analysis was inspired by research conducted in the early 1990s by David John Seel. See his dissertation, "The Evangelical Meltdown: Modernity and the Hysteresis of Habitus" (PhD diss., University of Maryland, 1992).

3. See Melissa Brown, ed., *Giving USA 2001: The Annual Report on Philanthropy for the Year 2000* (Glenview, Ill.: American Association of Fund Raising Council Trust for Philanthropy, 2001). The American Association of Fund Raising Council Trust for Philanthropy is now called Giving USA Foundation, and its reports from 2002–2005 are referenced below. *Giving USA* reports that giving to religion accounted for 36.5% in 2000 (88), 38.2% in 2001 (6), 35% in 2002 (106), 35.5% in 2004 (100), and 35.5% in 2005 (107) of total giving. The 2001 edition of *Giving USA* highlights trends in giving to religion from 1955 to 1999. From 1955 to 1977, giving to religion averaged about 45% of total giving with a high in 1977 of 48%. From 1978 to 1999 giving to religion averaged 47% with a high of 57% in 1985 and a low of 44% in 1999.

4. *Giving USA 2006*, 107.

5. *Giving USA 2001* reports that "giving by individuals has always been the largest component of charitable giving," 75% in 1999 (57). *Giving USA, 2003* cites "studies of individual or household giving (that) show that the largest share of contributions made by households supports religious organizations." It also quotes an Independent Sector report: "60% of all households in [the] U.S. contributed to at least one religious organization and that 53% of all household giving supported houses of worship or other religious purposes in 2000" (106–07). *Giving USA 2005* references a Barna Group study claiming that 65% of adults donated to a "house of worship" in 2004 (100). More to the point, Independent Sector's 2001 publication, *Giving and Volunteering in the*

United States, reports that 68.6% of "contributing households" give to religious organizations. See *Giving and Volunteering in the United States, 2001* (Washington, D.C.: Independent Sector, 2002), 34, 38.

6. According to *Giving and Volunteering, 2001*, the average household contribution to religious organizations was $1,358 (34).

7. See *Grants for Religion, Religious Welfare, and Religious Education 2006/2007* (New York: Foundation Center, 2006), vii–xiii. This report provides a list of 992 foundations that give grants of "$10,000 or more with a total value of $1,242,023,944, mostly in 2004 or 2005." There are a few important points about this list, however. The list of foundations includes organizations that give to a variety of religious faiths. Most significantly, there are a number of foundations that give exclusively to or that give a large portion of their donations to Jewish synagogues and organizations. The list also includes corporate or company-sponsored foundations and community foundations that allocate money (often at the direction of employees or community members) to religious organizations. In addition, the type of giving is important; the introduction to the report says the following: it covers grants for churches, synagogues, mosques, religious orders, missionary societies, associations, institutions, and organizations concerned with religious issues. Also included are grants for religious welfare for such activities as counseling, outreach, meal programs, and relief and volunteer programs. Religious education covers grants to religious educational institutions for operating support, facilities and equipment, curriculum development, staff endowments, scholarships, fellowships, professorships, ministry training, and research projects (iii).

8. The numbers in this list are from 2005 and can be found in the annual reports for each foundation.

9. The numbers in this list are found in *Grants for Religion, 2006/2007*. All numbers as listed in *Grants for Religion* are from 2005 except for the Gordon and Betty Moore Foundation, which lists numbers from 2004.

10. The Ford Foundation says the following about giving to religion:

> Religion, Society and Culture: examine the role of religious traditions of the world in shaping social values, with the goal of strengthening the contribution of these traditions to creating just, healthy and pluralistic societies. Grant making also seeks to support the participation of historically marginalized groups in the interpretation of diverse religious and cultural traditions and to examine the moral resources they offer contemporary societies.

It is worth noting that The Ford Foundation focuses almost exclusively on giving to interfaith agencies or projects designed to unite different faiths in some manner. The Lilly Endowment, in contrast, gives directly to many Christian organizations. Part of its mission statement says:

> Support for religion, education, and community development, with special concentration on programs that benefit youth and develop leadership. Giving emphasizes charitable organizations that depend on private support, with a limited number of grants to government institutions and tax-supported programs. Also supports limited grant programs in public policy research.

Both statements can be found in the Foundation Center Online Directory.

11. Of the foundations listed in the last three charts above, ten have a national or international focus (Batten, CIOS, Open Doors, DeMoss, Maclellan, NCCF, JTF, Weinberg, Raskob, and Koch), and fourteen identify a specific geographic focus (Mabee, Whittaker, Lazarus, DeVos, Lilly, Berger, Wiegand, Leavey, Connelly, Doheny, Ave Maria, Murphy, Valley, and Norcliffe). See Foundation Center Online Directory, fconline.fdncewnter.org.

12. This list can be found in *Grants for Religion*, xvii. The numbers for religious giving are also on page xvii and represent 2005 giving for the Lilly Endowment, Gates Foundation, John Templeton Foundation, The Duke Endowment, the Weinberg Foundation, and the Wayne and Gladys Valley Foundation. The numbers for the DeMoss Foundation, the Berger Foundation, the DeVos Foundation, and the Maclellan Foundation are for giving in 2004.

13. The numbers for religious giving come from *Grants for Religion, 2006/2007*, vii–xiii. The amounts for religious giving reflect gifts made in 2005 for the Valley Foundation, the Florik Charitable Trust, Koch Foundation, Inc., Leavey Foundation, and the Norcliffe Foundation. The numbers for Dan Murphy Foundation, Ave Maria Foundation, Doheny Foundation, Connelly Foundation, and Raskob Foundation for Catholic Activities are for spending in 2004.

14. In 1990, Timothy Clydesdale reported that approximately 88 percent give to evangelism, missions, and education. In addition:

> Eighty-three percent of these foundations support evangelistic activities within the United States, and two-thirds support the same overseas. Seventy-five per-cent of foundations support evangelical educational institutions (often the alma mater of the founder), where future evangelists and missionaries are trained. Two-thirds of the foundations do recognize their responsibility to the poor, donating money to organizations for relief, development, and social services; however, only one foundation places a high priority on supporting these groups. (Timothy T. Clydesdale, "Soul–Winning and Social Work: Giving and Caring in the Evangelical Tradition," in *Faith and Philanthropy in America* [New York: Jossey–Bass, 1990], 205)

15. The numbers cited in this paragraph are based on an analysis of the religious giving by the top ten Evangelical Foundations. These numbers do not reflect giving from the National Christian Charitable Foundation (NCCF). While it is difficult to assess NCCF giving, the NCCF generally gives to evangelical activities including religious education or religious schools, missions and evangelistic organizations, Christian ministries, and social service institutions with a religious orientation. The numbers listed for each of the categories mentioned also do not add up to $103,631,308 because they do not include giving by the Maclellan Foundation. The Maclellan Foundation gives most of its money to NCCF to allocate to Christian organizations. It is therefore impossible to trace what money given by NCCF is from the Maclellan Foundation.

16. The following two lists are based on analysis of the *Grants for Religion, 2006/2007* and 990s for some of the organizations included in the list. The lists are based on what each foundation gave to religious organizations in 2004 or 2005 and do not reflect total giving by each foundation.

17. The numbers listed in this section come primarily from *Grants for Religion*, vii–xiii. The religious giving for the National Christian Charitable Foundation can be found in the Foundation Center Directory Online (accessed on 18 April 2007). The religious giving for the Aimee and Frank Batten Jr. Foundation and the CIOS Foundation are from their 2005 990-PF.

18. The *Ford Foundation Annual Report 2005*, www.fordfound.org/publications; *William and Flora Hewlett Foundation Annual Report 2005*, www.hewlett.org; Annenberg Foundation 990-PF form, 2005; *John D. and Catherine T. MacArthur Foundation: Report on Activities 2005*, macfound.org.

19. The number for giving to the arts is based on an analysis of the 990-PFs for the Evangelical and Catholic foundations listed above. This number for giving to the arts does not include grants made through NCCF.

20. According to the 990-PFs for the Evangelical and Catholic foundations, there is no evidence that these foundations support a program or grant for talented intellectuals, artists, or social innovators.

21. See Richard Hofstadter, *Anti-Intellectualism in American Life* (New York: Vintage, 1963), and Mark Noll, *The Scandal of the Evangelical Mind* (Grand Rapids, Mich.: Eerdmanns, 1994).

22. The concept is drawn from Ernest R. Sandeen, *The Roots of Fundamentalism: British and American Millenarianism 1800–1930* (Chicago: University of Chicago Press, 1970).

23. Seel came to the very same conclusion in his dissertation, "The Evangelical Meltdown."

24. See, for example, D. Michael Lindsay, *Faith in the Halls of Power* (New York: Oxford University Press, 2007).

25. Seel, "The Evangelical Meltdown." This is another point that D. Michael Lindsay misses in his book *Faith in the Halls of Power*. Though there are some Evangelicals in positions of social and economic influence, there is little depth of theological reflection guiding them or uniting them.

26. Christian Smith and Melinda Lundquist Denton, *Soul-Searching: The Religious and Spiritual Lives of American Teenagers* (New York: Oxford University Press, 2005).

Essay II

CHAPTER 2

1. The education of the next generation, for example, would be impossible without such basic agreements about what is important to teach the young. Contracts—social and otherwise—to take another example, depend on agreements about language and principles of fairness. Interdependence in modern societies, then, only creates a certain degree of social solidarity, but not enough to keep them together and functioning smoothly.

2. The argument here is indebted to Michael Oakeshott, "The Claims of Politics," *Scrutiny* 8 (1939), and, even more, to Jacques Ellul, *The Political Illusion* (New York: Random House, 1967).

3. An important qualification should be made here. Prior to the twentieth century, news media made little effort to be unbiased. Newspapers openly took sides on behalf

of political parties or on behalf of certain issues. It is really only in the last century that the news made the concerted effort to remain free of political bias. What is new, then, is not that the news media is prejudiced one way or another, but that it is so under the pretext of being neutral.

4. Ellul, *The Political Illusion*, 12.

5. For Nietzsche, life, in its essence, is oriented toward domination. Life does not want to be channeled, contained, controlled, or negated, as the proponents of "slave morality" would have it. His description of the origin of what he calls the "higher cultures" illustrates this point:

[Anything which] is a living and not a dying body . . . will have to be an incarnate will to power, it will strive to grow, spread, seize, become predominant—not from any morality or immorality but because it is *living* and because life simply *is* will to power. . . . "Exploitation" . . . belongs to the *essence* of what lives, as a basic organic function; it is a consequence of the will to power, which is after all the will to life. (*Beyond Good and Evil*, trans. Walter Kaufmann [New York: Vintage, 1989], 259)

6. I will return to this at the end of Essay II.

CHAPTER 3

1. Peter McManus, letter to the editor, *Washington Post*, 27 January 1996.

2. Richard John Neuhaus, "One Nation under God," *Reflections* (Summer-Fall 1994,): 1–7.

3. From Joyce Meyer Ministries, www.joycemeyer.org (accessed on 13 July 2006).

4. From American Values, www.americanvalues.org (accessed on 17 July 2006).

5. Dr. Laurence White, in a session called "Pulpits Aflame with Righteousness" at the Vision America Conference, War on Christians, Omni Shoreham Hotel, Washington, D.C., 27–28 March 2006.

6. Rick Scarborough, introductory address, Vision America Conference, "Omni Shoreham Hotel, Washington," D.C., 27–28 March 2006.

7. From American Values, www.americanvalues.org (accessed on 17 July 2006).

8. Tony Perkins of the Family Research Council, quoted by Chris Hedges, "Feeling the Hate with the National Religious Broadcasters," *Harper's Magazine*, May 2005, 55–61.

9. Dr. James Kennedy, *Character and Destiny: A Nation in Search of Its Soul* (Grand Rapids, Mich.: Zondervan, 1994), 274. Gary Bauer uses tough language in a communication to James Dobson to say much the same thing at the time of the Clinton administration: "Robbers entered a church in the Washington suburbs this week and held-up the worshippers. Church-goers were stunned by the act. But the robbers were no more outrageous than the current gang running our country." Gary Bauer, Family Research Council, Memo to James Dobson, 20 May 1994.

10. Focus on the Family Action, "*Letter from 2012 in Obama's America*," 22 October, 2008. http://www.wnd.com/files/Focusletter.pdf. (accessed on 9 October 2009)

11. Sometimes the complaint is directed at specific people. According to *Christianity Today*, Jerry Falwell also "regularly berates his enemies. Moments after he told of the importance of witnessing for Christ in a recent sermon, he criticized 'liberals,' 'secular humanists,' and 'violent Muslims.' He called President Clinton an 'ungodly liar' and singer Madonna a 'despicable, highly paid prostitute.'" John W. Kennedy, "Jerry Falwell's Uncertain Legacy," *Christianity Today* 40, no. 14 (9 December 1996): 62–67.

12. Pat Robertson, Christian Coalition solicitation and information letter, 1996.

13. Robertson, Christian Coalition letter, 1996.

14. In a letter from the Christian Coalition, 1996, Pat Robertson wrote: "And the U.S. Government still spends tens of millions of dollars on the National Endowment for the Arts which makes a point of funding anti-Christian and pornographic 'art' projects . . . projects designed specifically to offend and outrage Christians and religious people."

15. Pat Robertson, Christian Coalition solicitation and information letter, 1994.

16. From American Values, www.americanvalues.org (accessed on 17 July 2006).

17. From American Values, www.americanvalues.org (accessed on 17 July 2006).

18. From American Values, www.americanvalues.org (accessed on 17 July 2006).

19. Robertson (Christian Coalition letter, 1996).

20. "1998 National Survey of Christian Voters," mailing, Christian Coalition.

21. The statement was made by Tony Perkins on the Family Research Council webpage about "Justice Sunday," 24 April 2005, organized by the Family Research Council. See David D. Kirkpatrick, "Frist Set to Use Religious Stage on Judicial Issue," *New York Times*, 15 April 2005.

22. "'Values Voters': Contract with Congress," www.valuesvoter.org (accessed on 9 October 2009) and, specifically, www1.valuesvoter.org/preamble.cfm?host id=VA1 (no longer available). This document was signed by 40 well-known leaders of the Christian Right.

23. This is a claim made about the American Civil Liberties Union. Alan E. Sears, "How the ACLU Grinch Steals Christmas: Are Public Nativity Displays Constitutional?," www.orthodoxytoday.org (16 December 2003).

24. James Dobson, "Restoring the Foundations: Repealing Judicial Tyranny," www.family.org (12 November 2004).

25. Dobson, "Restoring the Foundations." This is also the source of the quotation in the following subhead.

26. Mike Johnson in a conference panel entitled, "The ACLU and Radical Secularism: Driving God from our Public Life." Vision America Conference, War on Christians, Omni Shoreham Hotel, Washington, D.C., 27–28 March 2006.

27. Robertson, Christian Coalition letter, 1996. Here he also states that "Congress [was] ignoring the concerns of Christian and pro-family voters."

28. Robertson, Christian Coalition letter, 1996.

29. In a statement made at the Values Voter Summit. Washington, D.C., 12 September 2008.

30. These comments were made by Don Feder of Jews Against Anti-Christian Defamation, at the Vision America Conference: War on Christians, Omni Shoreham Hotel, Washington, D.C., 27–28 March 2006.

31. From www.visionforum.com (accessed on 13 July 2006).

32. Stanley J. Oakes, "1992 National Survey of Christians," Christian Leadership Ministries, mailing, 1–3.

33. Robertson, Christian Coalition letter, 1996.

34. Gary Bauer makes this claim on the American Values webpage, www.americanvalues.org (accessed on 17 July 2006). Elsewhere on this webpage, he reiterates the claim saying, "Recently, we have witnessed a substantial effort by secularist forces to prevent people of faith from continuing to acknowledge religion in the public square."

35. Robertson, Christian Coalition letter, 1994. In full the claim is that "Your gift will also help us survive the legal attack we're under from the Democratic National Committee, which is trying to close down the Christian Coalition in an effort to silence Christian voices and suppress the Christian vote in November."

36. Statement issued by the Family Research Council in defense of "Justice Sunday," 24 April 2005.

37. Staff reporters, "Some Say Christmas Banning Is Part of the Anti-Christian Agenda," *Citizenlink*, 30 November 2005.

38. Oakes, "1992 National Survey," 1–3.

39. Vision America Conference, War on Christians, Omni Shoreham Hotel, Washington, D.C., 27–28 March 2006.

40. At a time when Americans need to be reminded of our nation's
moral roots and the virtues that spring from those roots, secularists have worked tirelessly for such things as removing the words "under God" from our country's most sacred oath, an education system that forbids any mention or recognition of faith, and the removal of Judge Roy Moore as Alabama's Chief Justice because he refused to remove a 10 Commandments monument from the state's Supreme Court building.
American Values, www.americanvalues.org (accessed on 17 July 2006).

41. Oliver North gave voice to this anger in ways appropriate to the narrative. In his own words,

> It makes me angry when I meet trusting, decent Americans who naively believe they are getting the impartial truth from journalists who are actually hard-core, dedicated liberals! It makes me angry when I see so many honest, hard-working men and women who instinctively feel they are losing control of their lives, their children, their finances and their futures—but don't have a clue about why. And it's all because of the shameful disinformation they get from politicians and the liberal media alike!

Direct mail letter from Oliver North, April 1996.

42. Ralph Reed, "The Role of Religious Conservatives in the '96 Elections." Address to the Christian Coalition's "Road to Victory '95" Conference, 8 September 1995.

43. Pat Robertson, National Christian Voter Mobilization Campaign Letter, 1995.

44. Rick Scarborough, e-mail, 12 July 2006.

45. Focus on the Family, e-mail, 15 May 2006.

46. D. James Kennedy, "The New Tolerance." Sermon given at Coral Ridge Presbyterian Church, 28 February 1999.

47. "Anti-Christian Bigotry Threatens Americans." Advertisement. *WORLD* Magazine, 23 November 1996, pg. 25.

48. Dr. James Dobson and Gary L. Bauer, *Children at Risk* (Dallas, Tex.: Word Publishing, 1990), 19.

49. Quoted in Michael J. Gerson, "A Righteous Indignation: James Dobson—Psychologist, Radio Host, Family-Values Crusader—Is Set to Topple the Political Establishment," *Newsweek*, 4 May 1998.

50. James Dobson, "Restoring the Foundations: Repealing Judicial Tyranny," www.family.org (12 November 2004). Richard Land echoes this view in an interview with *Frontline*:

> I think there's a tremendous division in this country. . . . Basically, it breaks down to this enormous fault line. On one side of this fault line, you have people who have a traditional view of morality. . . . On the other side of this fault line, you have what I would call a post-modern worldview. . . . The problem with the left is that some of them don't think God has a side. George Bush and most of George Bush's supporters believe God has a side, and we believe that side is freedom. We believe that side is democracy. We believe that side is respect for basic human rights. We don't see the world starkly in terms of black and white. But we do see that there is a good and there is an evil, and that there is no moral equivalence between Saddam Hussein and the United States of America.

Interview by Richard Land, *PBS Frontline*, 29 April 2004.

51. Beverly LaHaye, "How Christians Make an Impact on Their Government," in *Citizen Christians: The Rights and Responsibilities of Dual Citizenship*, ed. Richard D. Land and Louis A. Moore (Nashville, Tenn.: Broadman and Holman, 1994).

52. James Dobson, "Why I Use 'Fighting Words': A response to John Woodbridge's 'Culture War Casualties,'" *Christianity Today*, 19 June 1995.

53. This was an announcement of a new ministry outreach of Joyce Meyer Ministries called Stand Up and Be Counted. See Joyce Meyer Ministries, www.joycemeyer.org (accessed on 13 July 2006).

54. Staff reporters, "Some Say Christmas Banning Is Part of the Anti-Christian Agenda."

55. Oliver North, letter, April 1996.

56. Alan E. Sears, "How the ACLU Grinch Steals Christmas: Are Public Nativity Displays Constitutional?" www.orthodoxytoday.org (16 December 2003).

57. In a statement made at the Values Voter Summit (Hilton Hotel, Washington, D.C., 12 September 2008).

58. In a statement made at the Values Voter Summit (Hilton Hotel, Washington, D.C., 12 September 2008).

59. LaHaye, "How Christians Make an Impact." Fourteen years later, at the Values Voter Summit, this remained the theme of the Christian conservatives.

60. "Citizen Christian Awareness Campaign: A Manual of Prayer and Action." Pamphlet, Christian Life Commission of the Southern Baptist Convention, 1992.

61. Gary L. Bauer, letter, Family Research Council, 9 July 1998.

62. "Christians and Politics." Pamphlet, published by Christian Life Commission of the Southern Baptist Convention, n.d.).

63. National Association of Evangelicals, "For the Health of the Nation: An Evangelical Call to Civic Responsibility," October 2004.

64. "Why Christians Should . . . Vote." Pamphlet, distributed by Focus on the Family and the Family Research Council. Focus on the Family Action created the website www.ivotevalues.com for the election.

65. From www.ivotevalues.com, "Pray for the Election" (accessed on 2 September 2004).

66. Roberta Combs, letter, Christian Coalition Action Alert, 1 July 2005.

67. From "Why Bother?" http://ivotevalues.org/get.cfm?i=WX07L14 (accessed on 9 October 2009).

68. Quoted in the program *God's Christian Warriors*, CNN, 23 August 23 2007, transcripts.cnn.com/TRANSCRIPTS/0708/23/cp.01.html (accessed on 9 October 2009).

69. This account is found in David D. Kirkpatrick, "Churches See an Election Role and Spread the Word on Bush," *New York Times*, 9 August 2004.

70. From the Christian Coalition, www.cc.org (accessed on 20 July 2006).

71. From the Christian Coalition, www.cc.org.

72. From the Christian Coalition, www.cc.org.

73. Michelle Ammons, a spokesperson for the Christian Coalition, quoted by Anne-Marie O'Connor, "A GOP Struggle for the Podium: Conservative Christians Feel Slighted by Party's Moderate Picks for Prime Convention Slots," *Los Angeles Times*, 18 August 2004. Steve Waldman wrote in his 2004 Convention Blog that "the most common religion buttons were: 'Christians for Bush,' 'When the righteous rule, the people rejoice. Prov. 29:2' (Photo of Bush, head bowed), and 'One Man, One Woman. Just as God intended. Bush Cheney 2004.' See "The Righteous Rule." www.beliefnet .com, 2 September 2004 (accessed 1 October 2004).

74. For one account, see David D. Kirkpatrick, "A Call to 'Win This Culture War,'" *New York Times*, 1 September 2004.

75. The Reverend Jerry Falwell was quoted as saying "[GOP political expert] Karl Rove called me this morning to say, 'Thank you for over 30 million evangelicals who visited the polls last Tuesday and who were a major player in what happened . . . And we have already formed a new group and begun meeting with a goal of getting 40 million people to the polls in 2008.'" Carol Eisenberg, "Election Poll: Morally Speaking, Iraq was the Bigger Issue," *Newsday*, 10 November 2004.

76. For example, in a telephone interview, Reed said he was proud of his campaign and glad that he had run: "I have been building the Republican Party and the pro-family movement for over 25 years, and I am looking forward to continuing that important work." See David D. Kirkpatrick, "What Next for Ralph Reed?," *New York Times*, 22 July 2006. To mention another figure, Michelle Ammons of the Christian Coalition said of the organization's president, Roberta Combs, that she had been a Republican delegate for 20 years, and "she knows politics better than anybody . . . She knows how to organize a precinct and how to organize a county. It's all about getting out the vote." O'Connor, "A GOP Struggle for the Podium."

77. For example, Richard Land of the Southern Baptist Convention ran an extensive get-out-the-vote operation in his denomination and took some credit for Republican victories. See Nina J. Easton, "Baptist Lobbyist Walks a Fine Line," *Boston Globe*, 10 October 2005.

78. Rick Scarborough, "Confronting the Judicial War on Faith." Address, Judeo-Christian Council for Constitutional Restoration Conference, Lufkin, Texas, 7–8 April 2005.

79. "Dr. Dobson Answers Questions about Focus on the Family's 20th Anniversary—and His Future," *Focus on the Family Magazine* (April 1997).

80. Pete Winn, "Dobson Credited with First Salvo in Court Battle," *Focus on the Family*, 4 January 2005.

81. In the first instance, Janet Porter, president of Faith2Action, made this case about those who planned to vote for Obama in 2008 (see www.worldnetdaily.com/?pageId=79276). Her article appeared on 28 October 2008. In the second instance, the Reverend Jay Scott Newman, a Catholic priest serving in Columbia, South Carolina, declared that those parishioners who voted for Obama should refrain from receiving Holy Communion before doing penance for their vote. The reason was that supporting him "constitutes material cooperation with intrinsic evil." See www.msnbc.msn.com/id/27705755/.

82. This was the book title of a former official of the National Association of Evangelicals: Robert P. Dugan Jr., *Winning the New Civil War: Recapturing America's Values* (Portland, Ore.: Multinomah, 1991).

83. Dr. D. James Kennedy, *Character & Destiny: A Nation In Search of Its Soul* (Grand Rapids, Mich.: Zondervan, 1994), 76.

84. Ralph Reed, *Active Faith* (Northampton, Mass.: Free Press, 1996), 249.

85. Kirkpatrick, "A Call to 'Win This Culture War.'"

86. Thomas B. Edsall, "Robertson Urges Christian Activists to Take Over GOP State Parties," *Washington Post*, 10 September 1995.

87. These statements are taken from www.Rightmarch.com, the Christian Coalition, Focus on the Family Citizen Link, among others.

88. Robertson, Christian Coalition letter, 1994.

89. Rod Parsley, public comments at the Vision America, War on Christians Conference, 27–28 March 2006, in Washington D.C.

90. Associated Press, Washington, 7 October 2004.

91. Associated Press, Washington, 7 October 2004.

92. Interview with James Dobson, *Day One: An ABC News Magazine*, 21 September 1995.

93. David D. Kirkpatrick, "Conservative Christians Criticize Republicans," *New York Times*, 15 May 2006.

94. Gerson, "A Righteous Indignation."

95. Gerson, "A Righteous Indignation."

96. Fred Barnes, "Family Feud: Religious Right versus Republicans," *New Republic*, 17 April 1995.

97. In 2004, a group of organizations within the Christian Right (including the Family Research Council, the Eagle Forum, and the American Conservative Union) held a press conference. The premise of the event was a warning: "if they don't take care of conservatives they may not be able to generate enough turnout of conservative religious voters." Steve Waldman, "Might Conservatives Stay Home?" 2004 Convention Blog, 30 August 2004, www.beliefnet.com (accessed on 1 October 2004). At the same convention, Paul Weyrich said, "If the president is embarrassed to be seen with conservatives

at the convention, maybe conservatives will be embarrassed to be seen with the president on election day." O'Connor, "A GOP Struggle for the Podium."

98. From the Christian Coalition, www.cc.org/vision.cfm.

99. From the Christian Coalition, www.cc.org/vision.cfm (accessed on 25 January 2008).

100. Tom Delay, "Challenge of Cultural Renewal," address given at the National Press Club Luncheon, National Press Club Ballroom, Washington, D.C., 4 May 2000.

101. James Dobson, mass e-mail, 20 April 2004. In full, Dobson writes, "I am convinced we can save traditional marriage and the traditional family if only we stand together for God's truth and tell our senators and congressmen by phone where we stand on marriage. Thank you for your continued partnership in this Campaign for Righteousness."

102. Roberta Combs, letter, Christian Coalition Action Alert, 24 April 2006.

103. Quoting from www.eagleforum.org (accessed on 23 March 2006).

104. "The Values Voters' Contract with Congress: A Declaration of American Renewal," www.valuesvoters.org (accessed on 22 July 2006).

105. Stuart Shepard, "It's Time to Vote," Focus on the Family, www.family.org, 1 November 2004.

106. Gary Bauer is quoted in Stuart Shepard, "It's Time to Vote," 1 November 2004. Focus on the Family Website.

107. From www.ivotevalues.com "My Church" (accessed on 2 September 2004).

108. Letter, Christian Coalition Action Alert, 1 July 2005.

109. James Dobson is quoted in Stuart Shepard, "It's Time to Vote," 1 November, 2004 Focus on the Family Website.

110. Tony Perkins, Family Research Council, www.citizenlink.org/, 15 August 2008.

111. Rick Scarborough, "It's All about the Judges," Vision America, 28 September 2007, www.visionamerica.us/article/its-all-about-the-judges (accessed on 18 January 2008).

112. Ralph Reed, at a 1995 Christian Coalition Meeting, Washington, D.C., 1995. Emphasis added.

113. Comment made by D. James Kennedy, February 2005, at a conference in Ft. Lauderdale sponsored by the Center for Reclaiming America for Christ.

In the war against Christianity . . . It's time to fight back! Introducing the Center for Reclaiming America. Millions of Americans sense that something is seriously wrong with the direction our country is heading. Many would like to do something about the problem but feel that as individuals they can have little, if any, impact. Others feel that they aren't properly equipped to get results. The CENTER for RECLAIMING AMERICA will provide the training and tools to allow you, as an individual, to be effective and link you with thousands of others to create an effective team to change your community, your state, and our nation. There are four vital areas for reclaiming America, and your efforts as a volunteer are desperately needed. As part of the Reclaiming America Information Network, the Telecommunications Message Center, the Christian Alert Bulletin or the Office of Traditional Values-based Legislation, you can make an important impact.

You can volunteer in one or more of these vital outreaches and join an army of volunteers whose purpose is to change our country.

D. James Kennedy, www.reclaimamerica.org (accessed on 31 December 1996).

114. Ralph Reed, Remarks, Road to Victory Conference, Washington, D.C. 16 September 1994).

115. Reverend Peter Marshall, "Prodigal Nation—Part II," *Washington Watch*, July 1998.

116. Tom Delay, "Rediscovering our American Values: The Real State of the Union" (address, Heritage Lecture #654, Washington, D.C. 1 February 2000).

117. See David Kinnaman and Gabe Lyons, *UNChristian: What a New Generation Really Thinks about Christianity and Why It Matters* (Grand Rapids, Mich.: Baker Books, 2007). Sentiments of disaffection have been growing for some time. For example, survey data from the *Religion and Politics Survey, 1996*, commissioned by the Pew Research Center for The People and The Press (Andrew Kohut, director). The survey was fielded by the Princeton Survey Research Associates between 31 May and 9 June 1996. The data show that the plurality of people of all faith traditions, by a substantial margin, preferred that Evangelicals, Protestants, Catholics, and Jews "have less influence in government and political matters than they have now." Another indication is that during the Bush administration, the support of white Evangelicals declined from 90 percent to 45 percent. David D. Kirkpatrick, "The Evangelical Crackup," *New York Times*, 28 October 2007.

118. Among these are Jonathan Falwell, Rick Scarborough, Janet Porter, Michael Farris, and Alan Sears.

119. "I am convinced Sen. McCain is not a conservative, and in fact, has gone out of his way to stick his thumb in the eyes of those who are. He has sounded at times more like a member of the other party. . . . But what a sad and melancholy decision this is for me and many other conservatives. Should Sen. McCain capture the nomination as many assume, I believe this general election will offer the worst choices for president in my lifetime. I certainly can't vote for Hillary Clinton or Barack Obama based on their virulently anti-family policy positions. If these are the nominees in November, I simply will not cast a ballot for president for the first time in my life. These decisions are my personal views and do not represent the organization with which I am affiliated. They do reflect my deeply held convictions about the institution of the family, about moral and spiritual beliefs, and about the welfare of our country." James Dobson, Focus on the Family Action "Citizen Link" (live webcast), 6 February 2008. Dobson changed his views when Sarah Palin was nominated as McCain's running mate.

120. Dobson accused Senator Obama of "deliberately distorting the traditional understanding of the Bible to fit . . . his own confused theology," of having a "fruitcake interpretation of the Constitution," and of appealing to the "lowest common denominator of morality." See Peter Wehner, "Dobson vs. Obama," *Washington Post*, 28 June 2008, www.washingtonpost.com/wp-dyn/content/article/2008/06/27/AR2008062702490.html.

121. Falwell made this statement on 12 September 2008 at the Values Voter Summit Hilton Hotel, Washington, D.C. James Dobson echoed this sentiment after the 2008 election, "The war's not over. Pendulums swing and we'll come back. We're going

to hang in there." Quoted in Lillian Kwon, "Dobson: Media Mistaken on the White Flag," *Christian Post*, 16 April 2009.

122. See Legacy Online, "Our Mission," www.legacyevents.org (accessed on 9 October 2009).

123. See The Clapham Group, www.claphamgroup.com (accessed on 9 October 2009)

124. See Reclaiming the 7 Mountains of Culture, www.reclaim7mountains.com/ (accessed on 9 October 2009).

125. See video "Reclaiming the 7 Mountains of Culture," www.youtube.com/watch?v=wQtB-AF41p8 (accessed on 9 October 2009).

126. T. M. Moore, "From Worldview Programs to Kingdom Movement: Forging Alliances for the Gospel," Washington, D.C.: Breakpoint, essay, December, 2008, pg. 3.

127. In this document, Moore identifies the central feature of the lie as "God is a construct; Man is the arbiter of truth." Out of this comes a worldview defined by "corollary lies and half-truths. Truth is relative and pragmatic; ethics are utilitarian, the cosmos is an accident, life is a fleeting and meaningless journey to oblivion, man is a product of evolution, the principal concern of man is man, spiritual concerns are private, merely, Christianity is a pliable, changeable thing; [and] Christ is one option among many as a way to eternal life." Moore, "From Worldview Programs to Kingdom Movement," 3.

128. Moore, "From Worldview Programs to Kingdom Movement," 4.

129. Moore, "From Worldview Programs to Kingdom Movement," 8. Emphasis added.

130. On its webpage, the Seven Mountains group explains the plan of reconquest this way:

> In the book of Joshua, God calls Joshua to cross the Jordan River and to take the Promised Land. However, in order to do that he had to drive out 7 enemies that were more powerful than the people of Israel at the time. *'This is how you will know that the living God is among you and that he will certainly drive out 7 enemies before you including the Canaanites, Hittites, Hivites, Perizzites, Girgashites, Amorites and the Jebusites'* (Joshua 3:10). There were 7 distinct enemies they were to drive out of the land. They were the rulers of seven mountains. Today, Christians have given over these 7 strategic mountains over to a liberal and secular leadership. God is calling his people to reclaim these mountains for His purposes.

www.reclaim7mountains.com (accessed on 31 January 2008).

CHAPTER 4

1. Georges Sorel, "Letter to Daniel Halevy," in *Reflections on Violence*, trans. T. E. Hulme and J. Roth (1908; repr. New York: Collier, 1950), 26–56.

2. See Paul Ramsey, *Who Speaks for the Church? A Critique of the 1966 Geneva Conference on Church and Society* (New York: Abingdon Press, 1967).

3. See Gustavo Gutiérrez, *A Theology of Liberation: Perspectives* (Lima, Peru: CEP, 1971).

4. "NETWORK envisions and works for a more humane world, one of justice and care for the common good. We act in solidarity with justice activists throughout the

global community. Our work is firmly rooted in our Catholic social justice tradition, which encompasses Scripture, Catholic Social Teaching and the lives of Jesus and people of faith who have followed the Gospel call to act for justice. We believe that faith has a public dimension. As the Church teaches us, 'Every citizen . . . has the responsibility to work to secure justice and human rights through an organized social response.' *Economic Justice for All*, #120. Our advocacy work with the 110th Congress focuses on critical issues such as a federal budget that adequately addresses human needs, the ongoing war in Iraq, a fair minimum wage, immigration, food security, global trade policies, and healthcare. In this era of globalization, we are always conscious of the fact that U.S. domestic issues are intertwined with the global common good." www.networklobby .org/issues/index.html.(accessed on 9 October 2009).

5. One can scroll through them on their websites: www.episcopalchurch.org/ peace_justice.htm, www.umc-gbcs.org/site/pp.asp?c=fsJNKoPKJrH&b=849409, www.elca.org/advocacy/federal/ (no longer available), and www.ucc.org/justice/index.html.

6. It was established in Washington, D.C., in 1946.

7. See "The Washington Office: a public policy ministry" www.pcusa.org/ washington/whatis.htm.

8. "The Justice and Advocacy Commission serves as the arm of the Council through which the member communions and their boards and agencies, together with partici- pating non-member communions and related organizations, cooperate in efforts to pursue justice in church and society, especially the elimination of poverty in the United States, racial justice, justice for women, environmental justice and responses to the urban crisis. This Commission works in collaboration with public policy ministries of the Council." www.ncccusa.org/about/justicehome.html (accessed on 9 October 2009).

9. Most prominent is the leadership of Michael Lerner and the Network of Spiritual Progressives. See Michael Lerner, *The Left Hand of God: Taking Back our Country from the Religious Right* (San Francisco: HarperSanFrancisco, 2006) and www.spiritual progressives.org/.

10. Though there are no formal ties, they share many strong affinities with such groups as The Center for Progressive Christianity, the Christian Alliance for Progress: The Movement to Reclaim Christianity, and Transform American Politics.

11. Clinton made these remarks at a service in New York's interdenominational Riverside Church on 29 August 2004. Reported by Mark O'Keefe, "Religious Progres- sives See Revival," *Contra Costa Times*, 3 September 2004.

12. Anne Farris, "Religion Proving an Important Piece of the Political Landscape," *Roundtable on Religion and Social Welfare Policy*, 16 August 2005, www.religionandsocial policy.org/news/article.cfm?id=3157.

13. See "Jim Wallis: Top Ten God's Politics Epiphanies," www.beliefnet.com/blogs/ godspolitics/2006/10/jim-wallis-top-ten-gods-politics.html. (accessed on 9 October 2009).

14. Sojourners/Call to Renewal, "From Poverty to Opportunity: A Covenant for a New America," mission statement, Pentecost 2006: Building a Covenant for a New America, 26–28 June 2006.

15. Bishop John Bryson Chane, quoted in Jim Wallis, *God's Politics* (San Francisco: Harper, 2005), 243.

16. Wallis, *God's Politics*, 249.

17. Jim Wallis, public comments, Pentecost 2006: Building a Covenant for a New America, hosted by Sojourners and Call to Renewal, Washington, D.C., 26 June 2006.

18. Tony Campolo, *Speaking My Mind* (Nashville, Tenn.: W Publishing Group, 2004), 169.

19. Jim Wallis, *The Soul of Politics* (New York: New Press, 1995), xxi.

20. Statements like "Disarm Iraq without War: A Statement from Religious Leaders in the United States and United Kingdom" are commonplace. They write:

> As Christians, we seek to be guided by the vision of a world in which nations do not attempt to resolve international problems by making war on other nations. It is a long-held Christian principle that all governments and citizens are obliged to work for the avoidance of war. . . . We, therefore, do not believe that war with Iraq can be justified under the principle of a "just war," but would be illegal, unwise, and immoral.

United for Peace and Justice, www.unitedforpeace.org/article.php?id=2837=. (accessed on 9 October 2009).
On the environment: "An Urgent Call to Action: Scientists and Evangelicals Unite to Protect Creation," letter, National Press Club, Washington, D.C., 17 January 2007.

> We declare that every sector of our nation's leadership—religious, scientific, business, political, and educational—must act now to work toward the fundamental change in values, lifestyles, and public policies required to address these worsening problems before it is too late. There is no excuse for further delays. Business as usual cannot continue yet one more day. We pledge to work together at every level to lead our nation toward a responsible care for creation, and we call with one voice to our scientific and evangelical colleagues, and to all others, to join us in these efforts.

Campolo makes a similar case: "We regard saving the environment from the degradation of polluters as a moral imperative. We are convinced that establishing fair trade policies with Third World countries is an ethical responsibility." See Campolo, *Speaking My Mind*, 200.

Launched in January 2006, the Evangelical Climate Initiative's Call to Action states that, "human-induced climate change is real," "the consequences of climate change will be significant, and will hit the poor the hardest," "Christian moral convictions demand our response to the climate change problem," and "the need to act now is urgent. Governments, businesses, churches, and individuals all have a role to play in addressing climate change—starting now." See "Christians and Climate," www.christiansandclimate .org (accessed on 9 October 2009).

Regarding immigration, "CCIR [Christian Coalition for Immigration Reform launched May 2007] represents a coalition of Christian organizations, churches, and leaders from across the theological and political spectrum united in support of comprehensive immigration reform." Sojourners, www.sojo.net.

21. Jim Wallis, public statement, Spiritual Activism conference, University of California, Berkeley, 20 July 2005. See Bob Burnett, "Rev. Jim Wallis Mobilizes the Religious Left," *Berkeley Daily Planet*, 22 July 2005.

22. Tom Sine, *Cease Fire: Searching for Sanity in America's Culture Wars* (Grand Rapids, Mich.: Eerdmans, 1995), 16.

23. Randall Balmer, *Thy Kingdom Come: How the Religious Right Distorts the Faith and Threatens America: An Evangelical's Lament* (New York: Basic Books, 2006), ix, xii.

24. Balmer, *Thy Kingdom Come*, ix, 177.

25. Balmer, *Thy Kingdom Come*, 34, ix.

26. Balmer, *Thy Kingdom Come*, 190.

27. Balmer, *Thy Kingdom Come*, 180, x.

28. Sojourners, "Confessing Christ in a World of Violence," Election 2004, www .sojo.net.

29. Balmer, *Thy Kingdom Come*, xii.

30. Balmer, *Thy Kingdom Come*, ix.

31. Balmer, *Thy Kingdom Come*, 186.

32. Christian Alliance for Progress, www.christianalliance.org/site/c.bnKIIQNtEoG/ b.592961/k.ABD2/About_the_Alliance.htm. (site no longer available)

33. Jim Wallis, "God Hates Inequality," *SojoMail*, 1 February 2007, go.sojo.net/ct/ PdzDenK14zoQ.

34. Sine, *Cease Fire*, 232.

35. Balmer, *Thy Kingdom Come*, ix.

36. Balmer, *Thy Kingdom Come*, 167. A minion is a servile or slavish follower.

37. Balmer, *Thy Kingdom Come*, ix, 167, 168, 170, 175, 177, 181, 190.

38. Balmer, *Thy Kingdom Come*, 167–169.

39. Christian Alliance for Progress, www.christianalliance.org/site/c.bnKIIQNtEoG/ b.592961/k.ABD2/About_the_Alliance.htm. (site no longer available)

40. Christian Alliance for Progress, www.christianalliance.org/site/c.bnKIIQNtEoG/ b.592961/k.ABD2/About_the_Alliance.htm. (site no longer available)

41. Consider, for example, the open letter by Jim Wallis to General William Boykin, republished in *God's Politics*. Wallis cannot contain his anger, castigating the general in the most condescending way for having made a foolish public statement about the spiritual battle America is in with Islam. Wallis, *God's Politics*, 155–57.

42. Call for Renewal, "The Cry for Renewal: Biblical Faith and Spiritual Politics," www.calltorenewal.com/about_us/index.cfm/action/history.html (site no longer available) 23 May 1995.

43. Jim Wallis, public comments in open session, Pentecost 2006: Building a Covenant for a New America.

44. Christian Alliance for Progress, www.christianalliance.org/site/c.bnKIIQNtEoG/ b.592961/k.ABD2/About_the_Alliance.htm. (site no longer available)

45. Balmer, *Thy Kingdom Come*, xii.

46. Jim Wallis, interviewed by Paula Gordon, *Paula Gordon Show: Conversations with People at the Leading Edge*, radio, episode "Religion & Democracy, Part I," 26 May 2005.

47. Wallis, *God's Politics*, 3–4. He repeats this statement often as he did at the conference on "Spiritual Activism," noted earlier. Burnett, "Rev. Jim Wallis Mobilizes the Religious Left."

48. Balmer, *Thy Kingdom Come*, 167.

49. Christian Alliance for Progress, www.christianalliance.org/site/c.bnKIIQNtEoG/ b.592961/k.ABD2/About_the_Alliance.htm. (site no longer available)

50. As it says in the "Cry for Renewal" vision statement: "But those Jesus told us to especially remember as 'the least of these' must be neither forgotten or [*sic*] scapegoated. To abandon or blame the poor for their oppression and affirm the affluent in their complacency would be a moral and religious failure, and is no alternative to social policies which have not succeeded." "The Cry for Renewal: Biblical Faith and Spiritual Politics," mission statement, 23 May 1995.

51. Sojourners, "Voting God's Politics: An Issue Guide for Christians" (pamphlet, 2006).

52. Jim Wallis, "Be Not Afraid," Huffington Post, 30 October 2008. www .huffingtonpost.com/jim-wallis/be-not-afraid:b_139362.html (accessed on 9 October 2009).

53. The Matthew 25 Network, www.matthew25.org/ (accessed on 9 October 2009).

54. ABC News, "Obama Friend Wants Abortion Reduction Plank," 25 June 2008, blogs.abcnews.com/politicalradar/2008/06/obama-friend-pu.html.

55. Katha Pollitt, "Jesus to the Rescue?," *The Nation* (7 February 2005), www .thenation.com.

56. Wallis, *God's Politics*, xxiv.

57. Amy Sullivan, an Evangelical progressive herself, acknowledges this fact as well; that while he doesn't "want to become the liberal equivalent of Pat Robertson," "on balance—particularly given his commitment above all to the elimination of poverty—Wallis's sympathies are more in line with Democratic policies and values." See Amy Sullivan, "The Good Fight: How Much Longer Can the Religious Left Remain Politically Neutral?" *Washington Monthly* (March 2005), www.washingtonmonthly.com/ features/2005/0503.sullivan.html (accessed on 9 October 2009).

58. The five reasons he offers are archived here: www.brianmclaren.net/archives/ blog/worth-comparing.html (accessed on 9 October 2009).

59. Wallis, *God's Politics*, 3–4.

60. Wallis, *God's Politics*, 2.

61. Jim Wallis, public comments, Pentecost 2006 reception at Hart Senate Building, Washington D.C., 26–28 June 2006. His full statement was, "The political leaders who lead on these issues are going to find a lot of support in the religious community. It will take a movement to support these leaders. We are here to announce that we are a new special interest group."

62. Some on the Christian Left criticize his leadership and the current direction of the movement as not being political enough. As the journalist Amy Sullivan puts it,

> In order to truly be heard, . . . Wallis and his compatriots need to face what they're up against—a conservative machine that uses two-way communication between religious communities and political institutions to coordinate policy and rhetoric. With the stakes high for issues they care about, religious progressives may have to set aside the pristine white choir robes for a time and get their hands dirty in practical politics. . . . If they want to protect the values they hold dear, and the country they love, they're going to have to start fighting the good fight.

See Sullivan, "The Good Fight."

63. Wallis, for example, accuses President George W. Bush of making "this mistake over and over again of confusing nation, church, and God. The resulting theology is more an American civil religion than Christian faith." *God's Politics*, 142.

64. Jim Wallis, interviewed by Paula Gordon, *Paula Gordon Show: Conversations with People at the Leading Edge*, radio, episode "Religion & Democracy, Part I," 26 May 2005.

65. The following statements accompany a list of beliefs published in a newspaper petition. Wallis reproduces these in *God's Politics*, xxiii–xxiv.

66. Wallis, *God's Politics*, 149, 126.

67. Wallis, *God's Politics*, 241.

68. Wallis, *God's Politics*, 250.

69. Wallis, *God's Politics*, 126–127.

70. Wallis writes, "What does the Bible have to say about the minimum wage? The prophet Isaiah said: 'my chosen shall long enjoy the work of their hands. They shall not labor in vain (65:22–23).'" Expressing the civil religious character of his position even more clearly, Wallis states, "But 9.2 million American families are. Somebody in all those households works hard, full time, and yet they're all raising their kids in poverty. That's wrong. *It's against our theology and it's un-American*" (emphasis added). See Wallis, "God Hates Inequality."

71. Wallis, *God's Politics*, 68. Wallis isn't the only one. As stated by the National Council of Churches, "Our values *must* be reflected in our nation's public policies." www.faithfulamerica.org/.

72. Amy Sullivan is quoted on this point in Alexander Bolton, "Clinton Hires Faith Guru," *The Hill*, 6 February 2007, www.thehill.com/.

73. Senator Harry Reid, "A Word to the Faithful," democrats.senate.gov/faith.cfm.

74. Reid, "A Word to the Faithful."

75. "Pelosi Names James E. Clyburn to Lead Faith Working Group," press release, Office of Congressman James E. Clyburn, 4 February 2005. clyburn.house.gov/press/050204faithgroup.html.

76. In early 2007, the major Democratic contenders had hired strategists from the faith community to advise them in these ways. See Alexander Bolton, "Clinton Hires Faith Guru," *The Hill*, 6 February 2007, www.thehill.com/.

77. Common Good Strategies has stated:

> Founded in the summer of 2005, Common Good Strategies (CGS) is a political strategy firm dedicated to helping Democrats reclaim the debate on faith and values. CGS works with Democratic elected officials, candidates, and social jus- tice-minded non-profits to develop and implement religious outreach programs that improve relationships and understanding with the religious community. CGS also helps Democrats understand how to effectively and authentically com- municate our principles and beliefs with people of faith and helps Democrats develop policy positions that will resonate with the faith community.

See www.commongoodstrategies.com/profile.html (site not longer available).

78. Faith in Public Life, www.faithinpubliclife.org/.

79. Broder, John M., "Obama Courting Evangelicals Once Loyal to Bush," *The New York Times* (July 1, 2008) (accessed on 9 October 2009) www.nytimes.com/2008/07/02/us/politics/01evangelicals.html.

CHAPTER 5

1. This is primarily due to the prominence of its founder, Shane Claiborne, author of *The Irresistible Revolution* (Grand Rapids, Mich.: Zondervan, 2006) and coauthor of *Jesus for President* (Grand Rapids, Mich.: Zondervan, 2008).

2. See www.communityofcommunities.info/ for a listing of these communities and information on each (accessed on 12 October 2009).

3. Matt. 19; John 12; and Acts 2:44–47.

4. According to its website,

> The Ekklesia Project is a network of Christians from across the Christian tradition who rejoice in a peculiar kind of friendship rooted in our common love of God and the Church. We come together from Catholic parishes, Protestant congregations, communities in the Anabaptist tradition, house-churches and more as those who are convinced that to call ourselves 'Christian' means that following Jesus Christ must shape all areas of life. Our shared friendship is one of God's good gifts. With deep gratitude for God's ongoing grace, we are unapologetically . . . [Here we abbreviate] God-centered, . . . church-centered, . . . shalom-centered, . . . [and] political. Seeing Christ's Body as our "first family," the Ekklesia Project aims to put discipleship and the Church as an alternative community of practices, worship, and integration at the center of contemporary debates on Christianity and society. We work to assist the Church as it lives its true calling as the real-world community whose primary loyalty is to God's Kingdom that has broken into the world in Jesus' person, priorities and practices, and that continues to do so in and through the gathered Body of Christ.

See www.ekklesiaproject.org (accessed on 12 October 2009).

5. John Howard Yoder, *The Priestly Kingdom* (Notre Dame, Ind.: Notre Dame University Press, 1984), 140.

6. John Howard Yoder, "Christ, The Hope of the World," in *The Royal Priesthood* (Scottdale, Pa.: Herald Press, 1998), 194–97.

7. "In addition to Hauerwas' initial indictment of liberalism, I would like to further specify that capitalism and market economics are no less imperial in their demands and must be considered as mutually supporting liberal political practices." Robert W. Brimlow, "Solomon's Porch: The Church as Sectarian Ghetto," in *The Church as Counterculture*, ed. Michael L. Budde and Robert W. Brimlow (Albany: State University of New York Press, 2000), 116.

8. Daniel M. Bell Jr., "What Is Wrong with Capitalism? The Problem with the Problem with Capitalism," *The Other Journal* 5 (4 April 2005), www.theotherjournal.com/article.php?id=76 (accessed on 12 October 2009); William T. Cavanaugh, "The Unfreedom of the Free Market," in *Wealth, Poverty, and Human Destiny*, ed. Doug Bandow and David Schindler (Wilmington, Del.: ISI Books, 2003), 103–128; William T. Cavanaugh, "Consumption, the Market, and the Eucharist," *The Other Journal* 5 (4 April 2005), www.theotherjournal.com/article.php?id=52 (accessed on 12 October 2009).

9. Eugene McCarraher, "Mammon's Deadly Grin: The New Gospel of Wealth and the Old Gospel of Life," presentation, Culture of Life Conference, Notre Dame Center for Ethics and Culture, Notre Dame, Ind., 30 November 2001.

10. As Hauerwas puts it, understanding Constantinianism is the basis on which "a genuine Christian critique of Christian America is to be made." Stanley Hauerwas, "A Christian Critique of Christian America," in *The Hauerwas Reader*, ed. John Berkman and Michael Cartwright (Durham, N.C.: Duke University Press, 2001), 459–80.

11. In summarizing Hauerwas's views, Mark Oppenheimer says,

> Today, the Christian remains loyal to the nation-state—and that's idol worship. The church needs to stop serving the Man and begin serving the Son of Man. Hauerwas believes that the true Christian ought to live on the social and political margins. The true Christian, recognizing that the story of the Cross requires pacifism, might refuse to fight the capitalist's wars. He also might find the world of market capitalism so inhospitable, so hostile to the formation of virtue, that he opts out—into separate schools and summer camps and circles of friends. He is a resident alien. He witnesses. ("For God, Not Country: The Un-American Theology of Stanley Hauerwas.

See www.Freerepublic.com (accessed on 7 June 2007).

12. Eugene McCarraher, "Smile When You Say 'Laity': The Hidden Triumph of the Consumer Ethos," *Commonweal* 124, no. 15 (12 September 1997).

13. As Hauerwas says of the mainline, the thrust of its ministry over the last several decades "has been built on trying to transform the church into the left wing of the Democratic party." See Stanley Hauerwas, *In Good Company: The Church as Polis* (Notre Dame, Ind.: University of Notre Dame Press, 1995), 56.

14. Stanley Hauerwas, sermon, Broadway United Methodist Church, South Bend, Indiana, 8 August 1993, as reprinted in Hauerwas, *In Good Company*, 39.

15. Michael L. Budde, "Pledging Allegiance: Reflections on Discipleship and the Church after Rwanda," in *The Church as Counterculture*, ed. Michael L. Budde and Robert W. Brimlow (Albany: State University of New York Press, 2000), 214.

16. E. McCarraher, "Christian Intellectuals, Embedded and Otherwise," *The New Pantagruel* 1, no. 1, www.newpantagruel.com/issues/1.1/christian_intellectuals. embedd_print.php (accessed on 21 May 2007, site no longer available).

17. John Howard Yoder, *For the Nations: Essays Evangelical and Public* (Eugene, Ore.: Wifp and Stock, 1997), 24.

18. John Howard Yoder, *The Politics of Jesus* (Grand Rapids, Mich.: Eerdmans, 1972), 61.

19. Luke 22: 26.

20. Matt. 26: 52–53.

21. See Yoder, "Christ and Power," in *The Politics of Jesus*, 134–161; and William Stringfellow, *Free in Obedience* (New York: Seabury Press, 1964).

22. Hendrik Berkhof, *Christ and the Powers* (Scottdale, Pa.: Herald Press, 1962), 30.

23. Berkhof, *Christ and the Powers*, 32–33.

24. Yoder puts the paradox sharply: "God permits human evil to keep itself under control by using evil against itself." See John Howard Yoder, *Discipleship as Political Responsibility* (Scottdale, Pa.: Herald Press, 1964), 18.

25. Yoder, *The Politics of Jesus*, 147.

26. John Howard Yoder, *The Christian Witness to the State* (Scottdale, Pa.: Herald Press, 1964), 8–9.

27. Berkhof, *Christ and the Powers*, 41f.

28. As Craig Carter puts it, "ecclesiology is the shape of Yoder's social ethics." See Part 4 in *The Politics of the Cross* (Grand Rapids, Mich.: Brazos Press, 2001), 179–224.

29. Yoder, *For the Nations*, 8.

30. In *The Original Revolution* (Scottdale, Pa.: Herald Press, 1971), 137–38, Yoder writes,

In the life and death of Jesus we find a reality and the possibility of all that the teachings say. It is possible to live that way if you are willing to die that way. In the personal case of Jesus it is made clear that He rejects not only unjust violence but also the use of violence in the most righteous cause . . . what Jesus was really tempted by was the proper use of violence. It was concerning the use of the sword in legitimate defense that Jesus said that they who take it will die by it! So we learn from the rooting of pacifism in the person of Jesus that the traditional tension between law and love or between the ideal and possible is artificial.

31. John Howard Yoder, "The Otherness of the Church," in *The Royal Priesthood* (Scottdale, Pa.: Herald Press, 1998), 64.

32. Yoder, *The Politics of Jesus*, 158, 199, 205, 214; see also Yoder, *The Royal Priesthood*, 63.

33. Stanley Hauerwas, "Why the 'Sectarian Temptation' Is a Misrepresentation: A Response to James Gustafson," in *The Hauerwas Reader*, eds. John Berkman and Michael Cartwright (Durham, N.C.: Duke University Press, 2001), 105.

34. Shane Claiborne and Chris Haw, *Jesus for President* (Grand Rapids, Mich.: Zondervan, 2008), 167.

35. Claiborne and Haw, *Jesus for President*, 212.

36. Yoder, *The Politics of Jesus*, 188. In making this case, Yoder cites Mark 10:42–43, Matthew 20:25, and Luke 22:5.

37. Yoder, *The Politics of Jesus*, 244.

38. Hauerwas, "Why the 'Sectarian Temptation' is a Misrepresentation," 106.

39. Yoder, *The Christian Witness to the State*, 9.

40. Yoder, "The Otherness of the Church," 56.

41. Yoder, "The Otherness of the Church," 56.

42. Yoder, *The Priestly Kingdom*, 92, 94.

43. John Howard Yoder, *Body Politics* (Scottdale, Pa.: Herald Press, 1964), viii; Hauerwas, *In Good Company*.

44. William Cavanaugh, *Theopolitical Imagination: Discovering the Liturgy as a Political Act in an Age of Global Consumerism* (London: T & T Clark, 2002), 15.

45. Stanley Hauerwas and William H. Willimon, *Resident Aliens* (Nashville, Tenn.: Abingdon, 1989), 43.

46. Hauerwas, *In Good Company*, 26.

47. Hauerwas, "Why the 'Sectarian Temptation' Is a Misrepresentation," 90–110.

48. Brimlow, "Solomon's Porch," 110.

49. Brimlow "Solomon's Porch," 113–14.

50. Yoder, *The Politics of Jesus*, 156.

51. Yoder, "The Otherness of the Church," 64. He goes on in this passage to say, "The church will be most deeply and lastingly responsible for those in the valley of the shadow if it is the city set on the hill."

52. Yoder, *The Politics of Jesus*, 157.

53. Yoder, *The Politics of Jesus*, 12, 100.

54. Hauerwas and Willimon, *Resident Aliens*, 30. To this one could add the statement, "The Gospel is itself, intrinsically, a politics enacted first in the *ekklesia*." Douglas Harink, "*Apolcalypsis* and *Polis*: Pauline Reflections on the Theological Politics of Yoder, Hauerwas, and Milbank," unpublished paper, brandon.multics.org/library/misc/harink1999apocalypsis.html (accessed on 12 October 2009). In this vein, Claiborne calls for a new kind of campaign, a different kind of party, and a different kind of commander in chief.

55. Yoder, *Body Politics*, viii.

56. Carter, *The Politics of the Cross*.

57. Consider the subtitle in Cavanaugh's book, *Theopolitical Imagination: Discovering the Liturgy as a Political Act in an Age of Global Consumerism*. In their book, *Jesus for President*, Claiborne and Haw present a "liturgy of resistance" that is framed by the political issues of the day. See Appendix 4.

58. Hauerwas, *In Good Company*, 8.

59. Yoder, *The Politics of Jesus*, 97.

60. Yoder, *The Politics of Jesus*, 132.

61. Claiborne and Haw, *Jesus for President*, 167.

62. Yoder, *The Politics of Jesus*, 158.

63. See "The Christian Case for Democracy," in John Howard Yoder, *The Priestly Kingdom* (Notre Dame, Ind.: Notre Dame University Press, 1984). Brimlow's contention is that "The challenge of the church as closed circle is [to] maintain our distinctiveness and our separateness while we simultaneously and steadfastly refuse to define 'other.'" Sociologically, this is impossible. See Brimlow, "Solomon's Porch," 121.

64. As Hauerwas put it,

> Niebuhr was, as I indicated in the last lecture, a child of the church. He spoke and preached about and prayed to God in a manner that leaves no doubt of his profound faith in the God of Jesus Christ. Yet exactly because he was such a vital Christian believer, Niebuhr felt free to provide an account of our knowledge of God that seems little more than a pale theism. In short, Niebuhr's practice, his use of Christian speech, prevented him, as well as those influenced by him, from seeing that metaphysically his "god" was nothing other than a Jamesian sense that "there must be more." . . . As it turns out, the revelation that is required for us to know Niebuhr's god is but a reflection of ourselves. This is a harsh judgement, but one that I think I can sustain. . . . Do we have anything more in Niebuhr than a complex humanism disguised in the language of the Christian faith? Probably not. . . .

Stanley Hauerwas, *With the Grain of the Universe* (Grand Rapids, Mich.: Brazos Press, 2001), 122, 131.

65. "At best it [Richard Neuhaus' "Christianity and Democracy"] is a form of Christian radicalism that, while morally impressive at certain times, is basically politically irrelevant, but at worst is politically immoral insofar as it fails to face the necessity of having to make judgments between lesser evils." Stanley Hauerwas, *Against the Nations: War and Survival in a Liberal Society* (New York: Winston Press, 1985), 123.

66. See Stanley Hauerwas and William H. Willimon, *Where Resident Aliens Live: Exercises for Christian Practice* (Nashville, Tenn.: Abingdon Press, 1996), 115.

67. Here is the larger statement by Hauerwas about G. W. Bush:

> And I think also, George Bush, his Christian faith, is the Christian faith of Alcoholics Anonymous. You can quite understand that. It never seems to occur to him what it would mean to be a part of a Church and under ecclesial authority, and to have your language tested by ecclesial authority. I mean, I'm sure he's very genuine in his religious faith, I just don't think very much of his faith. For someone like me to say that, you think well that's very arrogant. And it's true, it is very arrogant. And I think that one of the things that we suffer from in America is that religious people thinking secularity is such an enemy, that any religious faith is better than no religious faith. That is a deep mistake! There are very perverse forms of religious faith, that, give me a secularist any day compared to some of the forms of religious faith. And I must say, I think that Evangelicalism bears the brunt of a lot of this. I think that it is far too a-ecclesial and Evangelicals tend to turn the gospel into a system of belief rather than a body of people through which we are embraced through God's salvation that makes us different.

See Dan Rhodes, "An Interview with Stanley Hauerwas," *The Other Journal*, www .theotherjournal.com (accessed on 18 May 2007).

68. Hauerwas, *In Good Company*, 27.

69. Stanley Hauerwas, *A Better Hope: Resources for a Church Confronting Capitalism, Democracy, and Postmodernity* (Grand Rapids, Mich.: Brazos Press, 2000), 37.

70. Hauerwas, from a Sermon delivered 8 August 1993 to Broadway United Methodist Church, South Bend, Indiana, as reprinted in Stanley Hauerwas, *In Good Company*, 39. Hauerwas repeats this sentiment in a discussion with John Milbank. See John Milbank and Stanley Hauerwas, "Christian Peace: A Conversation between Stanley Hauerwas and John Milbank," in *Must Christianity be Violent? Reflections on History, Practice, and Theology*, ed. Kenneth R. Chase and Alan Jacobs (Grand Rapids, Mich.: Brazos Press, 2003), 212.

71. See "History of P.A.P.A." www.papafestival.org/history (accessed on 12 October 2009).

72. Claiborne and Haw, *Jesus for President*, Appendix 4.

73. See, for example, H. Richard Neibuhr, *Christ and Culture* (New York: Harper and Row, 1951); James Gustafson, "The Sectarian Temptation: Reflections on Theology, the Church and the University," *Proceedings of the Catholic Theological Society* 40 (1985): 83–94.

74. For example, Hauerwas says, "In short, I have never sought to justify Christian withdrawal from social and political involvement; I have just wanted us to be involved as Christians." Hauerwas, *A Better Hope*, 24.

75. Yoder, *The Politics of Jesus*, 151.

76. Hauerwas, *Against the Nations*, 7.

CHAPTER 6

1. It isn't just political language, metaphor, and practice that dominate Christian engagement with the culture, but one even finds the language of empire still used,

especially in Evangelical circles. Campus Crusade for Christ continues to use the word "crusade" without apparent recognition of its problematic heritage. More recently, Chuck Colson began "The Centurions Program" as a ministry of The Wilberforce Forum. The image and ideal of a military-controlled empire creates little cognitive dissonance with many conservatives.

2. Stanley Hauerwas and William H. Willimon, *Resident Aliens* (Nashville, Tenn.: Abingdon, 1989), 30.

3. See Michael Hamilton, "More Money, More Ministry: The Financing of American Evangelicalism Since 1945," in *More Money, More Ministry: Money and Evangelicals in Recent North American History*, ed. Larry Eskridge and Mark A. Noll (Grand Rapids, Mich.: Eerdmans, 2000), 104–38.

4. A search of all the religious, social welfare, and public affairs organizations listed in *Associations Unlimited* identifies at least 136 Christian organizations involved in some level of political activity. Of the 943 Christian organizations listed in *Associations Unlimited*, 51 percent were established prior to 1964, while 49 percent were established between 1964 and 2006. Of the 136 Christian organizations involved in politics, only 34 percent were founded before 1964; 66 percent were founded between 1964 and 2004. (This source did not have any organizations founded after 2004. There were also 14 organizations out of the 136 that did not list the founding date. The above numbers are based on the 122 organizations that list the founding date.) *Associations Unlimited* (Gale Research), www.galenet.com/servelet/AU (site no longer available).

5. For example, a search in Proquest Historical Newspapers for articles published in the *Washington Post* and *New York Times* between 1950 and 1990 and a similar search in Factiva for articles written between 1991 and 2006 indicated an increase in the numbers of articles written about religion and politics from 1950 to 2006. Although the numbers of articles about religion and politics would peak in presidential election years and drop off in the years between national elections, there is an identifiable upward trend in the numbers of articles written about religion and politics. This search focused exclusively on articles that included a combination of the words "Christian" or "Catholic" or "Protestant" or "Evangelical" and the words "politics" (or a derivation of that word) or "American politics" or "American" and "politics." In each case, an analysis of the numbers of articles meeting the search terms defined above revealed that the media has become more interested in and written more about Christian involvement in politics. For example, a search using the terms "Christian" or "Evangelical" or "Protestant" or "Catholic" and "politics" shows 210 articles written in 1950, 563 in 1960, 809 in 1976, 827 in 1984, 925 in 1996, 947 in 2000, and 896 and 871 in 2004 and 2006, respectively.

6. A majority of the Evangelical denominations have been involved in voter registration, not least, the Southern Baptist Convention, the nation's largest Protestant Christian denomination. The same has been true for para-church ministries such as Promise Keepers, the men's renewal movement. On the Left, the National Council of Churches became involved in voter registration through more than a dozen rallies in 2004 in its program, "Let Justice Roll." See Richard N. Ostling, "Religious Groups Left and Right Compete to Mobilize Voters," AP Worldstream, 30 September 2004.

7. Jacques Ellul, *The Political Illusion* (New York: Vintage Books, 1967), 171.

8. Michael Oakeshott, "The Claims of Politics," *Scrutiny* 8 (1939).

9. Ellul, *The Political Illusion*, 16.

10. More remarkable, this end is something that the Christian Left has actually articulated as a good. See Chapter 4, note 54.

11. David Brooks, "Party No. 3," *New York Times*, 10 August 2006.

12. Josef Pieper, *Leisure: The Basis of Culture* (1948; repr., South Bend, Ind.: St. Augustine's Press, 1998).

CHAPTER 7

1. Georges Sorel, "Letter to Daniel Halevy," in *Reflections on Violence*, trans. T. E. Hulme and J. Roth (1908; repr., New York: Collier, 1950), 26–56.

2. Sorel, "Letter to Daniel Halevy," 26–56.

3. This section draws heavily from the insights of Michel Foucault, Richard Adams, Steven Lukes, and Herbert Rosinski. See also the provocative work by Christian Smith, *What Is a Person?* (Chicago: University of Chicago Press, 2010).

4. Richard Adams, *Energy and Structure: A Theory of Social Power* (Austin: University of Texas Press, 1975).

5. The concept of symbolic violence is that of Pierre Bourdieu and it can be found in his book, *The Logic of Practice* (London: Polity Press, 1992). Its means are "gentle, invisible violence, unrecognised as such, chosen as much as undergone, that of trust, obligation, personal loyalty, hospitality, gifts, debts, piety." (127).

6. Hendrik Berkhof, *Christ and the Powers* (Scottdale, Pa.: Herald Press, 1962).

7. Robert Michels, *Political Parties* (Glencoe, Ill: Free Press, 1953).

8. Herbert Rosinski, *Power and Human Destiny* (New York: Praeger, 1965).

9. Rosinski, *Power and Human Destiny*, 23.

10. This was the whole point of Jacques Ellul's masterwork, *The Technological Society* (New York: Knopf, 1963).

11. "Our conviction is to remind Christians that we are in a fight. Do not make your practices relevant to the prevailing language. Do not withdraw, but rather engage the enemy." Stanley Hauerwas and William H. Willimon, *Where Resident Aliens Live: Exercises for Christian Practice* (Nashville: Abingdon Press, 1996), 33.

12. Stanley Hauerwas, *Against the Nations: War and Survival in a Liberal Society* (New York: Winston Press, 1985), 7:

> It is alleged that by definition a pacifist must withdraw from political involve-ment. However I refuse to accept such a characterization not only because there is no intrinsic reason why pacifists must disavow all political involvement simply because they refuse to kill on behalf of the state, but also I refuse to accept such a characterization because it implies that all politics is finally but a cover for vio-lence. That seems to be not only empirically unsupportable, but normatively a view that no Christian can accept. Rather than disavowing politics, the pacifist must be the most political of animals exactly because politics understood as the process of discovering the good we have in common is the only alternative to vio-lence. What the pacifist must deny, however, is the common assumption that genuine politics is determined by state coercion.

13. Stanley Hauerwas, "September 11, 2001: A Pacifist Response," in "Dissent from the Homeland: Essays after September 11," ed. Stanley Hauerwas and Frank

Lentricchia, special issue, *The South Atlantic Quarterly* 101, no. 2 (Spring 2002): 427. "In short Christians are not nonviolent because we believe our nonviolence is a strategy to rid the world of war, but rather because faithful followers of Christ in a world of war cannot imagine being anything else than nonviolent."

14. Stanley Hauerwas, *A Better Hope: Resources for a Church Confronting Capitalism, Democracy, and Postmodernity* (Grand Rapids, Mich.: Brazos Press, 2000), 40.

15. Stanley Hauerwas, "Why Truthfulness Requires Forgiveness: A Commencement Address for Graduates of a College of the Church of the Second Chance," in *The Hauerwas Reader*, ed. John Berkman and Michael Cartwright (Durham, N.C.: Duke University Press, 2001), 315–16.

16. Hauerwas and Willimon refer here to Niebuhr's typology, in particular "Christ Transforming Culture." See Hauerwas and Willimon, *Resident Aliens*, 41.

17. Robert W. Brimlow, "Solomon's Porch: The Church as Sectarian Ghetto," in *The Church as Counterculture*, ed. Michael L. Budde and Robert W. Brimlow (Albany: State University of New York Press, 2000), 112.

18. The term comes from John Howard Yoder, *The Politics of Jesus* (Grand Rapids, Mich.: Eerdmans, 1972), 244.

19. Craig A. Carter, *The Politics of the Cross* (Grand Rapids, Mich.: Brazos Press, 2001), 98.

20. See the end of Chapter 3 in this essay.

21. More will be said of this of a practical nature in Essay III, so here the focus is mainly on principle.

22. This echoes an observation made by James Fenimore Cooper.

23. This treatment is inspired by Hendrik Berkhof, *Christ and the Powers* (Scottdale, Pa.: Herald Press, 1977), especially Chapter Four, "The Powers in Redemption."

24. David Prior, *Jesus and Power* (Downers Grove, Ill.: Intervarsity), 32–48.

25. Prior, *Jesus and Power*, 34–35.

26. Alfred Plummer, *An Exegetical Commentary on the Gospel According to St. Matthew* (London: E. Stock, 1909), 12.

27. Prior, *Jesus and Power*, 54, 94.

28. Some manuscripts add, "You do not know what kind of spirit you are of, for the Son of Man did not come to destroy men's lives, but to save them."

Essay III

CHAPTER I

1. For an early and insightful take on this question, see Leslie Newbigin, *The Gospel in a Pluralist Society* (London: SPCK, 1989).

2. Peter L. Berger, *The Heretical Imperative* (New York: Anchor Doubleday, 1979), 18.

3. Peter L. Berger, Brigitte Berger, and Hansfried Kellner, *The Homeless Mind* (New York: Vintage, 1973).

4. Charles Taylor, *A Secular Age* (Cambridge, Mass.: Harvard University Press, 2007).

5. George Steiner, *Real Presences* (Chicago: University of Chicago Press, 1989), 88.

6. Steiner, *Real Presences*, 89.

7. Steiner, *Real Presences*, 89.

8. Steiner, *Real Presences*, 90.

9. From John Donne's poem, "An Anatomy of the World" (1611). I am most grateful to Richard Horner for his insights in this part of the argument.

10. Oral cultures were based on hearing; thus with writing, culture came to be dominated by a small number of elites who possessed the powers of literacy. Time and space did shrink in this culture in part because writing consolidated the power of elites over larger territories, over succeeding generations. Printing extended and democratized this revolution, making time and space shrink more for now written materials (and literacy) were not only the possession of elites but a privilege available to much larger swaths of a society's population. Because written culture cultivates linearity of thinking and pressures toward rational consistency, printing for the masses created conditions conducive to the development of the modern individualist, whose conscience and consciousness was duty-bound to cultivate and guard. See Harold A. Innis, *The Bias of Communication* (Toronto: University of Toronto Press, 1951).

11. See David Harvey, *The Condition of Postmodernity* (Oxford: Blackwell, 1989), 240.

12. The technologies of transportation only intensify this process. Harvey illustrates what has happened by showing how maps of the world have shrunk over time with the increasing speed of transportation. Because jet aircraft travel about fifty times the speed of a sailing ship, the size of the world in the middle of the twentieth century had become about one-fiftieth the size of the world of the sixteenth century.

13. Frank D. McConnell, "Seeing through the Tube," *Wilson Quarterly* (Autumn, 1993): 56–65.

CHAPTER 2

1. Fundamentalists and Evangelicals originally spearheaded this strategy but again, conservative Catholics have, in recent decades, followed suit.

2. Among younger leaders in the emerging church movement, the problems of consumerism, racial reconciliation, poverty, HIV/AIDs, modern slavery, and the damage to the environment are most often mentioned. See, for example, the workshops sponsored by the Catalyst Conference. www.catalystspace.com/about/history (accessed on 12 October 2009).

3. Brian D. McLaren, *A Generous Orthodoxy* (Grand Rapids, Mich.: Zondervan, 2004), 36.

4. McLaren, *A Generous Orthodoxy*, 323.

5. Pastor Charles Schmidt is quoted in Hanna Rosin, "Woolly Pulpit," *The New Republic* (13 March 1995): 12. The passion to be relevant could explain why emerging church leaders, such as McLaren, embrace a therapeutic approach to popular theology— a theology of the church that is highly self-referential and autobiographic; in which the main point of reference for ecclesiology is the author himself—his thoughts, his experiences, his feelings about the church.

6. David Kinnaman and Gabe Lyons, *UNChristian: What a New Generation Really Thinks about Christianity and Why It Matters* (Grand Rapids, Mich.: Baker Books, 2007), 22.

7. See the home page, Unchristian, for the book by David Kinnaman and Gabe Lyons, www.unchristian.com/book.asp (accessed on 12 October 2009).

8. Reggie Joyner, "The Catalyst Conference" (Gwynett Center, Atlanta, Georgia, 4 October 2007). Gabe Lyons, founder of Fermi, says it as well in an interview with Will Hinton: "We need to do something drastically different if the message of Jesus and his love is ever going to come across" (Good Will Hinton Podcast, 24 September 2007) goodwillhinton.com/good_will_hinton_weekly_podcase_gabe_lyons (accessed on 12 October 2009).

9. The online forum Street Prophets had a diary entry entitled "The Rebranding Christianity® Idea Jam: Results," posted on 18 November 2005. The brand attributes that were listed for Christianity included "extreme social conservatism, particularly on sexual matters," "materialistic concern for self," "reactionary bigotry," "dominionistic/theocratic political bent," "narrow-minded, legalistic approach even to Christianity itself and other Christians," "harsh, judgmental tone," and "fear of those who appear different from oneself." The conclusion of this discussion was that "the brand [of American Christianity] totally sucks." The consensus of the diary was that "we have to do something to change the perception of Christians® and Christianity® in this culture, and most folks seem to agree that the current situation is a disaster for all people of faith as well as for our nation and our democracy. So let's see what we can do to accomplish this in a way that is not shallow, not manipulative and that does not turn Christianity® into the spiritual equivalent of New Coke." One of the "Big Ideas" that followed was to "Define and drive awareness of new brand attributes." This entailed creating some brand attributes and then "promoting the hell out of them." Another idea was to "Create highly visible third-party spokespeople." Some of the names that topped the list for a spokesperson were Jimmy Carter, Barack Obama, Jim Wallis, and Tony Campolo. A third option was to "Change the Name." The top vote getters for this option were "Yeshuism," "Wayism," and "You-Don't-Have-to-be-God-ism." See www.street prophets.com/story/2005/11/18/85414/795.

10. Catalystspace. www.catalystspace.com/about/purpose.aspx.

11. Catalystspace. www.catalystspace.com/about/values.aspx.

12. This statement was made by a Catalyst employee, L. V. Hanson, at the 2007 Catalyst conference.

13. "Exclusive Access" to Filter and Fermi costs over $200. In the case of Filter, contributors are part of "a unique online community," and have access to "archives of Catalyst talks," "invitations to intimate events," "pre-release mailings of new re-sources," "private webcasts," and "much, much more" ("Filter." Magazine advertise-ment. Catalyst 2007: *Reverb*: 1). Some of the other products available from Catalyst are their *GroupZine* magazine, Volumes 1, 2, or 3, for $15 each, studies for "emerging-leaders who are courageous and willing to risk it all, but equally aware of their unique calling and in touch with their purpose God has placed on them" (*GroupZine*. Maga-zine advertisement. Catalyst 2007: *Reverb*: 2). There is also the first offering within the *Catalyst Film Series* that, for $59, "asks the big questions about culture, mission, and the gospel, and highlights answers from Christian leaders who will help your group envision how followers of Christ can be a counterculture for the common good." See estore.injoy.com/shopinjoy/. In addition, there is the *Catalyst Worship CD* for $15, *The Catalyst CD Package*, $129, *The Catalyst DVD Package*, $169, and *The Best of Catalyst: Andy Stanley*, $49, that includes in the 6 CD set his famous sermon "Challenging the

Process—The reason you question everything, have strong opinions, and a desire to share them is because God wired you that way." See www.injoy.com/store/ (accessed on 12 October 2009). Finally, there is *Catalyst Gear*, which boasts Catalyst T-shirts, Jackets, and Hats from $20 and up. Yet this is not to mention that in the wake of this Catalyst experience are numerous speakers, authors, and musicians whose books, CDs, and DVDs get promoted on stage, advertised in *Reverb* magazine, and sold at the Resource Center.

14. Interview with Gabe Lyons on CNN Headline News with Erica Hill: "Afraid to Admit You're Christian?" Posted on Fermi Project's blog at www.fermiproject.com/blog/ on 6 December 2007 by Jeff Shinabarger.

15. The entire list of commitments is noted on the New Monasticism website:

1) Relocation to the abandoned places of Empire. 2) Sharing economic resources with fellow community members and the needy among us. 3) Hospitality to the stranger. 4) Lament for racial divisions within the church and our communities combined with the active pursuit of a just reconciliation. 5) Humble submission to Christ's body, the church. 6) Intentional formation in the way of Christ and the rule of the community along the lines of the old novitiate. 7) Nurturing common life among members of intentional community. 8) Support for celibate singles alongside monogamous married couples and their children. 9) Geographical proximity to community members who share a common rule of life. 10) Care for the plot of God's earth given to us along with support of our local economies. 11) Peacemaking in the midst of violence and conflict resolution within communities along the lines of Matthew 18. 12) Commitment to a disciplined contemplative life.

See www.newmonasticism.org/12marks.php (accessed on 12 October 2009).

16. See Stanley Hauerwas's essay, "Why the 'Sectarian Temptation' Is a Misrepresentation: A Response to James Gustafson," in *The Hauerwas Reader*, ed. John Berkman and Michael Cartwright (Durham, N.C.: Duke University Press, 2001), 90–110.

17. John Howard Yoder, "The Anabaptist Dissent: The Logic of the Place of the Disciple in Society," *Concern* No. 1 (June 1954), 59. Elsewhere Yoder argues that in Christ, the distinction between the ideal and possible becomes "artificial." John Howard Yoder, *For the Nations: Essays Evangelical and Public* (Eugene, Ore.: Wipf and Stock, 1997), 24. One can make too much of remarks such as these, but qualifications nearly always get lost in the translation from theory to practice. It is not incidental, in this regard, that a large swath of the Anabaptist churches have actually become politically conservative Evangelicals. See, for example, Carl Bowman's studies of the Anabaptist community. Carl Bowman, *A Profile of the Church of the Brethren* (Elgin, Ill.: Brethren Press, 1987); Carl Bowman, *Brethren Society: The Cultural Transformation of a Peculiar People* (Baltimore: Johns Hopkins University Press, 1995); and Carl Bowman and Stephen L. Longenecker, eds., *Anabaptist Currents: History in Conversation with the Present* (Camden, Me.: Penobscot Press, 1995). This tells us something about the failure of translation of the neo-Anabaptist vision to those who would be its most natural constituency.

18. Beliefnet. www.beliefnet.com/story/177/story_17718_1.html (accessed on 12 October 2009).

19. Timothy C. Morgan, "Cyber Shock," *Christianity Today*, 3 April 1995, 78–86.

20. From a print ad from Biblesoft.com for the PC Study Bible.

CHAPTER 3

1. James Davison Hunter, *The Death of Character: Moral Education in an Age without Good or Evil* (New York: Basic Books, 2000).

2. I am grateful to Rabbi Jack Bemporad for his helpful comments in this regard. See his paper, "Biblical Views of Human Dignity," presented at Human Dignity in the Abrahamic Traditions (Oslo, Norway, 16–19 June 2008).

3. Of course Paul wrote in Greek not in Hebrew. The Greek translation of the Hebrew word *shalom* is *eirene* and, as with the Hebrew, the word speaks not only to tranquillity but also to wholeness and completeness in life. *Eirene* is the word Paul uses here and in the passages noted in the next paragraph. In the roughly ninety mentions in the Greek New Testament, *eirene* is used in much the same ways that *shalom* is used in the Hebrew Scriptures. I use the word *shalom* for the sake of continuity.

4. In Essay II, Chapter 7.

5. Miroslav Volf, "Soft Difference: Theological Reflections on the Relation between Church and Culture in 1 Peter," *Ex Auditu* 10 (1994): 15–30.

6. Volf, "Soft Difference," 21.

7. The pairing of "affirmation" and "antithesis" appears asymmetrical at first. Affirmation would seem better paired with negation, and antithesis would seem better paired with synthesis. There are several reasons why these are not paired. The first is that unlike "antithesis" which is constructive opposition, representing a contradiction and resistance but with the possibility of hope, the concept and practice of "negation" have become expressions of nihilism. It offers nothing beyond critique and hostility. It is antagonistic for its own sake. This, it would seem, is contrary to the gospel. "Synthesis" is problematic because it presupposes a blending and an accommodation with that which it opposes. "Affirmation," by contrast, does not require assimilation with its opposition to validate actions or ideas generated by the opposition of which it approves.

8. Ken Myers, *Christianity, Culture, and Common Grace* (Berea Publications, 1994), available at www.marshillaudio.org/resources/topic_detail.asp?ID=544 (accessed on 12 October 2009).

9. For my part, I take a minimalist view of "natural law." There are at least two problems with the maximalist view. First, if the laws of nature were so obvious, why is it that so few see these laws? The second reason is that much mischief has been done in the name of natural law, mischief that has legitimated political structures and social relationships that even the most conservative would now judge as not so natural.

10. James K. A. Smith, *Introducing Radical Orthodoxy* (Grand Rapids, Mich.: Baker Academic, 2004), 241–43 has a terrific discussion of this point. He, Milbank, Hauerwas, and I all agree that common grace as neutral moral space does not exist; and that all morality is rooted in particularities. The point of disagreement is that he, Milbank, and Hauerwas take the view that there is a "deep antithesis that brokers no overlapping consensus" between Christian morality and others, such as what one would find in modern liberal notions of the good (pg. 241). Smith himself argues "morality or authentic virtue is possible only for the community of the redeemed—which should

not, of course, issue in self-congratulations since even this is a gift. What appear to be instances of mercy or compassion or justice outside the body of Christ are merely semblances of virtue" (pg. 243 n. 38). I would contend that in our practices there can be and are numerous points of overlapping purposes that are in various degrees in conformity with God's purposes for human flourishing.

11. Broadly defined to include commerce and politics.

12. Isa. 2:4; Isa. 11:6–9.

13. See Graham Ward, *Cities of God* (New York: Rutledge, 2000), 227–37.

14. See, for example, Daniel M. Bell, "The State and Civil Society," in *The Blackwell Companion to Political Theology*, ed. Peter Scott and William Cavanaugh (Oxford: Blackwell Publishing, 2004). William Cavanaugh has written insightfully in this vein as well.

15. Walter Brueggemann, "Living with the Elusive God Counterscript," *Christian Century*, 29 November 2005.

CHAPTER 4

1. James Kunstler, *The Geography of Nowhere* (New York: Simon & Schuster, 1993).

2. What this means is that we end up with fewer and fewer reliable points of reference in our environment and in consciousness. The world we inhabit and our experience of it has fewer boundaries. This, of course, is reinforced by the most powerful and ubiquitous institution in world history—free market capitalism—which observes some but perhaps fewer and fewer borders, customs, loyalties, and commitments. It is also reinforced by an ideology of personal freedom that also beckons us to observe no binding authority, hierarchy, structure, nature, or ethics except as we, for however long we choose, consent to them.

3. Taken from *The Neuman Press Book of Verse* (Long Prairie, Minn.: Neumann Press, 1988). Tolkien here is commenting on Francis Thompson's important mystical poem, "The Hound of Heaven."

4. N. T. Wright, "Creation and New Creation in the New Testament," from a lecture series given and recorded at Regent College in Vancouver, British Columbia, in August 2003.

5. Jack Bemporad, "Biblical Views of Human Dignity," paper presented at Human Dignity in the Abrahamic Traditions, Oslo, Norway, 16–19 June 2008.

6. This is why biblical legislation mandated that there was one law for the home-born and stranger or alien alike. See Exod. 12:49.

7. See Essay II, Chapter 7.

8. Miroslav Volf, "Soft Difference: Theological Reflections on the Relation between Church and Culture in 1 Peter," *Ex Auditu* 10 (1994): 21.

9. Stanley Hauerwas, "Work as Co-Creation: A Critique of a Remarkably Bad Idea," in *Co-Creation and Capitalism: John Paul II's Laborem Exercens*, ed. John W. Houck and Oliver F. Williams (Washington, D.C.: University Press of America, 1983), 45.

10. Hauerwas, "Work as Co-Creation," 46.

11. Hauerwas, "Work as Co-Creation," 52.

12. Robert Brimlow, "Paganism and the Professions" (Ekklesia Project, 2002), 6. www.ekklesiaproject.org.

13. Brimlow, "Paganism and the Professions," 3, 6, and 12. Brimlow's animus toward the Catholic writer Michael Novak is shocking.

14. Hauerwas, "Work as Co-Creation," 50.

15. Hauerwas, "Work as Co-Creation," 50.

16. From an interview with Douglas J. Schuurman, Programs for the Theological Exploration of Vocation, www.ptev.org/interview.aspx?iid=5.

17. Brimlow, "Paganism and the Professions," 7.

18. Brimlow, "Paganism and the Professions," 14.

19. See Gary D. Badcock, *The Way of Life* (Grand Rapids, Mich.: Eerdmans, 1998). This statement is taken from an interview with Douglas J. Schuurman.

20. Brimlow, "Paganism and the Professions," 8, 10, 11.

21. Max Weber, "Science as a Vocation," in *Essays in Sociology*, ed. H. H. Gerth and C. Wright Mills (New York: Oxford University Press, 1946).

22. In one sense I am merely restating a classical view of vocation. Given the nature and conditions of the late modern world, the need for a rethinking and restatement of such a theology is of critical importance. Where I seek to build on this is in the institutional implications of this theological tradition.

23. What is more, all of these realms of experience, knowledge, and relationship are neither fixed nor are their directions predictable, but the future is infinitely open, wide-ranging, and contingent. We can imagine different directions in any of these realms of life depending on the choices we make. Indeed, each fragment of life is ever shifting, evolving, rearranging, and changing. To be sure, there is an unprecedented freedom to shape life, but the pressure to keep all of it synchronized and coherent and the anxiety about recent and future decisions are also unprecedented. One is always drawn elsewhere.

24. This phrase is used by Hauerwas, who attributes this sensibility to those who see vocation extending beyond the church. See Hauerwas, "Work as Co-Creation," 51.

25. See Essay II, Chapter 7.

CHAPTER 5

1. As my colleague Richard Horner has suggested, even if one goes to the better known, Matthew 28:19, "Therefore, go and make disciples of all nations," the word, "nations" could also imply the various spheres of life and governance. The fact that the "going" activity is a participle means that the mundane activity of "going" provides the setting in which we are to make disciples. In other words, we are to assume the going into all spheres of life where we are to make disciples of all sorts of people.

2. On this point I draw on the brilliant work on the dynamics of status and status hierarchies by Murray Milner, *Status and Sacredness: A General Theory of Status Relations and an Analysis of Indian Culture* (New York: Oxford University Press, 1994).

3. I say "on the face of it" because exclusion is not always practiced to ill-effect. Within the scientific community, exclusivity can spur a quality of discussion that leads to deeper inquiry, and in the arts and humanities communities it can create the competition that spawns higher levels of excellence. The same can be true in other realms of endeavor.

4. See Acts 22:3, 25–30, Acts 16:37.

5. See Essay II, Chapter 7.

6. See David Prior, *Jesus and Power* (Downers Grove, Ill.: Intervarsity Press, 1987), 59ff.

7. Though the word "marriage" is not used in the account, Jesus described it as such in Mark 10:2–9. He declared that this arrangement reflected God's will "from the beginning of creation" and that "what God has joined together, no one should put asunder."

8. See also the Song of Solomon.

9. See John 3:29; Mark 2:19; Matt. 22:1–14, 25:1–13.

10. See Eph. 5:21–33; 1 Cor. 6:15–17; 2 Cor. 11:2.

11. Nicholas Wolterstorff, *Justice: Rights and Wrongs* (Princeton, N.J.: Princeton University Press, 2007).

12. No one has inspired these thoughts more than Donald Flow.

13. This is language from "The Williamsburg Charter," 1988.

14. See J. D. Hunter, "Fundamentalism and Relativism Together: Reflections on Genealogy," unpublished paper, University of Virginia, 2007.

15. This is, of course, the aspiration of the "new urbanism." See, for example, Eric O. Jacobsen, *Sidewalks in the Kingdom* (Grand Rapids, Mich.: Brazos, 2003).

16. On a matter such as abortion, Christians have little ground from which to speak if they are not first caring for the needs of young women with unwanted pregnancies. On the matter of homosexuality, Christians have little room to say anything if they are not first loving gays as human beings and members of the community. On the matter of poverty, Christians have little to grumble about if they don't first understand the complexity of political economy and the contradictory pressures faced by business.

17. It goes without saying that there are also ways of engaging the world that are public without being narrowly political.

18. Rom. 12:5; 1 Cor. 12:12–27.

19. Consider one illuminating example of this. The 2 October 2000 issue of the Evangelical magazine *Christianity Today* offers a positive cover story on Christian Smith's book *Divided by Faith* (Oxford: Oxford University Press, 2000). The book argues for the importance of structural factors in shaping race relations and, therefore, dealing with its legacy. The book made clear that simply "having a friendship" with a person of a different race was an inadequate solution to the race problem, and yet the conclusion of the forum of Evangelical leaders commenting on the book and on the race issue was one that reverted back to the individualistic, relationalist mentality.

20. Robert Brimlow, "Paganism and the Professions" (The Ekklesia Project, 2002), 8, 10, and 11. www.ekklesiaproject.org.

CHAPTER 6

1. As the crow flies, the distance is about five hundred miles but the travel would have been by established trade routes that would have doubled the distance.

2. The single best work of political theology to unpack this view is Kristen Deede Johnson's important book, *Theology, Political Theory, and Pluralism: Beyond Tolerance and Difference* (Cambridge: Cambridge University Press, 2007).

3. Gabe Lyons, "Cultural Influence: An Opportunity for the Church," *Comment Magazine* (March 2008): 14–20.

4. For an important analysis of the ironic consequences of dealing poorly with difference, see Christian Smith (with Michael Emerson, Sally Gallagher, Paul Kennedy, and David Sikkink), *American Evangelicalism: Embattled and Thriving* (Chicago: University of Chicago Press, 1998).

5. This statement is drawn from James K. A. Smith, *Introducing Radical Orthodoxy* (Grand Rapids, Mich.: Baker Academic, 2004), 239.

6. George Barna, *Revolution* (Wheaton, Ill.: Tyndale House Publishers, 2005).

7. Barna, *Revolution*, 62 and 64. Barna's definition of culture is what one would expect from a pollster. "Culture," he writes, "is the accumulation of behaviors and beliefs that characterize a group of people. It is comprised of the attitudes, symbols, language, rewards, expectations, customs, and values that define the experience and context of those people" (108). His methodological individualism comports with his view of Christianity, in which the individual and his or her faith experience is the central dynamic. The common culture of his "revolutionary" Christianity is a market culture whose central actor is the Christian consumer, a consumer whose choices are driven by therapeutic exigency.

BIBLIOGRAPHY

Adams, Richard. *Energy and Structure: A Theory of Social Power*. Austin: University of Texas Press, 1975.

Ahlstrom, Sidney E. *A Religious History of the American People*. New Haven, Conn.: Yale University Press, 1975.

Aland, Kurt. *A History of Christianity*. Vol. 1, *From the Beginnings to the Threshold of Reformation*. Translated by James L. Schaaf. Philadelphia: Fortress Press, 1985.

Anatolios, Khaled. *Athanasius*. New York: Routledge, 2004.

Anderson, Carl. *A Civilization of Love: What Every Catholic Can Do to Transform the World*. San Francisco: Harper One, 2008.

Anstey, Roger. "A Re-Interpretation of the Abolition of the British Slave Trade, 1806–1807." *The English Historical Review* 87 (1972): 311.

Balmer, Randall. *Thy Kingdom Come: How the Religious Right Distorts the Faith and Threatens America; An Evangelical's Lament*. New York: Basic Books, 2006.

Bellah, Robert N. *The Broken Covenant: American Civil Religion in a Time of Trial*. New York: Seabury: 1976.

Bellah, Robert N., et al. *Habits of the Heart: Individualism and Commitment in American Life*. Berkeley: University of California Press, 1985.

Bercovitch, Sacvan. *The Puritan Origins of the American Self*. New Haven, Conn.: Yale University Press, 1975.

Berger, Peter L. *The Heretical Imperative: Contemporary Possibilities of Religious Affirmation*. New York: Anchor Doubleday, 1979.

———. *The Sacred Canopy: Elements of a Sociological Theory of Religion*. New York: Anchor: 1969.

Berger, Peter L., Brigitte Berger, and Hansfried Kellner. *The Homeless Mind: Modernization and Consciousness*. New York: Vintage, 1973.

Berger, Peter L., and Peter L. Luckmann. *The Social Construction of Reality*. New York: Anchor-Doubleday, 1966.

Berkhof, Hendrik. *Christ and the Powers*. Scottdale, Penn.: Herald Press, 1962.

Bourdieu, Pierre. *The Logic of Practice*. London: Polity Press, 1992.

————. *Outline of a Theory of Practice*. Cambridge: Cambridge University Press, 1977.

Bowman, Carl F. *Brethren Society: The Cultural Transformation of a Peculiar People*. Baltimore: Johns Hopkins University Press, 1995.

————. *A Profile of the Church of the Brethren*. Elgin, Ill.: Brethren Press, 1987.

Bowman, Carl F., and Stephen L. Longenecker, eds. *Anabaptist Currents: History in Conversation with the Present*. Camden, Me.: Penobscot Press, 1995.

Brimlow, Robert W. "Paganism and the Professions." The Ekklesia Project (2002). www.ekklesiaproject.org.

Brown, Peter. *Authority and the Sacred: Aspects of the Christianisation of the Roman World*. Cambridge: Cambridge University Press, 1995.

————. *Power and Persuasion in Late Antiquity: Towards a Christian Empire*. Madison: University of Wisconsin Press, 1992.

Brueggemann, Walter. "Living with the Elusive God Counterscript." *Christian Century* (29 November 2005).

Bryant, Joseph M. "The Sect-Church Dynamic and Christian Expansion in the Roman Empire: Persecution, Penitential Discipline, and Schism in Sociological Perspective." *The British Journal of Sociology* 44, no. 2 (June, 1993).

Budde, Michael L., and Robert W. Brimlow, eds. *The Church as Counterculture*. Albany: State University of New York Press, 2000.

Burke, Peter. *A Social History of Knowledge*. Cambridge, UK: Polity Press, 2000.

Carter, Craig. "Ecclesiology is the Shape of Yoder's Social Ethics." Part IV in *The Politics of the Cross: The Theology and Social Ethics of John Howard Yoder*. Grand Rapids, Mich.: Brazos Press, 2001.

Cavanaugh, William T. "Consumption, the Market, and the Eucharist." *The Other Journal* 5 (Spring, 2005).

————. *Theopolitical Imagination: Discovering the Liturgy as a Political Act in an Age of Global Consumerism*. London: T & T Clark, 2002.

————. "The Unfreedom of the Free Market." In *Wealth, Poverty, and Human Destiny*, edited by Doug Bandow and David Schindler. Wilmington, Del.: ISI Books, 2003.

Crawford, Michael J. "The Origins of the Eighteenth-Century Evangelical Revival: England and New England Compared." *The Journal of British Studies* 26, no. 4 (October, 1987): 371.

Crouch, Andy. *Culture Making: Recovering Our Creative Calling*. Downers Grove, Ill.: IVP Press, 2008.

Dunn, Geoffrey. *Tertullian*. New York: Routledge Taylor and Francis Group, 2004.

Eberly, Don, ed. *Building a Healthy Culture: Strategies for an American Renaissance*. Indianapolis, Ind.: Hudson Institute, 2001.

―――. *The Rise of Global Civil Society: Building Communities and Nations from the Bottom Up*. New York: Encounter Books, 2008.

Ellul, Jacques. *The Political Illusion*. New York: Random House, 1967.

―――. *The Technological Society*. New York: Knopf, 1963.

Ferguson, John. *Clement of Alexandria*. New York: Twayne Publishers, 1974.

Finke, Roger, and Rodney Stark. *The Churching of America, 1776–2005: Winners and Losers in Our Religious Economy*. New Brunswick, N.J.: Rutgers University Press, 2005.

Fletcher, Richard. *The Barbarian Conversion: From Paganism to Christianity*. New York: Henry Holt and Company, 1997.

Frend, W. H. C. *The Early Church*. Minneapolis, Minn.: Augsburg/Fortress, 1982.

Garreau, Joel. *The Nine Nations of North America*. New York: Avon, 1999.

Gouldner, Alvin. *Against Fragmentation: The Origins of Marxism and the Sociology of Intellectuals*. Oxford: Oxford University Press, 1985.

Guinness, Os. *The American Hour*. New York: Free Press, 1992.

Gustafson, James. "The Sectarian Temptation: Reflections on Theology, the Church and the University." *Proceedings of the Catholic Theological Society* 40 (1985): 83–94.

Gutiérrez, Gustavo. *A Theology of Liberation: Perspectives*. Lima, Peru: CEP, 1971.

Harland, Philip A. "Connections with Elites in the World of the Early Christians." In *Handbook of Early Christianity: Social Science Approaches*, edited by Anthony J. Blasi, Jean Duhaime, and Paul-Andre Turcotte, 394. Walnut Creek, Calif.: Alta Mira Press, 2002.

Harvey, David. *The Condition of Postmodernity*. Oxford: Blackwell, 1989.

Hatch, Nathan O. *The Democratization of American Christianity*. New Haven, Conn.: Yale University Press, 1989.

Hauerwas, Stanley. *Against the Nations: War and Survival in a Liberal Society*. New York: Winston Press, 1985.

―――. *A Better Hope: Resources for a Church Confronting Capitalism, Democracy, and Postmodernity*. Grand Rapids, Mich.: Brazos Press, 2000.

―――. "A Christian Critique of Christian America." In *The Hauerwas Reader*, edited by John Berkman and Michael Cartwright. Durham, N.C.: Duke University Press, 2001.

―――. *In Good Company: The Church as Polis*. Notre Dame, Ind.: University of Notre Dame Press, 1995.

―――. "September 11, 2001: A Pacifist Response." In "Dissent from the Homeland: Essays after September 11," edited by Stanley Hauerwas and

Frank Lentricchia. Special issue, *The South Atlantic Quarterly* 101, no. 2 (Spring, 2002).

————. "Why the 'Sectarian Temptation' Is a Misrepresentation: A Response to James Gustafson." In *The Hauerwas Reader*, edited by John Berkman and Michael Cartwright. Durham, N.C.: Duke University Press, 2001.

————. "Why Truthfulness Requires Forgiveness: A Commencement Address for Graduates of a College of the Church of the Second Chance." In *The Hauerwas Reader*, edited by John Berkman and Michael Cartwright. Durham, N.C.: Duke University Press, 2001.

————. *With the Grain of the Universe*. Grand Rapids, Mich.: Brazos Press, 2001.

————. "Work as Co-Creation: A Critique of a Remarkably Bad Idea." In *Co-Creation and Capitalism: John Paul II's "Laborem Exercens,"* edited by John W. Houck and Oliver F. Williams. Washington, D.C.: University Press of America, 1983.

Hauerwas, Stanley, and William H. Willimon. *Resident Aliens: Life in the Christian Colony*. Nashville, Tenn.: Abingdon Press, 1989.

————. *Where Resident Aliens Live: Exercises for Christian Practice*. Nashville, Tenn.: Abingdon Press, 1996.

Herberg, Will. *Protestant, Catholic, Jew: An Essay in American Religious Sociology*. New York: Doubleday, 1960.

Hofstadter, Richard. *Anti–Intellectualism in American Life*. New York: Vintage, 1963.

Hunter, James Davison. *American Evangelicalism: Conservative Religion and the Quandary of Modernity*. New Brunswick, N.J.: Rutgers University Press, 1983.

————. *The Death of Character: Moral Education in an Age without Good or Evil*. New York: Basic Books, 2000.

————. *Evangelicalism: The Coming Generation*. Chicago: University of Chicago Press, 1987.

————. "Fundamentalism and Relativism Together: Reflections on Genealogy." Unpublished Paper, University of Virginia, 2007.

Innis, Harold A. *The Bias of Communication*. Toronto: University of Toronto Press, 1951.

Jacobsen, Eric O. *Sidewalks in the Kingdom*. Grand Rapids, Mich.: Brazos Press, 2003.

Johnson, Kristen Deede. *Theology, Political Theory, and Pluralism: Beyond Tolerance and Difference*. Cambridge: Cambridge University Press, 2007.

Kee, Howard Clark. *Christianity: A Social and Cultural History*. New York: Macmillan, 1991.

Keynes, John Maynard. *The General Theory of Employment, Interest, and Money*. New York: Harcourt, Brace, and Co., 1960.

Kirk, Marshall, and Hunter Madson. *After the Ball: How America Will Conquer Its Fear and Hatred of Gays in the '90s*. New York: Penguin, 1989.

Kriegel, Abraham. "A Convergence of Ethics: Saints and Whigs in British Antislavery." *The Journal of British Studies* 26 (1987): 423–50.

Kunstler, James. *The Geography of Nowhere*. New York: Simon & Schuster, 1993.

Lambert, Frank. "The Great Awakening as Artifact: George Whitefield and the Construction of Intercolonial Revival, 1739–1745." *Church History* 60, no. 2 (June, 1991): 230.

Latourette, Kenneth Scott. *A History of Christianity*. New York: Harper and Brothers Publishers, 1953.

Lerner, Michael. *The Left Hand of God: Taking Back Our Country from the Religious Right*. San Francisco: HarperSanFrancisco, 2006.

Lindsay, D. Michael. *Faith in the Halls of Power*. New York: Oxford University Press, 2007.

Man, John. *Gutenberg: How One Man Remade the World with Words*. New York: John Wiley & Sons, 2002.

Mapp Jr., Alf J. *Thomas Jefferson: Passionate Pilgrim*. Lanham, Md.: Madison Books, 1991.

Marsden, George M. *Fundamentalism and American Culture*. Oxford: Oxford University Press, 1980.

Mathews, Thomas F. *The Clash of Gods: A Reinterpretation of Early Christian Art*. Princeton, N.J.: Princeton University Press, 2003.

McConnell, Frank D. "Seeing through the Tube." *Wilson Quarterly* (Autumn, 1993).

McGrath, Alister E. *The Intellectual Origins of the European Reformation*. Oxford: Blackwell Publishing, 1987.

McKitterick, Rosamond. *The Carolingians and the Written Word*. Cambridge: Cambridge University Press, 1989.

———, ed. *Carolingian Culture: Emulation and Innovation*. Cambridge: Cambridge University Press, 1994.

McLaren, Brian D. *A Generous Orthodoxy*. Grand Rapids, Mich.: Zondervan, 2004.

McManus, Peter. Letter to the editor. *The Washington Post*, 27 January 1996.

Meredith, Anthony. *Gregory of Nyssa*. New York: Routledge, 1999.

Michels, Robert. *Political Parties*. Glencoe, Ill.: Free Press, 1953.

Milbank, John, and Stanley Hauerwas. "Christian Peace: A Conversation between Stanley Hauerwas and John Milbank." In *Must Christianity be Violent? Reflections on History, Practice, and Theology*, edited by Kenneth R. Chase and Alan Jacobs. Grand Rapids, Mich.: Brazos Press, 2003.

———. "Mammon's Deadly Grin: The New Gospel of Wealth and the Old Gospel of Life." Address, Culture of Life Conference, Notre Dame Center for Ethics and Culture, 30 November 2001.

Miller, David Harry. "Sacral Kingship, Biblical Kingship, and the Elevation of Pepin the Short." In *Religion, Culture, and Society in the Early Middle Ages: Studies in Honor of Richard E. Sullivan*, edited by Thomas F. X. Noble and John J. Contreni. Kalamazoo: Western Michigan University, Medieval Institute Publications, 1987.

Milner, Murray. *Status and Sacredness: A General Theory of Status Relations and an Analysis of Indian Culture*. New York: Oxford University Press, 1994.

Murdock, Graeme. *Beyond Calvin: The Intellectual, Political, and Cultural World of Europe's Reformed Churches*. Houndsmills, U.K.: Palgrave Macmillan, 2004.

Myers, Ken. "Christianity, Culture, and Common Grace." © 1994 by Berea Publications. Transcript.

Neuhaus, Richard John. "One Nation under God." *Reflections* (Summer-Fall, 1994).

Newbigin, Leslie. *The Gospel in a Pluralist Society*. London: SPCK, 1989.

Niebuhr, H. Richard. *Christ and Culture*. New York: Harper and Row, 1951.

Nietzsche, Friedrich. *Beyond Good and Evil*. Translated by Walter Kaufmann. New York: Vintage, 1989.

Noll, Mark A. *A History of Christianity in the United States and Canada*. Grand Rapids, Mich.: Eerdmans, 1992.

————. *The Scandal of the Evangelical Mind*. Grand Rapids, Mich.: Eerdmanns, 1994.

Oakeshott, Michael. "The Claims of Politics." *Scrutiny* 8 (1939).

O'Brian, Susan. "A Transatlantic Community of Saints: The Great Awakening and the First Evangelical Network, 1735–1755." *The American Historical Review* 91, no. 4 (October, 1986): 811–32.

Ozmen, Steven. *The Age of Reform 1250–1550: An Intellectual and Religious History of Late Medieval and Reformation Europe*. New Haven, Conn.: Yale University Press, 1980.

Pettegree, Andrew, A. C. Duke, and Gillian Lewis, eds. *Calvinism in Europe, 1540–1620*. Cambridge.: Cambridge University Press, 1994.

Pew Research Center. *The American Religious Landscape and Politics, 2004*. Washington, D.C.: Pew Forum on Religion & Public Life, 2004. Based on the Fourth National Survey of Religion and Politics, conducted March–May 2004 by John C. Green and sponsored by the Pew Forum on Religion & Public Life and the Ray C. Bliss Institute of Applied Politics, Akron, Ohio.

Pieper, Josef. *Leisure: The Basis of Culture*. New translation by Gerald Malsbary. South Bend, Ind.: St. Augustine's Press, 1998. First published 1948 by Kösel-Verlag as *Musse und Kult*.

Plummer, Alfred. *An Exegetical Commentary on the Gospel According to St. Matthew*. London: E. Stock, 1909.

Prior, David. *Jesus and Power*. Downers Grove, Ill.: Intervarsity Press, 1987.

Ramsey, Paul. *Who Speaks for the Church? A Critique of the 1966 Geneva Conference on Church and Society*. New York: Abingdon Press, 1967.

Randall, Catherine. *Building Codes: The Aesthetics of Calvinism in Early Modern Europe*. Philadelphia: University of Pennsylvania Press, 1999.

Reichley, A. James. *Religion In American Public Life*. Washington, D.C.: Brookings Institution, 1985.

Riche, Pierre. *Education and Culture in the Barbarian West*. Columbia: University of South Carolina Press, 1978.

Rieff, Philip. "Toward a Theory of Culture." In *The Feeling Intellect*, edited by Johnathan B. Imber. Chicago: University of Chicago Press, 1990.

Rosinski, Herbert. *Power and Human Destiny*. New York: Praeger, 1965.

Sandeen, Ernest R. *The Roots of Fundamentalism: British and American Millenarianism 1800–1930*. Chicago: University of Chicago Press, 1970.

Schaff, Phillip. *History of the Christian Church*. 3rd ed. Peabody, Mass.: Hendrickson Press, 1996.

Seel, David John. "The Evangelical Meltdown: Modernity and the Hysteresis of Habitus." PhD diss., University of Maryland, 1992.

Sine, Tom. *Cease Fire: Searching for Sanity in America's Culture Wars*. Grand Rapids, Mich.: Eerdmans, 1995.

Skocpol, Theda. *States and Social Revolutions*. Cambridge: Cambridge University Press, 1979.

Smith, Christian. *American Evangelicalism: Embattled and Thriving*. Chicago: University of Chicago Press, 1998.

Smith, Christian, with Michael Emerson. *Divided by Faith: Evangelical Religion and the Problem of Race in America*. New York: Oxford University Press, 2000.

Smith, Christian, and Melinda Lundquist Denton. *Soul-Searching: The Religious and Spiritual Lives of American Teenagers*. New York: Oxford University Press, 2005.

Smith, James K. A. *Introducing Radical Orthodoxy*. Grand Rapids, Mich.: Baker Academic, 2004.

Sorel, Georges. "Letter to Daniel Halevy." In *Reflections on Violence*, translated by T. E. Hulme and J. Roth. New York: Collier, 1950. First published 1908.

Steiner, George. *Real Presences*. Chicago: University of Chicago Press, 1989.

Stringfellow, William. *Free in Obedience*. New York: Seabury Press, 1964.

Taylor, Charles. *A Secular Age*. Cambridge, Mass.: Harvard University Press, 2007.

Thomas, George M. *Revivalism and Cultural Change*. Chicago: University of Chicago Press, 1989.

Volf, Miroslav. "Soft Difference: Theological Reflections on the Relation between Church and Culture in 1 Peter." *Ex Auditu* 10 (1994).

Wallis, Jim. *God's Politics*. San Francisco: Harper, 2005.

———. *The Soul of Politics*. New York: New Press, 1995.

Ward, Graham. *Cities of God*. New York: Routledge, 2000.

Weber, Max. "Science as a Vocation." In *Essays in Sociology*, edited by H. H. Gerth and C. Wright Mills. New York: Oxford University Press, 1946.

Weingarten, Susan. *The Saint's Saint: Hagiography and Geography in Jerome*. Leiden, The Netherlands: Brill, 2005.

Werner, Jaeger. *Early Christianity and Greek Paideia*. Cambridge, Mass.: Harvard University Press, 1961.

Wilken, Robert. *The Christians as the Romans Saw Them*. New Haven, Conn.: Yale University Press, 1984.

Wolfe, Alan. *The Transformation of American Religion*. New York: Free Press, 2003.

Wolterstorff, Nicholas. *Justice: Rights and Wrongs*. Princeton, N.J.: Princeton University Press, 2007.

Wright, N. T. "Creation & New Creation in the New Testament." Audiobook on CD. Vancouver, B.C., Canada: Regent College, 2003.

Wuthnow, Robert. *Communities of Discourse*. Cambridge, Mass.: Harvard University Press, 1989.

———. *The Restructuring of American Religion*. Princeton, N.J.: Princeton University Press, 1988.

Yoder, John Howard. "The Anabaptist Dissent: The Logic of the Place of the Disciple in Society." *Concern* 1 (June, 1954).

———. *Body Politics*. Scottdale, Pa.: Herald Press, 1964.

———. "Christ and Power." In *The Politics of Jesus*. Grand Rapids, Mich.: Eerdmans, 1972.

———. "Christ, the Hope of the World." In *The Royal Priesthood*. Scottdale, Pa.: Herald Press, 1998.

———. "The Christian Case for Democracy." In The *Priestly Kingdom*. Notre Dame, Ind.: Notre Dame University Press, 1984.

———. *The Christian Witness to the State*. Scottdale, Pa.: Herald Press, 1964.

———. *Discipleship as Political Responsibility*. Scottdale, Pa.: Herald Press, 1964.

———. *For the Nations: Essays Evangelical and Public*. Eugene, Ore.: Wipf and Stock Publishers, 1997.

———. "The Otherness of the Church." In *The Royal Priesthood*. Scottdale, Pa.: Herald Press, 1998.

———. *The Politics of Jesus*. Grand Rapids, Mich.: Eerdmans, 1972.

———. *The Priestly Kingdom*. Notre Dame, Ind.: Notre Dame University Press, 1984.

———. *The Royal Priesthood*. Scottdale, Pa.: Herald Press, 1998.

INDEX

authenticity, 223, 224
authority, 206, 208, 211
autonomy, 133, 233, 279
avant-garde, 302n105
Ave Maria College, 86
Awakenings, 77

Babylon, 276–78
Badcock, Gary, 250
Baldwin, Stephen, 117, 120
Bale, John, 68–69
Balmer, Randall, 137, 140–42, 143
baptism, 161
barbarians, 57, 59
Barber, Rims, 136
Barna, George, 288n1, 336n7
Barth, Karl, 152
Basil the Great, 51, 55, 57
Bauer, Gary, 125, 307n9, 309n34
Baylor Institute for Studies of Religion, 19
Baylor University, 86
BBL Forum, 81
beauty, 248
belief, challenged by pluralism, 204, 224
Bellamy, Joseph, 71
Bell, Daniel M., Jr., 152
Bendix, Reinhard, 170
Benedict, 58
benefactors, of church, 59–60
Berger, Peter, 202
Berkhof, Hendrikus, 157, 158, 179
Bethel University, 5
Beza, Theodore, 70, 299n68
Bhabha, Homi, 44
Bible: authority of, 222; on justice, 136; language of, 237; reading of, 19; as standard for public policy, 13; undermining of confidence in, 221
Bible reading in public schools, 13, 215
Biola University, 86
bishops, 54, 63
Black, Jim Nelson, 293n23
Blackstone, William, 72
Boice, James, 10
Bolsheviks, 76
Boniface, 59, 60, 62
book-blurbing, 36
Books and Culture, 87
Booth, William, 16

"bottom up" social movements, 8, 15, 16, 31, 41
Bourdieu, Pierre, 34, 36, 327n5
Boy Scouts of America, 118
Brainerd, David, 71
branding, 30
BreakPoint Ministries, 130
Brethren, 151
Bright, Bill, 10
Brimlow, Robert, 181, 250, 324n63
British Empire, 73–74
Brooks, David, 173
Broughham, Thomas, 71
Brownback, Sam, 125
Brown, Peter, 53, 54, 56, 297n18, 297n32
Brueggemann, Walter, 237
Bucer, Martin, 66
Buchanan, Claudius, 73
Budde, Michael, 155
Bugenhagen, Johannes, 66
bureaucracy, 170
Burke, Edmund, 72
Burke, Peter, 66
Bush, George W., 137, 147, 165, 325n67
business, 265
Buxton, Thomas Fowell, 73

Caesarea, 50
Calderone, Mary, 25
Call to Renewal, 137, 138
Calvin College, 86
Calvinism, spread of, 67–68
Calvin, John, 16, 38, 66, 70
Campolo, Tony, 137, 139, 144, 317n20, 330n9
Campus Crusade for Christ, 4, 10, 326n1
capitalism, 76, 150, 198–99, 216: corruption of, 164, 275; erodes boundaries, 333n2; imperialism of, 321n7; neo-Anabaptists on, 154–55, 181, 250–51; transforms nature of work, 253
capital punishment, 146
Capito, Wolfgang, 66
Carlyle, Thomas, 37–38, 295n7
Carolingian Renaissance, 61–64
Carter, Craig A., 152, 181–82
Carter, Jimmy, 249, 330n9
Carthage, 50, 52
Cartwright, Michael, 152
Catalyst, 215, 217, 329n2, 330–31n13
catechesis, 237

Catholic left, 135
Catholics: and Constantinianism, 155; on cultural change, 11; cultural production of, 85–86; foundations, 82–83; and "defensive against paradigm," 214; in media, 86; and pluralism, 204
Catholic University, 85
Cavanaugh, William, 152, 161
celebrity, 209, 217, 222, 260–61
Celsus, 52
center, of culture, 37, 42–43, 78, 89–91, 270, 274
Center for American Cultural Renewal, 12
Center for Christian Statesmanship, 13
Center for Progressive Christianity, 316n10
Center for Reclaiming America for Christ, 122, 313n113
Centurions Program, 4, 288n6, 326n1
change, 210–12, 213
character, 15, 54
charisma, 38
charitable giving, 19, 303n5
charity, 55–56, 253
Charlemagne, 62–63, 64
Charles V, 299n61
child labor reform, 134, 215
choice, 203, 211, 283, 336n7
Christendom, 60, 64, 75
Christendom College, 5, 85
Christ for the Nations, 5
Christian Alliance for Progress, 141, 142, 143, 316n10
Christian America, 127–28
Christian Century, 85
Christian Coalition, 13, 80, 119, 122, 125, 308n14, 309n35
Christian Coalition for Immigration Reform, 139
"Christian colony," 161
"Christian culture," 234. *See also* Constantinianism
Christian difference, 231
Christianity: in America, 79–92, 260–61; as defender of social order, 204; divisions within, 244, 281; growth of, 48–56; legitimates political ideologies, 184–85; plausibility and persuasiveness of, 263
Christianity Today, 87, 142, 335n19
Christian left, 132–49, 321n62: politicization of, 168, 172; witness of negation, 174–75

Christian Life Commission (SBC), 120
Christian realism, 166
Christian Right, 46, 111–31; Christian Left on, 139–43, 150; disproportionate political power, 167; imitated by Christian Left, 145, 147–48; politicization of, 168, 172; witness of negation, 174–75
Christians in the Visual Arts (CIVA), 87
Christian Voice, 14
Christology, 187
Chrysostom, John, 51
church: as alternative community, 158 and aristocracy, 59–60, 62, authority of, 111–12; as community of resistance, 235; as conscience of society, 8; as consumer choice, 283; and cultural change, 16, 30–31; and imperial power, 300n79; intellectual and cultural production of, 61; legitimates political ideologies, 184–85; memory and identity of, 237; neo-Anabaptists on, 151; and networks of faithful presence, 270–71; as non-coercive community, 181–82; as *polis*, 283; power of, 182–84; as plausibility structure, 282; schism in, 281; as subversive, 235; and world, 160–62, 182; as utopian enclave, 218–19; as worshipping community, 161, 184, 244
church attendance, 19
Churchill, Winston, 17
Cicero, 63
"circulation of elites," 43
citizenship: in Roman empire, 55; in the church, 161
city states, 65
civic duty, 8, 12, 172
civil disobedience, 182
civil religion, 145–47
civil rights movement, 134, 135, 145, 216
Claiborne, Shane, 159, 165, 321n1, 324n54
Clapham Circle, 73
Clapham Group, 129
Clarkson, Thomas, 73
class, 105, 139
Clayton, John, 71
Clement, 52
clergy, orders of, 64
Clergy Leadership Network, 134
Clinton, Bill, 137, 308n11, 316n11

cloning, 23
Clydesdale, Timothy, 305n14
coercion, 159, 181–82, 192–93, 199, 263
coherence, 224
Colman, Benjamin, 71
Cologne, 65
Colson, Charles, 6–8, 12, 16, 21, 25, 130, 288n6, 326n1
Columba, 58, 60
Columbanus, 58, 60
Combs, Roberta, 311n76
commanding truths, 32
commerce, 265, 266
common good, 185, 251, 266, 271, 281
Common Good Strategies, 148, 322n77
common grace, 232–33, 332n10
communications technologies, 201, 208–10, 222, 238–39
Communism, 135, 215
community, 253: and cultural renewal, 16; of resistance, 235; and shalom, 227–30; in tension with world, 230–31; "community of saints," 72
compassion, 190–91
Concerned Women for America, 80, 122
conquest, 274, 280
consciousness, 26, 33, 35, 210
Constantine, 55, 153
Constantinianism, 153–56, 164, 167, 182, 184, 219, 233–34, 274, 279–80, 322n10
Constantinople, 50
consumer culture, 167; Christianity as, 336n7; trivialization of, 211
consumerism, 92, 198, 283, 329n2
"continuous partial attention," 252
conversion, and cultural change, 10, 46, 273
cosmopolitanism, of Reformation Europe, 68–69
counterpower, 179
covenant, 242
covenantal commitment, 261–65, 266
covetousness, 228
creation, goodness of, 231–33, 254
creation mandate, 3–5, 93, 99, 236
creedal confessions, erosion of, 221
Crisis, 85
cross, 156, 158, 163
Crouch, Andy, 27–30, 294n28
Crozier, Michel, 170
crusade, 326n1

"Cry for Renewal," 14, 80, 321n50
C. S. Lewis Institute, 130
cultural capital, 89
cultural change, 18, 40–44, 45, 273–74
cultural egalitarianism, 94
cultural materialism, 28, 30, 294n28
cultural power, 29, 30, 35–36
cultural production, 28–29, 30, 89–91
culture; as artifact, 27–31, 77; banality of, 211; complexity of, 47; commodification of, 39; conflict in, 44; as cumulation of values, 6; as dialectic, 34–35; essence of, 6; fields of, 39; as local and shared, 29; as logical and rational, 26; as materialist and secular, 19; naivete about, 27; not fully autonomous or coherent, 38–40; norms of, 32; as product of history, 33–34; resistant to intentional change, 45; as system of truth claims and moral obligations, 32–33; transformation of, 8–9, 16, 28; vs. worldview, 33
culture-making, 28, 231, 233
culture war, 14, 23, 25, 95, 124, 173, 201, 280, 285
currency, 258
cynicism, 263
Cyprian, 51
Cyril of Alexandria, 53
Cyril of Jerusalem, 51

"Dark Ages," 61
darkness, difference as, 220
Darwinism, 7
Day, Dorothy, 16, 17, 38, 134, 164, 251
debate, 266
deconstruction, 205, 208
"defensive against" paradigm, 214–15, 223, 226, 248–49, 272, 275; on difference, 219; on dissolution, 222
Delay, Tom, 13, 174
delegitimation, 43–44
Demetrius, 51
democracy, 101–2; in America, 108, 198; on differences, 202; spiritual and moral dimensions of, 15; vs. state, 170
Democratic Party: and Christian Left, 144, 148–49, 168–69; Christian Right on, 116, 124; Evangelical progressives and, 137
denominations, 244
Descartes, René, 8

evangelism, social change through, 9–11, 18, 45, 214, 216, 226, 249, 273

evolution, 7, 21, 134, 215

exclusion, 94, 258, 334n3

exile, 276–78, 281, 283

existentialism, 207

exploitation, 4, 64, 99, 250, 275, 307n5(1)

faith, 262–65; as other-worldly, 177; politicization of, 109–10, 128, 172

Faith and Action, 122

faith-based philanthropy, 81–84

faithfulness, 197, 213, 214, 237; and challenge of difference, 219, 223–24; and challenge of dissolution, 223–24; social conditions of, 203, 212; in totality of life, 227

faithful presence, 95–96, 241, 243–48, 252–54, 257, 272, 276, 286; in exile, 276–78; in institutions, 270–71; and leadership, 259–61; and obligation, 261–65; practice of, 265–69

Faith in Public Life, 148

Fall, 228, 232, 234

Falwell, Jerry, 128, 140, 147, 165, 308n11, 311n75, 314n121

Falwell, Jonathan, 129

family, 16, 103, 104, 111–12, 115–16, 117, 122, 171, 215

Family Research Council, 13, 80, 122, 130, 290n34, 312n97

fatherhood movement, 15

felt-needs, 216

female seminary movement, 134

feminism, 116, 215, 221

Ferguson, Adam, 72

Fermi Project, 215, 217, 330n13

Filter, 330n13

financial capital, 89, 270

First Things, 85, 87

Fitzroy, Robert, 302n102

Fletcher, Richard, 298n41

flourishing, 242, 252, 262, 263, 279, 283

Flow, Donald, 283, 284, 335n12

Focus on the Family, 5, 9, 13, 23, 80, 122, 123–24

Ford Foundation, 82, 83, 304n10

Ford, Henry, 20

Foreman, George, 249

forgiveness, 161, 184, 253

formation, 161, 226–27, 236–37, 281, 282–83

Foucault, Michel, 44, 179

Foundation for Moral Law, 122

foundations, 81–84, 304n7, 305n11

foxes and lions, elites as, 43

Foxe's Book of Martyrs, 112, 141

fragmentation: of American Christianity, 91, 92; of modern world, 252; of worldviews, 202–3

Francis of Assisi, 132

Franks, 61–62

fraternity, 132–33

Frederick the Wise, 69

free church, 159

freedom, 133, 136, 211

French Revolution, 132

Freud, Sigmund, 25, 207

friendship, 264

Fructosuosus, 58–59

fruitfulness, 248, 260

fundamentalism: affected by pluralism, 204; as "defensive against paradigm," 214; nihilism of, 264

Fundamentalists: on creation mandate, 5; on vocation, 248–49

Galen, 52

Gallagher, Sharon, 137

Gambold, John, 71

gatekeepers, 41, 43, 46. *See also* elites

gay community, disproportionate influence of, 20–21

gay rights movement, 20, 215

gender, 105, 110, 220

"generous orthodoxy," 216

Geneva, 65, 67, 70

genius, 38

genocide, 146

George, Robert, 8, 85

Georgetown, 85

German idealism, 24, 26

Ghent, 65

Gillespie, Thomas, 71

Gioia, Dana, 85

Gisbourne, Thomas, 73

Glendon, Mary Ann, 85

globalization, 197, 199, 200

gnosticism, of neo-Anabaptists, 251

God: faithful presence of, 241–43; love of, 242–43; no longer an inevitability, 203; sovereignty of, 48

God's World Publishing, 130

Goethe, Johann von, 24

Gordon College, 86
government. *See* state
grace, 184, 232–33, 263
Graham, Billy, 11
Great Awakening, 70–71
Great Commission, 226–27, 236, 256–57
great ideas, 7
"great man" view of history, 37–38
Greco-Roman culture, 49–56
Gregorian chant, 63
Gregory (the miracle worker), 51
Gregory of Nyssa, 51
Gregory of Tours, 51
Guggenheim, Peggy, 302n105
Guinness, Os, 11
gun ownership, 116
Gustafson, James, 166

habits, 33
habitus, 34
Harvard, 47, 71
Hauerwas, Stanley, 152, 155, 159, 160,
    161, 164–65, 169, 181, 249–50,
    322n10, 322n13, 325n67, 325n70,
    325n73, 327nn12–13, 332n10,
    334n24
Havel, Vaclav, 17
Hays, Richard, 152
Heaney, Seamus, 85
"hearts and minds" argument, 7, 10, 11, 16,
    20–22, 27, 45, 77, 273–74
Hegel, Georg W. F., 24, 25, 293n18
Hegelianism, 25, 35
Hegesippus, 51
Heidelberg, 67
Hellenistic Judaism, 49–50
Herder, Johann Gottfried, 24, 25
Heritage Foundation, 80
Herschiser, Orel, 249
Hervey, James, 71
Hewlett Foundation, 83
high culture, 89
higher education, 84, 103, 104, 118, 167,
    254, 264, 265. *See also* universities
history, 48, 95; and culture, 33–34;
    skepticism in, 207
Hitler, Adolf, 16, 302n103
Hittinger, Russell, 85
HIV/AIDS, 146, 329n2
Hofstader, Richard, 86
holiness, 253

Hollinger, David, 20
Hollywood, 116, 117
Holy Roman Empire, 65
Holy Spirit, 237, 248
homeschooling, 9, 39, 86, 92, 116
homosexuality, 20–21, 46, 112, 115–16,
    119, 145, 215, 266, 335n16
hope, 262–65; parodies of, 234–35; in
    politics, 126–27
Hopkins, Samuel, 71
Horace, 63
Horner, Richard, 334n1
hospitality, 253
household, 231
humanism, 66, 299n64
humanities, skepticism in, 207
humility, 253
Huns, 57
Hus, Jan, 69
Hutterites, 151
Hybels, Bill, 128

idealism, 24–25, 26–27, 29, 34, 44
ideas; consequences of, 40–41, 44; and
    institutions, 34; social conditions of, 44, 78
identity: and ideology, 105; management of,
    259; rooted in resentment, 173
ideology, 103–5, 110
idolatry, 228
image, 209
image of God, 183
imagination, 7
incarnation, 156, 223, 229, 236, 240–41,
    248, 252
indeterminacy, of human beings, 177
Indiana Wesleyan University, 5
individualism, 26, 31, 44, 92, 279, 283,
    293n24, 336n7
individuals: and cultural change, 16–17, 24,
    26, 30–31; and institutions, 35
industrialization, 200
inequality, 199, 228
influence, spheres of, 234, 247, 249,
    252–54, 255–60, 265, 269
information, 201
Ingham, Benjamin, 71
injustice, 228, 247, 263, 285
innovation, 41–43
Institute for Social Research, 303n106
institutions, 27, 30, 44, 45, 270; and cultural
    change, 38, 46, 76, 78;

institutions (*continued*)
and faithful presence, 246, 270–71; and
ideas, 35; and individuals, 34; power of,
88; of resistance, 235; and the state, 103
instrumentalism, 246, 264, 282
Interfaith Alliance, 80
International Arts Movement, 87
Iraq, 146
Ireland, 58, 59

Jaeger, Werner, 49
Jaurés, Jean, 76
Jefferson, Thomas, 9
Jeremiah, 276–78
Jerome, 51
Jerusalem, 50
Jesus: compassion of, 190–91; on leadership,
260; life and ministry of, 152–53, 156; as
New Adam, 3; as noncoercive, 191–92;
politics of, 162; and power, 187–93;
submission to Father, 188–89; suffering
of, 156, 191; temptation of, 157, 187–88,
189
Jews in America, disproportionate influence
of, 20
John D. and Catherine T. MacArthur
Foundation, 83
John Paul II, Pope, 11, 16, 17, 250
Johnson, Samuel, 12, 72
Jonas, Justus, 66
joy, 248, 262, 271
Joyce, James, 302n104
Joyce Meyers Ministries, 122
Judeo-Christian tradition, 114, 117, 126,
127, 129, 219
judiciary, 39, 116–17, 119, 290n34
Julian the Apostate, 53, 55–56
justice, 14, 18, 91, 132, 136, 159, 254, 262,
263, 285
Justin Martyr, 51, 52
Juvenal, 63

Kandlinsky, Wassily, 302n105
Kant, Immanuel, 24
Kennedy, D. James, 127, 128, 313n113
kenosis, 191
Keynes, John Maynard, 40
kingdom-building, as Constantinian project,
233–34, 279–80
Kingdom of God, 95–96, 156, 186, 229,
233, 269; Christian Left on, 134;

Christian Right on, 129–30; as noncoer-
cive, 192–93; not of this world, 12
King, Martin Luther, 17, 38, 134, 164
Kinkade, Thomas, 87
Kinsey, Alfred, 8, 25
Knights of Columbus, 8–9
knowledge industry, 39
Koch Foundation, 82
Kunstler, James, 239

labor movement, 215
LaHaye, Beverly, 119
LaHaye, Tim, 140
Land, Richard, 310n50, 311n77
Landry, Roger, 287n6
language, 33, 45; adequacy of, 205–8; of
politics, 103, 163–64, 168
late modernity, 201, 211, 214, 224, 231,
263–64, 282
Lawrence, D. H., 302n104
laws, and values, 171
leadership, 38, 226, 255–61, 269–71
Legacy, 129
Legionaries of Christ, 5
legitimacy, legitimation, 36, 43, 46, 102, 103
Leiden, 67
Leninism, 75–76
Lenin, Vladimir, 76, 301n101
Leo the Great, 57
Lessing, Gotthold, 24
Lewis, C. S., 249
liberal arts, 62
liberal democracy, 103, 199
liberalism, 204, 221, 248
liberation, 133, 134
liberation theologies, 135, 216, 221
liberty, 132–33
Liberty Council, 122
Liddell, Eric, 249
Liebknecht, William, 76
lifeboat theology, 4
lifestyle, 133
Lilly Endowment, 82, 304n10
Lincoln, Abraham, 17, 124
Lindsay, D. Michael, 306n25
literacy, 329n10
literary modernism, 76, 302n104
literature, 265
litigation, 102
"liturgy of resistance," 165
lobbying, 12, 13

Locke, John, 72, 75
Lombard, Peter, 66
lordship of Christ, 156
love, 161, 182, 190, 245–46, 262–65
Luther, Martin, 16, 38, 66, 70, 295n7, 300n79
Lyons, Gabe, 330n8

Macaulay, Thomas Babington, 73
Macaulay, Zachary, 73
Maclellan Foundation, 305n15
Madonna, 308n11
Magdalen College, 86
mainline Protestantism: decline of, 85; and
    Democratic Party, 322n13; political
    activism of, 12, 135
majority opinion, and cultural trends, 21–22
Mandela, Nelson, 17, 134
Man, John, 300n76
Marcion, 51
marginalization, of Christians, 117–18
market, 30, 39, 103, 154, 198, 264, 336n7.
    See also capitalism
marriage, 15, 111–12
    covenantal character of, 261–62
Marxism, 75–76, 135, 303n106
Marx, Karl, 76, 207
materialism, 28
material world, 24–25
Mathewes, Charles, 164
Mathewes-Green, Frederica, 287n1
Mathews, Thomas, 56
Matthew 25 Network, 144
McCain, John, 129, 314n119
McCarraher, Eugene, 152, 154, 155
McClendon, James, 152
McDermott, Alice, 85
McGrath, Alister, 66
McLaren, Brian, 137, 144, 216, 329n5
meaninglessness, 264. See also nihilism
mega-churches, 264
Melanchthon, Philipp, 66–67
Mennonites, 151
mercantilism, 74
mercy, 263
Merovingians, 61–62
Messiah College, 86
metaphysics, 24
Michels, Robert, 170
Milbank, John, 152, 325n70, 332n10
mind, 24–25, 26
missionality, 216

missionaries, 47, 59, 298n41
modernity, 201. See also late modernity
modern societies, 101
monasteries, 57–59, 61, 62. See also new
    monasticism
Montesquieu, 72
Moore, Roy, 309n40
Moore, T. M., 130–31, 315n127
Moral Majority, 13–14, 122, 140
More, Hannah, 73
More, Thomas, 132
Moses, 3
Mother Teresa, 11, 17, 134, 164, 251
Movement, The (Christian alliance), 130–31
multiple tasks, 252
Mumford, Lewis, 170
murder, 228
Murdock, Graeme, 68
Murphy, Nancey, 152
music, 63

National Abortion Rights League, 116
National Association of Evangelicals, 14,
    92, 121, 122, 291n44
National Christian Charitable Foundation,
    305n15
National Council of Churches, 85, 134,
    322n71, 326n6
National Education Association, 116
National Endowment for the Arts, 116, 117
nationalism, 154
National Organization for Women, 116
National Right to Life, 80
natural law, 332n9
Nazi Germany, 119
negation, discourse of, 166, 169, 173,
    174–75, 275, 332n7
neighborhood, 253
neo-Anabaptists, 150–66, 167, 283; on
    Constantinianism, 234; on difference,
    220; on dissolution, 223; and language of
    politics, 168; on power, 180; and "purity
    from" paradigm, 218–19; and ressentiment,
    169; witness of negation, 174–75; on
    work, 249–50
neo-Marxism, 76
NETWORK, 135, 315n4
networks, 42, 43, 44, 91, 274; and cultural
    change, 37–38, 76, 78; during Great
    Awakening, 71–72; of Enlightenment,
    75; in Reformation Europe, 66–68

Neuhaus, Richard John, 85, 113–14, 155, 165, 324n65
"new city commons," 279, 280–81
new creation, 3, 95, 243, 262, 265, 282
New Deal, 102, 108
New England Puritans, 71
New Jerusalem, 279
Newman, Jay Scott, 312n81
new monasticism, 218, 220, 223, 331n15
news media, 104, 118–19, 167, 265, 306–7n3
newspapers, 42
New York Review of Books, 87
New York Times, 36, 42
New York Times Book Review, 87
Niebuhr, H. Richard, 166, 214, 328n16
Niebuhr, Reinhold, 165, 166, 324n64
Nietzsche, Friedrich, 16, 76, 107, 109, 175, 179, 207, 302n103, 307n5(1)
nihilism, 207, 211, 264–65, 275, 332n7
Noah, 3
nobility, 54, 59, 60, 62, 64, 65, 69
noblese oblige, 301n90
nonprofit organizations, 123
nonviolence, 158–59, 328n13. *See also* pacifism
North American Christian Social Workers Association, 81
North, Oliver, 309n41
Notre Dame, 85
Novak, Michael, 155
Novak, Robert, 85
nuclear weapons, 47, 134
Nuremberg, 65

Obama, Barack, 116, 128, 129, 148, 314n120, 330n9
obligations, 33, 261–65
O'Brian, Susan, 71
O'Connor, Flannery, 85
Oppenheimer, Mark, 322n11
oppression, 228, 247
oral cultures, 329n10
Origen, 52
Orthodox Presbyterian Church, 218
"other," 219, 220, 224, 246
Ottoman Empire, 65
Ovid, 63
Oxford, 67, 71
Ozment, Steven, 299n61, 299n64

pacifism, 156, 158–59, 166, 181, 327n12(2)
Packer, J. I., 36
paideia, 53–55, 57, 297n18
Palin, Sarah, 314n119
Pantaenus, 52
PAPA Festival, 165
para-church agencies, 4, 82, 91
paradigms of cultural engagement, 213–19, 275
Pareto, Vilfredo, 43
Parsons, Jonathan, 71
partial-birth abortion, 22
patience, 253
Patrick, 58, 60, 298n41
patronage, 53–54, 64, 74, 78, 81, 104, 270, 302nn103–4
Paul, 49–50; as elite, 259; on imitating God, 253; on love, 245; on principalities and powers, 188; on work, 246–47
Pax Romana, 56–57
peace churches, 151
peace movement, 133, 134
Pearcey, Nancy, 25, 27
Peasant Revolt, 70, 77
Pemberton, Ebenezer, 71
Pentecostalism, 220, 223
Percy, Walker, 85
perfectionism, 165, 182, 219
periphery, of culture, 37, 42
Perkins, John, 137
Perkins, Tony, 127
persecution: of ancient Christians, 51; of contemporary Christians, 118, 119
Pew Forum on Religion and Public Life, 22
philanthropy, 81–84, 103
Philip the Arabian, 51
Philo, 51
Pickstock, Catherine, 152
pietism, 26, 45, 165, 182, 220, 223, 236, 286
Pippen the Short, 64
Pirmin, 59, 60
Pitt, William, 73
place, 238–39, 253
Plato, 24
Platonism, 53
plausibility structures, 202–3, 219, 227, 282
plenitude, 271
Pliny, 52

social power, 187
social reform, 14–15, 18, 27, 41, 45
social theory, 32
Society for the Propagation of the Gospel in Foreign Parts, 71
Sojourners community, 14, 80, 137, 138, 140, 144, 150
Solzhenitzyn, Alexander, 36
Sorel, Georges, 134, 176
Southern Baptist Convention, 120, 326n6
space, compression of, 208–9
Spalatin, George, 67
spectacle, 217
Stalin, Joseph, 16
state: and culture, 39; vs. democracy, 170; expectations of, 171; neo-Anabaptists on, 151, 153, 157–58, 160, 164, 181; and public weal, 103; and restraint of evil, 157
status, 190, 257–58
Staupitz, Joseph von, 66
St. Bartholomew's Day Massacre, 300n78
Steele, Michael, 120
Steiner, George, 205, 206
stem-cell research, 23
Stephen, James, 73
Stewart, Payne, 249
Stieglitz, Alfred, 302–3n105
stranger, 229, 245–46
Strasbourg, 65
Street Prophets (online forum), 330n9
Sturm, Johannes, 66
subjectivism, 206
substance, over style, 253
suffering, 156, 160, 175, 271
  as political suffering, 163
Sullivan, Amy, 321n57, 321n62
Summit Ministries, 5, 130
Supreme Court, 116–17
Swaggart, Jimmy, 140
symbolic capital, 35–37, 42, 43, 190, 258, 270
symbolic violence, 178, 266, 327n5
symbols, 28, 34, 35, 44, 46, 202, 203
syncretism, 204
synthesis, 332n7

Tacitus, 52, 63
Tackett, Del, 24
Taylor, Charles, 168
Taylor University, 86

technology, 104, 180, 198, 282; and cultural change, 76; and disembodiment, 239
teen-abstinence movement, 15
Teen Mania, 130
Teignmouth, Baron, 73
temperance movement, 46, 215
terrorism, war on, 146
Tertullian, 51, 52
Thayer, Scofield, 302n104
theocracy, 147
Theodosius, 153
theology: fragmentation of, 91; of power, 183–84
therapeutic ideologies, 92, 329n5
Thiel, Ernest, 302n103
Thirty Years' War, 154
Thomas Aquinas, 95
Thomas Aquinas College, 86
Thomas, Clarence, 249
Thompson, Francis, 333n3
Thornton, John and Henry, 73
time, compression of, 208–9
tithing, 89
Tocqueville, Alexis de, 113, 114
tolerance, 119
Tolkien, J. R. R., 241–42, 249
"top down," cultural change as, 41–42
torture, 146
traditional morality, 122
traditional societies, 101
Traditional Values Coalition, 122
travel, 200–201
tribalism, 166, 174
Trinity Forum, 5
triumphalism, 234
trivialization, of culture, 209, 211, 223
trivium, 62
true, the good, and the beautiful, 89, 90
truth, 27, 33, 111, 157, 205, 208, 315n127
"Truth Project" (Focus on the Family), 9, 23–24, 130, 292–93n16
Tutu, Desmond, 16, 134
two kingdoms view, 218

uncertainty, 203
unintended consequences, 47, 171, 179, 180, 221, 223, 251
United Church of Christ, 135
United Concert for Prayer, 72

United Methodist Church, 135
universities, 42; of early modern Europe, 74–75; and Great Awakening, 71; of Reformation Europe, 66–67. *See also* higher education
urban centers, of Mediterranean, 50–51
urbanization, 200–201
urban planning, 265
U.S. Catholic Conference of Bishops, 4

Valentinus, 51
Valerian, 51
values, 6, 9; degradation of, 13; and laws, 171; and politics, 172
Vandals, 57
vanity, 228
vengeance, 159
Venn, Henry and John, 73
victimization, 107–8
Vietnam war, 134, 135, 215
violence, 166, 179, 181, 218, 264, 275
Virgil, 63
virtue, 8, 14
Vision America, 122
Vision Forum, 122
Vladimir, 59, 60
vocation, 18, 95–96, 254, 334n22; neo-Anabaptists on, 159–60, 223
Volf, Miroslav, 230–31, 248
Volstead Act, 46
voluntary associations, 15
voter guides, 13
voter registration, 122, 169, 326n6

Wagner, Richard, 302n103
Waldensians, 132
Waldman, Steve, 311n73
Wallis, Jim, 14, 137–39, 140, 143–47, 150, 318n41, 319nn61–62, 320n63, 320n70, 330n9
war, 59–60, 146
Ward, Graham, 152
Warren, Rick, 128, 221
Washington Post Book World, 87
WASP establishment, 80, 84
Watson, James Sibly, 302n104
wealth, 50, 60, 65, 74, 138, 190, 199, 258
Weaver, Harriet Shaw, 302n104
Weaver, Richard, 40–41
Weber, Max, 170, 251

Weigel, George, 85, 155
Weil, Hermann, 303n106
Weiner, Anthony, 137
Wesley, Charles, 70, 71
Wesley, John, 16, 70, 71
West County Assembly of God (Missouri), 122
Western civilization, 59, 70, 95, 280
Westminster Shorter Catechism, 234
Weyrich, Paul, 128, 312n97
Wheaton College, 86
Whigs, 301n90
Whitefield, George, 70, 71, 72
Wilberforce Forum, 4, 130
Wilberforce, William, 38, 72–73
Wilfrid, 60
Wilken, Robert, 51
Willbrord, 60
William of Orange, 67
Williams, Charles, 249
Willimon, William, 161, 169, 181
will to power, 106–7, 109, 144, 173, 175, 186, 275
Wilson, John A., 122
wisdom, 237
Wisdom literature, 133
withdrawal, 166
witness, 248
Wolfe, Tobias, 85
Wolfowitz, Paul, 146
Wolterstorff, Nicholas, 262
women's rights, 134, 135
Word of God, 221, 239–40
words, and reality, 205–8, 210, 220–21
work, 246–50. *See also* vocation
World Council of Churches, 134
World magazine, 87
worldviews, 6–8, 9, 23–24, 25, 33, 202–3, 210, 288n2
worship, 283, 286
written cultures, 329n10
Wuthnow, Robert, 69

Yale, 42, 47, 71
Yoder, John Howard, 152, 156, 157, 158, 160, 163, 166, 181, 323n30, 323n51, 331n17

zealots, 156
Zurich, 65